W9-ANN-097

FLORIDA STATE
UNIVERSITY LIBRARIES

JUN 1 3 2001

TALLAHASSEE, FLORIDA

Structural Adjustment without Mass Unemployment?
Lessons from Russia

Edited by Simon Clarke

Professor of Sociology
Centre for Comparative Labour Studies
University of Warwick
Coventry, UK

Edward Elgar
Cheltenham, UK • Northampton, MA, USA

© Simon Clarke 1998. Copyright of individual chapters remains with the contributors.

All rights reserved. No part of this publication may be reproduced, stored in a retrieval system or transmitted in any form or by any means, electronic, mechanical or photocopying, recording, or otherwise without the prior permission of the publisher.

Published by
Edward Elgar Publishing Limited
8 Lansdown Place
Cheltenham
Glos GL50 2HU
UK

Edward Elgar Publishing, Inc.
6 Market Street
Northampton
Massachusetts 01060
USA

HC 340.12 .S83 1998

A catalogue record for this book
is available from the British Library

Library of Congress Cataloguing in Publication Data
Structural adjustment without mass unemployment? : lessons from Russia
/ edited by Simon Clarke.
    Includes bibliographical references and index.
    1. Structural adjustment (Economic Policy)—Russia (Federation)
2. Manpower policy—Russia (Federation) 3. Labor supply—Russia
(Federation) I. Clarke, Simon, 1946– .
HC340.12.S83   1998
331.12'042'0947—dc21
                                                                97-35420
                                                                    CIP

ISBN 1 85898 713 X

Printed in Great Britain by The Ipswich Book Company, Suffolk.

Contents

List of Tables   vii

List of Figures   xi

Contributors   xiii

Introduction *Simon Clarke*   1

1   Structural Adjustment without Mass Unemployment?
     Lessons from Russia   *Simon Clarke*   9

2   The Restructuring of Employment and the Formation of a
     Labour Market in Russia *Simon Clarke, Veronika Kabalina,*
     Irina Kozina, Inna Donova and Marina Karelina   87

3   Reviving Dead Souls: Russian Unemployment and
     Enterprise Restructuring   *Guy Standing*   147

4   The Economic Development of Industrial Enterprises and
     the Dynamics and Structure of Employment   *Pavel Smirnov*   186

5   How Vulnerable is Women's Employment in Russia?
     Galina Monousova   200

6   Russian Unemployment in the mid-1990s: Features and
     Problems   *Tatyana Chetvernina*   216

7   Economic Restructuring and Employment Promotion in a
     Russian Crisis Region: The Case of Ivanovo
     Maarten Keune   256

8   Aspects of Official Unemployment in Moscow and St
     Petersburg: The Views of the Registered Unemployed
     Kathleen Young   276

9   Households' Experience of Unemployment in Moscow,
     St Petersburg, and Voronezh *Nick Manning*   310

     References   332

     Index   345

List of Tables

2.1	Total Employment in Russia	72
2.2	Changes in Employment and Unemployment by Age and Sex, 1992–95. Labour Force Survey data	85
2.3	Changes in Employment and Unemployment by Age and Sex, 1992–96. RLMS data	86
3.1	Population and Employment, 1990–95	150
3.2	Mortality from Murder and Suicide, 1990–95	155
3.3	Women's Share of Occupational Categories, 1995–96	155
3.4	Distribution of Convictions, 1990–95	156
3.5	Characteristics of the Russian Labour Flexibility Survey, 1991–96	158
3.6a	Indicators of Surplus Labour in Russian Industry, 1996	173
3.6b	Indicators of Surplus Labour in Russian Industry, 1995–96	173
3.7a	Entitlement to Enterprise Benefits and Services, mid-1996	182
3.7b	Entitlement to Enterprise Benefits and Services, Change 1995–96	183
3.8	Benefits Entitlements for Worker Categories, mid-1996	185
4.1	Changes of Category of Enterprises, 1994–96	188
4.2	Proportion of Enterprises of Various Types, by Industrial Branch	189
4.3	Structure of Employment at Enterprises of Various Types	191
4.4	Separations of Particular Categories of Employee	193
4.5	The Main Reasons for Separations from Enterprises	195
4.6	Proportion of Pensioners at Various Types of Enterprises	196
4.7	Hiring Rate of Employees of Various Categories	198
5.1	Employment and Unemployment by Gender, 1992–96	202
5.2	Changes in Labour Market Participation, 1992–95 (%)	205
5.3	Changes in Labour Market Participation, 1992–95 (mill)	205
5.4	Average Duration of Job Search by Unemployed (months)	206

5.5	Total and Female Employment by Sectors, 1990–94	207
5.6	Relative Wages in Predominantly Male and Female Sectors	208
5.7	Indicators of Wages and Employment, by Gender, 1995	213
5.8	Perception of Employment Opportunities by Gender	214
6.1	Number of Unemployed Registered with the Employment Service and on ILO Definition	217
6.2	Distribution of Russian Regions by Registered Unemployment, 1992–96	217
6.3	Structure of Expenditure of the Employment Fund	223
6.4	Proportion of Employees Hired Through the Employment Service	228
6.5	Vacancies Reported to the Employment Service	229
6.6	Distribution of 75 Raions by Predominant Branch and by Rate of Unemployment	232
6.7	Some Labour Market Indicators of the Surveyed Regions	233
6.8	Distribution of Raions by Level of Unemployment, and Estimates of Director of Regional Employment Service	234
6.9	Distribution of Applicants by Educational Level	235
6.10	Distribution of Applicants by Marital Status	235
6.11	Employment Status of Respondents at the Moment of Application to the Employment Service	238
6.12	Reason for Visiting the Employment Service	238
6.13	Delays in Employment Service Procedure	239
6.14	Distribution of Unemployed by Size of Benefit	242
6.15	Main Sources of Subsistence of the Unemployed	244
6.16	Offer of Vacancies by Employment Service	246
6.17	Attitude of the Unemployed to Retraining	248
6.18	Reasons for Refusal of Retraining	249
6.19	Distribution of 75 Raions by Rate of Unemployment and Involvement of the Unemployed in Public Works	251
6.20	Preference for Specialism	253
6.21	Preference for Work Regime	253
6.22	Minimum Wage for a Suitable Job	254
7.1	Employment by Industry in the Ivanovo Region, 1990	258

7.2	Index of Industrial Production, 1994 compared to 1990	260
7.3	Production in Industry, 1990–95.	260
8.1	Dynamics of Employment in Russia 1992–95	281
8.2	Ownership of Previous Employer	285
8.3	Work Experience	286
8.4	Branch of Industry	287
8.5	Previous Position	288
8.6	Duration of Involuntary Administrative Leave	289
8.7	Official Reason for Loss of Employment	290
8.8	Duration of Registration with Employment Service	293
8.9	Additional Methods Used to Find Employment	294
8.10	Motivations for Turning to the Employment Service	295
8.11	Assistance Offered in Initial Visits to the Employment Service	296
8.12	Benefits Received from Previous Employer	299
8.13	Sources of Household Income in Addition to Unemployment Benefit	300
8.14	Approved Measures for the Reduction of Unemployment	303
8.15	Should Economic Reform Continue?	304
8.16	Actions of Protest Approved	306
9.1	Demographic Pattern for the Overall Sample	318
9.2	Age and Unemployment	319
9.3	Age, Skills and Discipline	319
9.4	Age and Family Circumstances	320
9.5	Self-reported Health Status	322
9.6	Income Sufficiency	325
9.7	Other Income from Self or Other Family Members	326
9.8	Previous/Current Employment	329
9.9	Age Structure in the Three Cities	329

List of Figures

3.1 Registered Unemployment, 1993–95, Russian Federation 152

3.2 Output Bartered, by Industry, 1995–96 160

3.3 Establishments Believing Bankruptcy Likely, 1996 160

3.4 Capacity Utilisation Rates, 1994–96, by Industry 161

3.5 Capacity Utilisation Rates, 1994–96, by Region 162

3.6 Percentage of Establishments that Could Produce Same Output with Fewer Workers, by Industry, 1996 166

3.7 Percentage Fewer Workers to Produce Same Output, by Industry, 1996 167

3.8 Working Time Lost due to Production Partially or Wholly Stopped, by Region, 1995–96 169

3.9 Workers on 'Administrative Leave', by Industry, 1995–96 170

3.10 Workers on 'Administrative Leave', by Property Form, 1995–96 171

3.11 Workers on Short Time for Economic Reasons, by Industry, 1995–96 171

3.12 Employment Change, by Industry, 1995–96 176

3.13 Employment Change, by Region, 1995–96 176

3.14 Employment Change, by Corporate Governance, 1995–96 177

3.15 Women on Maternity Leave, by Employment Change, 1996 177

3.16 Sales Exported, by Employment Change, 1995–96 178

3.17 Labour Turnover, by Region, 1995–96 179

3.18 Establishments Having Wage Arrears, by Region, 1996 180

3.19 Establishments Having Wage Arrears, by Employment Change, 1996 181

4.1 Proportion of Enterprises of Various Types, by Region, 1994–96 189

4.2 Proportion of Enterprises of Various Types, by Form of Ownership, 1994–96 190

4.3   Proportion of Enterprises of Various Types, by Number
       Employed, 1994–96   190
5.1   Relative Wages of Major Occupational Groups,
       by Type of Enterprise   211
7.1   Production and Employment in the Textile Industry,
       Ivanovo Region, 1991–95   262

Contributors

Simon Clarke is Professor of Sociology at the University of Warwick and Scientific Director of the Institute for Comparative Labour Relations Research (ISITO), Moscow.

Veronika Kabalina is a senior research fellow in the Institute of World Economy and International Relations of the Russian Academy of Sciences and director of the Moscow branch of ISITO.

Irina Kozina is head of the sociology laboratory of Samara Pedagogical University and director of the Samara branch of ISITO.

Inna Donova is a lecturer in Sociology of Labour at Kemerovo State University and a member of the Kemerovo branch of ISITO.

Marina Karelina is a researcher in the sociology laboratory of Samara Pedagogical University and member of the Samara branch of ISITO.

Guy Standing is Director of the Labour Market Policies Branch of the International Labour Organisation in Geneva.

Pavel Smirnov is a senior researcher in the Centre for Labour Market Studies of the Institute of Economics of the Russian Academy of Sciences.

Galina Monousova is a research fellow at the Institute of World Economy and International Relations of the Russian Academy of Sciences and member of the Moscow branch of ISITO.

Tatyana Chetvernina is director of the Centre for Labour Market Studies of the Institute of Economics of the Russian Academy of Sciences.

Maarten Keune is a member of the Central and Eastern European Team of the International Labour Organisation, based in Budapest.

Kathleen Young is a doctoral research student at the Institute of Russian and East European Studies, University of Glasgow.

Nick Manning is Professor of Sociology and Social Policy at the University of Nottingham.

Introduction

Simon Clarke

Contemporary economic, social and political developments in Russia are of global importance not only for geopolitical reasons, but also because of the historical uniqueness of the Soviet experiment and of the historical transition which the former Soviet Union and its erstwhile satellites are currently undergoing as they seek closer integration into the global capitalist economy. The direction and pace of transition has been heavily dependent on the transfer of experts and expertise from West to East, but there has been little recognition on the part of the multitude of Western advisers that they may have as much to learn from the East as the East has to learn from the West. The transition provides a unique opportunity not only to apply the liberal economic doctrines which underlie the modern panacea of stabilisation and structural adjustment, but also to evaluate those doctrines by assessing the consequences of their rigorous application. Success in Russia will surely vindicate the universalistic claims of these doctrines, while failure should send their proponents back to the drawing board. What is happening in Russia today could perfectly well be happening in our own countries tomorrow.

The process of transition from a Soviet to a developed capitalist economic system is as much of an unpredictable experiment as was the earlier Bolshevik effort to transform a nascent capitalist into a socialist system, both being driven forward against all the odds by the unshakeable faith of their proponents that their revolutions were built on solid scientific foundations so that all the undoubted suffering of transition would reap its inevitable reward in the future. But the liberal economists' faith in the applicability of their dogma to the process of transition is as much of a shot in the dark as was the faith of the Bolsheviks in the dogmas of Marxism-Leninism. The liberal economists share the Bolsheviks' conviction in the *a priori* truth of their doctrines, and are as ready as were the Bolsheviks to blame all their failures on the persistence of outdated attitudes and subversion by vested

1

interests. It was seventy years before the ideologues of the Soviet system acknowledged the need for a reassessment of their failure. Fortunately the parallel ends here, for we are free to assess the liberal experiment as its consequences unfold.

The papers in this book relate to one particular but extremely important aspect of the liberal experiment, the impact of stabilisation and structural adjustment on employment and on the formation of a labour market. This is an important field because labour market rigidities were initially identified by Western economists as potentially one of the most serious of the many barriers to a smooth transition, and labour market rigidities were indeed made a scapegoat for failure in the first years of transition, following the precedent already established in relation to other cases in which structural adjustment had failed to deliver the goods, from Western Europe to some of the poorest countries in Africa. And yet the argument that labour market rigidities were a barrier to adjustment became increasingly difficult to sustain as wages in Russia went into free fall, earnings differentials increased at a rate unprecedented in history, and labour mobility sharply increased to such an extent that the Russian labour market could be categorised, with little exaggeration, as perfectly flexible. Labour market flexibility, the fashionable panacea of the 1990s, only fuelled the persistent decline of the Russian economy, its benefits remaining constantly just over the horizon. A better understanding of the character of employment restructuring and labour mobility in Russia is clearly of considerable importance not only for Russia, but also for the understanding of the role of the labour market in any capitalist economy.

The papers presented here originally derive from contributions to a conference held at the University of Warwick in September 1996 to report on the results of the most recent research into the Russian labour market. The conference was financed by the British Overseas Development Administration as the concluding event of the first phase of a research project directed by Simon Clarke on the restructuring of employment and the formation of a labour market in Russia, the second phase of which began in October 1996 with funding from the British Economic and Social Research Council. The conference had been preceded by a seminar held in Moscow in July 1996, funded by the Ford Foundation, which brought the leading Russian researchers in the field together with Russian policy makers at national and regional levels.

The intention of the September conference was to bring together those currently researching employment restructuring and labour market formation in Russia and East-Central Europe, to debate the wider theoretical and policy implications of our findings with labour market specialists studying other parts of the world. Since various contending schools of thought were represented we had anticipated heated debate, but in fact the discussion was very constructive and achieved a high degree of consensus both as to the current situation and the need for further research. Following the conference the papers which make up this volume were more or less extensively revised and updated for publication. No attempt has been made in editing the volume to establish uniformity (or even consistency) between the contributions, which represent a range of different viewpoints. There is inevitably a small amount of repetition from one paper to another. This has been retained so that each can stand on its own.

The volume begins with an introductory chapter by Simon Clarke which sets the Russian experiment in the context of the theoretical debates among economists around the role of labour market flexibility in structural adjustment, and surveys the statistical and survey evidence to assess the extent of employment restructuring and the scale of hidden and suppressed unemployment in Russia. The chapter counterposes the view of the World Bank, that structural adjustment has been impeded by labour market rigidity represented by the hoarding of labour by worker-controlled enterprises, to Richard Layard's contrary view that extraordinary labour market flexibility has established a basis for Russia's coming economic miracle, broadly to endorse the position adopted by Guy Standing of the ILO, that Russia's labour market is extraordinarily flexible. It is this flexibility which has eroded any incentives to invest or to increase labour productivity, while disagreeing with Standing's conclusion that an appropriate policy is to force hidden unemployment into the open. The fact that three such different interpretations of the Russian experience can coexist is a striking indication of how little we know about the Russian labour market. The chapter ends with an assessment of the statistical sources on the forms and levels of Russian employment and unemployment which concludes that while only 3% are registered unemployed, at least 30% of the economically active population do not have regular employment, relying on subsistence production, casual employment, pensions and state benefits to survive.

The second chapter, by Simon Clarke, Veronika Kabalina, Irina Kozina, Inna Donova and Marina Karelina, reports the results of the first phase of a sociological research project on employment restructuring and the formation of a labour market in Russia, based on case studies of enterprises in two contrasting Russian regions, Kemerovo and Samara, which are undergoing dramatic restructuring but which still have low levels of unemployment. Since the overwhelming majority of labour market activity involves job-to-job transitions, this research project focuses on these processes, rather than the position of the unemployed, and on the processes themselves rather than on their aggregate outcomes. Following a methodological introduction which outlines a view of the enterprise as a social institution and the labour market as a social network, the chapter reviews the results of case-study research on management strategies, the collection and reporting of statistics, labour mobility and labour force stratification, internal mobility, external mobility, secondary employment, the behaviour of workers and the position of women in the labour market. The chapter concludes by indicating the policy implications of the research.[1]

The third chapter, by Guy Standing, reports the results of the last two rounds of the Russian Labour Flexibility Survey (RLFS), covering the years 1994–96, and updates the analysis presented in his recently published book (Standing, 1996b), which covered the first four rounds of the RLFS. Standing's paper chronicles the depth of the economic crisis which grips Russia and its impact on enterprises which have no incentive to displace or economise on labour because a flexible labour market has reduced the cost of retaining labour almost to nil. Thus open unemployment remains low, and politicians can deny that it is a problem, while hidden and suppressed unemployment builds up to explosive dimensions within enterprises.

The fourth chapter, by Pavel Smirnov, is also based on the analysis of data derived from the most recent rounds of the Russian Labour Flexibility Survey. This data set is invaluable since it is the only in-depth enterprise survey data which covers the period since the watershed year of 1994, when industrial enterprises began to reduce their labour forces in earnest. Pasha's paper explores a hypothesis which has been forming among all those actively involved in researching the

---

[1]   The full results of the next phase of this research will be published by Edward Elgar in 1998 in a volume edited by Simon Clarke and provisionally entitled *The Formation of a Labour Market in Russia*

Russian industrial enterprise over the past three years, that the economic situation of the enterprise is a fundamental determinant of management employment strategy in both quantitative and qualitative terms. This is a hypothesis which was investigated by the Warwick project using case study methods and is here explored using longitudinal data from the Labour Flexibility Survey. Pasha's paper represents only the first stage of analysis of this data, but even so it shows very striking differences in employment strategy between 'good' and 'bad' enterprises, expressed in differences in the structure of employment, in changes in the composition of the labour force and in hiring and separation rates for different categories of employee. The preliminary results of this analysis correspond very closely to the conclusions drawn by the Warwick group on the basis of its case studies: that management in unsuccessful enterprises has very little control of employment policy because it is not able to manage either hirings or separations, and so experiences very high rates of labour turnover with associated deskilling and degradation of the enterprise. The analysis also shows that the process of deskilling is one common to even the most successful enterprises, something which does not hold much promise for the future.

The fifth chapter, by Galina Monousova, addresses the issue of women's employment in more detail. This paper was not presented at the Warwick conference, which Galina was unable to attend, but was prepared within the framework of another project based at Warwick, on the restructuring of gender relations in Russia, funded by the Nuffield Foundation and directed by Elain Bowers, and linked to our research on employment restructuring in which Galya has also been involved. This chapter combines a review of the available statistical data on women's unemployment with a review of data from a variety of enterprise case studies in which Galya has been directly involved and in which she has explored the gender dimensions of employment restructuring. Galya's paper brings out clearly two features of employment restructuring in Russia: on the one hand, that women are not especially vulnerable to unemployment but, on the other, that women tend to be concentrated in the lowest paid work with the worst working conditions. The fact that they manage to hold on to their jobs, therefore, is a reflection of the fact that women tend to accept wages and working conditions which men will not. Galya's paper also shows clearly the way in which objective constraints and subjective perceptions of women's disadvantaged situation are mutually reinforcing.

The remaining four papers address the other side of the coin: the problem of unemployment in Russia. Unemployment is supposed by economists to be a symptom of labour market rigidity, and the low rate of registered unemployment in Russia a sign of the flexibility of the Russian labour market. Most economists are content to note the low rate of registered unemployment in Russia and then to pass on, concluding that unemployment in Russia is not a problem. All the papers in this volume are based on the supposition that unemployment in Russia is a problem, not least for those who experience it, and that in some of Russia's regions unemployment is a major and growing problem.

The first of these chapters, by Tatyana Chetvernina, surveys the current role and activity of the employment service on the basis of an examination of the pattern of its expenditure and activities, rather than its declared policy, and reviews the results of a detailed research project which studied those registering with the employment service in two contrasting regions of Russia in 1996, following up an earlier project which had been undertaken in 1992 soon after unemployment was first officially recognised in Russia. The paper makes grim reading, testifying to the seriousness of the problem of unemployment, the desperate situation of many of the unemployed, the inability of the employment service to meet the challenge presented to it, and the callousness of politicians who dismiss the problem and deny the unemployed support on the fashionable grounds that they must be cruel to be kind lest they foster the growth of a dependency culture.

The next chapter, by Maarten Keune, reviews the situation in Ivanovo oblast, which is recognised even by the optimists as a crisis region, dominated by a textile industry in catastrophic decline. The collapse of production has seen a very substantial decline in employment and increase in both registered and unregistered unemployment which is stretching the resources of the regional employment service and local administration to the limit. However, even this is only part of the story, since employment has still fallen by substantially less than production, with a considerable proportion of the labour surplus retained in enterprises, supported in some cases by local subsidies, at the expense of administrative leave, extremely low wages and long delays in their payment. As Maarten notes, there is a real danger that this labour surplus will be released on to the local labour market, leading to a further sharp increase in the unemployment rate. In the face of such a crisis the policy instruments available are relatively limited in scope and effectiveness. Drawing on comparative examples, Maarten argues that resources should be devoted to the implementation of a regional industrial development strategy based initially on the regeneration and diversification of the textile and engineering industries, and that labour market policy should be an active agent of such a restructuring, rather than being devoted to the continued support of jobs with no future in the vain hope that Ivanovo will eventually be pulled up by a national economic recovery. More broadly, although such a programme requires federal financial support, its success depends on the mobilisation and co-operation of regional actors and the systematic orientation of regional policy to the common aim.

Kathleen Young's paper reports the results of her own survey of the unemployed in Moscow and St Petersburg, at first sight as different as could be from the depressed regions of Vladimir and Ivanovo. Nevertheless, Kathy's results correspond very closely to those reported from those regions: the unemployed are by no means passive, although some are certainly more active than others; people register as unemployed not primarily to receive benefits, although this is an important consideration, but in the hope of receiving a job; unemployment is a sorry condition in which to find oneself and even the meagre unemployment benefit provided to those registered constitutes an important contribution to household income. Kathy's results also reinforce those of the other surveys, that while employers and those in employment are still dismissive of the Employment Service, and it does not have much success in providing appropriate training or placing people in appropriate jobs, its clients express a high degree of satisfaction with its services. The fact that the unemployed are so satisfied with so little perhaps indicates the degree of isolation which they otherwise feel.

The final chapter, by Nick Manning, derives from another comparative project which looks at unemployment in St Petersburg, Moscow and Voronezh. Unlike Kathleen Young's research, which focuses on the registered unemployed, this project focuses on the transition through registered unemployment, looking at those on administrative leave, those formally subject to redundancy, those who are registered as unemployed and those who have found jobs. The research reported on in this paper is the first stage of a longitudinal project in which those interviewed will be followed up in a year's time. Although the sample is very small, so the findings cannot claim statistical significance, the findings do correspond to those of other research projects, including that reported in previous chapters, and above all confirm the conclusion that the unemployed behave perfectly rationally in the situation in which they find themselves. The final conclusion can stand as a policy conclusion to the volume as a whole, that we need a lot more research before we can claim to know how the Russian labour market works and, in particular, we need to know much more about household survival strategies, about which very little is known but which are decisive in the design of appropriate social and labour market policies.

1 Structural Adjustment without Mass Unemployment? Lessons from Russia

Simon Clarke,
Centre for Comparative Labour Studies
University of Warwick

The Russian economy has seen GDP fall by over 40% and industrial production more than halved in the five years of radical reform and yet registered unemployment still stood at only 3.2% in June 1997, having fallen steadily for over a year, with the labour force survey reporting a relatively modest 8.6% unemployment on the ILO/OECD definition at the end of March 1996.[1]

[1] This is the most recent hard figure for ILO unemployment, since the October 1996 and March 1997 labour force surveys were cancelled. The extent of the decline in GDP, incomes and production has been hotly debated. The early Goskomstat figures showed a very substantial decline in GDP and production, but there were some reasons to doubt the extent of the decline, in particular the fact that consumption and income data, based on household surveys, indicated that income and expenditure had fallen rather less than output, while electricity consumption by industry had fallen far less than the reported decline in industrial production. Revisions to the data, including a substantial estimate for unrecorded activity, indicated a fall in GDP of just over a third rather than a half between 1990 and 1994 (Koen, 1996). Modest stabilisation in 1995 saw a fall of only about 3% in GDP and industrial production, leading to predictions of imminent recovery, but 1996 saw a further fall in GDP of 5–6% and in industrial production of 6–7% as the budget crisis led to a very tight squeeze after the Presidential election. These reported GDP declines were despite optimistic, if arbitrary, estimates for unrecorded activity of 20% of GDP in 1995 and 23% in 1996 (*Russian Economic Trends*, April 1997). A reported increase in GDP for the first quarter of 1997 was spurious, created by a further upward revision for unrecorded activity of 5% of GDP and soon neutralised by further decline through the second quarter. Even on the most optimistic measures, Russia has experienced a deeper and more sustained depression than any previously recorded anywhere in history. Most of the arguments claiming that the extent of Russia's decline has been exaggerated are completely specious (Hedlund and Sundstrom, 1996) – the currently published official figures are undoubtedly on the optimistic side. Both the ILO and the World Bank surveys of industrial enterprises found production declines in line with those reported by Goskomstat (Standing 1996b; Commander, Fan et al., 1996).

Is this low rate of unemployment an indicator of the failure of structural adjustment as state and former state enterprises continue to hoard labour, shielded by their soft budget constraints (as argued by Simon Commander)? Or is it an indicator of an extremely flexible labour market which is allowing extensive structural adjustment to take place without the intervening stage of mass unemployment (as argued by Richard Layard and Andrea Richter)? Or is reported unemployment only the tip of an iceberg, with a large proportion of the economically active population in a state of limbo: some with occasional casual work, some formally employed but laid-off without pay, some working but being paid wages far below the subsistence minimum or not being paid at all (as argued by Guy Standing)?

These three very different interpretations of the Russian experience have very different policy implications, not only for Russia but for all those countries that have been advised to pursue flexible labour market policies as part of a structural adjustment programme. However, to date there has been very little engagement between the three positions nor any attempt to confront them systematically with the available empirical evidence. In this paper I would like to review the evidence for and against these three interpretations before drawing some provisional conclusions.

STRUCTURAL ADJUSTMENT AND UNEMPLOYMENT IN TRANSITION

The dominant model applied in the early years of the transition was that which had been developed for the structural adjustment of market economies suffering chronic fiscal and payments imbalances. The structural adjustment model was based in the first instance on an evaluation of the experience of the structural adjustment of the developed market economies to the 1974 oil shock. The received wisdom was that those countries which had opened their economies to the world market and which had dismantled the barriers to the free play of the domestic market had been the most successful in making the major structural changes required to adjust to the new global economic environment and so to resume sustained growth through the 1980s. The generalisation of this model developed from the laudable desire to spread the benefits of the dynamism of the world economy in the

1980s to those relatively stagnant regions which had not participated in the world boom and which remained weighed down by the debts incurred in the 1970s. Structural adjustment would allow these countries to initiate or resume a process of economic growth and to restore fiscal and payments balances by reorienting their economies from protected and stagnant domestic markets to booming world markets. Macroeconomic stabilisation, privatisation and price liberalisation came to be seen as the *sine qua non* of structural adjustment programmes, both for their immediate impact on financial imbalances and as conditions for the effective operation of the market. In an ideal world a structural adjustment programme which stabilised the price level and allowed relative prices to adjust freely to market conditions would simultaneously encourage investment in the expansion of profitable branches of activity and free the human, material and financial resources for such expansion by accelerating the decline of unviable branches.

The appropriateness of the structural adjustment model appeared to be confirmed by the contrast between the fate of what became known as the 'newly industrialising countries', particularly the 'Asian tigers', and those economies which sought to protect themselves from the ravages of the world market. While the former rode the first punch before moving on to the offensive, the latter merely experienced economic stagnation as the cost of protection increasingly weighed on them in the form of a growing burden of domestic and international public debt and corresponding fiscal and financial instability. The short-term cost of adjustment could be high, as reductions in insupportable state expenditure and the impact of the market lead to the liquidation of unviable economic activity and rising unemployment. However, fiscal and financial stabilisation and the freeing of resources tied up in stagnant sectors would supposedly provide the means and the incentive for new investment in those sectors which enjoy a comparative advantage in the global market and so for the creation of new and viable jobs which alone can promise a rising standard of living.

The fact that many countries persisted with irrational protectionist policies and regulation of the domestic economy was explained in terms of a simple political economy of adjustment first proposed by Adam Smith in *The Wealth of Nations*, his critique of the mercantilist system in the eighteenth century. Those who benefited the most from the protectionist system, at least in the short-run, were those who were the most conscious of their own interests and the best-placed to defend them because they were those who were the most deeply embedded in the protectionist bureaucratic-political system. They secured a political base for themselves by ensuring that the employees of the state and of state-supported industry enjoyed security of employment, relatively high wages and superior working and living conditions. The principal victims of protectionism, the rural and urban poor involved in subsistence production and casual employment in the informal economy, were the least aware of their situation and the worst placed to do anything to remedy it. The beneficent hand of the market was therefore impeded in its liberating mission by the barriers of privilege, ignorance and narrow self-interest. Just as Adam Smith contrasted the virtues of enlightened despotism with the demagoguery of democracy, so the ideologues of structural adjustment presented themselves as the anointed representatives of the world's poor and dispossessed against the 'populism' of political regimes which masked the self-interest of a privileged minority (World Bank, 1995).

The record of structural adjustment programmes has been a very mixed one. In particular, many economies which have submitted to the initial shock have found themselves with high and persistent rates of unemployment without necessarily enjoying any of the benefits of recovery, while others have enjoyed the fruits of recovery without having to undergo the initial pain of shock therapy. Cynics might argue that such contrary experiences undermine the universality of the model, indicating that policy has a rather limited impact on the fortunes of a national economy in the global market, or even that the direction of causality is reversed: the successful can afford liberalisation, while continued regulation is the least-worst option for the unsuccessful. Those who are well-placed to respond to the challenge of globalisation, by virtue of location or of human or natural resource endowments or of the legacy (or absence of a legacy) of the past, enjoy a virtuous circle of export-led growth supporting rising domestic employment and living standards, drawing in young labour from the countryside, from backward industries or from abroad, without the need to destroy existing production facilities or social institutions and with bulging state coffers providing resources for growing public investment. Those who are burdened by a legacy of debt, an outdated industrial structure, unfavourable location, an absence of easily mobilisable reserves of labour or exploitable natural resources find themselves locked in to a vicious circle of decline as 'stabilisation' leads to rising unemployment, falling incomes, a deteriorating social fabric, rising inequality, a shrinking domestic market and an explosion of crime with few prospects for domestic investment, which is further discouraged by the need to retain high interest rates to stem capital flight. While the former can embrace the rhetoric, and even much of the reality, of liberalisation (though often retaining high levels of state intervention and state investment), it is hardly surprising that the latter take steps to try to arrest decline.

The structural adjustment model has remained impervious to all such criticism, despite the growing record of failure and the few examples of success. But no amount of empirical counter-examples can dent the model, or the self-confidence of its proponents, because the model is not presented as an empirical generalisation but as a statement of fundamental economic principles. Adam Smith's critique of the mercantilist system was based not any rigorous theoretical or substantive analysis but on the application of a few abstract ideological principles, the truth of which he insisted was self-evident. It is these same abstract ideological principles, whose truth is still regarded as self-evident, which have guided the ideologues of structural adjustment: the liberal economic model is an abstract model which rests on the supposedly self-evident foundations of human rationality. If the medicine of stabilisation and liberalisation does not achieve the miracle cure, it is because vested interest and timid politicians have prevented it from having its full effect. The limited success of structural adjustment programmes only feeds the radicalism of the ideologues and whets their appetite for more and deeper liberalisation.

The structural adjustment model is a three-stage model of transition from a regulated to a market economy. In the first stage, fiscal and financial 'stabilisation' force the reduction in the level of state activity, including the levels of social and welfare provision, and the closure of unprofitable state and private enterprises, leading to rising unemployment. In the second stage, the reduction in public borrowing leads to falling inflation and interest rates and the stabilisation of the exchange rate, while an increase in unemployment lubricates the labour market and allows wages to fall to levels which in the third, recovery, stage make new investment in new sectors profitable for domestic and foreign investors. The longer drawn out is the first stage, the more effectively are the benighted defenders of the old order able to mobilise support in opposition to reform, appealing particularly to its immediate victims, the state bureaucrats and urban industrial workers whose privileges have been eroded. At the same time, the longer reform is drawn out the longer it takes for stabilisation to create the environment for recovery. Thus, both political and economic arguments are in favour of a short sharp shock, a stabilisation package which works its wonders as rapidly as possible.

As noted above, structural adjustment programmes, in the broadest sense, have a mixed record. Even amongst those market economies which have taken a lead in adopting the package of stabilisation and liberalisation, have experienced structural adjustment and which have even tapped new sources of economic growth, some have experienced persistently high rates of unemployment: the most obvious contrast being between Western Europe, where unemployment rates have still not recovered from the sharp increases of the 1970s and 1980s, and the United States, which has seen unemployment rates below the historic average. According to the liberal model, such persistent unemployment can only derive from barriers to market adjustment. Once domestic and international product and financial markets have been liberalised, the only remaining culprit is the labour market.[2] During the 1980s the view became dominant that 'labour market rigidities' were one of the prime barriers to structural adjustment because they impeded labour mobility in response to the changes in relative prices that are induced by price liberalisation – a view which received the official support of the OECD and World Bank. The breaking down of 'barriers' to labour mobility therefore came to be seen as a prime task of the first stage of structural adjustment. These barriers are all those institutional and normative factors which prevent labour power from functioning as a commodity like any other: people's attachment to time and place, to their homes and their jobs, to forms of work, ways of living, and even to standards of living, that make them reluctant to uproot themselves and move to a new home, a new profession and a new way of life and induce them to look to

---

[2]   Not quite all the blame fell on the labour market. It was also recognised that capital markets did not function perfectly, in particular in their failure to provide funds for the development of small and medium enterprises which were seen as a prime potential source of new employment (often based on a confusion between gross and net employment creation: SMEs create a lot of jobs, but have a low survival rate). Labour market liberalisation has therefore generally been associated with various kinds of small business packages to provide a route into self-employment and to encourage the growth of SMEs.

government, trade unions and other social and political organisations for protection. The greater are these attachments, the more money people need to be paid to induce them to move and so the more difficult it is for new economic activities to attract people to work at wages sufficiently low to make the new jobs viable. Breaking the barriers involves breaking those attachments by destroying jobs that are no longer viable in market conditions. Once these ties have been broken, people will be willing to seek new jobs in new spheres at wages that make the jobs sustainable. This is claimed not to be the heartlessness of the banker, but the benevolence of the realist who appreciates that these jobs can no longer be sustained (and supposedly they have only been sustained at the expense of other, less fortunate or more enterprising, members of the population), so that it is necessary to be cruel to be kind. Only by destroying existing jobs can people be induced to seek new jobs in new spheres at wages which make the jobs sustainable. A relatively high level of transitional unemployment is therefore accepted as an essential feature of structural adjustment.

Providing that labour markets are flexible, this unemployment will only be transitional as investors take advantage of the abundance of low-wage labour to invest in the new opportunities opened by the market. The reform of labour market institutions through both passive and active labour market policies therefore came to be seen as an increasingly important component of structural adjustment packages. The purpose of such reforms was to increase wage flexibility, so that people would 'price themselves into jobs'; to increase the provision of training and retraining, so that people would have the skills required by the labour market; and to improve the functioning of employment services, to match the unemployed to available vacancies. The major barriers to wage flexibility were centralised collective bargaining, state regulation of wages and liberal unemployment benefit regimes, all of which set a floor to wages at a level above that sustainable by the market. The liberalisation of labour market institutions, therefore, implied decentralised wage bargaining, an end to state wage regulation and a stringent unemployment benefit regime. Those who could not find work at a tolerable wage as a result of specific disadvantages would be protected from the impact of liberalisation by the creation of a systematically targeted 'social safety net' providing income support for those unable to support themselves.

Although there were plenty of critics of this model in the West, and even within the multilateral organisations that promoted it, the model appealed to the elites in the so-called 'transition countries' in its most liberal form: the challenge of reform was to restructure an economy which had been distorted by the military and political demands of the Party-state and the rigidities of the administrative-command system, with an overdeveloped heavy industry and underdeveloped consumer goods and service sectors. The Party-state had tried in vain to reform the system over thirty years, and was now in a state of collapse. What could be more attractive than a programme of 'market Bolshevism' which promised an instant cure while absolving the state of all responsibility? Moreover, the promises of structural adjustment coincided precisely with the aspirations of a large part of the population of the transition economies: the opening of frontiers, access to world markets, participation in global society, the attainment of Western living standards were all goals worth suffering for, particularly if other people were to do the suffering.

The application of the structural adjustment model to the transition economies focused on a restructuring of the economy based on the decline of large state industrial enterprises which would free the resources to permit the growth of a new private sector, with little expectation that overdeveloped state enterprises, burdened with an excessively large labour force, outdated capital stock, poor product quality, inappropriate location and conservative management had much potential for internal restructuring. A tight stabilisation policy would subject the state sector to a 'hard budget constraint' leading to widespread lay-offs and large-scale bankruptcy. The resultant increase in unemployment would lead to falling wages, with labour market slack being absorbed by the new private sector, particularly in the underdeveloped branches of the economy (services, consumer goods production and extractive and processing industries oriented to the world market).[3] However, the extent of the structural maladjustment of the transition economies combined with a highly educated labour force, a generally favourable location with basic infrastructure in place and a strong resource base should have meant that, once freed from the straightjacket of state control, transition would be a rapid process.

---

[3] 'The presence of some unemployment is critical, at least initially if private sector growth is to occur in the transitional economy. Slack in the labor market will tend to reduce pressures for wage growth in the economy, and a low wage is a major factor motivating the creation of jobs in the private sector' (Michael Bruno, chief economist, World Bank in Commander and Coricelli (eds), 1995, p. vi).

According to this model, structural adjustment in Russia has still not got off the ground after five years of radical reform. The massive decline in industrial production has not been accompanied by bankruptcies, significant compulsory redundancies or a commensurate fall in employment, so that unemployment remains very low and labour which could be better used elsewhere remains tied up in unviable enterprises. The growth of the service sector has been limited, investment has collapsed and unrestructured light industry, unable to meet foreign competition, has been the hardest hit of all by structural shocks, while even the extractive and processing industries, despite being sustained by new export opportunities, have seen a fall in production of a third.[4] The proponents of the orthodox structural adjustment strategy have argued that employment restructuring in Russia has been blocked by 'labour hoarding' by state enterprises, which has been sustained by state subsidies and soft budget constraints (Commander, McHale et al., 1995).[5] The policy implication is that budget constraints should be hardened, bankruptcy effectively enforced, the Employment Service strengthened and a social safety net provided in preparation for mass unemployment. But what is the

---

[4]   Between 1990 and 1996 the physical volume of industrial production fell by 54%, while capital investment fell by 75% over the same period. However, this was not to the benefit of the relatively undeveloped consumer goods industries: the physical output of light industry (shoes, textiles, clothing etc.) fell by over 85% as import penetration soared, while the 'overdeveloped' branches of fuel and power and iron and steel were the least affected branches of industry, with electricity generation only 20% down, and fuels, iron and steel down by a third (*Rossiya v Tsifrakh*, 1996, 1997; *Sotsial'no-ekonomicheskoe polozhenie Rossii*, I and V, 1997; Tsentr Ekonomicheskoi kon'yunktury, *Rossii – 1996: ekonomicheskaya kon'unktura*, 4, 1996).

[5]   In the revised version of a 1995 paper Commander, Dhar et al. recognise that 'firms have generally been quite effectively constrained in their wage setting by their revenues, and they do not appear to have operated as if in the presence of a soft budget constraint' (1996, p. 49). The original version of the paper reported that 70% of enterprises in their sample received subsidies through the federal budget(1995, p. 3), revised to 25–30 per cent in the published version (1996, p. 22), recognising in both cases that these were 'at significantly lower real levels toward the end of the period'.

It is important to distinguish between the macro and the micro arguments for accelerated employment reductions. The macro arguments relate to the cost of subsidising jobs in unprofitable enterprises, the micro arguments relate to the freeing of labour to ease the labour market. We are concerned only with the latter aspect in this paper, although it should be noted that in the Russian context the macro argument cannot be sustained because the cost of subsidising jobs is minimal, jobs having been preserved at the expense of wages rather than the state budget. As Jackman and Pauna note, unemployment is very inefficient in transition countries because the opportunity cost of those remaining in employment is close to zero. Policies which increase unemployment 'have not eliminated the soft budget constraint, they have simply shifted it from firms to households' (Jackman and Pauna, 1996, p.9).

evidence for this argument that labour market rigidities have been the principal barrier to structural adjustment?

THE RESTRUCTURING OF PRODUCTION, INCOMES AND EMPLOYMENT IN RUSSIA

The almost universal expectation in the early stage of reform was that the transition to a market economy would involve a very substantial increase in unemployment as the reserves of surplus labour which were presumed to fill the Soviet enterprise were laid off and the large number of unviable state enterprises closed down. Shatalin expected that his '500 days' programme would lead to a five million increase in unemployment in the Soviet Union in the first year, with a further 20 million changing their jobs (IMF et al., 1991). Shokhin, Yeltsin's first Labour Minister, estimated in November 1991 that 30 million would lose their jobs in Russia in the first year of radical reform, of whom half were destined for long-term unemployment.[6] The ILO enterprise surveys in 1991 and 1992 indicated that enterprise directors believed that they had substantial surplus labour and were planning significant lay-offs, so that Guy Standing concluded that mass lay-offs were to be expected in early 1993, 'with drastic employment consequences' (Standing, 1994c, p. 259). Although interpretations differed, the general conclusion was that policy should focus on the provision of a social safety net and a system of job placement for the unemployed: 'The key requirement for the pursuit of effective labor market policies will be the build-up of a nation-wide public employment service' (IMF et al., 1991, pp. 137–8), although it was recognised at the time that only about one in five, mostly low-skilled, workers used the existing labour bureaux in looking for jobs (ibid., p. 159).

In the event everybody seemed to have been proved wrong. The 'big bang' of reform had a devastating impact on the Russian economy, leading to much higher inflation than had been expected, a

---

6   Such warnings of impending mass unemployment have been a regular feature of the Russian political scene, whether issued by the 'social' ministries anxious to secure funding, by opponents of liberal reform warning of its consequences or its supporters 'softening up' the population for the experience of mass unemployment. The fact that such cries of wolf have not yet been fulfilled does not mean that mass open unemployment is not a possibility for the future.

sustained fall in production far beyond the fears of even the most pessimistic of commentators, very little investment of any kind and yet,
although unemployment had risen rapidly in East Central Europe, with
the exception of the Czech Republic, there was no such dramatic
increase in Russia or the other republics of the former Soviet Union.[7]
Early estimates by the neo-liberal reformers were that the elasticity of
employment with respect to changes in production was between 0.1
and 0.15 in the first two years of reform (quoted Kapelyushnikov,
1994), although these estimates were based on rather dubious figures.
Nevertheless, it certainly is the case that while the physical index of
industrial production fell by 35% between 1990 and 1993, reported
employment in industry fell by only 9%. GDP was reported at the time
to have fallen by 31% over the same period, but the total fall in employment was originally reported as being only 4%.[8] Moreover, the
reduction in industrial employment was associated with only a relatively small rise in unemployment as some found jobs in other sectors
of the economy and others left the labour market altogether. According
to the Goskomstat figures at the time, total employment fell by 6%
over this period, but registered unemployment increased to only 1.1%,
although survey unemployment amounted to 5.5% at the end of 1993,
against an estimated 3.5% on the eve of reform.[9]

The failure of Russia to fit the neo-liberal model was taken, particularly by the World Bank Economic Development Institute (EDI)
team headed by Simon Commander, as an indicator of the failure of
reform to have the desired impact on state enterprises, 'pointing to the

---

[7]   Radical reform in Russia dates from January 1992, when wages and most prices were
      liberalised within an initially tight monetary and fiscal regime, provoking massive in-
      flation, a collapse of (statistical) real wages and devaluation of savings in the first half
      of the year. However, this aggregate shock came on top of the primarily structural
      shocks of 1991 as the Soviet system disintegrated, already leading to significant output
      falls. The aggregate shock of the first half of 1992 was dissipated by the accumulation
      of inter-enterprise debt and reversion to barter, which was then validated by credit ex-
      pansion in the second half of the year, allowing a substantial recovery of real wages.
      Since then inflation has been brought down to below 20% annual in 1996 primarily by
      a strict exchange rate regime which has co-existed with inconsistently tight money and
      credit and loose fiscal policies, the whole package being held together by arm-twisting
      the commercial banking sector which, while nominally private, depends severally and
      individually entirely on the state for its solvency.

[8]   The official figures for the fall in GDP and employment over 1990–93 were later re-
      vised to record a substantially lower rate of economic decline and a higher rate of
      employment loss.

[9]   Since October 1992 unemployment figures according to the ILO definition have been
      prepared on the basis of labour force surveys (annual apart from 1995, when two sur-
      veys were conducted).

immense inertia in the system' (Commander, Liberman et al., 1993, p. 1). Enterprise directors were supposedly able to avoid restructuring because they still faced soft budget constraints and so were able to continue their traditional practice of labour hoarding. This appeared to be confirmed by the fact that both the World Bank and the early ILO surveys showed little relationship between output (sales) decline and employment decline (Standing, 1992; Commander, Liberman et al., 1993).

This labour hoarding was explained by Commander, Liberman et al. as attributable to the 'implicit "moral economy" of the etatiste era' (p. 1) expressed in their model of the 'de facto worker controlled firm ... primarily concerned with employment stability' (p. 2) in which employment is maintained, with the availability of cash the main determinant of wages. On their analysis, in the first half of 1992 the aggregate shock imposed by acute cash shortages as a result of tight monetary and fiscal policy was absorbed by real wage decline while employment remained constant, insider bargaining power then pushing real wages back up in the second half of the year unconstrained by any budget constraint as monetary and credit policy eased, the result being a classic case of stagflation.

The World Bank judgement of failure might seem a little premature, apparently based on the expectation that the transformation from state socialism to capitalism could be achieved in a matter of months. Although 1992 was hardly an *annus mirabilis* of reform and 1993 was marked by a polarisation between the reformers and the conservatives, the reformers remained in the driving seat and the reforms remained on track, with a programme of crash privatisation dismantling state ownership and the success of stabilisation being manifested in the slow but steady fall in inflation. Industrial production and GDP continued their equally steady fall, but employment in the state and former state sector began to decline more rapidly, with industrial employment reported by Goskomstat as having fallen by 31% between 1991 and 1996, less than the 53% fall in industrial production but still a substantial decline. Unemployment also increased, although survey unemployment only reached a modest 8.6% at the end of March 1996 (and was estimated to have reached 9.5% a year later).

Amidst all the gloom, this avoidance of mass unemployment in the face of enormous structural shocks might seem to be the great achievement of the Russian transition. Not so for the World Bank team, which has continued to play down the extent of restructuring in the state and former state sector and to stick doggedly to its model of transition based on the pauperisation and demoralisation of the population through a spell of unemployment to prepare them for employment in the new private sector.[10] Privatisation appears to have had little or no impact on enterprise behaviour. There have been very few compulsory redundancies, with at least two-thirds of separations still being recorded as voluntary. According to the World Bank team, the high rates of labour turnover do not indicate labour market flexibility since the vast majority of job-to-job transfers take place within the state and former state sector as people move between existing jobs, while the new private sector provides only a limited number of new jobs, making extensive use of low-paid casual labour. The relatively low rate of unemployment and limited development of the private sector is for them an indicator of the failure of reform, which is explained by the continued hoarding of labour by worker-dominated state and former-state enterprises, facilitated by a soft-budget constraint and monopoly powers, and by various labour market rigidities. The implication was 'that every effort should be made to hit state enterprises as hard as possible' (Aslund 1993, p. 18). The shock of adjustment had been absorbed not by employment loss but by a substantial decline in wages: wage flexibility has been the price of employment inflexibility.[11]

Since this has tended to be the dominant analysis of the Russian situation, the elements of the argument merit closer consideration. The central thesis is that Russian enterprises entered transition with a substantial reserve of labour as a result of labour-hoarding in the Soviet era, and that this reserve has increased as enterprises have retained their old habits in the era of reform. Since this assumption of a freely disposable reserve of labour is widely held it needs to be examined more closely in both the Soviet and post-Soviet contexts.

---

[10] In fact the private sector throughout Eastern and Central Europe is a net contributor to the pool of unemployed, preferring to recruit directly from the state sector, so most of the flow out of unemployment is to state sector jobs or out of the labour market (Boeri, 1994).

[11] Commander, Liberman et al. see high labour mobility not as an indicator of significant restructuring but of institutional shocks which have disturbed wage relativities, but this argument is difficult to sustain since the flow is two-way: it is easy to understand why people should choose to move from low paid to higher paid jobs, but it is not clear why they should choose to move the other way.

DID SOVIET ENTERPRISES HOARD SURPLUS LABOUR?

The argument that Soviet enterprises hoarded labour has become a commonplace,[12] but it is one that is based on very little research or analysis. Soviet estimates in the first half of the 1980s, based on surveys of managers, were that enterprises employed somewhere between 15% and 25% more people than were required to make the production plan.[13] Phil Hanson's matched plant comparison in the chemical industry indicated that Soviet staffing levels were between 1.5 and 1.7 times the equivalent West European plants (Hanson, 1986). However, these estimates should be treated with caution. The fact that a Soviet enterprise had more employees than its Western equivalent, or than its director considered necessary for production, did not mean that it could simply dispense with a proportion of its labour force. Employers the world over think that they have more people than they need, if only they could make the remainder work 5, 10, 20% harder. Vladimir Gimpel'son reported from his surveys at the end of the 1980s that respondents more frequently identified redundant personnel in more distant parts of the enterprise – nobody thinks that their own workplace is overstaffed, but as for those people over there....[14] The complaints of labour shortage were genuine and the very large number of unfilled vacancies created serious difficulties for many enterprises, particularly if they had to storm to make the plan.

Labour hoarding is not necessarily the same thing as having a surplus of labour, although the two are commonly identified with one another. Phil Hanson's classic analysis saw labour hoarding as complementary to over-investment, so labour hoarding was quite consistent with labour shortage. There was a surplus of labour, not in the sense that people had nothing to do, but in the sense that many

---

[12]   'Given the initial conditions – firms entered the transition with large labour hoarding...' (Commander, Dhar et al., 1996, p. 15).

[13]   Oxenstierna, 1990, 31–4. Kapelyushnikov,1994, quotes the customary Soviet estimate as 20%. Over half a sample of émigrés interviewed by the Soviet Interview Project said that a given level of output could be produced with fewer workers and employees, although almost half of these claimed that the 'surplus' was only 5% (Linz, 1995, p. 706). The growing ideological emphasis on the labour surplus was closely connected with the attempt both to free labour for new projects and to encourage women with young children to leave their jobs.

[14]   Gimpel'son, 1993. Gimpel'son also reported that at this time managers did *not* think that they had surplus staff.

people could be dispensed with through technological rationalisation, particularly by scrapping outdated plant, mechanising auxiliary labour and improving the organisation and management of production. Without such rationalisation and investment, however, enterprises needed everybody they could get their hands on.

To understand the phenomenon of 'labour hoarding' it is necessary to understand the character of the Soviet enterprise, which was not just a unit of production, but was the fundamental institution of Soviet society, providing a whole range of social and welfare services to its employees and the surrounding community, and the principal locus of social control. Corresponding to the duality of function of the enterprise, the labour force had a dual structure, with the skilled core production workers responsible for meeting the production plan enjoying high status and a privileged position, surrounded by a mass of auxiliary and ancillary workers servicing production, providing housing, social and welfare services and constituting a labour reserve available for communal and seasonal work in municipal services and in agriculture (Kozina and Borisov, 1996). The productivity of labour in direct production was probably considerably less in Soviet enterprises than in contemporary Western plants, but this was a result of the poor organisation and management of production and the irrationalities of the administrative-command system rather than a result of labour hoarding. By the end of the Soviet era even the most highly privileged military plants faced the acute shortages of skilled labour which had always plagued the less privileged light industry, public services and construction. These shortages were not simply in relation to the insatiable demand for labour that supposedly marked the Soviet enterprise, but in relation to the complement required to operate the installed plant and equipment according to the technically determined norms, and the number actually required to meet the production plan. Very uneven work rhythms that were a result of the irregularity of supply and inadequacy of maintenance and repair of plant and equipment meant that production workers alternated periods of inactivity with periods of extremely intensive labour, working double or treble shifts to make the plan at the end of the planning period, and often working in appalling conditions.[15] Production labour was used very

---

[15]   One-fifth of industrial workers (and almost half the labour force in coal-mining) work in conditions which do not meet official health standards and almost a half of all industrial workers work in conditions recognised as being 'unpleasant'. While conditions have not improved in the transition to the market, there has been a significant reduction

inefficiently, at great cost to the health of the workers, but there is no evidence that enterprises disposed of significantly more production workers than they needed in the given technical conditions and with the given forms of organisation of production. There is similarly no evidence that a significant proportion of the substantial specialist staff employed to run the extensive social and welfare apparatus provided through large industrial enterprises was surplus to requirements, although those requirements again may have been inflated through the inefficient organisation of labour in this sphere.

The most marked 'surplus' of labour, in comparison to comparable Western plants, was to be found in the substantial reserve of unskilled auxiliary and ancillary labour which enterprises were required to maintain in the Soviet period to meet the demands imposed on the enterprise by local Party authorities to supply labour to perform communal, municipal and agricultural work, from the building, maintenance and repair of municipal facilities to the provision of agricultural labour at peak periods.[16] If the enterprise could keep a large body of unskilled workers engaged in various ancillary and auxiliary capacities, including the administration, construction, repair and maintenance of enterprise housing, social and welfare facilities, then it could meet the demands imposed on it for social labour without disrupting production. These demands for social labour are probably an important part of the explanation for the failure to mechanise the auxiliary and ancillary tasks performed by these workers and for the low disciplinary demands put on them, but in the absence of such mechanisation their labour was not superfluous. Finally, the social control and welfare function of the enterprise meant that it was obliged to provide employment for its pensioners, for the sick and disabled as well as for 'parasites' and released prisoners directed to it by the labour recruitment bureaux, all categories of people who could be employed in low productivity labour-intensive peripheral spheres such as cleaning, loading, cloakroom attending and so on. A significant proportion of the labour 'surplus', therefore, comprised people who, in a market economy, would be unemployable, and removed from the labour market by the social insurance or benefit system.

in the proportion of employees who are compensated for such unpleasant and harmful working conditions (Goskomstat, 1996e).

16   The scale of this work was considerable. In 1982 17 million people (16% of all employees outside agriculture) were detached from state enterprises on temporary agricultural assignments alone (Granick, 1987, pp. 38–9).

Enterprise directors certainly had an interest in enlarging their authorised labour force, since this gave them a large wage fund and increased their own status and income, which was normatively linked to the size of the 'staff list' of authorised personnel, although career advance for directors came through promotion rather than through marginal adjustments to the size of their current enterprise. The larger the labour force in relation to the demands of the plan the easier life was for the enterprise director. But the question of a labour surplus is not a question of whether directors would have liked to have had more labour, but of whether they were successful in thwarting the planners' attempts to confine the demand for labour within the limits of its supply.

In practice, of course, the planners were well aware that everybody wanted as much labour and as large a wage fund as they could get. For this reason the planners attempted to set the allocation of labour on a 'scientific' basis, with the staffing of every machine and the complement of ancillary, auxiliary, technical, managerial and clerical staff all being normatively defined, ultimately in relation to the technical characteristics of the stock of machinery and equipment. The authorised labour force was therefore linked normatively to investment and to output, so that it was at best only possible for an enterprise marginally to increase its labour force without at the same time committing itself to a higher output plan. The real constraint on the planned growth of the enterprise was not the size of the authorised labour force, but the investment funds allocated to it, while the constraint on the ability of the enterprise to meet its plans was not the supplies of goods and labour allocated to the enterprise by the plan, but the supplies it could actually secure and the labour it could actually recruit. This meant that the enterprise director had an interest in securing excess capacity rather than a surplus of labour. In other words, the tendency was to over-investment constrained by labour shortage, rather than to the hoarding of surplus labour.

The central argument in support of the existence of labour hoarding is the claim that enterprises were subject to a soft budget constraint, and therefore were not penalised for employing a surplus of labour.[17]

---

[17]   The idea that Soviet enterprises faced, and continue to face, soft-budget constraints is one of those taken-for-granted but manifestly false assumptions (derived from Kornai's characterisation of the Hungarian reform economy) on which most Western analysis is based. In the absence of a developed financial system and with virtually no working capital, enterprises faced and continue to face far harder budget constraints than their

Although this claim has become commonplace, arguments about 'soft budget constraints' are mis-specified in the Soviet context since Soviet enterprises did not have a single 'budget', but earmarked funds for a whole series of different categories of expenditure. While they could negotiate and re-negotiate their budgetary allocations, so that annual plans for wages and employment tended to be revised upwards, the negotiating process was extremely tough. As Granick argues, 'enterprise demand for labour is "effective" only within the constraint of its realised wage fund' (Granick, 1987, p. 68) so that over-investment and labour shortage only arise if the central authorities deliberately choose to allow it. In general, the Soviet authorities did not allow it, although they did deliberately maintain 'over-full' employment (ibid., p. 69).[18] Employment was very closely monitored by a state inspectorate to avoid precisely the kind of things which Western observers imagine were endemic in Soviet enterprises.

While Soviet enterprises could not be declared bankrupt, their expenditure was closely monitored and they had no access to bank credit. The primary constraint on the payment of wages was the wage fund, which was the source of 96% of the earnings of manual workers (Granick, 1987, p. 52) and whose expenditure was closely monitored. While an enterprise could overspend its allocation in the hope of negotiating a revision to its plan, the director who did so ran a high risk of incurring a heavy financial penalty and the loss of his or her job.

Western equivalents. It is true that no enterprise could go bankrupt, but this did not give the director *carte blanche* to run up debts, and nor can directors run up debts without limit today. It is true that some enterprises were consistent loss-makers, but this was a well-understood feature of the planning system, and the scale of losses was strictly, if informally, limited if the director was to keep his job. Russian enterprises had and have nothing like the scope for loss-making as a prelude or accompaniment to restructuring that is enjoyed by their Western equivalents because they have such limited access to credit and working capital and virtually no access to long-term finance. State and 'state-directed' bank credit is available to sustain enterprises but it is unpredictable, generally being provided only on a crisis basis, particularly to enable enterprises to pay their taxes, and so cannot be counted on by enterprise directors. In sum, the soft-budget constraint, as understood by Western economists, is a myth. Enterprises face very hard budget constraints, which is why they have to live from hand to mouth and can take only a short-term perspective. State subsidies to enterprises, outside coal-mining, agriculture and municipal services, have been slashed and are now below the level of many OECD countries (Halligan, Teplukhin et al., 1996).

[18] In fact it crept up within each plan period, partly because productivity targets were not achieved, but it could in principle be cut back and it was cut back for the next plan. The planning process was not completely effective: Malle, 1986, argues that adequate manpower planning was impossible because the planners didn't have the necessary information.

While the state bank covered over-spending on wages, this had to be repaid immediately or managers were heavily penalised.[19] This meant that an enterprise could only recruit beyond its authorised employment if it cut the wages of the labour force, which it would be most unlikely to do in a tight labour market, and which Soviet enterprises did not do: the problem was not to recruit more than the authorised number but to recruit up to the complement so as not to lose the unspent portion of the wage and related funds. Until the end of perestroika Soviet managers faced, and behaved as though they faced, far harder budget constraints and had far less discretion in their spending than a Western manager could even imagine. One result of these very hard budget constraints was the extremely low inflation which marked the Soviet period until the liberalisation of perestroika (Granick, 1987, pp. 57–9).

Under the 1987 Law on State Enterprise, enterprises were given more responsibility for defining their own wage and employment policies, determining the total number of workers, their skill and level of qualifications. However, the purpose of this reform was to strengthen the incentive for enterprises to shed labour as a means of increasing productivity, reinforcing the 1986 wage reform.[20] Thus, although they could pool the wage and material incentive funds and could carry savings on the wage fund over to the next year, there was still strict financial control of their allocation to wages (Malle, 1990), until these controls were reduced in 1990 and finally removed at the end of 1991. The inflationary pressure of the perestroika era came not from the softening of the budget constraint on state enterprises, but from the lack of any control of the new co-operatives and small enterprises. The result of this loss of control was not a growing labour surplus, but rapidly rising wages associated with a fall in employment as work was sub-contracted to formally independent co-operatives and small enterprises operating under the wing of state enterprises. This tightness of the budget constraint has left an important legacy for the inflationary

---

[19] Hanson, 1986, argued that the predominance of output targets meant that it was worth paying the fine for exceeding the wage bill rather than lose the bonus for making the plan. But in fact directors did not do this: the overspend was only 0.7% between 1975–80 (Granick, 1987).

[20] The 1986 wage reform gave enterprises a significant incentive to reduce their labour force, but by the beginning of 1990 only 5% of the labour force had been displaced, of whom one-third were redeployed within the same enterprise, one-third retired and one-third found jobs elsewhere (IMF et al., 1991). Zaslavskii and Moskvina, 1989, found that two-thirds of those made redundant remained in the same enterprise, usually moving to similar jobs. This would indicate that there were not substantial reserves of surplus labour secreted in state enterprises.

post-perestroika period, when state credits have been withdrawn without being replaced by a properly functioning banking system so that the industrial sector is extremely short of both working and investment capital, leaving all enterprises, profitable and unprofitable, to face acute problems of cash flow which can only be covered by delaying payment of taxes, inter-enterprise claims and wages.

The most striking aspect of the Soviet system is the poor organisation and management of work and of the allocation of equipment and materials which led to low levels of labour productivity, part of which was manifested in the extremely uneven rhythm of labour, but which was more generally manifested in the unproductive and unnecessary expenditure of labour, something which made workers extremely bitter and angry and fuelled their enormous hostility to management, which they regarded as parasitic and incompetent. Although the Soviet enterprise might use much more labour than its capitalist equivalent, this was not hoarded or surplus labour which could be released without any impact on production. The problem was not labour hoarding or a soft budget constraint, but a planning system in which enterprises had every incentive not to increase the productivity of labour, since norm overfulfilment led to an increased plan target, and so which used labour incredibly wastefully. This labour could only be released on the basis of a transformation of the organisation and management of production and, in many cases, significant investment in the rationalisation of production.[21]

WORKERS' CONTROL AND LABOUR HOARDING IN RUSSIAN ENTERPRISES

With the disintegration of the Soviet regime from 1990, and particularly with the liberalisation of wages and most prices at the beginning of 1992, enterprises took their fate into their own hands. While I have argued that Soviet enterprises did not hoard surplus labour, in the sense that they did not have reserves of labour which could easily be

---

[21]   This was partly a problem of production management. Nearly all Western 'technical assistance' in the area of management has been focused on developing the marketing and financial skills of senior managers and accountants, with almost no reference to the need to reform the system of production management if enterprises are to achieve the restructuring of production.

dispensed with, there was certainly very considerable scope for increasing productivity, especially of ancillary labour, and for reducing the need for labour by organising production more rationally. Moreover, the collapse of the Party meant an end to the demands for the provision of 'social' labour, which could be a substantial drain on enterprise resources, providing further scope for rationalisation. The rapid fall of production from 1992 further increased the scope for relieving the financial pressures on enterprises by cutting the labour force. So the question arises of why the decline in employment has lagged far behind the decline in production.

The first point to clarify is that of the existence or the extent of a labour surplus, in the sense of reserves of labour which can be dispensed with without the substantial reorganisation of production. Most of the evidence comes from enterprise surveys in which directors are asked questions such as whether they have surplus labour, or whether they could achieve their production plans with less labour than they currently employ, or whether they have more labour than they need for the next twelve months, and if so are asked to estimate the extent of the surplus and then are asked how much they plan to cut the labour force.[22]

---

[22]   The principal surveys of enterprises have been

- a survey carried out annually since 1991 by the ILO under the direction of Guy Standing, in collaboration originally with Goskomstat and more recently with the Centre for Labour Market Research of the Institute of Economics. This survey originally covered only Leningrad and Moscow, but its coverage has expanded in each round, with some duplication between rounds so it has a longitudinal dimension. The various rounds have covered between 200 and 500 firms. This survey is based on both questionnaires and interviews with managers. The results of the first four rounds have been summarised by Guy Standing (1996b) and those of the following two rounds in Guy Standing's and Pavel Smirnov's reports in this volume.

- the monthly postal survey of the *Russian Economic Barometer*, now covering 950 enterprises, with a monthly response rate of around 50%.

- the quarterly Goskomstat survey 'Monitoring employment in Russian industrial enterprises' carried out since June 1994 using a methodology developed by the Centre for Economic Analysis of the Russian Government. The October 1995 survey covered 1,843 enterprises, stratified by branch, region, property form and number employed, concentrating on managers' assessments of the present situation and short-term future trends. A similar survey of construction organisations is conducted. A number of other organisations, including the Gaidar Institute, conduct regular monitoring surveys of business expectations.

- the World Bank conducted a small survey of 41 firms in Moscow and the Volga region in November 1992 and April 1993 and a larger survey of a stratified random sample of 435 industrial firms, including 49 new ones, in June-July 1994. Analysis of the data from the latter survey formed the basis of a conference organised jointly by the World Bank and Ministry of Economics in St Petersburg in June 1995 and

In general, the evidence from these surveys is fairly consistent: between one third and a half of enterprise directors believe that they do have a surplus of labour, the amount of which varies considerably from one enterprise to another. However, it is by no means clear that this consistency reflects much more than the ideological and political climate. Thus, despite the fact that the decline in production continued to outstrip reductions in employment, fewer enterprises reported a labour surplus in the 1993 ILO survey than had done so in 1992, and the estimated surplus was considerably less (Standing, 1994b),[23] while the June-July 1994 World Bank survey found that about 45% of enterprises reported having surplus labour, the same as the 1992 ILO survey, although the reported extent of the surplus was less

---

some of the analysis has subsequently been published in (Commander, Fan et al., 1996).

- the Union of Industrialists and Entrepreneurs conducted a number of surveys in 1992 and 1993.

It is typical that there is a considerable amount of duplication between these surveys, apparently without any co-ordination between them, so that they all ask slightly different questions. None of the surveys provides sufficient information to be able to judge the quality of the data.

[23] The 1993 World Bank enterprise survey found that about one third of firms reported surplus labour, around the same as the ILO survey (Commander, McHale et al., 1995, p. 157n.). The *Russian Economic Barometer* surveys found that around 25% of respondents acknowledged a surplus (defined as current employment exceeding their needs over the next twelve months – a much higher proportion respond positively to an unqualified question of whether they have an excessive workforce) from 1993 to the end of 1995, while around 20% said they had too little labour, except in May 1994, when 34% estimated that they had a surplus and only 18% a deficit. The number who thought they had a surplus then shot up to 35% at the end of 1995, rising to 39% in the first quarter of 1997, while the number who said they had a shortage of labour fell correspondingly from 13% at the end of 1995 to 10% in the first quarter of 1997. The ILO surveys show exactly the same pattern, the June 1994 survey having about half the enterprises reporting surplus labour, falling to only 36% in the 1995 survey, although those who said they had a surplus claimed on average that it amounted to over 25% of the labour force. The ILO team attributed these variations to changing management priorities rather than the changing economic situation (Tsentr issledovannii rynka truda, 1995a, 21–2). The percentage claiming a surplus increased again to 45% in 1996 (Standing, this volume). These variations in subjective assessment are connected with the rate at which employment is actually reduced, with an increase in the second quarter of 1994 and from the end of 1995. In 1992 cash shortages meant that enterprises were having great difficulty in paying wages. In 1993 there was some hope that policy would be reversed, but Yeltsin's second putsch and the introduction of his new constitution put paid to such hopes, so that directors were convinced of the irreversibility of reform and the need for more drastic action by the beginning of 1994, turning their attention to employment reduction, with the rate of job cuts peaking in the first half of that year. The rate of job loss then fell again, until after the December 1995 election, when plummeting production and financial stringency led once more to falling employment as hiring was curtailed.

(Commander, Dhar et al., 1996, p. 25). This was despite the fact that in the meantime industrial production had fallen by a further quarter while employment had fallen by only one-eighth.[24] The fact of the matter is that senior enterprise management, at least in larger enterprises, is not in a position to know how much surplus labour exists in their enterprise since labour requirements are traditionally a matter for line management.

Although many enterprise directors reported that they had a labour surplus, as far as they were concerned the problem of surplus labour was not an issue, not least because wages are extremely low, while redundant workers can be put on short-time or sent on unpaid leave so that the enterprise is able to retain a reserve of labour at virtually no cost. The ILO survey in 1991 found far more enterprises concerned about shortages of skilled workers than were concerned about labour productivity or redundancy (Standing, 1994a), and in later years the problems of sales, availability of finance and high levels of taxation have loomed far larger than the excessive size of the labour force.[25] Nevertheless, whether or not Russian enterprises hoard reserves of surplus labour, the fact remains that employment reductions have lagged behind the decline in output, so we still have to explain why enterprise directors have chosen not to cut their employment at least in line with the output decline. The World Bank EDI explains this on the basis of its model of the '*de facto* worker-controlled firm'.[26]

---

[24] This would explain why there is not much relationship between reported surplus labour and changes in production and employment in the reporting enterprise. There is evidence from the ILO panel survey that a declaration of a surplus of labour is linked to an intention to reduce employment, since those reporting a surplus in one round had cut employment further in the next.

[25] In January 1994 only 7% reported to *Russian Economic Barometer* that they needed to cut the number of employees when asked to choose three of twelve priorities to adjust to the new environment, against 57% who needed to find new markets, 51% to get debts repaid, 38% to pay their own debts, 29% to change the output mix, 22% to repay bank loans. Only 3–5% of enterprises cited high labour costs as a barrier, so it would seem that maintaining employment (at very low or no wages) does not impose a significant financial burden on the enterprises. On the other hand, only about 5% complained of labour shortages (Kapelyushnikov and Aukutsionek, 1994a). The World Bank survey of June-July 1994 found that less than a third of firms considered employment reduction to be a high priority, with almost 40% attaching no importance to labour reductions (Commander, Dhar et al., 1996, p. 23 and n.).

[26] The reformers initially pinned great hopes on privatisation, which was expected to play a major role. But virtually all surveys find that privatisation has made little or no difference to firm behaviour (e.g. Commander, Liberman et al., 1993; Standing, 1994b; *Russian Economic Barometer*; Kapelyushnikov and Aukutsionek, 1994a; Commander, Dhar et al., 1996; Standing, 1996b). This is usually explained by the Russian form of privatisation, which reinforced insider control by putting the majority of

According to the EDI model, the reason that enterprises have not cut employment is that they are controlled by workers who choose to maintain employment even at the expense of wage reductions. This model of the '*de facto* worker controlled firm' is somewhat dubious, not only because of its lack of realism in the Russian context of authoritarian managerial control,[27] but also because it is not at all clear why the workers should choose to maintain employment at the expense of wages: indeed one would expect the opposite, that a majority of workers would form a coalition to dispense with a minority in order to maintain or increase the wages of those who remain, which is the more normal analysis of worker-controlled firms, as in the Yugoslav case (Kapelyushnikov and Aukutsionek, 1994a).[28] This is particularly

---

[27]   shares in the hands of the labour force.

Most surveys find no significant difference in the behaviour of 'worker-controlled' firms (e.g., in relation to employment cuts, Standing, 1994b), although the 1995 ILO enterprise survey found that 'worker-controlled' firms cut employment by *more* than the average (Standing, 1996a, p. 32). In a later paper Commander, McHale et al. distinguish more clearly between 'worker-controlled' and 'insider-dominated' firms, accepting that 'most Russian firms do not completely conform to' the model of 'firms dominated by inside coalitions of managers and workers, with the former having relatively small bargaining power' (Commander, McHale et al., 1995, p. 176), but continue to use their model of the labour-controlled firm on the grounds that management has to retain the support of its workers through the process of privatisation and for lobbying government and local authorities (Kapelyushnikov and Aukutsionek, 1994a), so that there is at least a temporary coincidence of interests (which then also begs the question of why management has an interest in maintaining employment). The majority of Russian enterprises are still undoubtedly 'insider-controlled', although creditor banks have considerable leverage and outsiders have very rapidly accumulated controlling shareholdings in desirable companies. The main threat to the position of the director comes not from the workers but from competing management factions and outside shareholders, one of which may seek to mobilise worker discontent, and this is the reason and the extent to which workers' collective views have to be considered. But the issue here is not whether insiders have control, but why insider coalitions should want to maintain employment. There have been very few cases in which trade unions have actively opposed redundancy programmes of enterprises or in which workers have taken any form of industrial action against job cuts in Russia. On the other hand, there have been many examples of strikes which have demanded job cuts (usually of office workers and managers) in order to maintain or raise wages – this was a central demand of the 1989 miners' strike (Clarke et al., 1995). It is the fact that management pursues policies counter to the implied and the expressed interests of the workers that leads one to doubt the model of the *de facto* worker controlled firm. *Russian Economic Barometer* found that around a quarter of labour-hoarding enterprises cited avoidance of conflict as a reason for hoarding, given a choice of three out of 13 options, but less than three per cent cited opposition from trade unions (Aukutsionek and Kapelyushnikov, 1996, p. 12). In a comparative study in 1996, 38% of Dutch enterprises cited trade union opposition (Rostislav Kapelyushnikov, personal communication, to be published in *Russian Economic Barometer*, 1997).

[28]   Commander and his colleagues work with a model in which the workers are a collective actor bargaining with management – 'assumed to act as a collective, maximizing

the case since unemployment still does not hold great fears for the majority of workers. Quite apart from the fact that 25% change job each year, in the January 1996 VTsIOM survey almost half those questioned expected that they would be able to find another job in their own trade or profession if they were laid off, which is a perfectly reasonable expectation since around half of those laid-off compulsorily do find new jobs almost at once.[29] One third of employees across the economy as a whole declared that they would prefer to keep their jobs at the cost of delayed wages if their enterprise was in difficulty, but an almost equal number declared that they would prefer to be laid off and one-third found it difficult to say. Almost twice as many of those under 29 years old chose to be laid off as chose to accept delayed wages.[30] Meanwhile, in January 1997 84% were dissatisfied with their pay, three-quarters believed that they earned less than they deserved and, despite continuing inflation, more people in the previous three months had had a pay cut than a pay rise. Rational argument and all the evidence supports the assertion that the interest of workers, in the absence of effective solidaristic trade unionism, is in reducing employment in order to maintain or increase wages.

More recently the World Bank team has recognised the inadequacy of its model, but retains its conclusions on the grounds of the declared concern of directors for the welfare of their workers (Commander, Dhar et al., 1996, p. 35). There is no doubt that directors do regularly

---

the aggregate utility of its members' (Commander, Dhar et al., 1996, p. 40), a degree of solidarity that even the Communist Party of the Soviet Union failed to achieve!

[29] VTsIOM (The All-Russian Centre for Public Opinion Research) has emerged as the main polling organisation in Russia. It has been conducting national polls with a two stage quota sample of between 1,200 and 2,500 individuals since late 1990, with a regular monthly (more recently bi-monthly) monitoring of economic and social change since 1993, using a sub-set of a standard set of questions each month, with additional questions for particular topics. There is a tendency to the substantial over-representation of educated urban professionals and under-representation of workers in their samples. Although the overall figures are adjusted for such sample bias, it means that the number of workers represented is relatively small. VTsIOM publishes a bi-monthly Information Bulletin which reports survey results and contains short analytical articles. The Russian Longitudinal Monitoring Survey (RLMS) has consistently shown people displaying a much lower level of confidence in response to a slightly different question, 24% in October 1996 being absolutely or fairly certain of being able to find another job no worse than their present job, down from 26% in 1994. RLMS is a survey of a national random sample of all members of 4,000 households which has been carried out since 1992 under the auspices of the University of North Carolina at Chapel Hill, which makes the raw data available by FTP. The first phase, covering 1992–93, is not strictly comparable to the second phase, covering 1994–96.

[30] By January 1997 almost 42% were saying that they would prefer to keep their jobs and only 28% that they would rather be dismissed (*VTsIOM Bulletin*, 2, 1997).

express such concern — the caring corporation is as alive (and as meaningful) in Russia as in the West.[31] But this explanation again depends on the unsubstantiated assumption that 'the collective' would prefer to maintain the size of the enterprise at the expense of their own incomes. This assumption might just be plausible in explaining the reluctance of enterprise directors to risk unrest or distress among the labour force by sacking surplus workers,[32] but is completely implausible in a situation in which there is a high level of voluntary separations, since what has to be explained is not any reluctance of management to fire workers, but their enthusiasm for continuing to hire additional workers even where this involves keeping down the wages of those who remain. In most enterprises any labour surplus could be eliminated by a freeze on recruitment for no more than a year or so. If the director wants to 'preserve the labour collective', i.e. to secure the jobs of loyal long-serving workers, the way to do so is to allow the drifters to leave and raise the wages of those who remain.[33]

---

[31] A survey by the Union of Industrialists at the end of 1992 found that 33% of directors chose as their first goal preserving the labour collective, 26% making profits, 16% increasing production and 16% increasing sales (Gimpel'son, 1994). In February 1994 *Russian Economic Barometer* found the maintenance of employment in second place among management objectives, cited by 47% of respondents and headed only by maintaining output (57%), followed by maximising wages plus profit (38%), maximising profit (35%) and maintaining average wages (36%) (Kapelyushnikov and Aukutsionek, 1994a). The June 1994 World Bank survey found that nearly a third of enterprises cited social and ethical reasons for not reducing employment (Commander, Dhar et al., 1996, p. 27). *Russian Economic Barometer* reported in its 1995 and 1996 enterprise surveys that over 70% of labour hoarding enterprises cited the social responsibility of the director as the reason for hoarding, given a choice of three out of 12 options (Aukutsionek and Kapelyushnikov, 1996, p. 12). We prefer to judge directors by what they do, not by what they say! However, there certainly are many enterprise directors who retain the Communist commitment to the retention of the 'labour collective' as the basic social unit. This is by no means the same thing as a commitment to the interests of the workers. In the past the interests of the 'labour collective' were represented by the Communist Party. Any attempt on the part of the workers to represent their own interests was denounced as a 'false collectivism' (Kharkhordin, 1996, p. 30).

[32] The *Russian Economic Barometer* surveys found the avoidance of conflict cited by a quarter of directors as one of the three reasons for hoarding labour. Compulsory redundancies are always referred to as 'painful' because they involve getting rid of 'our' people, but this is not the case for disciplinary dismissals. Redundancies are also more expensive, since the enterprise has to pay the average wage for the first three months of unemployment, whereas short-time working, administrative vacations, voluntary quits and disciplinary dismissals cost nothing.

[33] The bizarre suggestion is made in another report that labour hoarding exists because trade unions prevent the firing of workers (OECD, 1995a, p. 9), something which was virtually unheard of even in the Soviet period. Since 1970 the Labour Code has allowed redundancy if 'it is not possible to transfer the worker, upon his consent, to

Neither workers' control nor enterprise paternalism is sufficient explanation for a hiring rate which in industry in 1996 remained at 19%.[34]

Commander, Liberman et al. apparently appreciate the absurdity of this argument, explaining the high level of hirings not as a feature of employment policy, but as a result of 'semi-binding constraints on production exercised by technology and the associated level and structure of labour demand' (Commander, Liberman et al., 1993, p. 51). This would seem to undermine their whole argument since, if technology dictates that the majority of those who leave should be replaced, it can hardly be argued that the enterprises are harbouring reserves of surplus labour, particularly when the authors assert that separations have been concentrated at the lower end of the skill structure (ibid., pp. 18, 50), so that the demand is not for specific skills but for labour in general. So perhaps Russian enterprises are holding on to labour, to the extent that they are able to do so, not because they are induced to do so by worker control or by a benevolent concern, but because their managers believe that they do actually need these workers.[35] This is certainly the response that we have repeatedly encountered from line managers in industrial enterprises: although production has fallen by considerably more than has employment, there are periods of activity interspersed with long periods of idleness so that line managers feel that the production labour force has been cut to the bone to the extent that they find it difficult to resume production when and if orders are forthcoming.[36]

---

another job' (Malle, 1990, p. 71). A 1995 study by the Centre for Labour Market Research of the Institute of Economics found that in the majority of enterprises the trade union does not even have a right to be consulted about redundancies (Tsentr issledovannii rynka truda, 1995a, p. 50), despite the fact that this right is enshrined in the law.

[34] This was recognised by Commander and Yemtsov in 1995, when they noted that neither benevolence, nor adjustment costs, nor expectations of recovery 'can satisfactorily explain why so many state – often now privatized – firms continue to hire and report large hiring rates' (Commander and Yemtsov, 1995), but they still did not modify their model.

[35] Commander and Yemtsov also assert, without citing any evidence, that 'there are many reasons for thinking that employment, rather than, say, output, has been the main factor determining the size and distribution of subsidies' (Commander and Yemtsov,1995). The distribution of subsidies is a complex political matter, and it is certainly the case that the threat of mass lay-offs can be a source of leverage on local authorities, who have few resources themselves but who may be prevailed upon to press the case in Moscow. However, I know of no reason to think that employment *per se* is a significant factor in the distribution of subsidies. The power and prestige of an enterprise depends now on the level of the taxes, wages and benefits it pays, not the number it can continue to retain in penury.

[36] A 1995 survey of 21 firms in St Petersburg found that half of the top managers believed

I argued above that there was not and never had been a labour surplus in Russian enterprises in the sense that there was a proportion of the labour force which could be dispensed with without loss. There was always a body of ancillary workers, particularly the elderly and disabled, who were retained on very low wages as a social service and who made little contribution to production, many of whom were pushed out in the early stages of reform. There was a substantial group of workers, commonly as much as 25% of the labour force of large enterprises, who worked in the social sphere but made no contribution to production, and who have been displaced as social facilities have been transferred to municipalities that do not have the money to support them.[37] Beyond this, there was a large pool of auxiliary and ancillary workers, many of whose jobs could be reduced through relatively small investments in materials-handling equipment and so on, and the mass of production workers, which could be reduced by the scrapping of redundant equipment and by the reorganisation of production. However, reducing the direct and indirect production labour force requires an input of scarce managerial skills and time to identify those who can be dispensed with, make the appropriate changes in production organisation and, in many cases, the investment of funds which are not available.[38] Thus, even if the pay-off of such restructuring of production might be significant, enterprises do not have the financial and managerial resources to undertake it in a situation when they have other more pressing priorities, and when it costs them almost nothing to retain low-productivity labour. To retain production capacity without having to undertake significant reorganisation of production, however low might be the current level of capacity working, it may in many cases be necessary to retain a considerable

---

that they had surplus labour. The main reason for retaining labour was the cost and difficulty of re-hiring in the event of a recovery (Brown, 1996). About one-third of enterprises in the Russian Economic Barometer surveys cite the high costs of labour shedding, about one-fifth technological constraints and 4% opposition of lower managers to labour shedding.

[37] In the 1994 *Russian Economic Barometer* survey 12% of the labour force was still employed in the non-productive sphere, rising to an average of 23% in enterprises with over 1,500 employees (Kapelyushnikov and Aukutsionek, 1995b).

[38] Brown's survey in St Petersburg concluded that the shortage of adequate managers was the principal barrier to restructuring (Brown, 1996). The redundancies have to be implemented by line management, which is the principal source of resistance to cuts in employment, as our own research has shown. On conditions on the shop-floor of Russian industrial enterprises see the series of volumes *Management and Industry in Russia*, edited by Simon Clarke and published by Edward Elgar.

proportion of the workforce. This is by no means unreasonable in view of the extreme instability and uncertainty of the Russian economy.

This explanation, that enterprises retain labour because they need it and it costs them little to keep it, has the merit of simplicity and of corresponding to what directors themselves say.[39] In the June-July 1994 World Bank survey enterprises cited the expectation of a recovery of demand and output as the main reason for holding on to labour. Despite the continued decline of the Russian economy this is not unreasonable since, within the general decline, there have been considerable fluctuations in the fortunes of particular enterprises and industries and even the less successful enterprises get orders which require them to resume full capacity working for a period, so salvation might always lie over the horizon.[40] With very low labour costs, very

---

[39] There is also the argument that enterprises are politically constrained to retain workers. Enterprises are legally forbidden to lay off workers during the privatisation process (although they frequently induce them to leave voluntarily at this time, selling their shares to management as they go). Local authorities certainly press enterprises to maintain employment, both to avoid having to bear the social costs of the consequences of redundancies and because of their reliance on payroll taxes, and they may frequently offer employment subsidies, usually channelled through the Federal Employment Service, to preserve jobs, but enterprises responded to the *Russian Economic Barometer* survey in January 1994 that they had substantially more independence in hiring and firing than in wage, price and output decisions.

[40] Nearly 50% cited expected future output expansion as the reason for holding on to labour in the 1992 World Bank survey, while nearly 25% cited the lack of a financial burden (Commander, McHale et al., 1995, p. 157n.). The 1995 ILO survey found that 31% of enterprises kept a labour surplus because they expected output to expand, 16% because they wanted to keep skilled employees, 14% because there were no other jobs for employees (often connected with support from local authorities), 12% to preserve the collective, 8% because the surplus workers would leave of their own accord, 6% because they had no money to pay for redundancy, 6% because they were in the privatisation period and 4% because they needed a reserve of unskilled labour because the enterprise has old technology. Two-thirds reporting a surplus did not plan to reduce it (Tsentr issledovannii rynka truda, 1995a, p. 24). A September 1995 survey of enterprises on short-time or administrative vacation found that 40% of employers did not lay off workers because they expected the situation to improve, while 33% cited their sympathy for the workers (63% in Altai) (Garsiya-Iser, Golodets et al., 1995). *Russian Economic Barometer* in 1995 and in 1996 found around 40% citing expected demand recovery, given a choice of three options, a quarter a desire to maintain enterprise status, 17% technological constraints and 28% the high cost of labour shedding, in addition to the reasons already cited above (Aukutsionek and Kapelyushnikov, 1996, p. 12). The comparative Dutch study, referred to above, found that 31% expected demand recovery while 44% cited social responsibility (against 70–72% among Russian enterprises), 31% the high cost of labour shedding (28–35% in Russia), 31% technological constraints (18–19% in Russia) 19% a desire to maintain the status of the enterprise (18–25% in Russia), 38% trade union opposition (3% in Russia) and 6% avoidance of conflict (18–27% in Russia) (Rostislav Kapelyushnikov, personal communication, to be published in *Russian Economic Barometer*, 1997).

high mark-ups and very unstable markets it makes perfect sense to hold on to labour (Commander, Dhar et al., 1996).[41] In this case the problem with the Russian reform is not that unemployment has not risen sufficiently highly to drive wages down to a level attractive to private investors, but that the threat of unemployment has driven wages down so low that enterprises have little incentive to rationalise production and raise labour productivity, preferring instead to put their energies and resources into realising profits through marketing and financial speculation. Nevertheless, despite the proliferation of surveys, of theoretical models of enterprise behaviour and of regressions of everything on everything else, we have to conclude from a review of the literature that something is known about what enterprise directors say, but not much is known about what enterprise directors actually do and why they do it.[42]

EMPLOYMENT RESTRUCTURING AND LABOUR MARKET FLEXIBILITY

The World Bank claims that there has not been significant employment restructuring in Russia derives from its presumption that

---

[41]   Labour costs in 1996 accounted for only 15% of production costs across all branches of industry, and as often as not wages were not even being paid (*Sotsial'no-ekonomicheskoe polozhenie Rossii*, 1997, 1). In the 1994 ILO survey labour costs were less than 25% of the total costs in 64% of the enterprises surveyed (and enterprises bear little or no charge for the plant, buildings and land inherited from the state). Within metallurgy, labour costs amounted to less than 5% of the total in over a third of the plants surveyed. Only 3% regarded the cost of labour as their main problem in the sphere of employment. 33% regarded holding on to skilled labour as the main problem, 28% cited low wages and 10% the loss of labour (Tsentr issledovannii rynka truda, 1995).

[42]   There is a growing consensus among those Russian researchers who have been conducting panel surveys of enterprises (particularly the *Russian Economic Barometer* and ILO surveys) that it is necessary to differentiate enterprises according to their objective circumstances and management strategies (see particularly Kapelyushnikov and Auktsionek, 1995b and Tsentr issledovannii rynka truda, 1995a, both of which use a similar distinction between 'prosperous' and 'unprosperous' enterprises to that on which we have based our own case study research, and Pavel Smirnov's paper below). The heterogeneity of enterprises on both of these dimensions is what makes it very difficult to obtain useful statistical relationships using a more simplistic model of enterprise behaviour. Some enterprises appear to have cut employment in order to raise pay, some have been able to increase pay and employment despite a fall in production. All the signs are that enterprises are more concerned with paying good wages in order to hold on to their valued workers, rather than with maintaining employment for its own sake.

restructuring must involve a transfer of labour from state and former state enterprises to new private enterprises, rather than a restructuring of the state sector. It is this presumption that we now have to question.

Although state enterprises did not immediately cut their labour forces in line with the fall in production in the chaos and uncertainty of 1992, partly in the not entirely unreasonable expectation of recovery or government support, they were very quick to respond to the enormous challenge that confronted them, and the fall in employment has more or less shadowed the decline in production since 1993.[43] The third round of the ILO survey confirmed the findings of case study research, that a substantial proportion of enterprises had changed their product range, introduced new technology or made changes in work organisation (Standing, 1994b).[44] Although monopoly powers and inflationary financing enabled enterprises to avoid the full rigour of the market, prices and wages were becoming sensitive to market conditions once the latter stabilised and clarified, and enterprises were becoming sensitive to prices in their decision-making, while the restructuring of production and employment was proceeding apace despite continued instability and uncertainty. Twenty-eight per cent of industrial employees left their jobs in state and former state enterprises in the first year of radical reform (1992), 29% in the second, 32% in the third and 28% in the fourth year and 24% in the fifth. However, these employees did not pass into unemployment so as to depress wages sufficiently to make them attractive to private employers, but found new jobs predominantly in the state sector. Thus the hiring rates in state and former state industrial enterprises year by year were 22%, 20%, 18%, 21% and 19%.[45] The new private sector, meanwhile, remained primarily confined to banking and finance and various forms of trade, with some development of small business in the service

---

[43]   In the *Russian Economic Barometer* series the capacity utilisation rate in industry has fallen from 66% in the first quarter of 1994 to 54% in the last quarter of 1996, while the labour utilisation rate has fallen from 75% to 71% over the same period, indicating that enterprises have cut employment more than in proportion to the fall in capacity working. On the basis of the 1994 data Aukutsionek and Kapelyushnikov estimated that the relatively high costs of removal in relation to retention meant that it would take between one and three years to liquidate an employment overhang once production was stabilised (Aukutsionek and Kapelyushnikov, 1996, p. 14)

[44]   Guy Standing reviews the evidence from the subsequent rounds in this volume. See also closely comparable results from a Russian-French project (Vinogradova, 1996).

[45]   These are Goskomstat figures for large and medium enterprises (those with over 200 employees in industry until 1996, when the boundary was reduced to 100 employees), almost of all of which will be state and former state enterprises.

sector, making extensive use of self-employment, family and casual labour.

Although most of the labour turnover was within local labour markets,[46] and much of it comprised frequent job changes of the most mobile categories of labour,[47] and even some round-tripping, there have been substantial changes in the structure of employment.[48] While industrial employment and employment in construction both fell by 24% between 1991 and 1995 and employment in education, science and culture fell by 26%, employment in agriculture rose by 8%, employment in the state apparatus increased by 49% (mostly through the growth of local administration which almost doubled in size), employment in services grew by 60% and employment in credit, finance and insurance increased by 105% (based on Goskomstat estimates – according to preliminary estimates 1996 saw a further substantial shift from the 'productive' to the 'non-productive' sphere).[49] There has equally been very considerable restructuring within branches of production and between enterprises as the less successful, paying low wages, have lost workers to those able to pay more and more regularly.[50] Finally, although precise migration figures are not available,

---

[46] Many commentators see firm-provided housing and residence permits as major barriers to geographical mobility (Commander, Liberman et al., 1993, p. 18). However, the main barriers to mobility in Russia, as in the rest of the world, are poverty and the absence of a wide network of contacts.

[47] According to the *Russian Economic Barometer* 1994 surveys, about one half of hired workers leave within the year, with newcomers making up a quarter of all quits. Despite high turnover, average job tenure was 11.2 years, with 80% not having changed their workplace in the three years of reform and 65% still being in the job they held before 1990 (Kapelyushnikov and Aukutsionek, 1995). The Russian Longitudinal Monitoring Survey data for November 1996 show a mean tenure of 8.7 years, with 46% of respondents in work having held their job for over five years. VTsIOM in January 1997 found that 47% had worked in their present job for more than 5 years and 40% for less than 3 years (*VTsIOM Bulletin*, 2, March-April 1997, p. 87).

[48] There is not much survey data on the character of mobility, but a survey for Goskomstat in May-June 1992 of the first wave of redundancies in the wake of radical reform found that 50% of the men and 59% of the women who found new jobs had changed profession, similar to the US figures (cited in Gimpel'son and Magun, 1994). It is clear that there have been very substantial and very rapid changes in relative wages by region, by branch of industry and even between enterprises in any particular branch of industry (Stavnitskii and Solov'eva, 1994).

[49] It is difficult to apply the methodology developed by Richard Jackman for the evaluation of the extent of sectoral restructuring to the Russian case because it is difficult to identify an appropriate comparator for Russia (or at least one compatible with Russian national pride!) (Jackman, n.d.; Jackman and Pauna, 1996).

[50] *Russian Economic Barometer* estimates on the basis of its data that job creation was at the rate of 1–2% and job destruction at the rate of 10–16%, while 'churning' accounts for between two-thirds and three-quarters of job changes. Apart from 1994, Russian

there have been considerable population movements, some motivated by conflicts and by the disintegration of the Soviet Union, almost a million people a year returning to Russia from former Republics, but others motivated by labour market considerations.[51] Internal migration amounts to around three million per year (Zaionchkovskaya, 1994). Thus, the employed population of Moscow city increased by 11% more than the average in 1993, while that of Murmansk fell by 9% (Goskomstat, 1995a). However, very substantial differences in rates of unemployment between towns and settlements within regions indicate that labour is not very mobile geographically and in surveys about two-thirds of respondents indicate their unwillingness to move.

In the context of a massive aggregate shock, with an enormous overall decline in production, GDP and household incomes and a high degree of financial, economic and political instability, the Russian economy appears to have achieved an extremely impressive amount of restructuring, without having imposed the burden of open unemployment on more than a relatively small proportion of the population. By the end of March 1996 survey unemployment had reached 8.6%, but almost two-thirds of the registered unemployed had been on the register for less than eight months, and only 18% for more than a year, so that only about 1% of the economically active population was suffering the consequences of long-term unemployment.[52] This low rate of recorded unemployment is not therefore an indicator of the lack of employment restructuring and labour market rigidity, but an indicator of an extremely flexible labour market.

As we have seen, the reason for low unemployment in Russia has

---

industry shows a higher job creation and lower job destruction rate than comparable data for Polish state industrial enterprises in 1990–91, and a correspondingly higher rate of churning, which in Poland amounted to between half and two-thirds of job changes. The job creation rate is as high as the UK in the 1980s and the job destruction rate is higher, although the job creation rate is much lower than the US in the 1970s and 1980s (Kapelyushnikov, 1997). Gimpel'son and Lippoldt (1996) estimate churning at a significantly higher level, but this is on the basis of indirect estimates from official aggregate data.

[51] Although there are fewer than a quarter of a million foreign workers registered in Russian, the true number is vastly greater than this, Moscow's transport and construction industries being very dependent on such immigrant labour.

[52] Although long-term unemployment was increasingly rapidly through 1996. There are considerable regional variations in unemployment rates, but there are also very substantial variations in the unemployment rate between towns and cities within a single region. Thus, even in regions with very low levels of registered unemployment, such as Moscow region, there are towns where the collapse of the dominant employer has pushed registered unemployment to levels of 20% and above.

not been low labour-shedding, but a continued high rate of hiring. The majority of hires involve job-to-job transfers, but Russia also has a much higher rate of exit to jobs from unemployment than do the other ECE countries. The picture of labour mobility is not at all clear because the statistical data is ambiguous and incomplete, with very little statistical reporting from the new private sector and a certain amount of misleading reporting by former state enterprises and the Federal Employment Service. However, the statistical data can be complemented by a significant amount of survey data and by our own case study research.

Labour mobility in the Soviet Union, which had been very high in the period of forced industrialisation, had steadily declined until by the 1970s it was comparable to Western European and well below US levels. However, the Soviet ideal was to dedicate oneself to a single workplace, so that voluntarily quitting one's job was regarded in a strongly negative light and a high labour turnover was considered the mark of a poor enterprise. Thus campaigns to reduce turnover persisted through the 1970s and 1980s, leading to a continued sharp decline until 1986, when turnover rates began to increase again, although the official figure was still only 14% in industry (all employees) and 16.8% in construction (workers only) (*SSSR v tsifrakh*, 1990). According to the official figures, 45% of separations in industry in 1989 were voluntary, 8% for disciplinary reasons, 28% involved departure from the labour force, 8% were transfers and 12% terminations, most of which involved temporary contracts. A 1987 survey cited the need to change geographic location as the reason for a quarter of all quits, with living and working conditions, social facilities and wages all cited as other important reasons for quitting (IMF et al., 1991, Vol 2, pp. 143, 199). However, it should be remembered that voluntary quitting for pecuniary reasons was still socially frowned on at this time, so we would expect people to cite more acceptable reasons than dissatisfaction with wages.[53] By 1992 70% of quitters from state enterprises gave low wages as their reason for leaving (Standing, 1994a, p. 266).

---

[53] The change in responses to survey questions about work motivation following the collapse of the Soviet Union was dramatic. In 1989 only a quarter of Soviet people admitted that making a living was their main motivation for work, increasing to almost half only two years later, and reaching almost two-thirds by 1996 (Khibovskaya, 1996a, p. 33), with only one in eight in the November 1996 VTsIOM survey considering work to be important in itself.

It was expected that the separation rate would decline further as the labour market situation deteriorated. Thus the IMF study in 1991 regarded Goskomtrud's assumption that separations would remain at the 1990 level as 'most unrealistic as evidence from market economies suggests that quits should decline significantly in an environment of slack labour markets and rising unemployment' (IMF et al., 1991, Vol 2, p. 147). However, in fact there was a sharp increase in the separation rate, with voluntary quits retaining their traditional predominance, according to the official statistics, although there is ample evidence, strongly confirmed by our own research, that a substantial proportion of separations recorded as voluntary are the result of direct or indirect pressure on particular workers from the administration,[54] while the remainder were motivated primarily by dissatisfaction with low wages and, later, short-time working, compulsory unpaid leave and delays in the payment of wages.[55]

---

[54] One indication is the fact that the proportion of 'voluntary' redundancies is much higher in cities like Ivanovo, with very high unemployment, than St Petersburg and Moscow, where unemployment is still very low (Tsentr issledovannii rynka truda, 1995a).

[55] Large and medium enterprises report the reasons for separations directly to Goskomstat. Enterprises are also required to report anticipated redundancies to the Employment Service, and these numbers frequently include many employees officially registered as voluntary quits in the enterprise, but they also include a proportion who will in fact be redeployed within the enterprise, transferred to another enterprise or take retirement, so that the number recorded as having been made redundant when they register with the Employment Service is only about half the number notified to them by enterprises. The Employment Service collects data at local level from various sources, and reports this to Goskomstat, broken down into voluntary severances and redundancies. The figures derived from these two sources and published by Goskomstat report around two-thirds of separations as voluntary quits and between 6% and 8% as involving redundancy. It is not clear what figures enterprises use in responding to surveys. For example, *Russian Economic Barometer* found in 1994 that its enterprises reported voluntary quits at 50–60%, disciplinary dismissals at 15% and lay-offs at 15–20%, while the Goskomstat returns reported voluntary quits at 64% and lay-offs at 8% for the same year. In most enterprise surveys around half the enterprises do not report any compulsory redundancies, while most of the rest have very few (Goskomstat, 1996e; FES, 1995a; Kapelyushnikov and Aukutsionek, 1995a). Individuals specify the reason for leaving their last job when they register with the Employment Service, and around a third of those registering are recorded as having been made redundant. Labour force surveys also find that about one-third of the survey unemployed report that they were made redundant from their previous jobs, but the rate of registration of those made redundant is much higher than for others since they must register to qualify for redundancy payments. Finally, a significant proportion of those in fact dismissed for disciplinary reasons are recorded as voluntary quits. (The vast majority of offenders are willing to leave voluntarily rather than have a dismissal or redundancy recorded in their labour book. We have encountered examples in which the shop chief keeps signed but undated resignation letters for all employees to avoid the need for disciplinary procedures.) Thus, one-third of *Russian Economic Barometer* reporting enterprises in 1994

Compulsory and compulsory-voluntary lay-offs in the first instance, as elsewhere in ECE, seem primarily to have affected working pensioners and ancillary workers, particularly female clerical and professional employees, so that women predominated among the registered unemployed in the first stage of reform. This is partly a matter of the widely observed discrimination against these particular categories of the population, but also because these were the most reluctant to leave voluntarily and so the most liable to be compulsorily displaced.[56] The tendency through 1992–93 was for employers to try to hold on to the most desirable employees by guaranteeing work and stable wages, while putting the remainder on short-time, sending them on part-paid or unpaid leave, or delaying the payment of wages in conditions of rapid inflation, while the least desirable employees were forced out through retirement, disciplinary dismissal and 'compulsory-voluntary' redundancy. The first half of 1994, following the introduction of the new Russian constitution in December 1993, appeared at first to be the crunch time: administrative leave and short-time working rose, separations and the proportion of redundancies increased, while the hiring rate fell, so that there was a leap in unemployment over the first half of the year. However, in the second half of the year hiring resumed, the rate of growth of unemployment slowed and the proportion of compulsory redundancies fell back, although unpaid leave and short-time working have continued to affect up to 15% of the labour force in each quarter.[57] By the end of 1995 it appeared that

---

replied that they had had no disciplinary dismissals at all. (In the Soviet period only 1–2% of the labour force were recorded as having been dismissed each year for disciplinary reasons.)

[56] According to the March 1996 Labour Force Survey, 36% of unemployed women had lost their jobs through redundancy against 29% of men, while 31% of women against 40% of men had left their previous jobs voluntarily (Goskomstat, *Informatsionnyi statisticheskii byulleten'*, 13, November 1996).

[57] The number of stoppages shot up at the end of 1993, with 9.7% of working days lost to full-day stoppages in industry in 1994, falling back to 8.3% in 1995. It is noticeable that reported days lost to sickness and absenteeism have fallen over the period of transition, but the increase in public holidays, in holiday entitlement and in leave authorised by the employer have reduced the length of the working year by 5% since 1990 (Goskomstat, 1995a). Sixteen per cent of the entire labour force (37% of industrial employees) experienced a spell of administrative leave during 1996, the average duration being 40 working days, and 7.2% (16.1% in industry) worked an average of eight hours per week short-time, the total time lost to leave and short-time working amounting to 3.3% of working time (*Sotsial'no-ekonomicheskoe polozhenie Rossii*, 1, 1997). About 30% of enterprises were in arrears with wage payments in the second half of 1995, where almost half had been in arrears through 1994 (*Russian Economic Trends, 4 (4), 1996*), but wage arrears really took off from the end of 1995, amounting

the easy cuts in employment had been made, pushing out unskilled auxiliary and ancillary workers, the elderly, the disabled and the disadvantaged, and divesting a significant part of the social and welfare apparatus, leading to the destruction or decay of enterprise housing, social, welfare, health and cultural provision because municipalities lacked the resources to maintain the facilities transferred to them.

The result of the very high rate of hiring is that redundancy and unemployment are not the threat that they would otherwise be.[58] Most people still move directly from job to job, without an intervening period of unemployment, so that the inflow into unemployment remains low, given the high separation rate. Moreover, although the proportion of those unemployed who register with the Federal Employment Service has steadily increased, still only about one-third were registered in 1996, so the inflow rate into registered unemployment is lower still.

Even for those who do register as unemployed the outflow rate from unemployment, including the outflow rate to jobs, is much higher than in Eastern and Central Europe. In 1995 on average 18% joined the register each month, 16% left (calculated from *Russian Economic Trends, 4* (4), 1996), of whom 45% left the register for jobs, 12% for education, 5% for pension and 38% for other reasons (FES, 1995a). This is three times the outflow rate and three times the outflow rate to jobs of Poland. About 20% found work within ten days in 1994 (Kapelyushnikov, 1994). In the March 1996 labour force survey the average time of job seeking was 8.2 months (men 7.9, women 8.6), up from 4.4 months in 1992, with 7% finding work within a month (Goskomstat, *Informatsionnyi statisticheskii byulletin'*, 13, November 1996).[59]

---

[58] to 53.9 trillion roubles (over one month's wages – almost ten billion dollars) on June 2 1997 and still rising fast.

The hiring and quit rates remain high even as unemployment increases. In 1994 both the hiring and the quit rate in Ivanovo oblast, with registered unemployment of 8.9%, were higher than those in Moscow city, with a registered unemployment rate of 0.3%. Only in 1995 did the hiring rate in Moscow creep above that of Ivanovo, with registered unemployment rates of 0.5% and 12.5% respectively (Goskomstat, 1996e). Overall, hiring and quit rates in 1995 were almost exactly what they were in 1992 despite the massive increase in unemployment. Of course many of the jobs which people are leaving are extremely low-paid, with delayed payment of wages and spells of short-time working and unpaid administrative vacation. This is why for many there is little to fear from unemployment.

[59] Ten per cent of the labour force survey unemployed in March 1996 were first-time job-seekers post-education. The rate of unemployment among the under-20s had reached 31.8% and for the 20–24 year olds was 15.8% (Goskomstat, *Informatsionnyi statis-*

According to the data of the Employment Service, it succeeded in placing over a third of those seeking work through the service (1993: 39%; 1994: 32%; 1995: 43%; 1996:43%). However, a growing proportion of applicants are students seeking temporary work, who are much easier to place (in 1995 they made up 17% of applicants, 95% of whom were placed, falling back to 14 in 1996, of whom 96% were placed). The proportion of unemployed job-seekers placed was 36% in 1996. It should also be noted that this is one of the prime performance indicators of the Employment Service, so that local offices are inclined to take credit for all job placements, even if they had no part to play in them.[60] Even on its own account, however, the Employment Service is involved in fewer than 10% of job placements (Popov, 1995). A principal problem faced by the Employment Service is the skill mismatch between the registered unemployed, who tend to have relatively high qualifications, and the notified vacancies, the majority of which are for unskilled jobs. The Employment Service retains the reputation of the old recruitment bureaux from which it derived of being the last resort of those who cannot find work by any other means, and the last recourse of enterprises who cannot recruit through any other channels.

The Employment Service plays very little role in the labour market. The Employment Service is financed by a payroll tax at regional level with some redistribution between regions, which only breeds resentment on all sides. This leads to a situation in which the most prosperous regions have the highest income and the lowest expenditure on passive measures, while the Employment Service in those regions with the highest levels of unemployment, which tend also to have the lowest incomes, find their budgets exhausted by the payment

---

ticheskii byulletin', 13, November 1996). However, this does not mean that young people are being frozen out of recruitment to former state enterprises by 'insider control': enterprises complain that they have difficulty in recruiting young people and that those who come are inclined not to stay. The problem of youth unemployment is that young people will not tolerate working conditions which their parents had been drilled into accepting. The high *rate* of youth unemployment arises from the mass withdrawal of young people from the labour market rather than from an increase in the number of young unemployed, so it arises from a fall in the denominator rather than a rise in the numerator which is used to calculate the rate.

[60] The Goskomstat survey of the newly unemployed in 1992 found that while (only) 26% had sought help from the Employment Service, only 12% had received any help (Gimpel'son and Magun, 1994). The World Bank sponsored VTsIOM survey in April 1994 found that only one-third of those who turned to the Employment Service were even offered a job, 70% of the offers coming from the state sector and only 3% from private enterprises. Almost half those asked said that they did not believe that the Employment Service could help them to get a job (Yemtsov, 1994).

of benefit.[61] Nevertheless, with low levels of benefit and few benefit recipients, many regions have substantial funds available for active employment policy. However, most of this money is used to subsidise existing jobs, a lesser amount financing job creation by small businesses, with very little spending on retraining.[62] Moreover, while the Employment Service claims to find work for about a third of those who apply to it for help, it provides virtually no support for people other than the unemployed and those seeking temporary and supplementary jobs. Thus in 1996 only 150,200 people in jobs turned to the service for help in getting another job, of whom it claimed to place only 24,500. In 1996 the Employment Service claimed to have played a role in 2.3 million job placements, of which almost three quarters of a million were supplementary jobs, out of a total of 9 million hires during the year (this was a significant improvement on the previous year's performance).

Thus the Employment Service has very little part to play in making the labour market more or less flexible. Most job changes take place behind the back of the Employment Service, and about these almost nothing is known.

Finally, we should ask what is the relation between employer strategy and employee initiative in labour mobility? If we take the figures at face value, the fact that the bulk of separations are voluntary implies that employers are passive: they distribute the money and work available and if this means low wages then people leave. The *Russian Economic Barometer* team argued on the basis of their 1993 surveys that workers behaved in a much more market-oriented fashion than their employers, the only difference between low-wage and high-wage enterprises being in the rate of voluntary severance, the hiring and dismissal rates being the same (Kapelyushnikov and Aukutsionek, 1994b). But this implies that voluntary severance really is voluntary, rather than being the means by which management reduces the labour force. Some managements certainly are, or were, passive, but others use voluntary severance very actively. More recent reports by the same authors note significant differences emerging between enterprises,

---

[61] They then either cut or simply do not pay benefits. In April 1996 the President of the Komi Republic responded to the 'crisis situation' of 5% unemployment by issuing a decree slashing benefit entitlements.

[62] A substantial amount of Employment Service money is invested in financial instruments (14% in 1994), leading to a certain amount of scandal. This was one factor lying behind the cut in the contribution to the fund from 2% to 1.5% of payroll in 1996.

with prosperous enterprises being much more active in disciplining workers, while the less prosperous use more lay-offs (Kapelyushnikov and Aukutsionek, 1994a; 1995a). Our own research shows very marked differences in employment strategy between the relatively successful and relatively unsuccessful enterprises, the latter being able to use their more powerful position in the labour market to pursue a very active labour market strategy. These findings are confirmed by the results of the recent ILO surveys reported by Pasha Smirnov elsewhere in this volume.

LABOUR MARKET FLEXIBILITY: STRUCTURAL ADJUSTMENT WITHOUT MASS UNEMPLOYMENT?

Western trade unions, faced with the threat of large scale redundancy, have traditionally proposed job-sharing and short-time working as a means of weathering a crisis. The World Bank team argues that short-time working, administrative leave and the delayed payment of wages in Russia are another reflection of management's reluctance to fire, and thus an expression of workers' control, dismissing the possibility that this might be a form of flexibility to adapt to changes in relative demand on the grounds of the supposed scale of the hoarded surplus of labour (Commander and Yemtsov, 1995). However, if it is not the case that enterprises have these huge reserves, then short-time working and administrative leave, compounded by the delayed payment of wages of those still working, provide extremely rational responses of management to instability, even if they are not the best displays of benevolent paternalism. Managers in any country would relish the chance not to pay their workers. Only in the former workers' paradise is it possible for them to get away with it!

The argument that Russia provides us with an exemplary model of labour market flexibility has been developed primarily by Richard Layard and his colleagues, and endorsed by the prime exponents of labour market flexibility, the OECD (OECD, 1995b). The argument is essentially that the enormous wage flexibility displayed in Russia, together with very low unemployment benefits, has allowed the labour market to operate smoothly to facilitate structural adjustment without

the emergence of mass unemployment. In conditions of economic difficulty in any particular enterprise, falling wages and flexibility of
hours make it unnecessary for the management to declare redundancies and gives workers the choice of leaving for another job or
remaining on little or no pay. The fact that unemployment benefit is in
practice so low means that it does not provide any floor to the wage,
while the statutory minimum wage is far below any subsistence minimum.[63] Far from the stagnation depicted by the World Bank, there has
been very considerable employment restructuring, with an explosive
growth of the new private sector (if not now, at least on the immediate
horizon). Far from being an alternative to employment flexibility, as
the World Bank argues, wage flexibility is a means to employment
restructuring.[64]

Layard and Richter explain this wage flexibility not only in terms of
the low unemployment benefit, which means that unemployment is not
a realistic option, but also in terms of the worker's attachment to the
enterprise which means that an employee will continue to work even
when paid nothing at all.[65] They identify five reasons for continued
attachment to the enterprise: the extensive social support provided by
the enterprise; the importance of the workplace in the definition of
personal identity; the limited alternatives available with such low unemployment benefits; for some workers the access to tools and
equipment for secondary activity; and the fact that there is little

---

[63] A redundant employee receives his or her last monthly wage for the first three months,
paid by the employer, followed by 75% of the wage for the next three months, then
60% for four months and 45% for five months. After fifteen months the unemployed
person is entitled to support up to the minimum wage, which is about one-sixth of the
physiological subsistence minimum. Since lay-offs are a last resort, final monthly pay
of those laid off is usually very low in any case, while benefit payments are all unin-
dexed and so are eroded by inflation, but the floor is set by the (extremely low)
minimum wage. Average unemployment benefit in 1993 was 12% of average pay, and
18% of average pay in 1994 (between one-third and under one-half the very low subsistence minimum), the average length of receipt of benefit was 5 months
(Kapelyushnikov, 1994). By the end of 1995 about half those on benefit were being
paid at the minimum level. In addition the strength of the Soviet work ethic and the
continued identification, particularly among older people, of unemployment with parasitism leads to a considerable reluctance to register for unemployment and to draw
benefit.

[64] After the initial shock in 1992, cross-sectional and survey data has shown an increasingly close relationship between employment change and wage changes, with the
(relatively) more prosperous enterprises maintaining both wages and employment, and
the less prosperous paying low wages and failing to retain labour.

[65] Not without reason, Anders Aslund, a leading ideologue of liberal reform, is reported
as referring to wages in Russia as being 'perfectly flexible' (Aslund, 1996).

worker organisation to oppose pay cuts (Layard and Richter, 1995).[66]

The great advantage of this wage flexibility for Layard and Richter is that it allows for large-scale structural adjustment without the emergence of mass unemployment, a state which is particularly debilitating in a country which had lost the very concept of unemployment, in which work was the focus of people's lives and their identities. The downside for them is that the surplus workers hanging around the factory get in the way of the restructuring of production, so they argue that administrative leave is preferable to retaining people in the workplace. The implication, and the lesson of Russia, is that flexible labour markets work, that a low level of benefits reduces the incentive to leave work for unemployment, and that support needs to be for job-to-job transitions rather than for unemployment, which the benefit system should be designed to discourage. In the Russian context Layard and Richter propose a massive programme of retraining in the commercial skills required for the market economy; an increase in unemployment benefit for those made redundant, but minimal benefit for new entrants and returnees; a programme of public works in place of unemployment benefit for those unemployed for more than one year; and the removal of residence restrictions and the provision of hostels to encourage migration.

Our research undermines Layard and Richter's benign view of labour market flexibility. Employers do not offer employees a choice between job security with a low wage and mobility in search of a high wage. All employers would like to recruit and retain younger, skilled, male employees by paying good and secure wages, and to force out older, unskilled and undisciplined employees by paying them low wages or no wages. The relatively more prosperous enterprises are able to upgrade their labour force in this way, while the less prosperous are unable to hold on to their existing employees and have to be less selective in their recruitment. Thus labour market flexibility leads to a polarisation between 'good' and 'bad' enterprises.

While most people shuffle between existing jobs in former state enterprises, the significance of the new private sector as a source of employment has been considerably exaggerated. As we will see, comparison of various sources indicates that the official figures for private

---

[66]   Layard and Richter present this as involving an 'implicit contract between workers and managers. Workers accept highly flexible wages and hours, and managers may in return offer a high degree of job security' (Layard and Richter, 1994, p. 86). This seems rather a one-sided contract: if you work without pay, I won't sack you!

sector employment growth were hugely overestimated in 1992 and 1993 and that the rate of growth since then has been at best modest. Many jobs in the new private sector are casual and are not legally formalised, providing no security of employment and avoiding taxation and social insurance payments. Most people regard work in the private sector as undesirable because of this instability and absence of social protection, looking to it only for casual earnings. There are also indications that opportunities in the private sector are narrowing as it becomes more professionalised and competitive. Moreover, with incomes continuing to fall, it is unlikely that Russia can support a substantial private service sector outside the largest cities, which is where new enterprises are concentrated.

The significance of secondary employment has also been exaggerated. Only a minority has access to secondary employment, which provides additional opportunities for the privileged rather than a means of support for the disadvantaged. Most secondary employment is not in the new private sector, but takes the traditional forms of additional jobs at the main place of work or 'individual labour activity' providing goods and services. For those with skills that are in high demand, secondary employment can provide a way of trying out a new vocation or a new workplace, but these are only a small minority. Casual employment is typically not secondary employment, but the only source of income for those who are laid-off or unemployed.

Labour mobility for most people is a crisis phenomenon. People are driven by the need to survive in the face of low pay and the non-payment of wages, not by the attraction of a new job, a new life, or even a higher income. Although the young are highly mobile, most people retain the traditional values of hard work and are committed to their workplace and workmates. Many leave their jobs with real sorrow. When such workers leave, the home enterprise loses the irreplaceable benefit of his or her skill and experience, while the worker usually moves to a job that requires significantly less skill. Mobility therefore leads to the 'degradation' of the labour collective and of the skills and morale of individual workers as people shuffle between existing jobs or are driven into casual unskilled work in the new private sector.

The principal and most desirable channels of mobility for both employers and employees are personal connections. This leads to a closure and further segmentation of labour markets as enterprises close their doors to 'outsiders', except for those unskilled or highly-skilled posts that they cannot fill with 'their own people'. It also reinforces the marginalisation and the poor image of the Employment Service, which employers and employees use only as a last resort.

TOO MUCH FLEXIBILITY?

Layard and Richter are certainly right to emphasise the flexibility of the Russian labour market, in opposition to the view proposed by the World Bank. There are some labour market rigidities, particularly those social, political and economic factors which, as in any real economy, impede the geographical movement of labour, but there is no evidence that labour market rigidity presents any kind of barrier to the development of new capitalist activity: any employer who is able to guarantee to pay a living wage has the pick of the labour market. However, while there is plenty of evidence of the negative aspects of wage and employment flexibility, Layard and Richter offer little but wishful thinking on the positive side.

The price of labour market flexibility in the Layard/Richter model is low wages. Of course a job is better than no job, and low wages are better than no wages, but low wages tend to be self-reproducing, reducing incentives for both employers and employees to raise productivity and promoting the deskilling, casualisation and demoralisation of labour. Did Russia really set off on the route of perestroika to become a low wage economy, in which a very large proportion of the population live below the poverty line and work in conditions which give employers no incentive to invest or even to reorganise production to raise productivity and wages?

This brings us to the ILO position, put forward primarily by Guy Standing, which has underlain their enterprise surveys since 1991. The ILO starting point was the hypothesis, unfashionable at the time, that macro changes had to be accompanied by micro restructuring, and the basis of the ILO surveys was therefore to monitor the extent to which existing enterprises were indeed restructuring. The annual ILO surveys have shown that people are being kept on the payroll, and are not turning up as unemployed, but they are being used less and less productively and their wages, working conditions and living standards are falling steadily from levels which for many were already in the Soviet period at bare subsistence level.

According to the real average wage index, wages in Russia have fallen even more dramatically than production. As a result of Gorbachev's reforms statistical real wages peaked in 1990 at 32% above the 1985 level, reflecting an increase in unrealisable money incomes against relatively fixed prices rather than a sharp increase in living standards. By mid 1997, despite some recovery over the previous eighteen months, statistical real wages were still only a little over half of the 1985 level, or only 43% of the 1990 level.[67] Nevertheless, for a large proportion of the population the fall in wages has been much greater than this as inequality in Russia has doubled, the Gini coefficient increasing from 0.26 in 1991 to 0.29 in 1992 and 0.50 in 1993 (Goskomstat, 1996a). The 1993 figure is from the 1996 *World Development Report*, derived from an expenditure measure since income data is completely unreliable).[68] Wage dispersion between branches of production increased from 0.75 in 1991 to 1.46 by November 1995, with agricultural wages falling to less than half the average (*Russian Economic Trends, 4 (4), 1996*), increasing even more in 1996. Regional wage differences are also enormous, with the average wage in Moscow being between three and four times that in Dagestan, income per head in Moscow being 13 times as high as in Dagestan (Goskomstat, 1996e; Tsentr Ekonomicheskoi kon'yunktury, *Rossii – 1996: ekonomicheskaya kon'unktura*, 4, 1996). The result of falling wages and rising inequality is that even on official figures between one-quarter and one-third of the population live below the poverty line, which is defined as the physiological subsistence minimum in a crisis situation, a revision of the previous physiological minimum which reduced its level by one third (Chetvernina, 1994). Poverty, linked to alcoholism, no doubt lies behind the catastrophic increase in the mortality rate, which has seen the life expectancy of men fall from 62 years in 1992 to 57.6 years in 1994, recovering somewhat to 58.0 years in 1995 and 59.6 years in 1996 (that of women fell from 73.8 to 71.2, recovering to 72.0 in 1995 and then 72.7 in 1996).

Layard and Richter recognise that there are those who suffer, but

---

[67] The government's own research centre reports average real wages as having fallen to 24% of their December 1991 level by March 1995 (at December 1991 prices), recovering to 30% of the eve of reform level by September 1996 (Tsentr Ekonomicheskoi kon'yunktury, *Rossii – 1996: ekonomicheskaya kon'unktura*, 4, 1996).

[68] On the basis of its surveys VTsIOM estimates the Gini coefficient at 0.48 for 1995 and 0.45 for 1996 (*VTsIOM Bulletin*, 1, 1997, p. 35).

they appear to believe that all confront the same choices and all have the same opportunities opened before them by the dynamic new private sector. However, as in the case of enterprise behaviour, the behaviour of employees in the labour market cannot be reduced to a simplistic model of a homogeneous labour force. The experience and situation of different categories of employee are very different, with trade, age, branch of production, geographical location and sex being important objective characteristics, but with the subjective legacy of the Soviet past also bearing heavily on many, not only of the older generation. Unpaid administrative leave means something quite different for a driver who is able to use the enterprise's truck to run a market business than for a middle-aged female clerical worker with dependent children who cannot adapt to the new world and who has little chance of getting another job.

Layard and Richter considerably exaggerate the opportunities that are offered by the new market economy. There is no published data on employment in the new private sector, not only because of the absence of reporting but also because official data does not distinguish between privatised state and new private enterprises.[69] However, impressions gained in the centre of Moscow or large regional capitals are very misleading. If we look at the official sectoral employment estimates we find that fewer than half a million additional jobs have been created in credit, finance and insurance since 1990, about 600,000 additional jobs have been created in trade and public catering, while the rest of the service sector has seen a substantial employment decline. It has been science and technology and light industry, branches which should offer the best opportunities for new private enterprise, which have seen the largest employment declines of all. Even on Goskomstat's estimates, small business growth has ground to a halt, with the number of small enterprises in trade and catering falling by 10% and the number of employees in the small business sector as a whole falling, according to the Goskomstat figures, between 1994 and 1995 (Goskomstat, 1996c).

A significant proportion of employment in the new private sector is casual or secondary employment. A significant proportion of those whose wages are reduced by short-time and administrative leave and a

---

[69] Many apparently new private enterprises are in fact parasitic on state or former state enterprises, providing a cover for tax evasion and/or for the theft of enterprise assets by management.

significant proportion of the unemployed are engaged in casual employment and/or are producing for their subsistence on their private garden plots. This secondary activity is not only important in sustaining those on starvation incomes, but also in providing a means of adaptation to new economic conditions and a channel for transition to new jobs. Secondary employment combines flexibility in adapting to current changes while keeping options open for the future: both for workers and for their enterprises. However, it is important not to get carried away with the idea that secondary employment makes short-time working, administrative leave and low pay more acceptable. It is only a small minority who are involved in regular secondary employment, and those most actively involved and the best paid are those who are most competitive in both primary and secondary labour markets. Those with low or no incomes are more likely to be involved in low-paid casual work, self-employment or subsistence production which helps ward off starvation rather than promising new opportunities. For some, secondary employment is a vital element in a simple strategy for survival, but for those most active in the secondary labour market it is a means of realising an even higher standard of living.[70]

---

[70] The Federal Employment Service estimated in 1994 that about 10–12% of workers have at least two jobs, but the grounds for this estimate are not given (Kapelyushnikov, 1994, p. 3). Goskomstat estimates, on the basis of labour force survey data, that 70–80% of the 6 million people reported as working on contract in the first half of 1996 were doing so as supplementary jobs, which would give a figure of about 7% in secondary employment, and a further 2.8 million (4%) were in officially registered secondary jobs (*po sovmestitel'stvu*), which is the traditional alternative to overtime working (Goskomstat, *Informatsionnyi statisticheskii byulleten'*, 13, November 1996). However, only about 5% reply to VTsIOM surveys that they have second jobs (3.6% in November 1996, 5.6% in January 1997), with a further 10–15% reporting irregular secondary employment (9.9% in November 1996, 12.5% in January 1997), but this includes self-employment and is little more than the estimated extent of secondary employment in the Soviet period. The Russian Longitudinal Monitoring Survey, which is technically much the best of a bad lot of surveys, found in 1994, 1995 and 1996 that only 4% of people in work had second jobs, but fewer than half those who had second jobs in 1994 also had them in 1995, only half of which were in the same trade, while fewer than one in five had a second job in all three years. In the same survey, 7.3% of the total number of adults questioned in the autumn of 1996 had earned something from individual activity in the previous month, just over half of whom did not have any other paid work, but only one in five did this work on a regular basis, half had worked at it for less than 20 hours in the previous month and half had earned less than $40 for it. Only 0.8% of those questioned engaged in individual earning activity in all three years, 3% in two of the three years and 10% in only one of the three years. The 1992 RLMS had found that 3.4% had secondary employment and only 2.4%, evenly divided between those in work and those without other work, were involved in individual activity. Thus, most secondary and self-employment is unstable and of limited significance. The 1996 survey also showed that at most 10% of those on leave had any

While low wages discourage investment in the productive sphere, low wages and extensive short-time working in state and former state enterprises subsidise casual low-wage, low-skill employment in the new private sector, with employers avoiding taxation and social security payments. Thus low wages, far from encouraging the growth of a flourishing new private sector, underpin the informal and illegal character of economic activity in the new private sector and reinforce the continued deskilling and demoralisation of the labour force.

Low wages and the non-payment of wages also encourage employers to hold on to a substantial reserve of labour, in the sense discussed above. Guy Standing, on the basis of the findings of the annual ILO enterprise surveys, has argued that Russia has achieved a low rate of open unemployment as a result of labour market flexibility not because of the growth of a dynamic private sector, as Layard and Richter assert, but because of the enormous scale of 'concealed' and 'suppressed' unemployment. Standing distinguishes between 'short-term' and 'long-term' surplus labour, the former being those employees who currently have nothing to do or who could be dispensed with without any impact on production levels, the latter those who would be dispensed with in the event of significant structural changes, either through bankruptcy or new investment. The former together indicate the extent of hidden unemployment, the latter the further additions to unemployment that might arise in the event of serious structural change. In his analysis he focuses only on the former (Standing, 1996a and this volume).

According to the 1996 ILO survey, which covered industrial enterprises of all property forms, managers estimated that on average they could reduce employment by 9.6% without affecting output, which Standing takes as his indicator of the extent of 'concealed unemployment'. Standing estimated that during the first half of 1996 production stoppages for economic reasons, which he identifies as a major form

additional earnings (my calculations from RLMS data). This is in sharp contrast to the findings of other surveys. A September 1995 survey of enterprises with short-time or administrative leave found that 61% of the workers laid off said that they did not leave because they did not expect to be able to find similar work elsewhere, 31% because they did not want to lose social guarantees, but 71% had additional earnings and two-thirds said that they would leave if they had to go back full-time, unless pay was increased (Garsiya-Iser, Golodets et al., 1995). The May 1994 World Bank survey similarly found that most people on leave had secondary employment, half being self-employment (Commander and Yemtsov, 1995). On secondary employment see further Khibovskaya (1994a, 1995b, 1996b), Klopov (1996) and Donova and Varshavskaya (1996).

of 'suppressed unemployment', accounted for about 9.6% of total labour input. In addition Standing estimates the number of employees on
short-time and the number sent on administrative leave, to reach a
total estimated suppressed unemployment of over one-third of the
workforce, in addition to the 9.6% concealed unemployment. The implication is that well over a third of the industrial labour force is
effectively unemployed, despite the fact that industrial employment
has already fallen by at least a third. Enterprises have only held on to
these employees because they are a perfectly flexible labour reserve:
employers do not pay employees when they are laid-off or working
short-time, and increasingly do not pay them even when they are
working, although such practices are illegal under the Russian Labour
Code and repeated Presidential Decrees. Standing's conclusion turns
orthodoxy on its head: the labour market constitutes a major barrier to
restructuring, but the barrier is not labour market rigidity but excessive
labour market flexibility. It is excessive wage flexibility which encourages the deskilling and demoralisation of the labour force while
discouraging the investment and production reorganisation in existing
industrial enterprises which is the only realistic basis for economic
recovery. At the same time, the retention of surplus labour within enterprises conceals the extent of unemployment from public view and
allows the state to avoid addressing the issue.

While our own case-study research would strongly support Standing's substantive conclusion that Russia suffers from excessive labour
market flexibility, we would question his estimate of the extent of
concealed unemployment. We have already discussed the conceptual
aspects of this issue above. Managerial estimates of 'disguised unemployment' are more of ideological than substantive significance. No
doubt all enterprises and organisations could dispense with, say, 10%
of the labour force without any impact on production levels, but this
would not be without cost. The individuals surplus to requirements
have to be identified, the work they currently do has to be evaluated
and assigned to somebody else. Such an exercise requires an
investment of scarce managerial resources and implies some intensification of the labour of those who remain or some deterioration in the
quality of, for example, social and welfare provision. Faced with
higher labour costs, managers would be more inclined to undertake
such an exercise and to 'slim down' their labour force, but it is by no
means clear that such an exercise would be socially desirable in the

absence of any realistic alternative employment for those who would
be dispensed with.

The situation with the 'suppressed' unemployed is slightly different.
There are both conceptual and statistical issues involved here. The
first statistical issue concerns the extent of double-counting, since
Standing adds together the figures for production stoppages and the
figures for temporary lay-offs. He recognises that he has assumed that
'time lost from partial stoppages is separate from that lost to administrative leave or short-time working. It could be that such stoppages are
the immediate cause of some administrative leave' (Standing, 1996a,
p. 23), but the extent of such double-counting is unknown.[71] The second statistical issue concerns the estimates for the proportion of the
labour force temporarily laid off. Although a large proportion of the
labour force experiences short-time working and administrative leave,
the scale and duration varies quite considerably.[72] The Goskomstat
figures for loss of working time are actually rather higher than those
that Standing derives from his survey. While Standing estimates that
7.1% of time is lost to stoppages, Goskomstat figures show that about
8.3% of working time in industry was lost to full-day stoppages in
1995, a slight fall from 1994, when almost 10% of working days were
lost (and, as noted above, a further 5% reduction in working time is
accounted for by increased vacation and public holidays). While
Standing estimated that 18.7% of time was accounted for by administrative leave and 9.7% was accounted for by short-time working in
1996, the Goskomstat data for 1996 implies that about 1.2% of work-

---

[71] Large and medium enterprises report to Goskomstat days lost to work stoppages
(*prostoi*) for which, according to the Labour Code, employees must receive two-thirds
pay if the stoppage is the fault of the administration. Enterprises report separately the
number of employees working short-time, the number sent on leave on the initiative of
the administration (although these practices are illegal without the express consent of
the individual in each case) and the number of days lost to both. Conceptually short-
time and leave are distinct from the traditional conception of *prostoi* because in the
latter case the employees have reported for work, and in principle stoppages and absence are recorded differently on the time-keeping sheets, but it is not clear to what
extent the distinction is retained in practice and there may be some double-counting of
time lost.

[72] According to official statistics 15.8% of the entire labour force experienced a spell of
administrative leave of an average of 40 working days in 1996, 43% of whom were
paid nothing for that period, and 6–7% were working short-time at any one time. A
further 6% remained at work full-time but earned less than one-third of the physiological subsistence minimum. The average length of the working day in 1996 was 6.63
hours in the economy as a whole and 5.96 hours in industry (*Sotsial'no-
ekonomicheskoe polozhenie Rossii*, 1, 1997; Goskomstat, *Informatsionnyi statisticheskii byulleten'*, 13, November 1996, pp. 47–8).

ing time across all branches was lost to short-time working and 2.1% to administrative leave.[73] However, two-thirds of all short-time and administrative leave is found in industry, with 16% of the industrial labour force being on short time and 37% experiencing a spell of administrative leave in 1996, but still the total amounts to only about 8% of working time: a substantial proportion, but still much less than the 28.4% estimated by Standing.[74] Our conclusion is that the level of 'suppressed unemployment' in industry in 1996 did not amount to more than 16%, a substantial amount, but less than half that estimated by Guy Standing.

There is also a conceptual issue to address. Standing's 'suppressed unemployed' are people who are without employment for certain periods of the working week, or for weeks or even months at a time, but who are retained on the payroll because they cost the enterprise very little. However, for the rest of the week, month or year, these people are employed. The problem of short-time working and administrative leave is linked to the instability of production, which is linked in turn to the instability of the market. In our own case study research, shop management in most industrial enterprises insists that there is no surplus of labour on the shop floor, in the sense that they barely have enough people to resume production when orders are forthcoming and they recall everyone from leave. It is clear that short-time working and administrative leave are not used simply to retain surplus employees but also serve as an instrument of employment policy designed to preserve production capacity. In the event of a downturn management first makes use of short-time working to reduce labour costs. As the crisis continues management lays employees off on administrative leave, with or without pay (c.f. Aukutsionek and Kapelyushnikov, 1996, p. 9). On the one hand, managers know very well that a significant proportion of those laid off temporarily, particularly if they are paid nothing, will find other jobs and leave the payroll, so that it is

---

[73] The March 1996 labour force survey found that employees in all enterprises and organisations worked on average 5–6% less than the working week specified in their appropriate agreements (Goskomstat, *Informatsionnyi statisticheskii byulleten'*, 13, November 1996, p. 49).

[74] According to the UN Economic Commission for Europe, a Goskomstat survey in December 1994 found a rather higher level of lay-offs at 6% of the population (UN-ECE, Economic Survey of Europe in 1994–1995, Geneva, p. 112). Our research indicates that a significant proportion of lay-offs are unreported, as people are sent home after reporting for work, but our impression is still that Standing's figure is a considerable overestimate.

certainly the case that leave is used as a way of avoiding the bureaucratic and financial costs of compulsory redundancy. On the other
hand, temporary lay-offs provide a method of retaining employees
who will be required in the event of an upturn in production, while
allowing them to maintain their earnings through secondary and casual
employment, which is sometimes arranged by management itself.

This is a perfectly rational response to the unevenness of production
which is a feature of the instability that marks the Russian crisis. If
orders are not forthcoming and production is not resumed, those on
extended leave drift away and employment falls, but if there is an upturn those on leave are recalled, or those on short-time restored to full
working. There is certainly an element of labour hoarding involved
here, because enterprises do not sack workers as soon as production
falls with a view to rehiring later. However, this is not so much a matter of labour market rigidity as of the importance of firm-, shop- and
machine-specific technical and social skills which were an essential
aspect of the Soviet production system and which today, with ageing
equipment, make the existing skilled and long-serving employees even
more irreplaceable. It is, therefore, somewhat misleading to identify
those temporarily laid-off with the 'suppressed unemployed'. As with
the 'concealed unemployed', if enterprises met their legal obligation to
pay wages to those they had laid-off temporarily then a large proportion of these people would become unemployed, but this would
undermine the ability of the enterprise to resume production in the
event of a temporary or permanent improvement of its situation.

Our conclusion would be not that there is no hidden unemployment,
but that Standing's distinction between short-term and long-term hidden unemployment is not a useful one. At current wage levels
enterprises are discouraged from undertaking significant rationalisation of the labour force and are encouraged to retain those for whom
they currently have no work, in the expectation that they will be able
to resume production when new orders are forthcoming. In this sense,
at current wage levels there is not a substantial labour surplus, and
Standing's estimate of 'short-term' hidden unemployment is exaggerated. On the other hand, if wages were to be paid and if the minimum
wage were even to approach the subsistence minimum, enterprises
would no longer be able to afford to support not only those on short-
time and administrative leave, but also a substantial proportion of
those who appear currently to be in secure employment.

On any rational accounting principles the vast majority of Russian industrial enterprises must be insolvent:[75] any owner motivated solely by profit would cease production, force out all the employees, sell off the enterprise's assets and lease-out its premises, which indeed is what many 'outside' shareholders seek to do if they manage to acquire control. In this sense the vast majority of the industrial labour force can be considered to be a labour reserve, sustained by insolvent enterprises which receive little government subsidy, but which pay low or no wages, do not service their loans and build up growing debts, particularly to the tax authorities and energy suppliers. While Standing's estimate of 'short-term' hidden unemployment may be exaggerated, the scale of 'long-term' hidden unemployment – the number who would be dismissed if Russian enterprises were subjected to the normal legal and economic constraints of a market economy – hardly bears thinking about.

While we are sceptical of Standing's estimate of 'concealed' unemployment, we are equally sceptical of the published figures for open unemployment. As already noted, there is a substantial difference between the published figures for registered unemployment and those which derive from the labour force survey. However, there are considerable grounds for believing that these figures omit a large number of people of working age who are without any source of adequate income but who do not meet the definitional conditions of unemployment because they are not actively seeking and available for work.

HOW MUCH UNEMPLOYMENT IS THERE IN RUSSIA?

There are no data for unemployment in Russia before 1991, since unemployment did not officially exist. Nevertheless, there was undoubtedly a fair amount of frictional unemployment and quite high structural unemployment in some peripheral regions. The consensus is that unemployment in the late Soviet period amounted to something like 3% of the labour force. There are two sources of data on unemployment rates in Russia since 1991. The first is the data on registrations with the local offices of the Federal Employment Service,

---

[75]   In 1996 43% of all industrial enterprises were unprofitable on Russian accounting principles, when the vast majority have to pay nothing for land, premises or fixed capital (*Sotsial'no-ekonomicheskoe polozhenie Rossii*, 1, 1997).

the second is data derived from the labour force survey.

The Federal Employment Service was established in 1991, but it took some time for it to establish offices throughout Russia, so that its data only really has any significance from 1992. The Employment Service reports figures for the number applying to offices of the Employment Service in search of work, which includes students, pensioners and a small number of people currently in work; the number placed in employment with the assistance of the Employment Service; the number formally registering as unemployed; the number of those receiving benefits; and the number leaving the register each month. While the local offices of the Employment Service are eager to demonstrate a high demand for their services by registering people seeking work and a high success rate by recording job placements for which they can claim credit, they are less eager to register people as unemployed and even less to pay them benefit, which comes out of the unified budget of the employment fund and so reduces the sum available for active labour market policies and for the administration of the Employment Service itself.

A great deal of anecdotal and observational evidence points to the difficulties which are faced by those seeking to register as unemployed or to register for benefit, from the complexity of bureaucratic procedures through administrative obstruction to outright refusal. On the other hand, there is still a considerable, although declining, reluctance of large parts of the population to accept the stigma of unemployment which in the past was criminal 'parasitism'. The local offices of the Employment Service replaced the former 'labour recruitment bureaux', which were responsible for compulsorily placing the otherwise unemployable in work – those who had been repeatedly dismissed for disciplinary offences, released prisoners and 'parasites' – and so continue to be regarded by employers and employees alike as the last resort. Few believe that they will be able to secure an acceptable job through the Employment Service, so a growing proportion of the job placement activity of the Employment Service concerns the provision of temporary vacation work for schoolchildren and students. At the same time, the very low rates of unemployment benefit, the quite stringent conditions for its receipt and the bureaucratic obstacles in the way of registration discourage many who would otherwise be eligible from applying. There is therefore little incentive to register as unemployed either to find a job or to receive benefit. Taking all these considerations into account, it should not be surprising to find that the figures for registered unemployment remain very low, with 2.5 million people, 3.4% of the economically active population, being registered unemployed at the end of 1996, of whom 1.6 million, 2.2% of the economically active population, were receiving benefit.[76] This national figure masks considerable regional variations, with a high in December 1996 of 26% registered unemployment in Ingushetiya and a low of 0.9% in Moscow city.

If we were to believe the figures for registered unemployment, Russia has seen a fall in industrial production of more than 50% and a decline in officially estimated GDP of at least a third, but unemployment remains at the level estimated prior to the beginning of reform. Clearly the registered unemployed represent only the tip of an iceberg, but the question is how big is that iceberg?

The labour force survey has been conducted according to the ILO/OECD methodology since October 1992.[77] The first survey found that unemployment on the ILO/OECD definition was over six times the officially registered rate, at almost 5%, with over three million

---

[76] The proportion of registered unemployed receiving benefit fell from 68% to 59% over 1996 as conditions tightened, the long-term unemployed exhausted their entitlement and a growing number – three-quarters of a million by the end of the year – who were entitled to benefits simply did not receive them, delays in payment reaching four to six months in some regions by the end of 1996 (*Russian Economic Trends*, 1997, 1, p. 127), and many being paid in kind. These factors, and changes in terms of registration in the second half of 1996, explain a steady fall in the number officially recorded as unemployed, from a peak of 2.77 million in April 1996 to only 2.31 million by June 1997.

[77] The first labour force survey was in October 1992, followed by annual surveys in 1993 and 1994, based on a 0.55% two-stage random sample, with households sampled within selected census enumeration districts, which is rotated 20% each year (except 1994). In 1995 the survey was carried out twice, in March and October, with a sample of 0.2% of the population between the ages of 15 and 72. The October 1996 survey was cancelled, reportedly as a result of the lack of funds, but dissatisfaction with the results of the March survey was also reported. It was planned to return to an annual survey with a larger (0.4%) sample in April 1997, with a revised questionnaire, but shortage of funds led to its cancellation, but the October 1997 survey was expected to go ahead. The survey covers basic demographic characteristics of the population (sex, age, family position, education); type of economic activity; those in employment specify the type of activity of the enterprise, their profession, work regime, working conditions, basic working hours, additional work, employment status; the unemployed are asked about the reasons for lack of employment, means and duration of job search, profession, working conditions desired, willingness to start work, and whether they are registered as unemployed. The reliability of the survey is unknown. Although most of the staff of Goskomstat are undoubtedly diligent and honest, there appear to be technical problems with the sampling and there have been suggestions of a high refusal rate (although Goskomstat insists that this is the case only with its household budget survey). There is little monitoring or checking of the collection and reporting of data.

unregistered unemployed. Since then, however, survey unemployment has increased more or less in step with registered unemployment, to reach a rate of 8.6% in March 1996, 3.7 million more than the registered unemployed. The gap between registered and survey unemployment is open to a number of different interpretations. On the one hand, we may believe the labour force survey figure and conclude that the Employment Service is becoming more efficient at registration, while the population is overcoming its reluctance to register, so that the proportion of the unemployed who are failing to register has fallen from 84% in 1992 to 59% in March 1996.[78] On the other hand, we may be more inclined to believe the Employment Service figures, which are based on the rigorous application of ILO/OECD criteria rather than on self-reporting, which would indicate that there is a pool of between three and four million people who claim to be unemployed in response to the survey, but who do not turn to the Employment Service because they would not be recognised as eligible for benefit if they did so. Thus Commander and Yemtsov (1995, p. 4) doubt the reliability of the labour force survey data as a measure of unemployment, partly because 20% of the survey unemployed in October 1992 were reported as being students and pensioners (the figure had fallen to 6% by March 1996). However, the latter are only recorded as unemployed if they are actively seeking and available for work, and many students and around one-third of all pensioners do work (it should be remembered that the pension age is low in Russia, with even earlier retirement for the large number of people working in harmful conditions). On the basis of their own April 1994 survey Simon Commander and his colleagues estimated the 'true' rate of ILO/OECD unemployment as lying about halfway between the survey and the registered rate of unemployment.[79]

---

[78]   The rates of registration vary enormously across the country (Gorbacheva, Breev et al., 1995), so that those regions with the highest rates of registered unemployment are not necessarily those with the highest survey unemployment. The most extreme example is the small Jewish Autonomous Region, which in March 1995 had an official unemployment rate of less than 2%, although according to the labour force survey the rate is the highest in the country, at 23% (Tkachenko, 1996).

[79]   This was part of the regular VTsIOM monthly survey of the population, which tends substantially to over-represent those with higher education, who are both much less likely to be unemployed and much more likely to have secondary employment, and substantially under-represent workers, who are much more likely to be unemployed and much less likely to have secondary unemployment, although VTsIOM corrects for bias in its overall figures. The labour force survey uses a two-stage random sample which is two hundred times as large as that of VTsIOM.

Commander and Yemtsov also point to the proportion of the registered and survey unemployed who themselves report in surveys that they have significant earnings from employment. In their own survey with VTsIOM almost one fifth of the registered unemployed and over a quarter of those claiming benefit had significant informal or secondary work, while 'nearly a third of those working to a significant degree in the informal sector were registered as unemployed and just under a quarter were receiving benefits' (ibid., p. 10). In a VTsIOM survey in April 1995 one-third of those who described themselves as unemployed were earning above the average wage from their supplementary jobs (Khibovskaya, 1995b). The head of the Moscow Employment Service was quoted in *Izvestiya* as estimating that 60% of his registered unemployed people had jobs (*Izvestiya*, 15.10.93, cited Gimpel'son, 1994).[80]

Commander and Yemtsov aside, there is no special reason to doubt the labour force survey estimate of the rate of unemployment according to the strict ILO/OECD definition. People may have an incentive to conceal the fact that they are employed from the Employment Service, but they have no incentive to lie to the labour force survey. Moreover, as Commander and Yemtsov note (ibid., p. 10n), it is hardly surprising that many of the unemployed have additional earnings, given the low level of benefit. Since the usual level of benefit is considerably below the physiological subsistence minimum, those without additional income and/or the support of family and friends will, by definition, die. In these circumstances, when ILO/OECD unemployment is not a realistic option, the official definition of unemployment is misleadingly restrictive.

In Russian conditions, where many of the employed are working short-time or are laid-off without pay, where the payment of wages for those in work may be delayed for months at a time, where many earn below the subsistence minimum, where there is a wide range of opportunities for casual and self-employment, even if low-paid, and where a large proportion of the population is engaged in subsistence agriculture and domestic production, the dividing line between employment and unemployment is a very fine one, with a substantial

---

[80]   The RLMS estimate of ILO unemployment, which eliminates all those with any form of employment from its count, closely corresponds to that of the labour force survey, while its November 1996 survey showed a 'self-reported' unemployment rate of 14%. The 1996 survey found that 14% of the registered unemployed had incidental earnings, although only 2% worked on a regular basis and had significant earnings.

proportion of the population in a limbo between the two. We can therefore perhaps best try to categorise the population not into employed and unemployed, but into at least three groups, the employed, the unemployed and those between the two statuses. For this purpose we need some indication of the number employed.

HOW MANY PEOPLE ARE EMPLOYED IN RUSSIA?

This might seem a simple question to answer. If we want to know how many are employed we have only to turn to the published official statistics on employment in Russia.[81] These figures tell us that 65.4 million of an economically active population of 72.3 million were employed in June 1997, the remaining 6.9 million being those identified on the basis of the labour force survey as being unemployed.[82] This marks a fall in total employment of 12% since 1990. According to the labour force survey, employment fell by 8.7 million between October 1992 and March 1996 while unemployment increased by 2.9 million. Since the population of working age increased by 1.7 million over this period, this implies that 7.5 million people, equally men and women, withdrew from labour force participation in this period.[83]

Although Goskomstat officials are very helpful, the presentation and explication of published data leaves much to be desired. The employment totals derive from estimates prepared in the regional Goskomstat offices using guidelines issued from Moscow. The figures for medium and large enterprises and organisations, which are overwhelmingly state and former state enterprises, are reported to Goskomstat regional offices by the enterprises themselves and, according to our own research into the collection and reporting of

---

[81] I am very grateful to Veronika Kabalina for help in collecting statistical data and to Zinaida Ryzhykova, deputy head of the labour statistics department of Goskomstat, for clarifying a number of issues. They bear no responsibility for any of my misinterpretations of the data!

[82] The estimate of employment includes both full-time and part-time, permanent, temporary, seasonal and casual employees and all those who derive any kind of income from 'self-employment' or who work without payment in family businesses. Double-counting is supposed to be compensated for on the basis of information about multiple-job holding from the labour force survey (Goskomstat, 1996b, pp. 54–5).

[83] One should not ignore the third form of exit, through death. Women outnumber men by over 2 million in the age range 15–60 (and by three-to-one among pensioners). The increase in the death rate of middle-aged men has meant that the population of working age has only increased a little since 1990.

employment statistics by industrial enterprises, they are reported reasonably accurately, at least in the case of state and former state industrial enterprises.[84] Figures for employment in small enterprises are gathered on the basis of a sample survey of such registered enterprises, but the regional statistical offices do not have an adequate sampling frame and our research indicates that the numbers returned

---

[84] Medium and large enterprises were defined until 1996 as all those with more than 200 employees in industry and construction, 100 in science, more than 50 in other productive spheres and more than 25 in non-productive spheres. From 1996 the definition is all those with more than 100 employees in industry, transport and construction, 60 in science and in agriculture, 30 in retail trade and services and 50 in other branches. According to Goskmostat, large and medium enterprises still employ 85% of the industrial labour force.

Russian Economic Trends claims that the Goskomstat employment figures 'apply mainly to the state and former state sectors' (*Russian Economic Trends*, 1996, 4 (4), p. 92), implying that they overstate the decline in employment. This is true only in the sense that most employment is in the state and former state sectors, but the totals include Goskomstat's estimates of private sector employment as well.

Some commentators have argued that enterprises inflate their reported employment figures in order to reduce their average wage and therefore their liability to the excess wage tax, which was in force until the end of 1995, although there is no evidence of such a practice, and we have found none in our research. Enterprises with whom we have discussed the issue claimed that if they wanted to distort the figures it was much easier to distort wage than employment figures, and this was also much more to their advantage since various local taxes were based on the number of employees, so that if they inflated employment figures they would only pay more in local taxation than what they had saved on the excess wage tax.

Roxburgh and Shapiro have proposed the tax as an explanation for the hoarding of low-wage labour in order to reduce the average wage (Roxburgh and Shapiro, 1996). However, the tax cut in at such a low wage that this would have been a very costly way of reducing tax liability (since the wage and social insurance and other overheads of the surplus employee still had to be paid in order to save a relatively small amount of tax: the excess wage tax accounted for only between 3 and 10% of the total wage bill in 1994, depending on the branch of production. *Statisticheskoe obozrenie*, 12, 1995, p. 68). Workers on unpaid or minimally paid administrative leave would reduce the average wage more significantly, since technically they are counted in the number employed (the only legal basis for 'administrative leave' is unpaid compassionate leave), whereas short-time workers are only counted in the number employed *pro rata* (accounting for wages and numbers employed is still according to the Soviet Goskomstat Instruction of 17.09.87). However, only 4% of labour-hoarding enterprises gave *Russian Economic Barometer* saving on the excess wage tax as one of their three reasons for hoarding labour in January 1995 (Aukutsionek and Kapelyushnikov, 1996, p. 12). A survey of 21 enterprises in St Petersburg reported six managers as having mentioned the excess wage tax as a factor in their employment decisions, although only two of the six reported that they had any surplus labour, so that the author concluded that the tax was not a major factor in the explanation of labour retention (Brown, 1996, p. 819). The excess wage tax was abolished at the end of 1995, with no obvious effect either on reporting practices or on the scale or pattern of separations. Although there was a sharp increase in short-time working from the beginning of 1996, there was no decline in the scale of administrative leave and there was a continued rapid increase in the non-payment of wages.

to the statistical offices, particularly by new private enterprises, are almost entirely fictitious. The regional statistical office then supplements this data and adds its own estimates for employment which is not covered by official reporting, in particular for non-reporting small enterprises, self-employment and employment by unincorporated employers, using a variety of sources, including the labour force survey. It appears that tax records are used only in relation to partners in registered private businesses not engaged in economic activities (Goskomstat, 1996b). This data is cumulated and the gross figures are reported to Goskomstat in Moscow, where they are revised and returned to the regions for publication locally. Goskomstat in Moscow does not have access to the raw data collected at regional level. This means that nobody really knows what these figures actually mean, because nobody knows where they have come from.

The alternative source for estimates of employment is the labour force survey. This is carried out through the regional Goskomstat network, with preliminary data processing taking place in the regions. This data is based on a large sample survey and should be much more reliable than that collected through the old system of statistical reporting by enterprises and organisations. However, Goskomstat continues to fly in the face of international practice and place primary reliance on its administrative data, on the grounds that this reflects the annual average situation, while the labour force survey refers only to one week in the year. The labour force survey figures are used primarily for internal purposes and the results are only published partially and with considerable delay – the results of the October 1994 labour force survey were not published until July 1995, in an edition of 150.[85] Until the end of 1996 the labour force survey data was cumulated regionally so that detailed breakdowns of the data (for example, by forms of employment) were not available to Goskomstat in Moscow.[86]

Goskomstat does not publish the absolute figures revealed by the labour force survey, only distributions.[87] However, it is possible to

---

[85] The results of the 1995 surveys were only published in *Trud i Zanyatost* in April 1997, although summary data had been published in Goskomstat's monthly *Statisticheskoe obozrenie* and other publications.

[86] Each region collects and codes its data using its own methodology and computer systems, only the figures required by Moscow being prepared in standard form, so that it is technically not possible for Goskomstat to aggregate the primary data.

[87] The absolute figures published in the reports on the 1992–95 labour force surveys are the Goskomstat estimates based on administrative data, not the labour force survey figures, although the latter are used for the distributions.

interpolate the labour force survey totals from the published participation rate figures, which cover the age range 15–72,[88] giving us a total employed in that age range.[89] This gives a figure of 63.4 million employed in 1994, over 5 million fewer than the published Goskomstat total.[90] Goskomstat has begun to provide a set of figures which are said to derive from the labour force survey to the OECD, which publishes these figures in its review of short-term economic indicators, alongside and in unexplained contradiction with the 'official' employment figure.[91] The published figure for 1994 is exactly the same as that calculated from the participation rates, although that for 1993 is actually 1 million less than the figure calculated from participation rates, making the employment decline between 1993 and 1994 appear correspondingly less. The labour force survey figure reported to OECD for 1995 is only 340,000 lower than the figure for 1994 and over half a million higher than the figure of 62.529 million for March 1995 published (inadvertently?) by an official of the Ministry of Labour (Tkachenko, 1996, p. 39), although it is almost the same as the figure calculated from participation rates for October 1995.[92] Since

---

[88] The various figures are not entirely consistent. Participation rates derived from the 1992–95 surveys are published in *Trud i Zanyatost'* 1996, which also publishes the age and sex distribution of the employed and the unemployed population. However, the published overall participation rate is not consistent with the sex and age-specific participation rates published in the same table, which imply a significantly larger overall participation rate, and neither is consistent with the age and sex distributions of employment and unemployment, which taken together imply a participation rate of over 100% for some sections of the population. The most likely explanation is significant sample bias in the labour force survey in favour of women and the young and old. If this is the case, estimates derived from the age and sex specific participation rates will be more accurate than the overall estimates published by Goskomstat. Table 2.1 provides the totals calculated by both methods, the difference in total employment year by year being between 1.5 and 2 million, somewhat narrowing the gap between labour force survey and administrative estimates.

[89] Employment is defined by the labour force survey as any kind of income-generating activity, for as little as one hour, in the week of the survey, including any agricultural production, hunting, fishing, picking berries or mushrooms for sale, or any kind of work from which the individual is temporarily absent, or unpaid family labour. The total includes those on administrative leave, whether paid or unpaid, and also includes around 2 million women on maternity and child care leave, who are not included as employed in the administrative statistics.

[90] The labour force survey covers the population in the age range 15–72. There were 5.4 million women and 1.6 million men over 72 in 1995. The RLMS found that 4% of men and 2% of women in this age range worked in 1976, which would add only 80,000 to the economically active population.

[91] This reduces the denominator of the calculation of the unemployment rate, which the OECD reports as 9.2% against Goskomstat's officially published 8.2% (OECD, 1996c, A20).

[92] Allowing for the increase in population of working age, the reported participation rate

these figures include women on maternity leave, who are excluded from the Goskomstat published totals, this means that since 1994 labour force survey employment has been consistently about seven million less than the estimated figure published by Goskomstat.[93]

A third source for estimates of employment is provided by the Russian Longitudinal Monitoring Survey. Although the sample is much smaller than that of Goskomstat, technically the survey appears to be superior to the labour force survey and should give reasonable estimates of employment totals. However, the questions asked are not strictly comparable to those of the labour force survey.[94] Figures are

---

for October 1995 implies a fall of only half a million in employment over the previous year, against a rise in unemployment of one million, which seems unlikely, particularly as employment in large and medium enterprises fell by 2.5 million over 1995, while even Goskomstat estimates of self-employment and employment in small enterprises showed barely any increase. Goskomstat believes that it has lost about one million self-employed in the service sector in the labour force survey, one aspect of the revision of the questionnaire for 1997 being to try to find these 'lost souls' by asking explicitly about the provision of services by the self-employed. It may be that the October 1995 labour force survey data, including that reported to OECD and that on which estimates of participation rates are based, has been 'corrected' to account for this, although Goskomstat denies that labour force survey data is corrected. However, it should be noted that the RLMS data actually indicates an increase in employment and fall in unemployment over the same period (November 1994 to November 1995), concentrated among women. Both surveys were conducted immediately before the 1995 duma election, but there was no pre-election boom nor any let-up in the incidence of leave, although the shift to non-payment of wages during 1995 might have temporarily stemmed the employment decline as employees stayed in jobs in the hope of receiving back-pay, while employers postponed lay-offs. In 1996 all the data sources agree that misery was piled on misery: RLMS shows a very substantial fall in employment and rise in unemployment, while Goskomstat shows a fall in employment in large and medium industrial enterprises of over 10% alongside a massive increase in administrative leave, short-time working and non-payment of wages.

Statisticheskoe obozrenie, 2, 1996, publishes participation rates derived from the labour force surveys since 1993, including age-specific rates for age groups under 30. The overall rate for 1993, 65.9%, is as originally published, 1994 is given as 68.1%, against the 63.1% originally published, and the rates for the two 1995 surveys as 67.5% and 67.4%. These are certainly misprints, since *Trud i Zanyatost'*, 1996, gives figures of 63.2% for both October 1994 and for October 1995.

[93] The labour force survey is a household survey which does not cover such facilities as barracks and hostels (as well as penal and mental institutions), which could account for some of this discrepancy. However, this seems unlikely since the sampling frame is the 1989 population census and the labour force survey figures are reported to OECD as the labour force survey-based employment totals.

[94] For the key question RLMS (1994–96) simply asked: 'do you now work, are you on paid or unpaid leave, or do you not work?', later asking about supplementary earning activities. The LFS asks 'have you done any paid work or had an income-earning occupation in the week of the survey?', with supplementary questions for other self-employment (examples are producing agricultural products, catching fish, hunting, gathering mushrooms or berries for sale), unpaid family labour and to identify the reasons for not working so as to include those on leave in the estimate. On this question

therefore provided both for total employment and for those who say that they worked in the last week, the former being comparable to Goskomstat's administrative statistics, the latter to the labour force survey (which include those on maternity leave).[95]

There is clearly a substantial discrepancy between the survey data, relating to current employment status, and the administrative figures. What is the source of this discrepancy? Technically the most likely source is double-counting in the Goskomstat aggregate figures. As

---

RLMS shows a substantially higher number working than the LFS. However, 5% of those who responded to RLMS in 1996 that they worked went on to say that they had not worked in the previous month, while 11% said later in the interview that they had not worked in the previous week (comparable figures for 1995 were 5.1 and 8.3% and for 1994 were 5.3% and 9.5%). Only a third of people engaged in individual economic activity said that they had worked in the previous week (this is plausible – two-thirds of those engaged in individual economic activity said that they had performed less than 40 hours of such activity in the previous month). On the other hand, RLMS produces a rather low proportion who say that they are on leave (only about half the number that would be expected from the Goskomstat figures on administrative leave alone). In 1996 0.6% of those who said that they worked later indicated that they were currently on administrative leave, but half these said they worked at secondary activity in the previous week. On the other hand, about 1% of those who said they worked last week had previously said that they did not work and did not engage in individual activity. It seems most likely that these people were engaged in subsistence activity, since the relevant question was 'Did you in the last 7 days work at an enterprise, in an organization, including part-time work, work at home, entrepreneurial activity, and farming?', and half these people had worked their gardens in the previous week. The conclusion is that this question is the most likely to produce comparable results to that of the LFS, when supplemented by those on various forms of leave. It is not likely that many people take their regular vacation at the time of the interviewing, in October and November. The discrepancy between the two sets of figures indicates the scale of casual and irregular employment, 5.7 million people telling RLMS interviewers in October and November 1996 that they worked, but had not in fact worked the previous week, well over two million of whom had not worked in the previous month.

The 1992 RLMS survey used a different questionnaire, the first question asking whether you 'now work at an enterprise, organization, collective farm, or cooperative?', later asking how many hours were worked last month, and whether this was a typical month. 85% of the 9% of people who did not work last month said this was not typical. Later in the questionnaire respondents were asked whether in the last week they had worked 'in the production sector or at an office, including part-time work, work at home, entrepreneurial activity, farming or individual economic activity?', 16% of those who earlier had said that they worked responding that they had not worked in the previous week, but this question is probably too narrow. 63.2 million said they had worked in the last month, against the 60.5 million who said they had worked in the last week.

[95] All RLMS figures are my calculations from RLMS data, based on age and sex specific rates to compensate for any sample bias. RLMS shows considerably higher unemployment for 1992 and lower for 1995 than does the labour force survey data, with an apparently anomalous substantial rise in employment in 1995. The RLMS estimates include around 2 million women on maternity leave who are included in the LFS but not in the administrative data, in addition to those on other forms of leave included in both.

noted above, Goskomstat combines figures from administrative reporting by enterprises with estimates, derived in part from the labour
force survey, of unregistered employment and self-employment.
Goskomstat uses the labour force survey data on dual job-holding to
correct for this form of double-counting, but a substantial proportion
of those who are active only in unregistered and self-employment will
have left their labour books in a registered enterprise in which they
perhaps once worked, but do not work now. This has tax advantages
for the enterprise and allows the unregistered employee to accumulate
years of work service to qualify for pension and other benefits without
having to deal with the bureaucratic and financial burdens of registering as self-employed. The labour force survey does not ask people
where they are registered as being employed, so these people will be
double-counted.

Table 2.1: Total Employment in Russia, various sources, million

	1990	1991	1992	1993	1994	1995	1996
Goskomstat (av. of quarterly data)	75.3	73.8	72.1	70.9	68.5	66.4	66.0
Goskomstat (large and medium enterprises)			58.9	56.8	53.3	50.8	47.5
Labour force survey (October)			70.5	67.6	63.5	62.9	61.8 (March)
Labour force survey (age and sex-specific participation rates)			72.1	69.9	65.7	64.5	
RLMS who work			72.3		69.0	70.0	67.2
RLMS worked last week or on leave			60.5		62.1	63.1	57.5

There is also a philosophical difference between the two sets of figures, in that the administrative figures are formulated within the
framework of the Soviet tradition of the 'balance of labour resources',
which is why they include many people who are currently not working, such as those on child-care leave, laid-off or on administrative
vacation. This also underlies what is most likely a considerable overestimate of the number engaged in self-employment, many of whom
the RLMS shows to be employed only on a casual or occasional

basis,[96] and in the new private sector, arising from an overestimation of the dynamism of the new private sector.[97]

In principle we would expect the figures for large and medium enterprises, which are overwhelmingly state and former state enterprises and which account for over 80% of total employment, to be reasonably accurate, since these continue to report and, on the basis of our research, it seems that they report accurately. These figures show a decline in employment between 1992 and 1995 of 8.2 million, to 50.8 million, against a decline of 7.5 million reported by the labour force survey, which would imply that there has been very little growth in individual employment or in employment in small businesses since 1992.[98] This might seem implausible at first sight, but it is conceivable when we consider the scale of the economic decline, the extent to which the new private sector involves secondary employment which will not lead to an increase in the number employed, and when we remember that there had already been an extensive growth of employment in co-operatives and individual labour activity in the late 1980s. The number of small businesses grew rapidly between 1991 and 1994, but many of these were former co-operatives and many were paper companies created for tax purposes.[99] According to

---

[96] The biggest overestimate was in 1993, the administrative figures having fallen in line with those reported by the labour force survey between 1993 and 1995, with a further substantial overestimate in 1996.

[97] Many have argued that official data underestimates the growth of the new private sector, but little or no evidence is ever cited for this claim, while the weight of available evidence is to the contrary. Goskomstat prepares its own estimates for private sector economic activity and, as an arm of government, has a strong incentive to prepare the most optimistic projections. Moreover, it is important to remember that there was a large but completely unrecorded private sector in the Soviet period. It is a myth that the small business sector is dynamic. The most thorough survey of the small business sector to date found in 1994–95 that only a quarter of small businesses established *de novo* since 1990 considered themselves to be profitable with prospects for future development. The principal goal of over a third of such newly created small businesses was simply to survive, one-sixth were mostly concerned with finding new kinds of activity and only 6% were looking to maximise current profits (Institute for Strategic Analysis and Development of Entrepreneurship, 1995).

[98] Some of those reported as employed by large and medium enterprises may be 'dead souls' who are in fact self-employed. However, a pilot project which we have conducted on the self-employed indicates that the overwhelming majority keep their labour books in friendly new private enterprises (former co-operatives), which can reduce their tax liability by reporting them as employed and receiving wages. We have found few cases of such 'dead souls' in medium and large former state enterprises, where the more complex accounting and traditional reporting systems make the practice much more difficult, although research and higher education institutes are certainly an exception to this rule!

[99] According to Goskomstat estimates, the number of small enterprises increased from

Goskomstat estimates, 8.9 people were formally employed in small businesses in 1995, up from 8.5 million in 1994, with a further 4.9 million working as a registered second job or on a part-time basis, but this is almost certainly an overestimate (1996 figures, which show 6 million employed, are not comparable because of the change in the definition of a small enterprise). A further 4.7 million were estimated to be self-employed in 1994 (so far as I am aware no figure has been published since then), up from 128 thousand in 1990 (1 million in 1991, 3 million in 1992 and 2.6 million in 1993) but, as noted above, the vast majority of these are likely to be officially recorded as working elsewhere.[100]

The available data is clearly very unsatisfactory, but the general trend is common to all the data sets. It would seem that employment fell by somewhere between 12% and 24% between 1990 and 1996, while the population of working age increased slightly. What has happened to between nine and 18 million people, the overwhelming majority of whom used to work full-time? If we assume that about 2.5 million were unemployed in 1990, we can estimate that about four million have joined the ranks of the unemployed: they have no form of employment, are available for work and are actively seeking work. This leaves between five and 14 million people unaccounted for. We might be tempted to assume that these are people who have taken

---

268,000 in 1991 to 897,000 in 1994, but has since fallen back. One-third of all small businesses are in Moscow and St Petersburg city and regions (*Statisticheskoe obozrenie*, 10, 1995, p. 66; *Rossiiskii statisticheskii ezhegodnik*, 1996). A sample survey of 1,628 small enterprises found that 12.5% had been formed within a larger state enterprise, 8.0% were spin-offs of a larger enterprise, 12.2% formed out of the dismemberment or collapse of a larger enterprise, 11.7% transformed from a co-operative and 55.7% were new start-ups. However, the new starts were substantially smaller than the older enterprises, with 60% having fewer than 15 employees, so that new starts employed only about half the total number of employees (Institute for Strategic Analysis and Development of Entrepreneurship 1995).

[100] Goskomstat reported 6.7 million involved in non-waged labour in 1995, up from 6.5 million in 1994, 5.9 in 1993 and 4.4 in 1992. This comprises an estimated 1.1 million employers, those working on contract, the self-employed and unpaid family labour. This is not an unreasonable estimate: 3.6% of adults in the Russian Longitudinal Monitoring Survey in 1995 who did not have other jobs had in the last month received money for some kind of individual work, examples in the question being 'maybe you sewed someone a dress, gave someone a ride in a car, assisted someone with apartment or car repairs, purchased and delivered food, looked after a sick person, or did something else that you were paid for?', although fewer than one in four regarded this as regular work. This equates to about 4.3 million people for Russia as a whole. The comparable figure for 1994 was 3.8 and for 1996 4.0 million. Goskomstat reports 9.1 million self-employed to the OECD, based on the labour force survey, but this includes those estimated to be working in subsistence production.

advantage of their new-found freedom not to work and have chosen to leave the labour force – perhaps there has been a mass withdrawal of women from work, back into the home? According to the Goskomstat administrative statistics 3.6 million women withdrew from the labour force, as opposed to only 0.9 million men, between 1992 and 1995, which would appear to confirm this common conception. However, examination of the labour force survey data tells quite a different story, with men's employment falling by more than that of women. Unemployment among men has increased more than among women, because more men than women who have lost their jobs seek work, and more men of working age than women have died, but still the economically inactive male population has increased by slightly more than the inactive female population. In a period of deep economic crisis with a rapid fall in wages and sharp increase in inequality it is unlikely that many can afford to withdraw voluntarily from the labour market. With savings having been destroyed by inflation and reserves exhausted by years of penury there are few who can survive without earning a living in one way or another. Russian women remain strongly attached to the ethos inherited from the Soviet and peasant past: they are committed to work and it is they who take primary responsibility for the survival of their families. The men may take to the bottle and/or die in despair, but the women battle on (Ashwin and Bowers, 1997).

Withdrawal from the labour market in Russia is much more a matter of age than of gender, as can be shown by examination of the sex and age-specific participation rates derived from the labour force survey covering the period 1992–95 (Table 2.2). The reduction in labour force participation is heavily concentrated among young people (15–19), whose participation rate fell by a quarter, and those past retirement age, whose participation rate fell by over a third, with a less dramatic fall of just over 10% in the pre-retirement age group (men of 55–60 and women of 50–55) against a fall of less than 5% for all other age groups. These categories account for two-thirds of the increase in the economically inactive population between 1992 and 1995.[101] The

---

[101] Total unemployment increased by almost three million (almost 80%) between 1992 and 1995, but there was virtually no increase at all in unemployment recorded by the labour force survey in the age group 15–19 or among those aged 50 and above (as calculated by applying the age and sex distribution to the annual totals), although these were the groups experiencing the largest falls in employment, strongly indicating that non-employed teenagers do not want regular jobs at the kind of wages on offer, while those over 50 do not see any point in seeking jobs. According to Goskomstat, only a small number give up looking for work in the current year (300,000 in 1994 (Popov, 1995)),

number of 15–19 year-olds in employment fell by three-quarters of a million, almost a third, between 1992 and 1995, despite the fact that the age group grew by half a million over the same three years.[102] The reduction in participation among the young is most likely explained not by a mass return to education, which has not taken place, but by the growing tendency for urban teenagers to live on their wits rather than to look for a job – according to the RLMS data, 30% of the 15–19 year-olds who work are self-employed against 7% of those in the 20–24 age group, while the universal fear is that those who have withdrawn from the labour market have turned not to philosophy but to crime. Meanwhile, those pre-retirement and of pension age are predominantly those who have been pressed or forced to give up their jobs, but who are not eligible for unemployment benefit and are not actively seeking work because they know that they have no chance of getting another job, reduced to living on their pensions and scraping a living as best they can. The image of the teenager robbing the pensioner who has just sold her last possessions on the street corner has become the modern icon which Russia's flexible labour market presents to the world.

The boundaries between unemployment and non-participation are statistically imprecise because the dividing line between them in reality is equally hazy. Unemployment benefits are so low, for those who negotiate all the hurdles, secure registration and then are lucky enough to be paid on time, that the unemployed and 'economically inactive' alike inhabit a limbo world between employment and unemployment, living on meagre pensions and benefits supplemented by handouts from friends and relatives, from subsistence agriculture, from occasional casual labour, petty trading or petty crime. The only difference is that the unemployed report that they are still seeking regular employment.

But neither of these groups differs radically from the employed.

---

which would imply that Russian 'discouraged workers' are so discouraged that they never even start looking for jobs. This broad pattern is confirmed by the RLMS data, summarised in Table 2.3.

[102] This growth in numbers implies that the proportion of 15–17 year-olds within the age-group increased and this would account for a small part of the decline in the participation rate (at most one-sixth of the fall), since one would expect the 18 and 19 year-olds to be the most economically active. The large fall in participation means that the unemployment rate among the young has increased sharply, although the number unemployed has not. Although the population of working age has barely changed, there have been considerable changes in the age distribution of the working population.

Many of the employed also have to find other ways to make a living because, although they may work, they may not receive their wages for months. Many of them are regularly laid-off or put on short-time with little or no pay. A growing number, particularly in the private sector, are only working part-time or as casual, seasonal or temporary employees, all of whom are included in the Goskomstat employment total. And even many of those who work and are paid their wages on time do not earn enough to support even one person at the minimum subsistence level. In short there is a wide range of statuses in the Russian labour market, with a series of gradations between the small minority who are in regular full-time employment, are paid on time and who earn enough to support themselves at or above the socially established subsistence level and, at the other extreme, those who are entirely without employment or any apparent means of subsistence.

How many such people are there living in this world-in-between? There has been no fall in the population of working age, and we can assume that given the catastrophic fall in income levels, particularly among the more vulnerable sections of the population, there has been no fall in the desire or need of people to engage in paid employment, so we can assume that at least 75 million people need to work in order to live, the number reported employed in 1990.[103] A best guess on the basis of the most recent available data would be that in the autumn of 1996 about 60 million people were formally employed, including around three million part-time employees,[104] although over two million of these were on administrative leave (average duration of two months), of whom over 40% were paid nothing, and a further three million were working an average of eight hours per week short-time (Goskomstat, *Sotsial'no-ekonomicheskoe polozhenie Rossii*, 1,

---

[103] This is an underestimate since, although the population of working age has hardly changed, there are almost three million more people of pension age, around one-fifth of whom normally work. Although the plight of the pensioners is a sorry one, the nominal value of their pensions is not significantly different from the Soviet period, so we would expect their need to work to be neither greater nor less than in the past.

[104] Six per cent of employed adults in the Russian Longitudinal Monitoring Survey in 1996 normally worked less than six hours a day and 3.5% worked four hours or less in their primary jobs. This would indicate that around 3 million people work part-time, of whom about 1.8 million work half time or less. This corresponds quite closely to Goskomstat's estimate that 6 million people are employed on individual agreements (which are used for non-standard terms of employment). Goskomstat estimates that 70–80% of these people are in second jobs, but the survey evidence on secondary employment would indicate that this is a considerable overestimate.

1997).[105] Only 52 million of these people were actually working in any one week and only 55 million in the course of the month (RLMS), which would indicate that at least six million were employed on a more or less casual basis in their primary jobs and/or that many more are laid-off than are recorded by Goskomstat.[106] Of the 55 million actually working in a given month, only around 16 million had received their most recent wages on time and in full while around 20 million had been paid nothing at all in the past month, about 17 million were three months or more in arrears and about three million people were over 6 months in arrears (VTsIOM Bulletin, January/February 1997; RLMS).

According to the RLMS data, the median wage of those in employment who were lucky enough to be paid in October 1996 was 500,000 roubles, 35% above the official physiological subsistence minimum, while the two-thirds of those in employment who were owed money by their employer were owed on average 1.5 million roubles.[107] Around 2 million people supplemented their incomes by holding second jobs, although over half worked less than two hours per day at their second job and one-third of these people had received no wage for their second job in the previous month. Around three million supplemented their basic wage through additional self-employment, although only a quarter did so on a regular basis and only 10% for more than two hours per day. Even with their supplementary earnings, however, the median total income of those who worked last month was 400,000 roubles, just above the subsistence minimum, and of those who were actually paid was 600,000 roubles. Although those in industry bear the brunt of lay-offs and short-time, the 27% of the population living in the countryside are by far the worst off, with even the average wage far below the subsistence minimum, very substantial

---

[105] Eighteen per cent of those working had worked less than 32 hours in the previous week in RLMS, indicating that short-time working is more extensive than this.

[106] The latter possibility would help to reconcile the Goskomstat data with Guy Standing's finding of a much higher rate of disguised unemployment in RLFS.

[107] According to Goskomstat figures the average wage due (but not necessarily paid) in October-November 1996 was 840,000 roubles, just above the RLMS average of 790,000 for those who were actually paid. The subsistence minimum was 370,000 roubles and the minimum wage was 75,900 at the time of the survey, when Goskomstat reported that 20% of the population had an income below the subsistence minimum. Respondents in the VTsIOM survey in November 1996 defined the poverty line as 290,000 roubles per head, the minimum required for subsistence as 535,000, an income required to live normally as 1,453,000 and an income to be rich as 4,302,000. The official subsistence minimum at that time was about 380,000 roubles per head.

wage delays, no alternative employment and a growing rural population as people leave the towns in search of food.

About four million people were self-employed, including those engaged in occasional trade, sale of agricultural produce and so on, although two-thirds only did this work on a casual basis, fewer than a third having worked in the last week and two-thirds worked less than half time, with a median monthly income of 250,000 roubles, two-thirds of the subsistence minimum. A further one million people defined themselves as entrepreneurs but this by no means meant that they were all rich – their median total income was less than one million roubles, although a third made more than two million a month.

This leaves around 13 million people (those not reported as having worked or been on leave during the previous month) making a living as best they can, of whom 2.6 million were registered as unemployed, of whom 1.6 million were receiving a median benefit of 128,000, just over one-third of the subsistence minimum (RLMS), a further four million reported that they were unemployed and seeking work, while at least another six million (around three million of whom are pensioners – women over 55 and men over 60 and one and a half million are under 25) were working in subsistence activity or unrecorded casual labour in order to survive.

The median household income of the 4,000 households questioned by RLMS in November 1996 was 680,000 roubles (the mean household income was 1,150,000 roubles), and the median income per head was 290,000 (the mean was 436,000 roubles, which is only just over half Goskomstat's estimate for income per head). Sixty-four per cent of households had a total income per head below the physiological subsistence minimum, three times Goskomstat's estimate of 20%.[108] Half the households had only one-third of the amount which they estimated that they needed to live normally, 83% had less than two-thirds of the amount they needed to live normally and only 7% had what they considered to be sufficient to live a normal life. One-quarter

---

[108]   The RLMS data on wages are very close to the published Goskomstat estimates. However, Goskomstat adds a substantial estimate for unreported income, the purpose of which is essentially to reconcile its income data with its (optimistic) consumption and expenditure estimates. *Russian Economic Trends*, 1997, 1, pp. 86–7, offers an alternative official estimate which reduces personal income by 14% by modifying Goskomstat's absurdly unrealistic assumptions about household saving. According to Goskomstat data, 1996 was the year in which wages rose sharply, inequality was reduced and poverty ameliorated, although a growing number were not actually paid their so generous wages.

of households depended on state benefits (pensions, child benefit, unemployment benefit) for more than 50% of their income. It should hardly be surprising to find that a growing proportion of people's needs are met by their own subsistence production. Two-thirds of households in the Russian Longitudinal Monitoring Survey grew some of their own food but only 2–3% sold any of the produce. In 1996, 56% of households grew their own potatoes, with a median harvest of 400 kilos and a mean of 700 kilos against estimated *per capita* consumption in 1996 of 108 kilos. In 1996 an estimated 46% of total agricultural output, including about 90% of all potato production and three-quarters of all vegetables, came from household plots (*Russian Economic Trends*, 1997, 1, pp. 104–5). In short, extreme labour market flexibility has allowed Russia to endure an unprecedented economic collapse while both registered and survey unemployment remain relatively low, but it is doubtful that this can be considered a great achievement since labour market flexibility and the absence of adequate provision for the unemployed has condemned the majority of the population to living and working conditions which cannot be considered acceptable by any standards. Far from promoting the transition to a market economy, labour market flexibility is promoting the reversion to subsistence production as wages fall below the minimum necessary for physical survival. In parallel with the reversion to subsistence production on the part of individuals is the reversion to barter on the part of those enterprises which are still doing business. *Russian Economic Barometer* reported that barter accounted for 40% of the sales of its reporting industrial enterprises in December 1996, while the government itself estimated that 'almost 70% of deliveries were exchanged on barter terms' in 1996 (Goskomstat, *Sotsial'no-ekonomicheskoe polozhenie Rossii*, 1, 1997, p. 11). While the real economy is largely demonetised, the shrinking supply of money circulates incestuously between government and the financial system.

CONCLUSION

Russia has been the test bed of the theory that labour market flexibility is a key to successful structural adjustment. The most important policy conclusion that we would draw from our research, that cannot be reiterated too strongly, is that Russia has definitively established that *labour market flexibility does not work.* Far from promoting structural adjustment, a flexible labour market has proved to be one of the major barriers to such adjustment by allowing employers and the government alike to transfer the costs of continued decline on to the mass of the population and by depriving management of any incentive to rationalise production or to invest in order to raise labour productivity. The lesson to be drawn from Adam Smith is not that free markets are always right, but that the 'liberal reward for labour' is socially beneficial, not only because 'no society can surely be flourishing and happy, of which the far greater part of the members are poor and miserable', but also because high wages encourage the 'industry of the common people'. As Smith noted: 'Our merchants and master-manufacturers complain much of the bad effects of high wages in raising the price, and thereby lessening the sale of their goods both at home and abroad. They say nothing concerning the bad effects of high profits. They are silent with respect to the pernicious effects of their own gains' (*Wealth of Nations*, Book 1).

The tendency since the beginning of the 1980s has been for governments progressively to dismantle more and more of the institutions which had been built up over the previous century to provide some stability in the wages and employment of the working population. It was recognised that in the short-term such 'liberalisation' of the labour market would lead to rising unemployment, falling wages and growing inequality, and in this respect the liberalisers have been proved correct, but these were supposed to be transitory manifestations of the flexibility which would remove the barriers to investment. New investment would promote the sustained economic growth which would promise real jobs and higher living standards for all. In fact nowhere has the liberal dream come to fruition.

In the United States, labour market flexibility, a euphemism for an extremely repressive benefit regime, has been one factor underlying a fall in unemployment, but at the cost of steadily falling wages and living standards for the majority of the population. In Western Europe there has been a growth of wages and living standards, but unemployment has shown no signs of turning down. In most of the rest of the world, apart from East Asia, liberalisation has been accompanied by both rising unemployment and falling living standards.

The negative consequences of labour market liberalisation led in most countries to sufficient trade union and electoral reaction to induce governments to hold back, allowing the more radical liberalisers to argue that policies of labour market flexibility had not achieved the promised results because they had not been implemented sufficiently rigorously: trade unions retained certain powers and privileges, legislation restricted the employer's right to hire and fire, governments imposed a range of costs on employers and continued to provide 'over-liberal' benefit regimes. However hard the screw was tightened, for the radicals it was never tightened hard enough. As usual, the more extreme exponents of the neo-liberal panacea have been able to proclaim that shock therapy has not performed the miracle cure because it has not been implemented sufficiently rigorously, but in Russia the screw has been tightened so hard that it can be turned no more. Certainly social and political opposition to ultra-radicalism has modified the pace and character of reform sufficiently to prevent the complete implosion of the Russian economy which many of its critics feared would result from the full-blooded implementation of shock therapy, but nevertheless Russia shows what happens when the labour market becomes 'perfectly' flexible.[109] A quarter of the labour force changes jobs every year, unemployment is not an option, wages at the margin have fallen close to zero, with no sign of recovery anywhere in the economy after six years of continuous and continuing decline in output and investment. Russia has tested the flexible labour market hypothesis to destruction, at enormous cost in human suffering.

The Russian case strongly supports the alternative, and currently less fashionable, view that labour market rigidities are not, in general,

---

[109] One can reformulate the question of the role of labour market adjustment in terms of the question of the consistency of macro and micro policy and objectives, an effective structural adjustment programme being one which reconciles the two (Mosley, Harrigan et al., 1995; Toye, 1995). A regressive macroeconomic stabilisation policy generates resistance from those unfavourably affected by its microeconomic implications which is directly expressed through political channels and indirectly through the steps taken to avoid the negative impact of policy (non-payment of taxes, bribery of officials and so on), thereby forcing modifications in macroeconomic policy. The effectiveness of this resistance cannot simply be put down to the inordinate strength of vested interests, for all policies are backed by interests and all interests are vested. Its impact may be for the better or it may be for the worse, but the extent of such resistance is a strong indicator of the extent to which the stabilisation and structural adjustment programme has failed to reconcile macro and micro objectives. The response should not be to attempt to circumvent the political process, as was the temptation in the 1980s and is the temptation in Russia today (with General Lebed regarding Pinochet's Chile, which many see as structural adjustment's biggest failure, as his preferred model), but to bring policy formulation and evaluation out of the air-conditioned conference rooms of international hotels and back into the political system.

a major barrier to structural adjustment. Labour is by no means as mobile as capital, but labour power is never a commodity like any other, it can never have the fluidity of money. Forcing down people's wages and destroying people's jobs does not transform labour power into a flexible resource, it merely demoralises people, deprives them of the resources to take control of their lives and even induces them to cling more tightly to their customary attachments. The result of wage flexibility and employment insecurity is not the creation of a flexible reserve of labour, but of a stagnant pool of the unemployable. There is not, therefore, a choice between the stick and the carrot in inducing labour mobility: those who move to better jobs are those who are drawn by the carrot of new opportunities and a better standard of living, not those who are deracinated and demoralised by low wages and the threat of unemployment. In the imbalance between the mobility and flexibility of capital and the immobility and inflexibility of labour power it is the former not the latter that is the problem. The successful examples of structural adjustment are, therefore, those which have managed to reconcile the two by inducing capital to create the new opportunities which have generated jobs, attracting new entrants to the labour market and drawing people out of other sectors of the economy.

The failure of one set of policies does not automatically define the set of policies which should take its place. Labour market regulation on its own will no more secure the long term stability of wages and employment than has labour market flexibility. But the disastrous consequences of liberalisation should at least dispel the taboo which has until recently prevented serious consideration of appropriate forms of labour market regulation. The liberal critique of protective regulation has some force: to some extent there has to be a trade-off between wages and employment. This is an unavoidable policy dilemma, not one which can be dissolved with the magic wand of flexibility, but it is one which is made immeasurably more acute by economic decline and which can be softened by economic recovery. The key is to develop a policy package which can reconcile stable levels of employment with stable levels of wages by facilitating, encouraging and promoting the redeployment not only of labour, but also of capital. Labour market policies have been constructed on the presumption that if the labour is there, appropriately trained and ready and willing to work, capital will be forthcoming to set the labour in motion. But if that investment is not forthcoming, the policies directed at securing a supply of appropriately trained labour are utterly pointless.[110]

It is interesting in this context to observe the activity of the multinational corporations, presumably the world's most sophisticated investors, in Russia. There is no sign that these corporations are moving into Russia in search of cheap and flexible labour. Apart from Macdonald's, we do not know of a single green-field investment in Russia which has recruited its own labour force *de novo*. International real estate developers and construction companies rarely employ Russian labour, but bring in their entire labour force at huge expense, while other investors buy into existing state and former state enterprises, however much these might have been maligned by the liberal reformers, to take advantage not of the cheapness of deracinated labour but of the experience and skills of an established work collective.[111] This was the comparative advantage of Russia which underlay the hopes of perestroika and the promises of transition and it is, above all, this that labour market flexibility is destroying.

---

[110] This is not a matter of institutional barriers, as those who focus their attention on the currently fashionable topics of corporate governance and financial institutions appear to believe, but of the simple fact that private productive investment in a declining economy with an uncertain future will never be judged to be profitable. Institutions are never the most significant barriers: where there is a will there is a way.

[111] Of course there are multinational investors and 'partners' who are interested in no more than using their investment as a means of securing access to supplies of exportable natural resources or in milking an enterprise of its assets.

Table 2.2: Changes in Employment and Unemployment by Age and Sex, 1992–95. Calculated from Labour Force Survey data (age and sex-specific, total male and female and total participation rates) Trud i Zanyatost' 1996, p. 8. (* totals from administrative statistics)

	Population Increase (million)	Fall in Ec. Active Population (million)	Employment Fall (million)	Unemployment Rise (million)	Ec. Inactive Increase	Activity Rates % Decline
15–19 Men	0.2	-0.4	-0.4	0.0	0.6	23.2
15–19 Women	0.3	-0.3	-0.4	0.1	0.6	24.3
20–24 M	0.3	0.2	-0.1	0.3	0.1	1.8
20–24 W	0.3	0.1	-0.2	0.3	0.2	4.6
25–29 M	-0.2	-0.3	-0.6	0.2	0.1	2.9
25–29 W	-0.4	-0.6	-0.7	0.2	0.2	5.5
30–49 M	1.5	0.7	-0.4	1.0	0.8	3.6
30–49 W	1.8	0.7	0.0	0.7	1.1	4.4
50–54 M	-1.7	-1.7	-1.7	0.0	0.0	6.9
50–54 W	-2.1	-1.9	-1.9	0.0	-0.2	9.8
55–59 M	0.6	0.1	0.0	0.1	0.5	12.0
55–59 W	0.9	-0.2	-0.2	0.0	1.1	23.9
60–72 M	0.2	-0.6	-0.6	0.0	0.8	38.6
60–72 W	0.0	-0.6	-0.5	0.0	0.6	39.4
Sum of above	1.7	-4.8	-7.7	2.8	6.5	
Sum men	0.9	-2.1	-3.8	1.7	3.0	
Sum women	0.8	-2.7	-3.9	1.2	3.5	
Total (15–72)	1.7	-4.9 (-2.8*)	-7.7 (-5.6*)	2.8	6.6 (4.5*)	8.0 (5.1*)
Total men	0.9	-2.6 (0.0*)	-4.2 (-1.7*)	1.7	3.5 (0.9*)	8.2 (1.7*)
Total women	0.8	-2.6 (-2.8*)	-3.8 (-4.0*)	1.2	3.4 (3.6*)	8.8 (8.8*)

Table 2.3: Changes in Employment and Unemployment by Age and Sex, 1992–96. RLMS data

	1992–95 Population Increase (million)	Fall in Ec. Active Population (million)	Employment Fall (million)	Unemployment Rise (million)	Ec. Inactive Increase	Activity Rates % Decline
15–19 Men	0.2	-0.2	0.0	-0.3	0.4	17.4
15–19 Women	0.3	-0.4	-0.4	-0.1	0.7	30.8
20–24 M	0.3	0.3	0.3	0.0	0.0	-2.4
20–24 W	0.3	-0.1	-0.2	0.1	0.4	9.8
25–29 M	-0.2	-0.5	-0.5	0.0	0.3	5.6
25–29 W	-0.4	-0.4	-0.7	0.2	0.0	1.8
30–49 M	1.5	0.5	0.0	0.6	1.0	4.2
30–49 W	1.8	0.6	0.2	0.5	1.2	4.9
50–54 M	-1.7	-1.7	-1.7	0.0	0.0	6.4
50–54 W	-2.1	-1.9	-1.8	-0.1	-0.2	6.8
55–59 M	0.6	0.1	0.0	0.1	0.5	10.5
55–59 W	0.9	0.5	0.3	0.2	0.4	-7.2
60–72 M	0.2	-0.5	-0.6	0.1	0.7	27.9
60–72 W	0.0	0.2	0.1	0.1	-0.2	-15.6
72– M	-0.1	0.0	0.0	0.0	-0.1	25.9
72– W	-0.2	0.0	0.0	0.0	-0.2	13.6
Sum (over 15)	1.4	-3.6	-5.1	1.5	5.0	7.8
Sum men	0.8	-1.9	-2.5	0.6	2.7	7.9
Sum women	0.6	-1.6	-2.6	0.9	2.2	6.6

2 The Restructuring of Employment and the Formation of a Labour Market in Russia

Simon Clarke, Veronika Kabalina, Irina Kozina, Inna Donova and Marina Karelina
Institute for Comparative Labour Relations Research, Moscow, Samara, Kemerovo

HOW MUCH FLEXIBILITY? STRUCTURAL ADJUSTMENT AND THE LABOUR MARKET IN RUSSIA

The dominant model applied to the 'transition economies' has been that developed by liberal economists on the basis of the experience of the structural adjustment of the market economies to the oil shock of 1974 and the subsequent explosion of domestic and international public debt. Those economies which were best able to recover from the structural shock imposed by the oil price hike were those which pursued rigorous policies of financial stabilisation and which liberalised domestic and international markets to allow competitive pressures to erode those sectors which could not compete and to stimulate the growth of those which could take advantage of new global opportunities. The lesson drawn from this experience by liberal economists was that the relation between policy and outcome was a simple causal one: the recovery was the result of the adoption of the package of stabilisation and liberalisation policies – there was no serious consideration of the possibility that the relationship might be reciprocal or even inverse: that those countries which were structurally and institutionally well-placed to adapt were those which were able to enter a virtuous circle of growth which allowed them to maintain stability and reconcile liberalisation with rising incomes. According to the liberal diagnosis, those countries which sought to protect employment by means of government intervention merely intensified the problems of structural maladjustment, building up a burden of domestic and international debt, the servicing of which undermined financial stability and impeded the development of new economic activity. The remedy was apparently very simple: embrace the structural adjustment package of stabilisation and liberalisation and, although the short-run economic and social costs might be high, the forces of enterprise would be freed to achieve a rapid recovery. The limited success of structural adjustment programmes through the 1980s only reinforced the radicalism of the message. Those which failed had been insufficiently committed to reform. There were no half measures: the more radical the shock, the more dramatic would be the therapy.

One major blot on the liberal copybook was that the era of structural adjustment was also an era of rising unemployment on a global scale with long-term unemployment even rising in some of those core economies, particularly of Western Europe, which had otherwise responded to the cure. The orthodox interpretation of this phenomenon was that persistently high unemployment was the result of various kinds of labour market rigidities, including strong trade unions, state regulation of wages and excessively liberal benefit regimes, which prevented wages from falling sufficiently low to make it profitable for investors to absorb the labour surplus. Labour market rigidities became a prime scapegoat for the failure of structural adjustment, and 'liberalisation' of labour market institutions, accompanied by active labour market policies, therefore came to be seen as a central component of any structural adjustment package.

The focus of structural adjustment in the transition economies was expected to be the decline of the overblown state sector of the economy and the rise of a new private sector exploiting new opportunities opened up by liberalisation. The short-run costs, particularly in terms of rising unemployment, were expected to be high because of the extent of the distortions to which the economies of the Soviet system had been subjected, but the recovery was expected to be equally dramatic, provided that the remedies were strictly adhered to, for the same reason: the technological gap, the under-development of the service sector, unexploited opportunities for export, were all indicators of opportunity as much as signs of backwardness.

In practice, if structural adjustment programmes have had mixed results in the transition economies, with no dramatic success stories to tell, the outcome in Russia has been nothing short of disastrous. Between 1990 and 1996 the Russian economy was in continuous decline to experience the deepest recession experienced by any economy in peacetime in world history. GDP had fallen by almost a half, industrial production by over a half and investment by over eighty per cent. Moreover, although in 1995 the exchange rate had been stabilised and the battle against inflation was declared to have been won, the decline in the real economy accelerated through 1996, with even the most optimistic of commentators not daring to predict even stabilisation before 1998. The decline not only hit the 'overdeveloped' branches of the national economy: the hardest hit branch of all was light industry, with output down by over 80%, and even the extractive industries, well-placed to orient themselves to world markets, saw a fall in output of around a third. By 1995 the small business sector was also in decline, with the number of enterprises and employment in retail trade falling by ten per cent. Cuts in state expenditure, including the virtual elimination of subsidies to industry, by no means matched the decline in state revenues.

Of course, there is a substantial gap between models and the real world. While the critics of liberal reform see this disaster as the predictable result of an inappropriate policy package, the proponents of the model see it as the equally predictable result of an inconstant and inconsistent commitment to reform. So, is this disaster a result of the reform strategy? Or is it the necessary price of a radical transformation which is just over the horizon? Or is it the result of the failure to reform sufficiently radically. Is the remedy to reverse policy, is it to hold course, or is it to take still more radical steps? These are the issues which have divided analysts and policy makers in Russia and in the international community. The labour market has turned out to provide a principal focus of this debate.

There is no doubt that, for all the twists and turns, the principal elements of a macroeconomic stabilisation policy and of market liberalisation have remained in place throughout the period of radical reform in Russia. The issue, therefore, is why the real economy has not responded positively to market freedom and price flexibility, plunging into generalised recession rather than experiencing a structural adjustment. Of course, a part of the reason is the extent of the structural adjustment required by the multiple shocks to which the Russian economy has been subjected. But the fact remains that very little structural adjustment has taken place, at least in the anticipated direction. According to the liberal model, this could only be a result of barriers to the perfect operation of markets. Following the example of the market economies, the scapegoat in Russia was found in the rigidities of the labour market. Attention soon came to be focused on the fact that, despite the substantial fall in industrial production, Russia had experienced no bankruptcies, there had been only a small fall in industrial employment and very little increase in unemployment. This was explained by the World Bank's Economic Development Institute (EDI) team, led by Simon Commander, as a result of labour hoarding by state and former state enterprises which were sustained by continuing state subsidies. The implication was that reform had been insufficiently far reaching, privatisation had not broken 'insider' control, and the former state sector had not been hit hard enough. What was needed was the imposition of 'hard budget constraints' on industrial enterprises through the withdrawal of state subsidies and the introduction of effective bankruptcy procedures, backed up by active labour market policies, measures to increase the geographical mobility of labour, and an adequate social safety net to make the package socially and politically acceptable.[1]

Although bankruptcy remained rare, the reduction of subsidies and tight credit policies led to a deepening industrial crisis, with industrial employment beginning to fall sharply and unemployment beginning to rise, although the scale of the changes remained a matter of dispute and the official statistics for employment and unemployment continued to show only a relatively small decline in total employment and a small rise in unemployment. At the same time, wages and living standards continued to fall and levels of inequality rapidly increased, with large increases in regional and sectoral wage dispersions.

This phenomenon of growing wage flexibility but relatively little flexibility in numbers was open to two very different interpretations.

---

[1]   One of the barriers to enterprise closure was identified as the importance of the enterprise in the provision of health, housing, social and welfare facilities to the local community and in its contribution to local budgets. The divestiture of social assets and the reform of local government finance therefore played a central role in the liberal programme. The result was the collapse of large parts of the social infrastructure as facilities were transferred to municipal authorities which had neither the means nor the staff nor the competence to administer them.

On the one hand, the EDI team focused on numerical inflexibility and persisted with the argument that the problem remained labour market rigidity sustained by labour hoarding by worker-controlled state enterprises. Workers had chosen to accept wage flexibility as the price of continued employment security, the package sustained by the continuing soft budget constraint. On the other hand, Richard Layard and his colleagues focused on the 'perfect' flexibility of wages, which allowed employees to choose between retaining a job at low or no pay and moving to a new job at higher wages. Wage flexibility was possible because of the attachment of Russian employees to the workplace and the absence of an effective floor to wages provided either by the minimum wage or the level of unemployment benefit. The low rate of unemployment was an indicator of the perfect flexibility of the labour market, not of its rigidity, this flexibility also being manifested by the continuing high labour turnover, at levels typical of the United States rather than Western Europe. The Layard view was that Russia has the ultimately flexible and dynamic labour market, it is the test case of labour market flexibility and it has passed the test with flying colours in allowing substantial structural adjustment to take place with very large movements of labour but without any significant rise in levels of unemployment, and with virtually none of the long-term unemployment which hangs over the other transition economies and has proved so debilitating in Western Europe. Far from Russia learning from the West, it is now the West which can learn from Russia: 'The main news in Russia is good news',[2] and the news is that flexible labour markets work.

While many would support Layard's view that the Russian labour market has proved remarkably flexible, and even parts of the World Bank appear to have come round to the view that the labour market is not a significant barrier to transition,[3] few observers share Layard's optimism about the growth of employment in the new private sector or

---

[2]   Richard Layard, *Financial Times*, 20 September 1995, cited in Standing, 1996a, p. 1.

[3]   The current World Bank position is somewhat schizophrenic. The 1995 World Development Report, *Workers in an Integrating World*, proclaimed labour market flexibility as a key to global prosperity. However, the 1996 World Development Report, *From Plan to Market*, barely discusses labour market issues, except to note that 'at the start of transition many [the many are not named - 'we' might be more appropriate - S.C.] doubted the ability of labor in the CEE and the NIS to adjust rapidly to the enormous structural and macroeconomic changes. But labor *has* responded...' (World Bank, 1996, p. 73, emphasis in original). The institutional barriers in the 1996 report are identified as being in capital markets, not in the labour market.

the extent of small and medium enterprise growth, which appears at best to have levelled off while production and investment in the state and former state sector continue to fall. Although open unemployment is only slowly creeping up, production stoppages, short-time working and administrative leave, usually without pay, are increasing, and delays in the payment of wages, sometimes of several months, have become the rule rather than the exception. Although there is a very high level of labour mobility, most of this involves people shuffling between existing jobs within the state and former state sector, while the bulk of new jobs are casual, low-paid, unregistered and insecure. On this basis Guy Standing and his ILO team have argued that Russia suffers from too much labour market flexibility. Flexible wages (a euphemism for extraordinarily low wages) sustain labour hoarding by state and former state enterprises, which in total amounts to very substantial disguised unemployment, while removing any incentive to reorganise or invest in production. Far from finding the key to structural adjustment without mass unemployment, as Layard argues, Standing believes that Russia has experienced little structural adjustment but is experiencing mass unemployment, disguised only by the fact that the unemployed remain attached to enterprises which pay them low or no wages.

We therefore have three fundamentally different interpretations of the Russian situation, with very different policy implications and very different significance as examples for other countries undergoing radical structural adjustment. Within the liberal camp there are two sharply contrasting interpretations which declare Russia to be the ultimate negative or positive example. On the one hand, it is argued that Russia is plumbing the depths of recession as a result of labour market rigidities which impede structural adjustment. On the other hand, it is argued that Russia has developed a perfectly flexible labour market which is the key to structural adjustment without mass unemployment. The third, sceptical position, combines the latter view that Russia has an extremely flexible labour market with the former view that Russia has undergone little structural adjustment, while contesting the position common to both that Russia has avoided mass unemployment.

How is it possible for three such starkly contrasting interpretations of the same phenomenon to coexist? Part of the problem of resolving the disagreement is the limited scope and the inadequacies of the available statistical and survey data, although none of the parties has conducted a systematic review of the data that is available, each largely confining itself to the analysis of data from its own chosen source. In his paper in this collection Simon Clarke has carried out a review of the existing analytical literature, both Western and Russian, and the limited statistical and survey data which is available in order to arrive at a preliminary assessment of the issues and definition of research priorities. Merely getting hold of the data is not such an easy task: the state statistical agency does not go out of its way to make its data accessible or comprehensible, while the distribution of analytical reports by academics and government departments leaves equally much to be desired.[4]

A review of the existing research material casts considerable doubt on both variants of the liberal interpretation of the Russian experience. In particular, although the fall in employment lagged behind the fall in output, it has more or less shadowed that fall since 1993, while the published employment statistics almost certainly considerably under-estimate the fall in employment in the state sector. It is very far from being the case that state and former state enterprises face soft budget constraints or that they enjoy significant subsidies from the local or federal budgets. There is no evidence that management decisions are significantly constrained by worker preferences, and all the evidence indicates that if it were then the most active workers would favour employment reductions in order to maintain or raise their wages. There is no substantial evidence that these enterprises are hoarding significant reserves of surplus labour, although there is a low rate of labour and capacity utilisation because of the extreme unevenness of production. High rates of labour turnover persist, so that numbers are determined by hiring decisions rather than by firing decisions. In short, enterprise managements are severely constrained by the financial

---

[4]   Most academic reports are printed in editions of one hundred or fewer copies, with summary versions sometimes being printed in newspapers or later in more or less accessible academic journals. Neither Russian researchers nor multilateral agencies normally make their data freely available. Government analytical reports are rarely published for wider circulation. Federal statistics are no more accessible: the Goskomstat monthly statistical report *Statisticheskoe obozrenie* is published in a Russian edition of 400. According to the publication information at the back, Goskomstat's 'Basic Indicators of Labour Statistics' for 1995 was published in an edition of 150. It is true that much of this data was also published in the collection 'Labour and Employment 1995' in a larger edition — 260 copies were printed in February 1996 (although, according to the publishing information, the material had been ready in July 1995). Data is also published only with considerable delay: the latter two reports are based primarily on the October 1994 labour force survey.

situation but appear to be little constrained by worker preferences in making their wage and employment decisions. Employment has been substantially reduced in state and former state enterprises and there is ample cheap labour available for absorption by the new private sector.

On the other hand, while wages have halved and inequality doubled, there are no signs of the 'Layard boom' in private sector employment, at least outside the centre of a few large cities. While political instability and the absence of a framework of strong legal and financial institutions are certainly barriers to recovery, all the evidence would support a 'Keynesian' interpretation of the Russian recession and of the failure of recovery to occur. Instability and criminality are as much consequences of the absence of legitimate investment opportunities as they are causes. The absence of opportunities in the service and light industrial sectors, which should be the focus of domestic recovery, is to be explained primarily by the simple fact of the dramatic and continuing decline in the incomes of the mass of the population, much the largest employment growth having been in subsistence production.

The policy implication is that the barriers to recovery in Russia are not institutional but macroeconomic. In particular, rapid turnover indicates that the labour market does not present any significant barriers to recovery, but that labour market flexibility can only play a positive role in a favourable macroeconomic environment. This means that labour market policies can only be formulated within the wider framework of a comprehensive macroeconomic recovery programme which has to include targeted industrial and employment policies. In this context the enforced transition from disguised to open unemployment proposed by Guy Standing would only add another twist to the cycle of decline.

A review of existing survey and statistical data can indicate the parameters of the problem, but it cannot take us very far in understanding how the Russian labour market actually works, and so cannot provide much help in the design of labour market and employment policies appropriate in the Russian context. The fundamental problem is that what is in question is not so much the scale of the changes taking place as the character of the underlying processes. It is clear that there is a very high rate of labour mobility in Russia, but very little is known about the character of this mobility. We need to understand the *processes* of employment restructuring, on the side of both employers and employees,[5] if we are to understand the character and role of the labour market in Russia. In particular, we have to ask what is the significance of high labour mobility? How extensive is labour hoarding, and what is its significance? How can the collapse of production be reconciled with a continued high rate of hiring? What is the role of secondary employment? These were the questions which our own research project was designed to address using qualitative methods of case study research.

THEORETICAL AND METHODOLOGICAL FOUNDATIONS OF THE RESEARCH

The use of the case study method was dictated partly by the object of research, the processes of employment restructuring, which cannot be identified using the available statistical and survey data, but also by the theoretical framework of the research, which takes a sociological rather than a narrowly economic view of the labour market, based on a conception of labour power as a distinctive kind of commodity.

Most of the research on employment restructuring and the development of a labour market in Russia has been conducted by economists of a more or less liberal inclination whose view of the world is based on the interaction of individual actors who are differentiated from one another socially only by the commodities which they own and bring to market and whose behaviour is determined by their rational responses to economic stimuli. Social institutions are evaluated only to the extent that they promote or impede the realisation of the supposed aims of these rational economic actors although, since the analyst has no knowledge of what these aims are, the evaluation is in fact based on a theoretical model of how free competitive markets ought to work.

Existing research, based primarily on the analysis of statistical data prepared by the state statistical service and the Federal Employment Service, has produced few conclusive results. This is in part because

---

[5]   The EDI survey of labour market restructuring in transition concluded that 'further research will be required to understand more satisfactorily the options facing state and privatized firms and their subsequent choices over employment and wages' (Commander and Coricelli, eds, 1995, p. xxi), but it takes two to tango: we also have to understand the options facing employees in their choices.

of the quality of the data but, in our view, it is primarily because the analysis does not take account of the heterogeneity of enterprises and of the labour force which derives from the fact that enterprises and labour markets are social institutions. This means that the opportunities confronting economic actors are structured and constrained by the social relations within which they are inserted. For example, the restructuring of production and employment within an enterprise is not simply a matter of redeploying physical resources, it is a matter of restructuring a social organisation which comprises many individuals, each with their own aims and ambitions, capacities and constraints, organised in various institutional sub-systems which together make up the organisation as a whole, which in turn interacts with other social institutions. This social framework is not in itself a barrier or an opportunity to economic actors, it is the framework within which alone they are constituted as actors, within which they formulate their intentions and within which they are able to act. Employment restructuring is therefore a process of transformation of a complex social organisation in response to diverse internal and external pressures and constraints.

Similarly the labour market is quite different from other commodity markets in that the labourer is never detached from the commodity which he or she sells. If I sell coals to Newcastle I do not need to know where Newcastle is, but if I take a job in Newcastle I have to go there, live there, and attend my place of work every day. The workplace is a social environment in which I carry out my work in social interaction with others. But the labour market is also a social environment: I find out about work through others, I establish some kind of interaction with a representative of the employer, the employer finds out about me through others. The employer wants to know not only about my formal qualifications and technical capabilities, but also about what I can actually do and how I will fit into the social environment of the workplace. It should not be surprising, therefore, to find that most people find jobs through various kinds of social network, and that one's possibilities of labour mobility depend to a considerable degree on the density and extent of the social networks in which one is inserted. Thus employment restructuring and the formation of a labour market is a social process which takes place through various institutional forms, these forms themselves not being static but being transformed and developed through the activity of social actors.

The focus of our research, therefore, was not so much the scale as the *processes* of employment restructuring, based on qualitative methods of sociological case study research, the purpose of the research being to discover the interaction of subjective and objective factors and the identification of the institutional forms within which restructuring takes place. In particular, since at least 90% of employment restructuring occurs through job-to-job transitions, we were concerned to identify the channels through which mobility takes place within and between enterprises.

Our research is not designed to be comprehensive. In particular, it focuses primarily on large state and former state industrial enterprises, which still employ around 85% of the industrial labour force, and a small number of the few new private enterprises oriented to the productive sphere. With some exceptions it does not cover agriculture, construction, public administration or the service sector which, broadly defined, employ three-quarters of the economically active population. Nevertheless, this emphasis is justified because it is the industrial sector which is expected to bear the brunt of restructuring and it is large industrial enterprises which are considered by some to present the main barrier to such restructuring.

As the starting point of our research we distinguished between three different labour markets, which we anticipated would operate in rather different ways and within different institutional frameworks.

The 'internal' labour market operates within large industrial enterprises and is based on the redeployment of the labour force within the enterprise. In the Soviet period internal transfers were relatively rare, but redeployment has always been a primary way of avoiding redundancy and our preliminary research indicated that redeployment is systematically used today both to avoid redundancy and to restructure the labour force.

The 'informal' labour market is the principal channel for job-to-job transitions between enterprises and the main segment of the labour market through which people seek and acquire secondary employment. It is the segment of the labour market in which personal connections play a primary role in job changes. This informal labour market is institutionalised through social networks and may involve some degree of employer sponsorship through traditional connections between enterprises.

The 'external' labour market is the principal channel for job transitions through unemployment, with people individually seeking work 'from the street', through advertisements or through public and private employment services. In the course of our research we came to distinguish more sharply independent job search from job search through employment agencies.

Our hypothesis was that these different institutional channels of mobility defined different segments of the labour market and involved different processes and therefore needed to be analysed separately from one another.

The second fundamental distinction on which our research was based is that between three types of enterprise: 'successful' and 'unsuccessful' state and former state enterprises and new private enterprises. Within the former categories we do not distinguish between enterprises which are still state-owned and those which are privatised since all the research evidence, including our own, indicates that at this stage of transition this is not a fundamental distinction. Some analysts believe that there is a fundamental distinction between enterprises which are controlled by insiders and those which have come under the control of outsiders. Although there are differences (Kabalina, 1996), and our own research indicates that these differences are beginning to harden, at the present stage of Russian development it is too early to assess their significance. Two of our case-study enterprises came under outsider control during the course of this research, with the new management proposing much more radical employment reductions, but the present stage of fieldwork ended before the new management had attempted to put these reductions into effect.

The distinction between state and new private enterprises should not require any justification. A number of researchers, including ourselves, have independently come to the conclusion that there is also a qualitative distinction between 'successful' and 'unsuccessful' state and former state enterprises, and that there is a tendency towards the polarisation of enterprises into these two types (Kapelyushnikov and Auktsionek, 1995b and Tsentr issledovannii rynka truda, 1995a). We consider this issue more fully below.

A final aspect of the research was to contribute to the analysis of the differentiation and stratification of the Russian labour force. It is clear that there are substantial differences in labour market behaviour between different categories of employee, particularly those defined by skill, occupational, age and gender differences, although it is not easy to disentangle the independent influence of these different variables. While labour turnover in Russia is relatively high, it is clear that some workers are highly mobile, while others remain committed to the Soviet ideal of a job for life. A number of researchers have applied and developed the distinction between 'core' and 'peripheral' workers in the Russian context, and one of our objectives has been to deepen this analysis by relating the position of different groups of employees within the labour process to differences in their behaviour in the labour market (Kozina and Borisov, 1996; Tsentr issledovannii rynka truda, 1995a). This part of our analysis is still at a relatively early stage.

The focus of our research was therefore to identify the processes of employment restructuring and redeployment within and between large industrial enterprises and new businesses by identifying the operation of the 'internal' and 'informal' and 'external' labour markets and the interaction between these three labour markets.

RESEARCH METHODOLOGY

The research methodology employed in our research has been centred on the use of a range of qualitative methods of intensive case study research, supplemented by the collection of statistical and local labour market data. The case studies were conducted in twelve enterprises in two regions of Russia, Kemerovo (Kuzbass) and Samara (six enterprises are located in Samara, three in Kemerovo city, one is based in Kiselevsk and two are in the town of Osinniki, the latter towns both being in the south of the Kemerovo region). The focus of research was the processes of employment restructuring and labour market formation since 1985, allowing us to compare the present situation with that under the old system. The research was designed as a pilot project for a larger project which began in October 1996, funded by the British Economic and Social Research Council and covering four regions. The method of case-study research was adopted in order to focus on the *processes* of employment restructuring and the formation of a labour market which are not revealed by the analysis of statistical data, although one aspect of the research was an investigation of the collection and reporting of statistical data from enterprises, which forms the basis of state statistical reporting.

The research was conducted between July 1995 and September 1996 by groups of sociologists from the Kemerovo, Samara and Moscow branches of the Institute for Comparative Labour Relations Research (ISITO), directed respectively by Petr Bizyukov, Dr Irina Kozina and Dr Veronika Kabalina, and the project was directed by Professor Simon Clarke (Centre for Comparative Labour Studies, University of Warwick and ISITO). The research was funded by the Overseas Development Administration of the British Foreign and Commonwealth Office. The fieldwork was carried out by the Samara and Kemerovo groups, with the Moscow group participating in the collection of statistical and other research materials and in the analysis and writing up of the data.

This research is part of a wider programme of research on enterprise restructuring which has been under way since 1991 in Kemerovo, Samara, Moscow and Komi.[6] In this particular project we have been able to draw on the results and experience of our previous research and knowledge of a wide range of industrial enterprises, and members of all four groups have participated in the discussion and elaboration of research reports. The research teams have met regularly to discuss the progress and preliminary findings of the research, and a number of substantive papers were presented to a residential seminar in May. Draft enterprise reports were discussed with the management of each enterprise and with representatives of the local employment services between March and May 1996, and a series of analytical reports were prepared collectively in Britain during June 1996 on the basis of earlier drafts and detailed reports on each case-study enterprise, including field notes and interview transcripts. Provisional results were presented to a conference in Moscow in July 1996 which was sponsored by the Ford Foundation and also included presentations by the other leading Russian research groups in this field and was attended by representatives of the Kuzbass and Samara employment services and by key policy makers from a number of Federal

---

6   Some of the results of this research have been published in a series of volumes edited by Simon Clarke and published by Edward Elgar: *Management and Industry in Russia* (1995); *Conflict and Change in the Russian Industrial Enterprise* (1996a); *Labour Relations in Transition* (1996b); *The Russian Enterprise in Transition* (1996c). Details of this programme and many of the research materials on which this report is based are available on our website: www.warwick.ac.uk/fac/soc/complabstuds/russia/russint.htm.

Ministries. The reports were revised and then translated and edited by Simon Clarke for presentation to a second conference held at the University of Warwick in September 1996 attended by the leading Western researchers currently working in this field.

It is important to stress that the research is systematic, but it is not intended to provide an exhaustive account of employment restructuring and the formation of a labour market. The methodology was therefore determined by the relatively limited aims of the research.

The enterprise was chosen as the unit for case-study research because the processes of employment restructuring take place primarily within and between enterprises, with relatively few job changes taking place with an intervening period of unemployment. The enterprise is therefore the primary context of labour market behaviour, and the principal actors are the enterprise administration and employees. The case-study research was complemented by a study of the local labour market as a whole and the role of the employment service in the cities which were the principal focus of the research.

Within each enterprise research focused on two levels. On the one hand, the level of the administration of the enterprise as a whole. At this level statistical data on the structure of employment and labour turnover was collected and interviews were conducted with management representatives in order to determine the employment strategy and policies of senior enterprise management. However, our previous research had already indicated that the employment strategy of higher enterprise management is often very remote from the actual practice of employment restructuring and hiring and firing, which is determined primarily at shop level. The case-study research therefore focused particularly on interviews with and observation of actors at shop level. This research was supplemented with work-history interviews with a sample of workers drawn from the shops which were the object of the case studies.

As indicated below, the enterprises chosen for case study were not selected as a representative sample of local enterprises, nor was the sample of workers interviewed randomly drawn. It is important to stress that the purpose of the research at this pilot stage is typological rather than quantitative. Our aim was to identify the different types of processes of employment restructuring and labour mobility to be found in the emerging Russian labour market, rather than to determine the scale of restructuring or rates of labour mobility, either overall or within particular categories, which might be the object of further research using more conventional survey methods. Nor is our research exhaustive. We have focused on large and medium industrial enterprises in the state and former state sector, which are still the dominant employers, and, with one exception, on new private enterprises in the productive sphere. We have not studied former state municipal and service or small enterprises, nor (with the one exception) have we studied new private enterprises in the service sector (mainly commerce and finance) in which they are most active, except to the extent that employees of our case-study enterprises have either work experience or secondary employment in these spheres.

Having said this, in order to set our case-study research in a wider labour market context we have also carried out a review of the local labour market in the cities in which the bulk of the enterprises researched are located (Kemerovo, Kiselevsk and Osinniki in the Kemerovo region and Samara city) on the basis of a review of available statistical data and free interviews with staff of the employment service and city administration in these two regions. In Samara we also had the opportunity of appending a set of questions on secondary employment to a representative sample survey of the population of the city.

Finally, we have conducted a review of the existing statistical material and research literature on employment restructuring and the formation of a labour market in Russia.

The primary data on the basis of which this report has been written therefore comprises:

1. Statistical data, including that provided by state statistical agencies and enterprise management as well as internal statistical records maintained at enterprise and shop levels.
2. Personnel data maintained within enterprises in the form of record cards on employees, the labour books of individual employees, registers of hirings and firings, disciplinary records, attendance and work-time records and pay records. We are very grateful to the staff of the case-study enterprises for providing us with free access to such records.
3. Free interviews with experts, including senior and middle management in the enterprises, staff of personnel and economic-planning departments at shop and enterprise level and staff of the local employment service and private labour exchanges.

4. Other documentary materials, including enterprise reports, policy documents and orders.
5. Semi-structured work-history interviews with a total of 260 employees drawn from the twelve case-study enterprises.
6. Representative survey of the population of the city of Samara focusing on secondary employment (800 people).

The two regions selected as the focus of research were selected not as representative of Russia as a whole, but as typical of heavily industrialised regions in which there has already been extensive employment restructuring as a result of structural economic changes, but in which there is still a relatively low level of registered unemployment. This is in keeping with the focus of our research, which is processes of employment restructuring in labour market situations in which there is no mass unemployment. Samara was one of the regions most heavily dominated by military needs in Russia, which has seen dramatic changes as a result of the cuts in military orders, but which is generally viewed as one of the regions most likely to succeed. Kemerovo, in Western Siberia, is part of the industrial periphery, dominated by coal-mining, steel and chemicals, all three of which have seen a substantial decline in production and face massive reductions in employment, with little prospect of ever competing in a market economy. The two regions are of similar size, each with a population of a little over three million, Samara city having a population over about one and a quarter million and Kemerovo of half a million. The results of our research cannot be generalised to those towns, cities and regions in which there is already large scale unemployment. There is extensive research being undertaken by others in such crisis cities and regions as Vladimir, Ivanovo or Dagestan, which can be compared with our research results. We plan in the near future to look at the situation in smaller towns which have very high levels of unemployment within regions of low unemployment.

The enterprises selected for case study were selected as typical examples of three broad categories of enterprise, which we call 'successful', 'unsuccessful' and 'new', two of each type being chosen in each region (quality of access to the enterprise and availability of data was also a consideration in the selection of the objects of case-study research). This classification was based on the hypothesis that the process of employment restructuring and labour mobility would be different in these three types of enterprise.

The distinction between 'successful' and 'unsuccessful' enterprises is not one that is easy to make using quantitative indicators because, for various reasons, such figures as reported profits, production, turnover, wage levels or employment are not necessarily correlated with one another and do not necessarily reflect the relative prosperity of an enterprise as commonly understood. Moreover, in a very unstable economic and financial environment, the fate of an enterprise can be fundamentally transformed from one day to the next by a turn in the market or by a change in the political situation. The distinction is therefore not a hard and fast or a stable distinction, and some of our case-study enterprises have experienced phases of success and failure in the period under review. Nevertheless, the distinction has allowed us to make some comparative analysis of the differences between these two types of enterprises, within the framework of features that appear to be common to all medium and large enterprises.

'New' enterprises are those which have been formed since 1990. Access to such enterprises for purposes of research is notoriously difficult, not least because many of their practices are in more or less flagrant violation of the law. Our task was made the more difficult because we wanted to research private industrial enterprises with more than a handful of employees. In the end we did select one enterprise in the financial services sector in Kemerovo, primarily because there are virtually no private industrial enterprises in Kemerovo, but also because we were offered exceptional access to this enterprise. The other new enterprise selected for study in Kemerovo region was not entirely new, because it had emerged on the basis of a coal mine which had been one of the first enterprises in Russia to privatise, but is now closed.

The size and representativeness of our sample of enterprises is obviously not sufficient for us to generalise from any quantitative analysis of differences between the enterprises, so our conclusions regarding the characteristic differences are based on a qualitative evaluation of the processes within our case-study enterprises. While the conclusions may be regarded as plausible, and consistent with other data and the findings of other researchers, we would not be confident in generalising those conclusions without further research. Before summarising the results of the research, however, a little more needs to be said about the analytical basis of the distinction between successful and unsuccessful enterprises.

SUCCESSFUL AND UNSUCCESSFUL STATE ENTERPRISES

The distinction between successful and unsuccessful enterprises is not a hard and fast one, but it is nevertheless fundamental to our research. It therefore merits further consideration before we look more closely at our research results.

In a market economy, competition in principle establishes a uniform price for a particular commodity and an equalisation of the rate of profit between different employments of capital against which the success and failure of each capitalist can be judged. The tendency is, therefore, for the relative advantages and disadvantages of particular producers to be evened out, the marginal differences in profitability then being attributed to the skill, foresight and luck of management. The market thus provides *ex ante* incentives for good management and *ex post* penalties for poor management. But this analysis of the beneficent role of the market and the decisive role of management qualities depends on enterprises competing on more or less level ground. This has by no means been the case in the transition economies, and above all in Russia, where investment decisions were in the past made on strategic and political as much as on economic grounds, leaving enterprises with inappropriate locations, extended supply chains, excessive autarchy, more or less substantial social overhead costs and so on. Moreover, the investment process in centrally planned economies was extremely 'lumpy': a giant plant would be constructed and then might have little investment for twenty, thirty or more years before undergoing a major reconstruction. Even then, the tendency to over-investment inherent in the Soviet system of planning meant that much old plant and equipment would not be retired. Finally, there were substantial differences in wages and social provision between branches of production depending on whether or not they belonged to priority sectors. There was no tendency for these differences to be evened out by competition: differences in conditions were compensated by subsidies and administered prices, while managers were assessed against their plan targets.

The collapse of the Soviet system and the transition to the market imposed massive structural shocks which superimposed yet another extraneous determinant of the relative prosperity of different enterprises by leading to the uneven disruption of supplies and markets expressed in dramatic changes in relative prices and in the absolute and relative demand for particular products. The form of privatisation adopted in Russia, which effectively transferred assets to the enterprise free of charge, further exaggerated the inequalities between competing enterprises as those with modern plant and equipment and large stocks of parts and raw materials carried more or less the same capital charges as those with antiquated equipment and no stocks. All of these differences dwarfed the undoubted relative advantages enjoyed by those with monopoly powers and good political connections on which most commentators have focused their attention.

In such circumstances it hardly needs to be stressed that the primary determinant of relative success and failure is not so much the strategy pursued by management as the objective situation in which the enterprise finds itself as a result of its historical legacy. Of course, management makes a difference and the kinds of managerial qualities required in the transition economy are very different from those which had been demanded by the administrative-command system. However, the qualities required are also very different from those appropriate in a market economy. The extreme price and exchange rate instability of the transition period, the withdrawal of virtually all investment subsidies to industry and the very limited development of financial institutions and capital markets denied enterprises the access to investment resources which are the means by which the market economy enables those with an unfavourable legacy to take advantage of favourable future prospects. The name of the transition game is survival in unstable conditions with existing resources, to retain as much of the enterprise's material, human and social infrastructure intact as possible so as to provide a diversified basis for weathering the storm of transition and on which to build in future, and the historical legacy and transitional fortunes of the enterprise are far more powerful determinants of the ability of the enterprise to survive than are the skills of its management.[7] This is by no means to argue that management is irrelevant, but only that the transitional economy severely constrains management's ability to determine the fate of an enterprise. An enterprise which is in a more favourable situation has much more freedom

---

[7]   The fate of the 'pioneers of privatisation', enterprises with an innovative market-oriented management which were quick to exploit the opportunities opened up by the disintegration of the old system, clearly demonstrates this point as such enterprises were forced back into a more conservative orientation as their historical legacy caught up with them (Clarke, Fairbrother et al., 1994; Clarke, 1996c).

in the strategies and policies it pursues, which means that management can certainly make decisions which undermine the position of the enterprise: an enterprise which fails to adapt to the increasing quality demands of a market economy, which fails to seek new markets or develop new products, may slide into failure. An enterprise which took advantage of a privileged position to borrow heavily from banks at negative real rates of interest during 1992 and 1993 in order to maintain wages and avoid redundancies might find itself in growing financial difficulties as real interest rates rose to astronomical heights from 1993, perhaps sliding towards failure until taken over by its creditor bank. On the other hand, an enterprise which is unsuccessful, often through no fault of its own, has very little freedom of manoeuvre, however good its management. With limited access to credit and working capital it has difficulty in securing supplies, augmenting or replacing equipment, developing new marketing and financial services and even paying its wages. It therefore finds itself caught in a vicious circle of decline, out of which it can only break if external factors take a turn for the better.

The priority of survival is often expressed by managers in terms of their determination to 'preserve the labour collective'. This is often interpreted by Western observers as expressing a desire to maintain employment out of some paternalistic concern for the fate of the labour force. However, the Soviet concept of the labour collective is not an empirical but a transcendental concept: it does not refer to the actual individuals who work in the enterprise, but to the Soviet conception of the enterprise not as an entry in a balance sheet or a stock of means of production but as a 'collective labourer'. 'Preserving the labour collective' in this context means preserving the productive capacity of the enterprise, which includes its ability to reproduce itself as a productive organism. This is quite consistent with what is sometimes referred to as the 'qualitative cleansing' of the labour collective: the dismissal of pensioners, drunkards and absentees and their replacement by younger, better disciplined and more highly-skilled employees. It is also quite consistent with reduction in the size of the labour force by removing unproductive employees, particularly the army of unskilled ancillary workers, in which case the phrase 'preserving the skeleton of the labour collective' might be used by management to describe its strategy.

The emphasis on the labour collective as the basis of the enterprise is in part an ideological legacy of the Soviet conception of labour as the agent of production and the enterprise as the institution responsible for the reproduction of the labour force. It is also a legacy of the reality of the Soviet experience of labour scarcity, in which the priority branches of production were able to recruit and retain a skilled and disciplined labour force by offering higher wages and better social and welfare facilities, while low priority enterprises had to make do with a low-skilled undisciplined labour force recruited 'from the street'. However, this is also an enduring reality to the extent that the quality of the labour force is an important mediating factor in the determination of the fate of an enterprise. This is particularly the case in the Russian context in two respects. First, the traditional Soviet system of production and production management relied heavily on the skills and commitment of the core of the labour force, the *kadrovyi* workers. On the one hand, the uneven quality and quantity of supplies, the inconsistency of operation of ageing machinery and equipment and now fluctuating demand for the product and growing quality demands, meant that the core shop-floor production and maintenance workers have to show considerable initiative to keep things running at all. On the other hand, production management was delegated to the shop floor to a much greater extent than has been seen in developed capitalist countries since the 1930s. Second, the transition to the market economy requires marketing and financial personnel with scarce new skills. A prosperous enterprise has the resources to recruit new specialists who have an opportunity to display their skills and it is able to retain and recruit the skilled and diligent shop-floor workers and line managers who constitute what is often referred to as the 'skeleton of the labour collective'. This makes it possible for the management of the enterprise to respond to the challenge of the market by developing new methods of production and new product lines, improving quality and so on, even in conditions in which there is very limited scope for new investment. An unsuccessful enterprise is not able to offer adequate wages and opportunities to new specialists, nor to pay sufficiently high and sufficiently regular wages to recruit and retain skilled shop-floor workers and line managers and for this reason alone is unable to take advantage of opportunities that present themselves, let alone to seek out such opportunities. In the sphere of employment policy, therefore, the successful enterprises find themselves in a virtuous circle, as success enables them to recruit and retain the staff essential to preserve their position, while the unsuccessful enterprises find themselves in a vicious circle, with an ageing staff of management and specialists, experiencing not only the loss of valued workers, but eventually the disintegration of the nucleus of the labour collective on which the manageability of production depends. We therefore find a progressive polarisation of enterprises, with what has often been referred to as the 'degradation' of the unsuccessful and the 'rejuvenation' of the successful enterprises, with relatively few enterprises occupying the middle ground.

There is growing agreement among researchers that the distinction between relatively successful and relatively less successful enterprises is much more meaningful than distinctions based, for example, on the property form or the form of corporate governance. In any particular town or city everybody knows which are the 'good' and which are the 'bad' enterprises, so that for the purposes of case study it is not difficult to assign enterprises unequivocally to one or the other category,[8] but it is not easy to derive appropriate objective indicators which can be used to assign enterprises automatically to one or the other category for the analysis of survey or statistical data.[9] For example, falling unit labour costs may be a result of increasing productivity, or they may be a result of falling wages and the loss of higher-paid skilled workers and specialists (Lippoldt and Gimpel'son, 1996). A relatively small decline in production may be an indicator of successful adaptation to the market or it may be an indicator of a conservative management producing without regard to its costs. A large decline in employment may be an indicator of a radical cost-cutting management or of a loss of labour by an enterprise which cannot pay its wages. A high level of investment may be the result of a sophisticated evaluation of long-term prospects, or it may be a residue of the Soviet fetishism of technology. A high level of net indebtedness may be an indicator of insolvency, or it may be an indicator of a close integration into powerful financial and political networks. The published accounts of an

---

[8]   In Russian conditions 'prosperous' and 'unprosperous' are relative terms. In Kemerovo region there is not a single unambiguously prosperous industrial enterprise, although a handful of food-processing enterprises (brewery, sweet factory) were at least solvent (until recently).

[9]   In Russian conditions the health of an enterprise is determined by its historical legacy and its current political standing and/or monopoly powers much more than by any evaluation of its future economic prospects, which are equally uncertain for all. When the name of the game is survival those who can best survive are those with the best current resources, not those with the best long-term prospects.

enterprise are hardly an adequate indicator of its true economic position or of the financial resources at its disposal because a punitive rate of taxation on profits provides a strong incentive to conceal resources.[10] The proof of the pudding is in the eating: the only reliable indicators of the financial position of an enterprise are to be found on the expenditure side: the ability of the enterprise to preserve the housing, social and welfare apparatus and, above all, the level and regularity of payment of wages, which are both a sign of success and the means of its reproduction by reproducing and increasing the quality of the labour force. However, the use of such measures as indicators to categorise enterprises into the more and less successful would introduce an element of circularity into an analysis which is designed to explain differences in employment strategy on the basis of the greater or lesser freedom of manoeuvre of enterprise management.

Each of the following sections summarises the conclusions of a fuller report. These sections are: the collection and reporting of enterprise employment statistics; employment policy in different types of enterprise; the structure of the internal labour market; secondary employment; the behaviour of workers in the labour market: methods of job search and recruitment; internal mobility; external mobility; and women in the labour market.

THE COLLECTION AND REPORTING OF EMPLOYMENT STATISTICS

The collapse of the Soviet system has seen fundamental changes in the collection and reporting of statistics, including those relating to the sphere of employment. In the Soviet period all manner of detailed personnel statistics were collected and reported by enterprises and organisations. These statistics had both a control and an ideological function. On the one hand, the planning authorities required detailed

---

[10] The best simple indicator is probably capacity utilisation. Pasha Smirnov, see Chapter 4, uses the closely correlated indicators of capacity usage, volume of production, scale of production stoppages and the average wage as the basis for classifying enterprises into the three categories of 'good', 'normal' and 'bad'. The *Russian Economic Barometer* uses the closely correlated indicators of capacity and labour utilisation rates as their indicators of success and failure. In both cases the differences between the good and the bad on a whole range of indicators are dramatic, while property form or form of corporate governance produce few, if any, significant correlations.

and accurate information to formulate and monitor the implementation of their plans. From this point of view the accuracy of reporting was enforced by an army of inspectors who had extensive powers to ensure that false returns, for example of the number of employees or the payment of wages, were not made. On the other hand, statistics had an important ideological function in displaying the success of this or that organisation in accomplishing its tasks and in contributing to the building of socialism. From this point of view enterprises, for example, had a strong interest in presenting a picture of a steady increase in the educational level of their employees and to show labour turnover in the best light, while the labour recruitment bureaux had a strong interest in showing how many people they had successfully placed in work. Despite the common view that statistics were systematically falsified in the Soviet period, our interviews lead us to believe that, at enterprise level at least, the statistics reported to state agencies were conscientiously compiled and that, for those figures which were significant as plan indicators, the inspectorates were sufficiently effective to prevent falsification. While there were many 'snowdrops' – people who were registered for one job but actually did something quite different (providing personal services for managers, members of sports teams, workers in the social sphere) – and many pensioners might have been retained in sinecures – there were very few 'dead souls', people who did not exist or were not working in some capacity in the enterprise. On the other hand, figures which had primarily ideological significance, such as the educational level of the labour force, were often not systematically collected at all, but were merely returned on the basis of what one could call 'an improvement from the reported level', corresponding to targets set in the enterprise's 'social development plan'. Other figures were simply misleading, such as those on the skill structure of the labour force, because formal grade increases were often used as the means of increasing the pay of particular individuals or groups of workers, with no corresponding skill improvements in reality.

Nowadays, in keeping with the de-regulation of wide spheres of economic activity, enterprise statistical reporting has been enormously simplified and the whole apparatus of inspection, apart from matters of taxation, has been dismantled. This gives enterprises considerable freedom to misreport even those few data which they are obliged to report to the state statistical agencies. This is particularly true of the inflation of employment returns in a situation in which the size of an enterprise, as measured by the number of its employees, still has some importance as an indicator of its success in weathering the storm of the transition to a market economy and in determining the political weight of the enterprise. An additional factor, to which many Western commentators have drawn attention, is the excess wages tax under which, until January 1996, the wage bill was taxed as profits to the extent that it exceeded an average wage of six times the derisory minimum. In principle enterprises could reduce their liability to this tax quite simply by inflating their returns of the number of employees, so increasing the size of wage bill which could be paid without incurring additional tax liabilities.

Our own previous research had led us to the conclusion that there was systematic misreporting of employment data by enterprises, because of the gross disparities which we found between data reported at enterprise level and data collected at shop level, and between reported data and our own observations in the shops (Kozina, 1996). For these reasons we conducted a systematic investigation of the collection and reporting of enterprise statistics in our case-study enterprises, in particular to discover whether there was systematic distortion of the data which would be amenable to correction. It should be emphasised that this research concerns only the collection and reporting at enterprise level. What is done with these statistics in the oblast and federal statistical offices we do not know and the production of aggregate data does require a considerable amount of guestimation of data relating to non-reporting enterprises and organisations, particularly those in the new private sector. In reviewing the results of this research we need to distinguish between 'old' and 'new' enterprises.

Old enterprises

Large and medium enterprises (those with more than 200 employees in industry and construction – 100 from 1996) return forms 2-T and 1-T on labour to the regional statistical administration. Form 2-T is the traditional form inherited from the Soviet period, although it has been simplified and is modified almost every year, and is returned annually (quarterly returns have also been required in some years). Form 1-T is a return which partly duplicates 2-T and is supposed to have been submitted quarterly since 1993, with a summary of employment and total wage payments for intervening months being submitted since 1995. A sample of registered small enterprises provide less detail on employment and wages as part of their return on Form MP, although other employment data is collected through surveys of enterprises and through the labour force survey.[11]

The data used to complete Forms 1-T and 2-T derives from two sources. First, data on the registered number of employees and on the hiring and departure of employees maintained by the personnel department of the enterprise on the basis of their personnel records. Second, data on the actual number working and the hours worked which are prepared at shop level by the time-keeper and reported monthly to the planning-economic department of the enterprise, which is the department responsible for filling in these forms.

In addition to information about wages, prepared by the department of labour and wages, Form 2-T requires data on the registered number of employees (that is, the total number registered as working in the enterprise) by certain categories (which change slightly year by year), the average registered number of employees (that is, the average number of full-time equivalent personnel), losses of working time, the number of industrial-production and non-productive personnel, the number of industrial-production personnel hired and the number leaving in the given period, and the formal reasons for departure of those leaving.[12] Form 1-T requires similar data, with less detail on wages and on the composition of the labour force and more detail on short-time working, administrative leave and forms of employment (contract and supplementary).

In general, although there are many sources of inaccuracy and there are discrepancies between data collected from different sources, our

---

[11]   Some of our case study enterprises only began to return form 1-T during 1996, and one appears still not to return this form, in which case the regional Goskomstat office presumably estimates the unreported data. The 1997 revised forms 1-T only reached our case-study enterprises in May. Large and medium enterprises are also required to notify the local employment service of vacancies and of impending redundancies, although they do so rather lackadaisically. This is then reported to the statistical agency with the employment service data. Health and safety reports on working conditions and industrial injury also have to be returned. We are very grateful to Galya Monousova for preparing a survey of statistical sources for us and to Zinaida Ryzhykova, deputy head of the labour statistics department of Goskomstat, for clarifying a number of issues.

[12]   Until 1996 Form 2-T recorded only the total separations and the numbers of 'voluntary' quits and disciplinary dismissals, while 1-T reported the number made redundant and the number separating voluntarily. From 1996 2-T also reports the number made redundant.

conclusion is that the data are conscientiously collected and accurately reported. The figures on registered numbers and on average registered numbers can be considered an accurate reflection of the absolute and the average full-time equivalent numbers employed. The reorganisation of enterprises can lead to changes in the accounting units, for example if an enterprise is broken up into smaller units, but this does not affect the aggregate figures. In particular, we have no evidence that any of our enterprises have over-reported their numbers with a view to evading the tax on excess wage payments and have no reason to believe that they have done so.

The breakdown between production-industrial and non-productive personnel is not particularly meaningful because there are no standard definitions employed, and definitions can change over time.

The figures on turnover are accurately collected and reported, but may overestimate the extent of turnover partly because it is not uncommon for people to register without ever coming to work, so being counted as both a hire and a quit, and partly because some people who change their employment status are registered as both a quit and a hire.

The most misleading figures are those which give the formal reasons for departure. The proportion reported as leaving voluntarily is substantially exaggerated because many disciplinary dismissals and compulsory redundancies are officially registered as voluntary quits. This is in addition to the obvious fact that many voluntary quits occur under pressure from the administration (non-payment of wages, low pay, transfer to other work). Differences in the data relating to different types of enterprise are as likely to result from differences in reporting practice as from real differences, although we would expect those paying better wages to have lower natural wastage and so to make greater use of compulsory redundancy or disciplinary dismissal to reduce employment.

In addition to the reported data, a large amount of personnel data is still maintained in enterprises, although this is not usually aggregated or analysed. The most reliable data is that prepared at shop level, which may differ substantially from data held in enterprise records so we have used shop-level data to provide the most accurate picture of labour mobility in our research. We had no problems in securing access to this data, including the personal record cards and labour books of individual employees, which proved to be a very rich source of data as a supplement to and check on our work-history interviews.

In addition to forms 1-T, 2-T and returns to the tax inspectorate, enterprises are surveyed by various state agencies and researchers. Where the data required is readily available we have no reason to believe that enterprises misreport the figures, but where data has to be specially prepared we suspect that returns are based on guesses or are quite arbitrary, and may frequently express impressionistic estimates which are at variance with reality. In relation to questions regarding enterprise policy and practice it is important to be aware that question-naires are completed by central management bodies whereas, in the area of employment, much policy-making in practice takes place at the level of the subdivisions.

New enterprises

The situation is quite different in new enterprises, which are usually sufficiently small as not to have to complete forms 1-T and 2-T, but which are haphazardly surveyed by the statistical services. Their only reporting requirements beyond this are to the tax authorities, whose records are not normally available to Goskomstat. New enterprises do not maintain systematic employment records beyond, in the best cases, those records of recruitment, departures and disciplinary measures required by the Labour Code, which may themselves be handled sum-marily. In general, enterprises do not have summary data on the structure or changes in employment, and their reporting to outside bodies, including the tax authorities, is based on arbitrary or system-atically distorted figures. New enterprises are frequently reorganised, for tax or other purposes, so that there can appear to be substantial fluctuations in the number employed as a result of changes in juridical form. New enterprises are also far more likely than former state enter-prises to harbour 'dead souls', holding the labour books of people who are in fact not in formal employment and reporting the payment of wages to these people in order to reduce tax liability. No reliance is therefore to be placed on state statistical data derived from the report-ing of small, and particularly new, enterprises.

At the same time, we found that the enterprises which we selected for case study were very willing to give us access to their employment records, and in several cases to prepare data for us.

Our overall conclusion is that the data submitted to the state statistical service by large and medium enterprises is, in general, accurate so far as numbers, time worked and turnover are concerned, although the reasons for turnover are seriously distorted. Although there are substantial discrepancies in data from different sources, apart from the latter point we have not found any source of systematic error or distortion in the collection and reporting of employment statistics from state and former state enterprises. Whether this data is accurately aggregated and reported by the regional and federal offices of the statistical service we do not know on the basis of the present research. We do know that the data submitted by small enterprises is unreliable and that submitted by new enterprises is worthless.

EMPLOYMENT POLICY IN DIFFERENT TYPES OF ENTERPRISE

In this section we review the findings of our analysis of employment policy in the three types of enterprises which we have defined: unsuccessful, successful and new enterprises. The most general finding is that all state enterprises have pursued a positive strategy of 'preserving the labour collective', but this can mean very different things in different contexts. As noted above, the 'preservation of the labour collective' means the preservation of the productive capacity of the enterprise as a social organism and is not inconsistent with the pursuit of a very active employment strategy, including large scale reductions in employment if these do not compromise the productive capacity of the enterprise. This can be exemplified by the changing attitudes to enterprise housing, social and welfare provision which not only provided for the needs of the labour collective, but which could employ as much as a quarter of the entire labour force of a large enterprise.

In the Soviet period, labour shortage and the very limited development of alternative sources of social and welfare provision meant that the large enterprise had to take responsibility for all aspects of the reproduction of the labour force. Social and welfare provision by the enterprise was therefore an essential part of its reproduction as a labour collective, as was the provision of education and training both for new entrants and for current employees, and its allocation was used as a means of tying employees to the enterprise. It should not, therefore, be surprising to find that enterprise directors in the first stages of the transition sought to retain not only the direct productive capacity of the enterprise, but also its social and welfare infrastructure. While this may have been motivated in part by a genuine humanitarian concern on the part of the enterprise director, it was also dictated by the fact that the problem of recruiting and retaining labour had not eased, but had become more acute as state enterprises faced growing competition from smaller and new private enterprises. State enterprises could not compete with the wages paid in the new private sector, in part because of the internal conflicts unleashed by attempts to reform the wages system (Clarke, 1995, 1996b), but sought to compete by offering stability and security, including the provision of housing and welfare benefits which were not available through the market.

Foreign advisers and the Russian government saw the divestiture of the housing and welfare infrastructure and their transfer to municipal authorities as a vital element of the development of competitive product and labour markets. At first, large enterprises were reluctant to follow this course but, as the crisis continued to deepen and labour market pressures to ease, the rising costs of maintaining a large housing stock and social and welfare apparatus came increasingly to be seen to outweigh their declining benefits and enterprises began to transfer social provision to a commercial basis, to sell their profitable social assets and to transfer all their loss-making assets to municipal authorities. The barrier to divestiture soon became, not the reluctance of enterprises to reduce provision, but the absence of private buyers and the reluctance of municipal authorities to assume responsibility since they lacked the financial and managerial resources to maintain the facilities. The priority of 'preserving the labour collective' was retained unchanged through all these changes: the employees of the social sphere were only considered to be a part of the labour collective to the extent that they contributed positively to its reproduction as a productive unit and were only retained for as long as the benefits of social provision were considered to outweigh their costs.

The same phrase, the 'preservation of the labour collective', can cover a strategy of seeking to preserve the *number* of the labour collective and a strategy of seeking to preserve the '*quality*', 'skeleton' or 'nucleus' of the labour collective. Most state enterprises entered the transition committed, at least nominally, to preserving the number employed, although a few of the more dynamic 'pioneers of privatisation' pursued employment cuts from very early in the transition process.[13] The size of the labour force of an enterprise was a decisive planning indicator in the Soviet period and one of the principal bases on which the enterprise competed for resources, including investment funds. The size of the enterprise continued to be an important determinant of the political weight of an enterprise in the post-Soviet period, particularly in relation to local authorities,[14] but the size of the labour force was only one among a number of factors, including the political connections of management and the export and tax-paying capacities of the enterprise, and one which became rapidly less important as state subsidies to industry were slashed from 1994. On the other hand, the attempt to maintain numbers in the face of falling production and the withdrawal of state financial support meant that most enterprises found it increasingly difficult to maintain wages. As real wages fell, their payment was delayed and workers were put on short-time or laid off, the more mobile younger and unskilled workers would move from job to job in search of better pay, while even the traditionally more stable skilled and experienced workers would begin to leave the enterprise.[15] Sooner or later it became clear that the attempt to preserve the number of the labour collective was proving self-defeating, as enterprises saw their workers drain away in response to falling wages, while high labour turnover, which extended to the best and most highly-skilled and experienced workers, was undermining the productive capacity of the labour collective. As a result, sooner or later virtually all enterprises have moved from the first to the second variant of the strategy of preserving the labour collective, seeking to maintain not the number but the 'quality' of the labour collective. Such a change was usually initiated not from above but from below, as line managers responded to the actions of workers by manipulating payment systems, the allocation of work and administrative leave to retain their most prized workers while encouraging the less desirable to leave

---

13   These tended to be small enterprises which cut the labour force primarily by divesting themselves of peripheral activities (Clarke, 1996a, 1996c).

14   A number of local taxes are payroll based, giving the municipal authority an interest in preserving the number employed. More significantly, the cost of providing for those dismissed from the enterprises falls on the local authority. Local authorities frequently use their power to delay large-scale redundancies, directing the local offices of the Federal Employment Service to provide subsidies to preserve jobs.

15   Some enterprises borrowed large sums of money at negative real interest rates to pay wages in the early stages of the transition, only to find themselves burdened with astronomical debt servicing costs when interest rates shot up (by 1995 one of our case-study enterprises was paying more in interest on its accumulated debt than its entire wage bill).

voluntarily. Changes in policy at the level of senior management of the enterprise were then most frequently a response to changes in practice at the level of the shop floor initiated spontaneously by workers and line managers (Romanov, 1995).

Every enterprise faces the choice between a strategy directed at preserving the number and preserving the quality of the labour collective and its ability to reconcile the two depends primarily on the financial resources at its disposal. This means that within the common rhetorical framework of 'preserving the labour collective' there are significant differences to be observed between successful and unsuccessful enterprises, the latter being unable to do more than to try to limit the decline in numbers, the former aiming to upgrade the labour collective.[16] In neither case is it the rule that enterprises seek to retain labour for its own sake: the least successful enterprises face shortages of key production workers because they are unable to pay adequate and regular wages, the more successful force out less desirable employees in order to upgrade the labour force. Only the most stable and secure of enterprises, many of which, ironically, remain in state ownership, have been able both to maintain numbers and to pay sufficient wages to maintain or improve the quality of the labour force.[17]

The principal motivation of enterprises in seeking to preserve the labour collective is to retain their productive capacity in the hope or expectation of increasing production once circumstances improve. Although the economy as a whole has been in consistent decline, there have been significant fluctuations in demand for particular branches or enterprises so that even the least successful have received orders from time to time. Political and policy instability meant that at least for the first two years of reform the hope of many conservative managers of a restoration of the old order was not entirely unrealistic. The success of Yeltsin's second putsch at the end of 1993 dashed such hopes, but the possibility of a change of course on the part of the government

---

[16] The findings of our case-study research are entirely consistent with the striking differences in the dynamics of employment in 'good' and 'bad' enterprises uncovered by the last three rounds of the Russian Labour Force Flexibility Survey carried out by the Centre for Labour Market Research of the Institute of Economics in conjunction with Guy Standing. A panel element of the survey, covering 263 enterprises in five regions, found very substantial differences in the changes in labour force composition and substantial differences in turnover rates of different categories of employee in the contrasting types of enterprise (see Chapter 4 by Pavel Smirnov below).

[17] These are in such branches as energy, transport and communications and parts of construction.

remained at least until Yeltsin's victory in the Presidential election of 1996. The conservative policy of preserving productive capacity in the hope of recovery was, therefore, a perfectly rational one from the point of view of enterprise management, particularly when it was the labour force that bore the costs as discipline was tightened, wages fell and went unpaid for months on end, workers were laid off and sent on leave with little or no pay. On the other hand, preserving the productive capacity of the enterprise was not inconsistent with realising its assets to the benefit of the enterprise and/or its management and/or outside owners: the land and buildings of the enterprise could be leased out and valuable assets of the enterprise could be sold off while the shrinking core of the enterprise survived.

The 'preservation of the labour collective' remained a rational strategy for an enterprise management while it had sufficient resources to expect to be able to sustain its productive capacity until an anticipated recovery. However, both the means and the expectation of recovery were steadily eroded through 1995 and 1996. On the one hand, the less successful enterprises built up growing debts to their employees, tax authorities, suppliers and banks, which were no longer being eroded by inflation as the inflation rate fell sharply from 1995, while direct and indirect government subsidies were substantially reduced and valuable assets progressively leased or sold off. On the other hand, expectations of economic recovery and/or a change of government course were progressively eroded, finally being dashed by Yeltsin's election victory in 1996. With the erosion of both means and incentive to sustain productive capacity and firms coming under growing pressure from banks and tax authorities, a marked tendency was emerging at the end of the period of our research (the middle of 1996) for both successful and unsuccessful enterprises to introduce much more radical programmes of employment reduction and realisation of the enterprise's assets, often with a change in management, sometimes associated with a change in ownership, under direct pressure from bank creditors.[18] This change is reflected in the increasing number of

---

[18]   The fact that the preservation of the labour collective was a perfectly rational management strategy explains why ownership does not appear as a significant variable in the analysis of data from enterprise surveys, even outside owners leaving management to pursue its 'traditional' strategy, subject to financial constraints. The abandonment of this strategy is often linked to ownership changes as creditor banks move in, but the change in formal ownership is only a means of changing strategy which is itself a reflection of the change in circumstances.

reported job losses and of registered unemployed through 1996, although the most recent figure for survey unemployed dates only from the March 1996 labour force survey.

Unsuccessful enterprises

As noted above, within the common strategy of the 'preservation of the labour collective' there are significant differences between the more and the less successful enterprises. The least successful enterprises have been in a state of crisis, from which they have been quite unable to extricate themselves, since the beginning of radical reform in 1992. These are particularly the once-privileged enterprises of heavy industry and the military-industrial complex which have experienced the most dramatic change in their fortunes. Others have joined the ranks of the unsuccessful more recently. In particular, the enterprises manufacturing for domestic consumer markets which have faced growing foreign competition as the exchange rate has steadily appreciated. These are enterprises whose market situation and limited resources leave little scope for innovative responses, so they have tended to continue to pursue conservative employment policies. With limited financial resources and facing high levels of labour turnover the management strategy of these enterprises has been focused on the attempt to hold on to labour and, in this sense, to limit the fall in the number of the labour collective in the face of high natural wastage.

Within this common framework of conservatism at the level of senior management, we find that line managers pursue a more or less active strategy aimed at the 'qualitative cleansing' of the labour collective, forcing out the less skilled and less disciplined and taking every step to hold on to their key workers so that in practice numbers steadily fall. This initiative of line management trickled up to senior management as the economic situation continued to deteriorate. Despite the subjective intentions and declared purposes of senior management, staff reductions for economic reasons began to occur in all unsuccessful enterprises during 1994–95, although the majority of separations were still officially recorded as voluntary.

Faced with high levels of natural wastage, the main attention of the management of unsuccessful enterprises is directed at the control of separations, while hiring is the most passive element of their employment policy. The need to recruit and retain desirable workers within the constraints of severely limited resources means that line managers enjoy a great deal of autonomy in hiring and firing, so that employment policy in depressed enterprises is marked by a high degree of decentralisation, the actual practice often diverging considerably from the rhetorical declarations of senior management. The administration does not impose any significant restrictions on recruitment for work, and few demands are made of new workers because of the difficulty of attracting them. As a result, the enterprise conducts an 'open door' recruitment policy, taking on all comers. At unsuccessful enterprises we observed few innovations in the field of hiring staff and the use of flexible forms of employment. These enterprises, which remain in the traditional situation of facing labour shortages at the level of wages which they can pay, tend to work in traditional ways and seek employees through traditional channels, working much more actively with the employment services than others.

Despite distinctions in the subjective approach of senior management and in the timing and sequence of steps taken in response to the crisis, objective circumstances – financial difficulties and the absence of real levers of employment policy – have played the leading role in determining that depressed enterprises have ended up with a common result: the number of employees has fallen sharply and the technological and social personnel nucleus of the enterprise is in the process of being destroyed.

Successful enterprises

The financial limitations on employment policy faced by successful enterprises are less rigid and consequently there are more possibilities of their persisting with the traditional policy of preserving the number employed. At the same time, their more favourable financial and economic position gives them the resources to pursue a more active labour market strategy aimed at improving the quality of the labour force. The commitment to the preservation of numbers does not, therefore, imply a commitment to preserving the jobs of those employed in the enterprise at any particular point in time. Although a small number of enterprises was able both to preserve numbers and to improve the quality of the labour force, for most of the more successful enterprises, as for the less successful, 1994 marked the watershed when change became unavoidable.

These shifts were connected with the complication of the financial position caused by a sharp deterioration in the general economic situation, aggravated for some enterprises by adverse changes in the exchange rate and in domestic and world markets. The initial response of the more successful enterprises was no different from that of the less successful – short-time working and compulsory lay-offs – but, unlike the latter, the management of the more successful enterprises had the resources to bring the process of employment restructuring under its control before this began to occur spontaneously. Sooner or later, therefore, the management of the more successful enterprises undertakes an active strategy of forcing less desirable workers out of the enterprise in order to preserve employment stability and relatively high wages for those who remain or who can be recruited.

The greater resources at the disposal of the enterprise, which permit a more active employment policy, are also linked to a higher degree of centralisation of control of employment strategy. While in the unsuccessful enterprises it tends to be line management that determines employment strategy in accordance with the perceived needs of production, within the limits of financial constraints imposed from above, in less successful enterprises strategy tends to be determined by senior management which is increasingly preoccupied with financial considerations, within the limits of the constraints of the needs of production which are communicated from below. Thus it is not uncommon to find the enthusiasm of senior management of successful enterprises to reduce their staff to a minimum for financial reasons, running up against resistance to reductions from line managers which arises from their perception of the need to preserve the enterprise as a purposive industrial and social organism.[19] At least until recently, new external owners of the enterprises find themselves compelled to act within the framework of the same limits, initial plans for radical reductions being thwarted by pressure from line managers to preserve productive capacity.

The management of more successful enterprises is able to exert much more control of hiring than that of the unsuccessful enterprises, which have to take anyone they can find and so can only pursue an active employment policy through the attempt to control separations.

---

[19]   This is not just a matter of conservatism. We have observed a number of cases in which enterprises have had great difficulty in meeting new and profitable orders because of an inability to recruit appropriately skilled labour which has been lost as a result of previous job-cutting exercises.

Corresponding to the more active employment policy of successful enterprises we find a higher degree of innovation and adaptability. This particularly concerns the hiring of managerial personnel trained in the new commercial and financial skills required for the market economy. Alongside the continued domination of the traditional policy of hiring through friends and relatives for management and skilled workers' posts, external hiring on a competitive basis is increasingly used for the recruitment of these new specialists. Corresponding to the more centralised control of hiring, these enterprises are also marked by a higher degree of formalisation of the demands made on newly hired employees and of the recruitment procedure itself, even where recruitment takes place through traditional informal channels. These enterprises also make more active use of flexible forms of employment, including multi-skilling and the use of contract and temporary labour.[20]

New enterprises

As against the 'old' enterprises, with their traditional employment policy of 'preservation of the labour collective', new enterprises have first to create a labour collective. A necessary condition for the development of new firms is the formation of a staff which forms the technological and social nucleus of the enterprise, whose existence then makes the reproduction and expansion of the enterprise possible. With an increase in the size of the enterprise and the complexity of its activity the problem of structuring the staff arises.

A two-sector model of internal employment, consisting of a 'core' and a 'periphery' seems to be characteristic of newly created private sector enterprises. The two parts of the labour force differ in the structure and forms of employment and the payment of labour. The chiefs (owners) and some of the specialists who are included in the 'core' work on a permanent basis (are part of the staff). The workers and specialists who belong to the periphery work on a temporary basis on contractual terms.

Different channels of hiring are applied to different categories of staff: personal connections are used for hiring the chiefs and specialists who form the core, while for the peripheral workers competitive

---

[20]   Although flexible forms of employment are still not widespread (Tsentr issledovannii rynka truda, 1995a).

recruitment and free hiring are used. The transition from hiring through family connections to those through friends, acquaintances and professional contacts is characteristic of developing new firms operating in a competitive environment.

In new firms more formal procedures of selection are used more often and formal criteria of selection (age, training and practical experience) are given considerable significance while decision-making regarding personnel questions is concentrated in the hands of the founder-proprietors.

While in many medium and large concerns experiencing financial difficulties the system of professional training and retraining of staff is in decline, the new firms which we studied, all of which work in new lines of business, organise their own systems of staff training. Having devoted significant resources to training staff, who have also built up specific knowledge on the job, new firms begin to develop a policy of retaining key workers in order to preserve the nucleus of the enterprise. At the same time, the existence of a stable nucleus is one of the preconditions for the expansion of the firm and the hiring of new 'peripheral' workers. This is particularly the case in unstable Russian economic conditions, where it is typical for new firms (although not for those which we selected for our case study) to change their line of business as opportunities change, the continuity of the business lying in the skills and experience of its core employees. Thus, once the nucleus of the labour collective has been formed in private concerns they face exactly the same problem as former state enterprises, of the effective utilisation of the potential of the labour force and the creation of the conditions for its preservation.

The overall conclusion of our investigation of management strategies is that there is some convergence of strategy between all three types of enterprise, as the unsuccessful are forced to abandon their attempt to hold on to employees at all costs and the new enterprises are forced to pay attention to the need to preserve the nucleus of the labour force, in both cases the primary constraint being the need to ensure the reproduction of the enterprise as a purposive social and technical organism, this in turn being the condition for the adaptation of the enterprise to changing circumstances and its expansion to grasp new opportunities.

This convergence of employment strategy to focus on the reproduction of the labour collective as a productive unity takes place within the framework of a perennial contradiction between financial constraints and the retention of productive capacity, a contradiction which is expressed within enterprise management in a conflict between the newly emerging financial specialists and the engineering specialists who were traditionally dominant in the Soviet enterprise. This increasingly frequently coincides with a conflict between senior management, preoccupied with financial questions, and line management, which is responsible for production, and where the balance has increasingly shifted in favour of the former. The likelihood is that sooner rather than later all enterprises will be compelled to cut their labour force to the level required for currently profitable production and to scrap redundant productive capacity, unleashing a tidal wave of unemployment.

THE STRUCTURE OF THE INTERNAL LABOUR MARKET

Western economists regard the retention of labour in readiness for an upturn of production as completely irrational in a situation in which labour market pressures are being relieved by growing unemployment, so that any enterprise will be able to hire new employees if and when production resumes. However, there are both technical and social constraints on relying on the external labour market to recruit employees as and when they are required. On the one hand, the nucleus of the enterprise which the directors seek to retain comprises a core of technically skilled workers, familiar with equipment which is often unique to the factory and which they alone are able to keep going. On the other hand, the nucleus of the enterprise is also defined socially, as the reliable and dedicated workers at the heart of the network of social relations on the shop floor on whom the operation and reproduction of the enterprise as a social organism depends. The nucleus is therefore as much a social as a technical conception.

The distinction between the technical and social skills and attributes of the labour force leads us to a preliminary classification of the labour force which can be applied to both production and non-production workers and, in principle, to any branch of production. This classification is a little more complex than the traditional dichotomy of core and periphery, which we ourselves use in relation to 'new' enterprises.

This classification is based on the two cross-cutting axes of technical skill and social attributes.

We define the *internal segment* of the labour market as those employees who have high technical or professional skills and who are also at the heart of the social networks of the enterprise. Their skills tend to be firm-specific, acquired over many years of service, but they also tend to have a wide range of such skills and to be the most flexible workers. These are above all the employees who in the past were referred to as *kadrovyi*. The *industrial segment* is that which has relatively low technical and professional skills, but has long service and a record of loyalty and commitment and is a social mainstay of the enterprise. The *professional segment* is those workers who have high technical or professional skills, but not necessarily a high degree of commitment to the enterprise. The *marginal segment* is those with neither technical skills nor social commitment.

These four segments differ in their role within the enterprise, but also in their labour market behaviour. The internal segment are well able to defend their position in the enterprise and are able to control entry to their group but, having firm-specific skills and being older, they have few prospects in the external labour market. They tend, therefore, to hold on at an enterprise until the last. If they have secondary work it is usually also within the enterprise, whether official or unofficial. Those who have not yet gained access to the inner sanctum, not having built up their social position, tend to be much more mobile and much more active in secondary employment, particularly if opportunities within the enterprise are blocked.

The industrial segment is those workers with a lower skill level, usually also firm-specific, who have established a position for themselves on the basis of long-service, commitment and a network of social contacts. They also have low levels of voluntary mobility because they have few opportunities outside, but have lower pay and independence at work. This category includes many women, particularly in the offices, and younger workers. They tend more than other groups to be sent on administrative leave, because they are technically dispensable and there is less risk of them leaving voluntarily; also they are more likely to be laid off in the event of the need for compulsory cuts because they are unlikely to leave voluntarily.

The professional segment have high but not firm-specific technical or professional skills. This is the group which is in the strongest position on the external labour market but which, in the past, tended to be lower paid because they were predominantly involved in auxiliary sections rather than in direct production. They are also the most affected by the reorganisations of management structures which have become common in recent years. They therefore display relatively high voluntary labour mobility and are heavily involved in secondary employment.

The marginal segment is the most unstable group, comprising low-skilled workers, and is typically highly mobile with low levels of discipline, seeking higher earnings not by committing themselves to one place or building up their skills but by moving from job to job to exploit whatever opportunity offers the best return at the moment.

SECONDARY EMPLOYMENT

Secondary employment plays a crucial role in the development of the labour market, increasing its flexibility and smoothing the transition, but its novelty and importance should not be exaggerated or its negative consequences ignored. Secondary employment was widespread in the Soviet period, both as formally registered additional jobs and as (until 1987 usually illegal) individual labour activity providing goods and services for the population, usually on a barter rather than a sale basis. These remain the dominant forms of secondary employment today. The largest growth in the sphere of secondary labour activity is in subsistence production, which we do not include within secondary employment.

Contrary to the popular stereotype, secondary employment is not a mass phenomenon, participation not being much greater than in the Soviet period, and it is not predominantly informal employment in the new private trading sector. At least two-thirds of the working population have no access to secondary employment, and the most disadvantaged groups of the population — women, the elderly and disabled, the unskilled — have the fewest opportunities for secondary employment. Thus secondary employment plays more of a role in improving the material situation and life chances of the most competitive groups of the population than protecting the most impoverished and disadvantaged groups from destitution. The majority of people who do have second jobs take these jobs within the formal sphere of employment (they are officially registered in one way or another), many within their own enterprise. Only a relatively small proportion are involved in trading activities as their second jobs, and this tends to be more on a casual and episodic basis, helping out friends and relatives. Thus trade is increasingly a full-time occupation, not particularly marked as a sphere of secondary employment.

The conclusions of our research on secondary employment can be summed up briefly:

1. Secondary employment serves a number of important labour market functions:
    - For some workers secondary employment is a means of survival in conditions of partial employment or low salary, while for others it is a means of satisfying high economic and social aspirations.
    - For state structures, secondary employment is a 'shock-absorber' of social tension. For managers at all levels it is a means of holding on to staff, and even of maintaining a surplus in case of the growth of production.
    - Secondary employment indirectly influences the level of labour mobility. This is in those cases when the additional, secondary, work becomes the testing ground for trying out other opportunities, a way of checking on the 'marketability' of additional skills and capabilities, and also simply a period of adaptation before the transition from the former 'main' job to a new one. In other cases the need to do additional work results in the destruction of the habit of always working in one place and widens the spectrum of possibilities the person considers.
    - In small organisations, where there are natural limits to individual transfers within the framework of the organisation, secondary employment partly replaces the functions of vertical and horizontal internal mobility.

2. The behaviour of people in the sphere of secondary employment is defined by a complex set of characteristics, the main ones of which are sex and education. In the final analysis the boundary between those engaged in additional work and those not so engaged is not determined by biographical data, but by socio-psychological and socio-cultural features of the workers.

3. The position of employers of all types in relation to secondary employment is expressed in the phrase 'we won't help, but we won't hinder it'. At unsuccessful enterprises this position is clear and unavoidable: if you cannot provide your employees with work and wages, you should not interfere in people's attempts to earn enough to live and you should be thankful that they still pin some hopes in you and have not all left. If the administration hardens its policy in relation to additional work the likelihood is of a mass departure of workers involved in secondary employment from the enterprise.

   At successful and new enterprises the situation is slightly different. Here the administration is much quicker to exert control over additional work so that it does not develop to the detriment of the main activity.

4. There are obvious negative consequences of involving a large number of workers in the sphere of secondary employment:

   • reduction of the social protection of workers in the present and future (the incomes of the majority of kinds of additional employment are not subject to the normal deductions for sick pay, holiday pay and, eventually, pension).

   • professional degradation at the main place of work, deskilling and the further undermining of already low labour morale.

5. The sphere of secondary employment is gradually narrowing. First, because the jobs which have traditionally been available in enterprises for subsidiary employment are either being cut or being filled by permanent workers from among those who have been made redundant but redeployed by the enterprise. Second, particularly in the informal external labour market, by virtue of the increasing competitiveness and professionalisation of work in trade and services. The narrowing of the secondary labour market is likely to lead to a further deterioration in the situation of the less advantaged members of the labour force.

BEHAVIOUR OF THE WORKERS IN THE LABOUR MARKET: METHODS OF JOB SEARCH AND RECRUITMENT

The study of methods of job search was based on the analysis of semi-structured interviews, a leading theme of which was the labour biography of the respondent. A total of 260 interviews were conducted with workers of the twelve enterprises in which case studies took place. It should be emphasised that this data relates only to those currently employed in these enterprises, so it does not touch on the unemployed or those working, for example, in budget organisations or in agriculture, although some additional interviews were conducted with former employees. It is also important to note that our research was conducted in areas of 'normal', low unemployment.

In spite of the fact that distinctions of biographical situation, psychological features and life circumstances determine distinctions of individual recruitment strategy it has been possible to distinguish some general factors influencing people's behaviour in the labour market. The following factors prove the most significant: *temporal*, as the modern employment situation significantly differs from the situation prior to the beginning of the 1990s; *socio-cultural*, as people of different generations, different sexes and belonging to different social strata behave differently in the labour market. And, finally, the *prestigiousness* of the job has an influence on labour market behaviour (in our research this is analysed from the point of view of the type of enterprise). The principal conclusions of our research can be summed up as follows.

Despite fundamental socio-economic changes, including those in the labour market, personal employment strategies have not really undergone significant change. The first thing that can be stated is the existence of a series of traditional methods or channels of recruitment which are common to all:

1. Recruitment with the help of personal connections. In the Russian system of labour relations the role of personal connections in job search and recruitment has become pre-eminent. Patronage in job placement is by no means a new phenomenon in Russia, connections of friends and relatives playing a very important role in Soviet times. However, in recent years this method of job search

and recruitment has not only become much more common, but its specific application has also changed somewhat, as became clear from our interviews. Within this category there are really three distinct methods of recruitment: direct help in getting work through patronage or recommendation; the provision of information about a job; and recruitment through professional contacts.

2. Independently – active search for a job on one's own. This is also a common method of finding work, but less so than in the past.

   The opportunities for independent recruitment have narrowed very considerably as there have come to be fewer jobs, but recruitment 'from the street' is also limited by the protectionist policy of the administration of the majority of enterprises who prefer, as a rule, to recruit new employees from among the relatives and friends of the existing staff. Independent recruitment as a specific personal employment strategy is now characteristic only of certain groups of employees: pensioners, low-skilled and unskilled workers, some young workers, and some occupational groups, such as building workers, whose skills are still in high demand.

   There are also some new variants of independent recruitment, through participation in competitions and through the creation of one's own job, but these are still only rarely used.

3. Recruitment with the help of the employment service. This is not a significant channel, except for the least employable sections of the population: unskilled youth, pensioners and those near to pension age, general labourers — those sections of the labour market which in the past were served by the notorious labour placement commissions. The employment service, as a rule, is only able to offer low-paid and low-status jobs and its main function in practice is to administer the benefit system and to collect statistics. Both employers and employees tend to be highly dissatisfied with the work of the employment service and regard it as a last resort. Active labour market policies are confined to the provision of unsophisticated short training courses and the subsidisation of existing jobs, largely on a political basis at the direction of the local administration.

   Non-state, private, labour exchanges are beginning to emerge to service that segment of the labour market which involves high-skilled high-paid jobs. Private agencies are used mainly for the recruitment and placement of skilled specialists, where employer and employee are willing and able to pay the fee. However, employers report considerable dissatisfaction with the services provided.

4. Placement through the compulsory distribution of graduates of educational establishments. This was the principal route into employment in the past, but has now lost its compulsory dimension and is becoming much less significant as a means of job placement. The few job placements through distribution which we have recorded since 1990 all involved the use of personal connections.

These four categories exhaust all possible methods of recruitment. The methods have not changed, but the distribution between them has changed quite markedly in the period of reform.

The most preferable and widely used source of information about vacancies is relatives and friends. The next most significant sources are announcements of vacancies posted in factories and in the streets and published in newspapers, including specialist newspapers set up to service the labour market. The employment service and independently visiting personnel departments of enterprises do not now appear to be important sources of information about vacancies.

Personal employment strategies have not changed and do not vary a great deal. As a rule, possibilities of recruitment through personal connections are explored first of all, and for the majority these prove successful. If personal connections do not work then people turn to independent search for work, first of all looking for announcements and advertisements and then, much less often, touring round personnel departments. Only in the last resort do people turn to the employment service.

The high levels of labour mobility should not conceal from view the fact that the stereotype of behaviour in the labour market has remained as it was in the past. For the majority of people the priority is to find a permanent place of work with a stable income where they can work for many years.[21] In this sense a large part of labour mobility today is forced, a feature of the crisis period. Once people have found themselves an acceptable job, most people leave that job in only one of two circumstances. Either when the size of wages or delays in its payment makes a normal existence impossible (and in this case people, as a

---

[21]   Despite high labour turnover, the Russian Longitudinal Monitoring Survey found that 43% of those in work in late 1995 had been in their jobs for more than 5 years.

rule, try to keep going by taking on secondary employment rather than leaving), or when people are effectively forced out of the enterprise in order to reduce the size of the staff (and here most people try to get another job at the same enterprise, even if it involves a drop in pay and status).

The majority of people have no desire to leave for another enterprise, and many of those who have left speak of the pain and anguish it caused them, even if they are now in much better work, and they often express a desire to return to their 'home' enterprise if the situation there stabilises. Most people who do decide to leave prefer to stay on in their old job while they look for another, with secondary employment providing one of the channels through which they explore other possibilities.

INTERNAL MOBILITY

The ideal of remaining in one enterprise for one's entire working life meant, to the extent that it was realised, that the principal site of labour mobility was within the enterprise. However, there has been very little research on the internal mobility of labour within enterprises.[22] In order to understand the processes of internal mobility we conducted interviews with workers and shop management, and also conducted a systematic analysis of internal mobility in those enterprises for which data was available, based on the examination of the internal enterprise records and the personal cards of employees which, at least in principle, record every change of status and change of post.

The first conclusion to draw from this research is that just as the ideal was to make one's career within one enterprise, so within that enterprise most people tended to stay within a single shop, with very low levels of inter-shop transfer. This means that in all but the largest enterprises people were much more likely to leave the enterprise than to move to another shop (up to ten times more likely on our data). This is not only explained by 'shop patriotism' but also by the fact that shops tend to be technically specialised and Soviet/Russian occupational definitions are very narrow so that skills would not nec-

---

[22]   Kathryn Hendley's research in 1990 in six enterprises found an inter-shop transfer rate of between one and two per cent. Inter-shop transfers did not enter into the calculations of either management or workers (Hendley, 1993).

essarily be transferable from one shop to another. This limitation on transfer, together with the limitations on promotion inherent in a small unit, is one reason why people breached the ideal of stability by changing enterprise in order to advance their career, particularly in smaller enterprises.

The very narrow band of occupational classification and the fairly flat hierarchy within the shop also meant that occupational and intra-shop mobility were very limited, with only two principal transitions: one from apprenticeship to the appropriate skill grade and the second after at least ten years' service when the worker could expect promotion to the ranks of the *kadrovyi* workers. In general, therefore, the Soviet worker would spend his or her early career moving around looking for an enterprise and/or a shop within which to settle down and then stay there, only expecting promotion and additional benefits after about ten years. There was accordingly very little flexibility either within or between shops.

In the Soviet period internal mobility was primarily on the initiative of the worker, but the scope for this kind of voluntary mobility has been considerably narrowed by the pressures of staff reduction and insecurity which reduce the scope for transfer and induce people to hold on to their jobs. The frequent reorganisations of enterprises in the attempt to develop new management structures have involved a higher level of 'paper' transfers, where a unit is transferred nominally from one subdivision to another. Much more important, the attempt to hold on to core workers and to cope with sharp fluctuations in production in response to sales and financial instability has involved a substantial increase in administratively sponsored transfers as redundant workers are redeployed and as workers are transferred from one section or shop to another to meet the changing demands of production. The reduction in the scope for voluntary internal mobility and the increased scale of administrative internal mobility is one of the factors which has induced an increase in external mobility, as those who want to advance their careers or who are dissatisfied with the changes imposed on them are more likely to leave.

Our conclusion is that internal mobility is an important instrument in management's attempt to preserve the nucleus of the labour collective. But this does not mean that it is a negative phenomenon from the point of view of the development of the labour market, since it substantially increases flexibility in the use of the labour force and so increases the ability of the enterprise to withstand the shock of transition. In this sense internal and external flexibility are alternatives.

EXTERNAL MOBILITY

Our research into external labour mobility was based on internal enterprise statistics, the examination of personnel records and interviews with personnel department staff and with workers. Here we only sum up the results of this research.

In the past the external labour market was dominated by the movement of low-skilled and undisciplined 'peripheral' workers, while the core of skilled *kadrovyi* workers was stable. A new model of mobility has emerged in the transitional situation which co-exists with the old model rather than displacing it. This new form of mobility is connected with the differentiation of the position of enterprises and the deepening differentiation of pay.

For successful enterprises external mobility is typically moderate. In some of them there is a tendency to close the internal labour market even more, reflected in the weakening of connections between the internal and external labour markets and increase in internal mobility. Recruitment is restricted, but this does not mean that it has ceased. On the contrary, the level of recruitment of new workers in particular periods may exceed the level of separations.

The closure of the labour market is displayed in the fact that vacancies for well-paid jobs for skilled workers are not advertised but are filled, as a rule, through informal channels of internal or external hiring on the basis of personal connections. Low-paid work which can easily be combined with another primary job is also taken by existing employees. Low-paid jobs involving simple physical work are normally filled through the internal redistribution of workers nearing or beyond pension age. Access to the enterprise from the external market is open only for unskilled, low-paid, physically heavy work in bad working conditions. These jobs are filled from the external labour market by young people, unemployed sent by the employment service and former employees. Although recruitment may officially be closed, successful enterprises are still keen to take on high-skilled workers from less successful enterprises. Thus the successful enterprises improve the composition of their labour force at the expense of those enterprises which find themselves in a crisis situation.

Unsuccessful enterprises are more open to the external market, which is reflected in a higher level of turnover and a significantly larger number of quits than hires. Voluntary quits, provoked by low pay and delayed payment of wages, prevail over compulsory lay-offs. The first to leave are the workers with all-round skills who are the most mobile, then workers with basic trades and engineering-technical employees join the outflow. As a result those who remain are those close to or beyond pension age and those with narrow skills applicable only in this branch of production. Such depressed enterprises also become the last resort for people who for one reason or another have fallen out of networks of social connections.

The employment service and the formal external labour market plays an insignificant role in placing the unemployed in vacant jobs because nobody wants to recruit 'from the street'.

New private enterprises are marked by high levels of mobility of staff. The main inflow is from state enterprises, with managers and specialists settling into permanent jobs, while the peripheral workers and specialists are very mobile and often take the jobs as secondary employment.

WOMEN IN THE LABOUR MARKET

Our research did not set out to address the problem of gender as a factor in the labour market in Russia because this is an extremely complex issue which needs to be the focus of specific research. In the early stages of transition women predominated among the registered unemployed and women continue to constitute the majority of those formally made redundant, although this is primarily because women are much more reluctant to leave their jobs voluntarily than are men. Discrimination against women is overt and unimpeded by the law, with many employers expressing a preference for men. Men have rapidly moved into occupations such as those in economics and finance, which were once overwhelmingly low-status female professions but which have acquired new prestige and importance with the growth of the market economy. In the two regions which were the focus of our research, unemployment continues to have a predominantly female face, although in Russia as a whole women

constitute about half of both the registered and the survey unemployed, and this is not because women have been pushed out of the
labour force, the participation rate for women having fallen less than
that for men. Despite the discrimination against women, the fact that
employment reductions have been achieved predominantly by natural
wastage has enabled women to hold on to their jobs, so that the proportion of women employed has actually increased in almost all
branches of industry, although women's greater reluctance to move
also means that, as can be seen in all our case-study enterprises,
women are increasingly concentrated in the low-wage/no-wage enterprises as the men leave for jobs with better prospects. Women are also
very active in the new service sector, in retail trade and in public catering. On the other hand, while there is certainly very considerable
overt discrimination against women, women are more highly educated
than men and they are concentrated in those professions and those
branches of the economy which ought in theory to be the growth areas
in the transition to the market economy, the service sector and light
and consumer industries, while men have been concentrated in heavy
industry and the military-industrial complex which should bear the
brunt of restructuring. Many employers consider women to be more
diligent, responsible, reliable and docile employees than men so that,
even while expressing a preference for men, in practice they go on
hiring women. It is not, therefore, obviously the case that women have
been the principal victims of the crisis, although it certainly is the case
that men have sought to shift the burden on to women and that to some
extent they have succeeded.

The issue of gender is complex because the high degree of gender
differentiation and segregation in employment makes it very difficult
to disentangle the independent influence of gender as a factor determining employment patterns. Our own research, and in particular our
work-history interviews, indicate that although men everywhere have
a wider range of choices and opportunities than do women, gender
cannot be isolated as a single independent variable which has a uniform impact. On the one hand, gender is not nearly as important as
education, training and experience in determining the careers of
women specialists and managers, until they hit the ceiling (and in Russia it is not made of glass) which largely excludes them from top
management in all spheres. On the other hand, among workers we
observe very different kinds of career patterns and labour market

behaviour among men and women, with husband, home and children serving as determinant constraints in the employment choices faced by women. While men can choose their occupation and workplace and can make themselves a career, women have to bow to other demands and to change jobs in response to those external pressures. One consequence is that women are far less likely than men to build up the continuity of service and the depth of experience in one trade or profession which makes them desirable employees even as they grow older, so that women's employment prospects decline much more rapidly with age than do those of men, and women live in much greater fear of unemployment than do men.

POLICY CONCLUSION

Our research was not intended to provide quantitative assessments of the extent of employment restructuring or of the use of different channels of labour mobility, but to identify their qualitative characteristics. The starting point of our research was the belief that we have to consider people not as atomised individuals but within the social networks and social institutions within which they live their lives. We believe that this is true of any society, but it is particularly true in Russia where the Soviet sense of the labour collective, shorn of its Communist rhetoric, remains a very meaningful reality in people's lives, the basis of Russian society to the extent that other social and cultural institutions which can provide people with a point of reference are still very undeveloped. Thus the problem of employment is not that of re-deploying people as individuals so much as that of transforming and re-directing their labour collectives.

The process of structural adjustment has been able to take place without mass open unemployment because of the very substantial flows of labour directly from unsuccessful to more successful enterprises, with wage differentials being the primary incentive to labour mobility and social networks the primary means by which people move jobs. These same networks provide access to secondary and casual employment, to participation in subsistence production, and to social and material support which are essential for survival in Russian conditions and are the basis of continued social stability in the face of a catastrophic economic decline. Large warge differentials have been maintained by the willingness of a substantial part of the labour force to continue to work in (or at least to remain registered at) enterprises which pay extremely low wages with very considerable delays. One reason for this is certainly the very low level of unemployment benefit, although even unemployment benefit is more generous than unpaid leave or unpaid wages. A further reason is the importance of retaining registration as an employee in an enterprise in order to maintain one's work record to qualify for pension and other benefits, which is particularly significant for employees working in conditions officially designated as 'harmful' who enjoy enhanced pension rights. Registration also provides access to a further, although diminishing, range of social and welfare benefits. In the past many people worked in a particular enterprise to qualify for free or subsidised housing, but this benefit has largely gone as enterprise housing construction has been cut back, and what there is is usually sold at prices beyond the reach of the ordinary worker, even on privileged terms. The third, and very important reason, why people continue to work for insignificant pay, often at considerable risk to their health, is the persistence of the Soviet work ethic, particularly among older people. This ethic involves not only a commitment to labour and a horror of 'parasitism', but also an attachment to the 'labour collective' which many workers refer to as their 'second home', and many even regard as their first home.

The importance of social networks in the recruitment of labour, particularly by the more successful enterprises, means that those who remain in the less successful enterprises are not necessarily those who lack the technical qualifications necessary for work elsewhere, but in many cases are those who are unable or unwilling to move because their social networks do not extend far beyond their native enterprise, so that they lack the confidence to move and the connections necessary to find a good job elsewhere. This is one reason why labour mobility occurs through more or less dense institutionalised informal networks which connect neighbouring or kindred enterprises with one another (and these networks can cover large geographical distances: in cases, for example, when an enterprise was founded on the basis of a transfer of staff from a parent enterprise elsewhere, or of the recruitment or drafting of labour from a particular geographical location, channels of mobility are established which can persist for decades).

Labour market flexibility has thus far protected Russians from the scourge of mass unemployment, but this is its one redeeming feature.

The high level of labour mobility should not conceal from view the fact that around half the working population have not changed their jobs but hold on, despite low pay, unpaid wages, short-time and compulsory leave, retaining their old values and clinging to the hope of a more stable future: the flexibility of wages is an indication of people's (often ambivalent) attachment to their workplaces. This is also manifested in the fact that many who have changed jobs have done so with great reluctance under pressure of economic circumstances and would return to their old workplaces if they could.

While labour market flexibility has provided the opportunity for some to improve their position and for others to avoid the worst effects of the crisis, the fact remains that the crisis of the Russian economy continues to deepen, the number of available jobs is in steady decline and wage levels remain extremely low. Labour market flexibility within the state and former state sector, which still employs at least three-quarters of the working population, has involved a reshuffling of a diminishing pool of jobs (among largely the same group of people, since new entrants to the labour market are reluctant to take such jobs on anything but a temporary basis), with a growing pool of young and older workers pushed to the margins of the labour market and who survive on the basis of subsistence production, casual labour and support from friends and relatives given that there is little or no investment in the creation of new jobs in the productive sphere, in either state or private enterprises.

This reshuffling of jobs has led to a polarisation of enterprises which presents acute problems for future industrial and employment policy. The degraded enterprises, usually burdened with debt, endowed with outdated and deteriorating equipment and producing products which are uncompetitive in a market environment, are the prime candidates for bankruptcy. While they may have some realisable assets, if these have not already been sold off as the price of survival of the enterprise and/or for the enrichment of managers and their associates, these assets usually amount to no more than their premises and real estate, stocks of raw materials, and the scrap value of their equipment. As a result of the process of employment restructuring the labour force which remains in these degraded enterprises comprises those who have not left despite everything, who are predominantly the older and less flexible manual workers, managerial and professional staff who have little prospect of finding work elsewhere, and those who have come to the enterprise because this is the only place that will give them a job – the notorious 'misfits, drunkards and absentees' who are the bane of every manager's life. In both cases these are not necessarily people with limited technical skills and capacities so much as people engaged in limited or restricted social networks.

With the younger, more enterprising and flexible managers and workers having left over the past five years, these enterprises have little prospect of adapting to new conditions, even if the opportunity was presented to them. However, the bankruptcy of these degraded enterprises will throw a mass of people on to the labour market who are ill-equipped, or completely unequipped, to work in competitive conditions, and who have been working in these enterprises only because they have been unable or unwilling to take a job anywhere else. The problem posed by a large-scale transition from disguised to open unemployment, which would be the consequence of widespread bankruptcies, would be compounded by the fact that these people have continued to work in the given enterprise either because it has been the focus and primary source of meaning of their entire lives, or because they are deracinated. To throw these people out of work would literally be to throw them on to the streets, in the sense that it would tear them from the primary social networks through which they have been integrated into society. These are the people for whom the social and psychological consequences of unemployment would be the most acute. These enterprises, which still account for a significant proportion of the labour force, are a time bomb waiting to explode.

The relatively prosperous enterprises have in many cases been able to use their situation to 'upgrade' the labour force, getting rid of unskilled and ill-disciplined workers, forcing out pensioners and those close to retirement age, bringing in younger skilled workers and professionals. However, in most of the prosperous enterprises this is the limit of their restructuring. Their prosperity derives, in general, not from advanced production methods or sophisticated products but from a favourable legacy from the past, whether it be large stocks of valuable equipment and raw materials, prime real estate, a strong political position or monopoly powers. Because most enterprises were privatised effectively without charge many have been able to make large profits, despite a sometimes catastrophic decline in production, by trading on this legacy. Their prosperity is expressed not in a high rate of return on capital invested, but in a positive cash flow. And even if a progressive management has upgraded the labour force, introduced new management systems and improved current operations, prosperity cannot last without new investment which, in the continued absence of any significant long-term private investment in industry, can only come from government or on the basis of government guarantees.

Labour market flexibility has provided considerable benefits to the new private sector, but this too cannot be considered to be entirely positive for society as a whole. On the one hand, new private enterprises have used their resources to attract the most highly-skilled and innovative managers and specialists from state enterprises, depriving the latter of the people who could otherwise have played a leading role in their transformation, while employing such people in jobs which frequently make little use of their skills. On the other hand, new private enterprises use state enterprises as a reserve from which they can draw temporary and casual employees on terms which provide no job security, make no social insurance or tax payments and generally imply de-skilling and the intensification of labour.

Russia has a highly trained and highly educated population whose skills in the past have been underused and misdirected and are now being discarded. Market-led restructuring is not leading to the emergence of dynamic new sectors and enterprises to displace the overdeveloped heavy industry and military-industrial complex, primarily for familiar Keynesian reasons that continuous economic decline does not provide a favourable environment for long-term investment, while low and falling incomes do not provide a basis for the long overdue expansion of consumer services. The extractive and raw material processing industries should face profitable prospects in world markets, but their geographical location alone means that they cannot be insulated from the domestic economy, while their eventual technical restructuring and re-equipment will lead not to the creation but the substantial reduction of jobs. While few new opportunities are being created, the sustained industrial recession implies not only the deterioration of outdated enterprises but also the progressive destruction of the technological base of the economy with the decline in military spending and in the face of foreign competition. The problem is not a problem of the labour market and employment policy, but of an industrial strategy which can not only exploit Russia's natural resources, but also use its abundant human resources.

The failure of Russia to conform to the neo-liberal model of a state sector in terminal decline, with a new private sector ready to rise from the ashes of destruction, is a failure of the model, not a failure of Russia. The new private sector has a role to play in the sphere of trade and services, although it should be brought within the tax and legal systems, but if Russia is to recover it can be and will be only through the restructuring of the state and former state enterprises and organisations which remain the dominant employers and which will remain the dominant employers for a very long time.

A growing number of commentators have reached the conclusion 'that unemployment is not a necessary element of the restructuring process, and indeed may not even be helpful' (Jackman, n.d., p. 3), indeed it can be argued that the most successful cases of structural adjustment have been precisely those which have not been associated with large-scale unemployment.[23] The policy conclusion is then that 'the objective of policy should be (or should have been) to try to balance the growth of jobs in the private sector with the decline in employment in the state sector, by encouraging the former and restraining the latter' (Jackman and Pauna, 1996, p. 10). This implies a fundamental change in policy, from a policy focused on unemployment, which has encouraged low wages and the emergence of a casualised and de-skilled shadow economy by attempting to accelerate the decline of the state and former state sector in the hope that a vibrant private sector will emerge, to a policy which seeks to encourage the state sector to maintain employment, while at the same time inducing it to restructure.

The policy dilemma is that the former goal is attained by keeping wages at a level which undermines the incentives required to induce the latter. If wages are forced up, for example by raising the statutory minimum wage to something approaching the subsistence minimum, then enterprises will be forced to lay workers off in their millions. It is at this point that our research would endorse the conclusions of Layard and Richter rather than those of Standing, in showing the importance of continued employment both to the individual and society in main-

---

[23]   Toye, 1995. Horton, Kanbur et al., 1994. This is not a new conclusion: 'A number of countries have shown that substantial structural adjustment can be achieved without any period of high unemployment, strongly suggesting that high unemployment is neither necessary for structural adjustment nor preferable to other forms of market adjustment. These countries that have achieved structural adjustment without mass unemployment or severe cuts in wages should surely be emulated. Or could they?' (Standing, 1991, pp. 40–41).

taining individuals' integration into the work-based social networks which provide the focus of their social existence as well as the channels through which they find secondary employment and new jobs. Russia certainly needs effective collective bargaining institutions, a minimum wage which at least approaches the physiological subsistence minimum, and the enforcement of elementary labour rights. It may even be that Russia needs to restore the former legislation that imposed a responsibility on the employer to train and place a redundant employee. But Russia needs such policies as part of a wider programme that can enable enterprises to provide employment at wages which at least meet the minimum subsistence needs of the employees and in working conditions which do not destroy their health.

Although the support and counselling of the unemployed always has a role to play, employment policy should focus on job preservation rather than on attempting to place those who have become unemployed. To date such job preservation measures have amounted to the subsidisation of enterprises on primarily political grounds at the direction of local authorities, with no reference to the long-term sustainability of the jobs being preserved. There is always going to be a tendency for political factors to play a role in the direction of employment-supporting measures, even an open democratic society, but this is not grounds for rejecting such measures outright: the implementation of any policy is politically constrained, the important issue is that policy formation should take place in an open, democratic and consistent manner.[24] Employment-supporting measures should therefore be provided within a framework of systematic policy evaluation in which the productiveness and sustainability of the jobs preserved is taken into account.

In the short run, there are very large reserves of human and productive resources locked up in state and former state enterprises which could be put to good use within programmes of social and public works, many of these resources being idle because of the over-hasty dismemberment of the housing, social and welfare apparatuses of the enterprise, where municipal authorities lack the material, managerial and financial resources to fill the gap. A programme of maintenance,

---

[24] The various packages to support self-employment and the formation of small and medium enterprises which are favoured by foreign consultants are even more distorted in their implementation, but by personal interest and corruption rather than political constraint. Such packages need to be evaluated much more critically than they have been hitherto to determine to what extent they contribute to net job creation.

repair and construction of housing, communal facilities and roads, of environmental restitution and improvement could be undertaken at minimal real cost by mobilising these currently idle resources, the provision of such works being the condition of employment subsidy. Such a programme could avoid the stigma that was attached to such public and social work in the past by ensuring that those employed on such programmes are paid directly for their contribution, rather than being directed to such work by an enterprise which receives state or municipal subsidies which it is free to use at its discretion. Corruption and the misdirection of funds could be minimised by organising such a programme on the basis of tendering for work, with employment subsidies being provided in the form of payments conditional on the necessary work being done.

This kind of employment-creation programme can only be a stopgap measure, and its scope is bound to be limited when government finances are in such a sorry condition. In the longer term no employment policy can be successful unless it is combined with an industrial policy which encourages investment-led restructuring. Despite the poverty of the mass of its population, Russia is an extremely wealthy country, with the most favourable endowment of natural resources of any of the world's major economies, with a highly educated, skilled and motivated labour force and with a very favourable balance of international trade, currently being dissipated in huge outflows of capital. It does not require the invisible hand of the market, which threatens all enterprises with closure, or the bureaucratic apparatus of Gosplan, which keeps them all open, to identify the branches of the economy and even the individual enterprises which have the potential to be the long-term winners and losers in Russia. The problem is not one of the absence of the knowledge and/or of the means required to implement a state-directed industrial programme, but it is a political problem which goes far beyond the issue of labour market and employment policy. This is a problem which cannot be avoided by bypassing the state in favour of the market: it is a problem which has to be confronted within the democratic political process.

3 Reviving Dead Souls: Russian Unemployment and Enterprise Restructuring

Guy Standing
Employment Department
International Labour Organisation

INTRODUCTION

This paper is about several aspects of the Russian labour market, and is divided into two parts. The context is one of extraordinary economic, social and political upheaval, in which a large number of economists have been claiming that the statistics on economic and labour market trends have been misleadingly pessimistic. Ever since 1991, there has been a stream of books, articles, reports and speeches claiming that economic and social decline has been mild, and that an economic upturn is either about to occur or has already started. One could give numerous examples, and it is perhaps unfair to select a few. However, one recalls Anders Aslund writing in 1994 that the economic decline had 'bottomed out' and Richard Layard claiming in 1995 that 'the main news coming out of Russia is good news'. In 1995–96, the IMF, World Bank and EBRD all forecast that there would be positive economic growth in 1996. The boom may be coming, but Keynes's famous aphorism seems peculiarly apt.

One has to be careful about interpreting any Russian statistics. But one should try to be objective. There has been a tendency among some observers, particularly those supporting the 'reformers', to question – or dismiss with scorn – statistics showing continuing and huge decline in the economy, while accepting without question those statistics that suggest positive developments. Of course, there *are* positive developments. Yet there is enough evidence to assert with regrettable confidence that on average living standards have plummeted, that the economic slump has been prolonged and is continuing and that the consequences for poverty and economic inequality have been very severe.

This paper does not try to support that contextual conclusion.[1] Rather it draws on research done since 1990 on aspects of the labour market to examine the vexed issue of surplus labour and unemployment, linked to a book summarising the initial research (Standing, 1996b). Anybody working on the Russian labour market should be blessed with a sense of humility, for its features defy any easy generalisation, it has been changing so extensively and rapidly and it is not blessed with an abundance of reliable information. The work reported in the book, here and in other articles, draws mainly from a multiple-round survey of industrial enterprises, which the writer initially designed in 1990 and which has been refined or extended with colleagues in Moscow over the past six years. From the outset, we have recognised the limitations of the Russian Labour Flexibility Survey (RLFS); others with more resources and skills could have surely done a better job. Yet in its defence it has been conducted by a small team with very limited resources, and it remains the largest and most detailed survey of labour market developments between 1990 and 1996, covering hundreds of factories employing hundreds of thousands of workers.

In addition, although not discussed in this paper, the analysis draws on two small surveys of jobseekers and a small survey of women workers, as well as from secondary data collected from employment service offices, government agencies, trade unions and enterprises.

INTERPRETING RUSSIAN UNEMPLOYMENT

Until recently at least, there have been three interpretations of Russian unemployment. The first is that it has not happened. According to this view – which was at its most popular in 1992–94, although it still has adherents – enterprises have not shed labour because they are still operating under a 'soft budget constraint', so that employment has not been cut to anything like the extent of the decline in production.

---

[1]   Evidence to do so is presented in the 1996 Human Development Report for the Russian Federation, which the writer co-ordinated (UNDP, 1997).

Supporters of this view have typically pointed to the low rate of registered unemployment, which hovered around 1.5% during 1993–94, after rising in 1992 in the wake of the 1991 Employment Law, which effectively permitted unemployment for the first time since the 1920s.

A second interpretation is that there has been little rise in unemployment because the labour market has been 'buoyant' and highly 'flexible', such that workers have 'preferred' to take real wage cuts in return for preserving their employment. This view has been based, explicitly or implicitly, on the view that workers have been holding on to their jobs.

Both these interpretations have relied on official statistics in claiming that there is very little unemployment and both have led to the policy conclusion that there is no need to worry about unemployment. Intriguingly, economists who have questioned almost all other Russian statistics have found the unemployment data sufficiently reliable to be cited as demonstrating that unemployment is low and not a major worry.

A third interpretation is that unemployment actually has been high, and in part has been concealed in the most cruel way possible. This is the view taken in the book, and in earlier papers. There are various elements in this interpretation.

First, there has been a very substantial cut in total employment since the 1980s. It is possible that informal economic activities have been spreading, and there have been many who have claimed that this has been the case. Probably that is correct, although it should not be forgotten that in the Soviet era secondary employment was common. However, there is reason and some evidence to suggest that much of the 'informal' activity (much of it 'black') is 'secondary employment' taken by those already counted as employed.[2]

The official statistics on employment are such that head-scratching should be a reasonable reaction to any review of them. However, on one point we should be reasonably sure: *since the late 1980s, there has been a steady and very substantial cut in employment*. We are contemplating a decline that has been continuous for a decade. Yet we are

---

[2]   Besides the old 'secondary' jobs of those employed in 'primary' jobs, there are three main types of informal economic activities. One is productive and/or financially rewarding and legal, which requires capital, savings and contacts. Another is criminal in some way, and the third is marginal survival activity, as in selling the odd Coca-Cola bottle or old piece of clothing in Nevsky Prospect, to update the famous image of Joan Robinson describing disguised unemployment in the British Depression.

supposed to believe that there is and has been very low unemployment.

Table 3.1 shows that, according to traditional Goskomstat sources, between 1990 and 1995 total employment fell by 8.2 million, while the size of the working age population and the overall labour force participation rate rose slightly. Somewhat different figures come from the national Labour Force Survey, which has been evolving in difficult circumstances since the end of 1992. According to the latest available (with difficulty) figures from this source, in March 1996, total employment was 61.8 million. The difference in employment between the two sources is very substantial. One factor might be a legacy of the Soviet practice of reporting on the employment forms sent to Goskomstat the number of 'employment places'. This used to be done as a means of inflating the wage fund allocated to the enterprise, and its persistence into the 1990s was encouraged by the misguided 'tax-based incomes policy', i.e., the excess wage tax. One recognises that this is a speculative interpretation, and the difference may have other explanations. What is beyond doubt is that according to both sources the level of employment has declined very substantially in the 1990s, and was doing so from the outset of the 'reforms'.

Table 3.1:   *Population and Employment, Russian Federation, 1990–95 (in millions or %)*

Years	1990	1991	1992	1993	1994	1995
Total population	148.2	148.3	148.3	148.0	148.0	147.9
Working age population	–	83.9	83.7	83.8	84.1	84.7
• Labour force participation rate (%)	–	56.6	56.8	56.6	56.9	57.2
Employment	75.3	73.8	72.1	70.9	68.5	67.1
• Employed as % of working age pop.	–	–	85.5	84.2	81.3	79.2
Employed in industry	22.8	22.4	21.3	18.6	18.6	17.2
• Share of employed in industry (%)	30.3	30.4	29.6	27.2	27.2	25.6

Source: Rossiski Statisticheski Ezhegodnik, 1995, p.9.; *Sotsial'no-ekonomicheskoe polozhenie Rossii*, 1995, 12, pp. 237–38, 276. Note the inconsistency between the participation rate and employment total. The employed include those over the ages of retirement.

According to labour force survey data, between October 1993 and March 1996 the size of the working age population (ostensibly, 15–72) grew by 3.21 million (i.e., by 3%). The level of employment fell by 4.56 million (-6.9%), recognised unemployment rose by 2.52 million (63.8% – scarcely a modest rise), and the labour force participation rate fell by a substantial 3.8%. The measured unemployment rate rose by 3.9 percentage points, to 9.5%. However, these figures imply some disappearing souls. Had the labour force participation rate of 1993 held for 1996, then the size of the labour force should have been 4.18 million larger than the measured size. Although one should not add all those to the unemployed, if they were regarded as 'discouraged' or 'passive' unemployed, the unemployment rate would have been 14.7%. If the labour force participation rate fell by 3.8 percentage points over two-and-a-half recessionary years in the United Kingdom, for example, most economists would be eager to claim that this was concealing the true growth of unemployment. Given the poverty of those on the margin of the Russian labour market, and the lack of social protection, those claiming that Russian unemployment has remained low should ponder on the statistical treatment of the four million people. The point is strengthened by the fact that the male participation rate declined much more, by 4.7 percentage points.

Second, the cut in employment has been very much greater than the rise in registered unemployment. Everybody agrees on that now, yet for several years adherents of the first two views cited the registered unemployment rate as evidence that there was minimal unemployment and that employment was not falling. There have been numerous reasons for non-registration, which are summarised elsewhere (Standing, 1996b, Chapter Two). Modifications to the administration of benefits have made it more likely that those who do manage to register receive them. However, their level is extremely low and the average benefit has comprised about 10% of the income needed for survival.

As significantly, the number of employment offices and the number of staff in them have lagged well below what would be required for the rising number of unemployed. Travelling long distances, at rising cost and inconvenience, to stand in long queues for hours often in adverse climatic conditions, in the dim hope of successfully registering and receiving a very low unemployment benefit scarcely amounts to a way of inducing people to register as unemployed.

The registered unemployment rate has risen modestly, and was still below 3.5% in 1996 (Figure 3.1). This compares with an unemployment rate of 9.5% estimated from the Labour Force Survey for July 1996, which is itself deflated by several factors to be discussed.[3] It is also interesting that, according to the LFS, while the employment figure has been declining and the unemployment rate rising, the overall labour force participation rate has been falling from a low level, particularly for men.[4] In October 1995, the male participation rate (age 15–72) was 70.9%; in March 1996, it was 69.7%. According to the 1993 LFS, the male participation rate was 75.6% in December 1993. Given that the population structure has shifted marginally towards those age groups with typically relatively high participation rates and that participation in post-secondary educational institutions has been dropping, this *suggests* a growth in 'discouragement' unemployment.

Figure 3.1:   *Registered Unemployment, 1993–95, Russian Federation (per cent of labour force)*

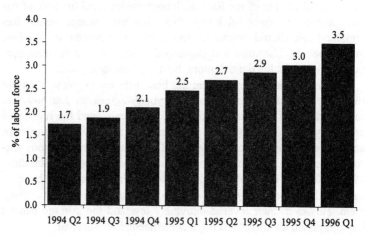

Source: Goskomstat, RF, Moscow.

This leads to the *third* factor in the under-recording of unemploy-

---

3   Actually, the difference between registered and measured unemployment was even greater in earlier years. In December 1993, the LFS estimate was *five* times the registered rate.

4   Contrary to many claims, the female unemployment rate has been lower than the male. In March 1996, the male rate was 9.8%, the female 9.2%. Reasons for this are discussed in Standing, 1996b, Chapter 9. Women have had a much higher propensity to register as unemployed.

ment and the deflation of the unemployment rate, which is the statistical and administrative treatment of *older workers*. The Goskomstat figures on employment and the Labour Force Survey estimates give employment for the age category 15 to 72. However, a woman becoming unemployed at age 54 is not usually counted as unemployed but as in retirement (officially from age 55, although any woman going to an employment exchange at age 54 has been put into early retirement), while a man aged 59 or above becoming unemployed is also counted as in retirement. In both cases, they are excluded from the count of unemployment, *even if they are looking for paid employment and needing it to compensate for a meagre pension.*[5] However, anybody in those older age groups who has an *attachment* to a job is counted as employed. The result is that the statistics inflate real employment and deflate real unemployment.

A *fourth* element in the under-recording of unemployment – and in the over-recording of employment – is that a substantial number of workers have been *laid off*. We will consider the character of this below. It has been widely reported, and has been extensive for several years. However, it is notable that those claiming that employment has scarcely declined and unemployment scarcely risen have made no adjustment for this development. The treatment of lay-offs in international labour statistics has long been a source of controversy. Probability of recall to employment should be one factor in classifying the laid-off person as employed or unemployed. In the Russian case, there are grounds for believing that many of those laid off have an extremely low probability of recall, in which case one could reasonably argue that they should be called unemployed.

In most countries, the statistical treatment of lay-offs would not make much difference to the unemployment rate. In Russia, it certainly does. At present, the statistics doubly deflate the unemployment rate by not counting them as unemployed and by counting them as employed. The problem is compounded by the fact that there have been considerable financial incentives to induce firms to put workers on lay-off rather than make them formally unemployed and there is no real restraint to making lay-offs.

---

5   It should be borne in mind that a substantial number of people under the age of 60 are classifiable as 'retired' in that they qualify for some special 'pension'. But many of those have been receiving 'pensions' that are well below what would be required for survival. Should a person receiving the equivalent of $10 a month who is seeking and available for employment be excluded from the count of unemployment ?

A *fifth* factor, which raises a difficulty with respect to the second interpretation of unemployment in particular, is that *labour turnover* has always been high and has remained high. If there were considerable churning in the labour market, it would signify that employers are not holding on to workers in any rigid manner and suggests that they could easily reduce employment simply by not recruiting to replace those who leave jobs. This issue will be discussed further in a later section.

A *sixth* element in concealing the extent of unemployment is the most significant. It is scarcely hyperbole to claim that the rise has been held down by the real disappearance of workers – in premature death. Since the late 1980s, average life expectancy at birth has declined by over five years. For males, it declined from about 65 in 1987 to 58 in 1995. With male life expectancy falling relatively to female, the gender differential has become the largest in the world. Mortality rates rose fastest for young and middle-aged men, and actually fell slightly for infants. While declining public healthcare has played a part in the rising mortality, it seems that economic insecurity and stress have been the main factors.

Morbidity has also been significant in reducing the numbers counted at the margin of the labour force. The number of registered alcoholics has risen by a small amount, and the number of registered drug addicts has risen by a substantial relative amount. The number of working-age people who died from alcohol-related causes more than tripled between 1990 and 1995. In the same period, the number of murders more than doubled and the number of suicides rose by 1.6 times. The number of registered disabled rose by 1.4 times.

All these trends have helped remove people from the margins of the labour force. For instance, in the 1980s there was a very high number of people with disabilities in employment, whether in regular enterprises, sheltered workshops or in special institutions. The employment of people with disabilities was decimated in the early 1990s, and yet very few turned up in employment service statistics of registered unemployment, because they were not counted as unemployed.

The growth in *suicides* is extraordinary. Suicide has been increasingly concentrated among young and middle-aged men, although the number of suicides by women has also risen sharply. Although empirical studies are required, suicides and deaths among working-age people seem disproportionately concentrated among the jobless.

Table 3.2: *Mortality from Murder and Suicide, Russian Federation, 1990–95*

| | Thousand | | Per 100,000 | |
Whole population	Murder	Suicide	Murder	Suicide
1990	21.1	39.2	14.3	28.4
1991	22.6	39.4	15.2	28.5
1992	33.9	48.1	22.8	31.0
1993	45.1	56.1	30.6	38.1
1994	47.8	61.9	32.6	42.1
1995	45.3	81.0	30.6	41.3
Males				
1990	16.0	30.4	23.2	43.9
1991	17.3	30.9	24.9	44.5
1992	26.1	37.0	37.6	53.2
1993	34.5	46.0	49.5	68.2
1994	38.6	51.5	52.8	74.1
1995	34.5	50.3	–	–
Females				
1990	5.1	8.8	8.5	11.1
1991	5.3	8.5	8.7	10.7
1992	7.8	9.1	9.8	11.6
1993	10.6	10.1	13.5	12.9
1994	11.3	10.4	14.4	13.3
1995	10.8	10.7	–	–

Table 3.3: *Women's Share of Occupational Categories, 1995–96 (%)*

	1995	1996
Managerial	43.3	41.5
Specialist Employees	72.9	72.5
General Service Employees	82.2	81.2
Supervisory Workers	33.4	36.3
Technicians	62.4	64.4
Qualified Manual Workers	46.6	45.1
Unqualified Manual Workers	52.2	55.7

Source: RLFS6, n = 497.

Anecdotally, in mid-1996 during the second round of our survey of jobseekers, the director of one city's employment service reported that in the three months before the survey date 23 registered unemployed had committed suicide.

Although one cannot be certain that rising mortality has contributed to the underestimation of unemployment, one can be reasonably confident that this has been the case, and that this has been a major factor, both indirectly and directly. Any analysis which neglects this tragic dimension is woefully incomplete.

Table 3.4:   Distribution of Convictions, Russian Federation, 1990–95 (%)

	1990	1991	1992	1993	1994	1995
Convicted (total)	100	100	100	100	100	100
Age distribution of those convicted (%):						
14–17 years	14.7	14.3	13.6	13.2	12.0	11.3
18–24 years	22.9	22.9	23.6	25.0	25.0	24.0
25–29 years	20.3	18.8	17.7	16.1	15.9	15.6
30–49 years	38.4	38.2	39.5	40.1	41.6	43.2
50 years and over	5.7	5.8	5.4	5.8	5.6	5.9
Percentage of total:						
– women	8.5	8.6	7.2	8.6	9.2	11.7
– students	39.6	37.9	38.8	37.1	35.2	33.5
– unemployed	20.3	21.3	26.1	34.9	40.6	44.1

A *seventh* means by which unemployment has been concealed is through *crime*, both because low incomes and joblessness have been powerful recruiting agents for the 'dangerous classes' and because many men and women, having drifted into crime in desperation or in response to market signals, have proved less than adept at avoiding being caught and convicted. While total crime and the number of people convicted of crime more than doubled in the 1990s, the percentage of all those convicted who were without employment also more than doubled between 1990 and 1995, when they accounted for over 44% of the total (Table 3.4). By no means all those convicted would have been taken out of the labour force, but the number in prison has been growing along with the rise in crimes, so one can be confident that this has been taking place.

In sum, unemployment and the economically more significant phenomenon of 'dis-employment' have been greater than casual inspection of official unemployment statistics would suggest. Nobody should put any credence in the figure on registered unemployment as an indicator of either the level or underlying trend; it is essentially an administrative artefact. And one should be wary of putting much reliance on official statistics on employment, beyond believing that they understate the extent of the decline.

Perhaps as interesting is an assessment of the dynamics of employment, and for this we need data from firms, to which we now turn. One underlying thesis is that it is inadequate to analyse the Russian labour market through the prism of conventional labour force statistics designed from the 1930s onwards to coincide with 'Keynesian' policy requirements. Simple distinctions of employment, unemployment and labour force participation are scarcely adequate for the institutional and behavioural complexities of the type of labour market that has been emerging in Russia.

THE RUSSIAN LABOUR FLEXIBILITY SURVEY

In 1990, we organised an international conference in Moscow on the 'Soviet labour market', and it was apparent that there were remarkably few data with which to assess the labour market developments and considerable restructuring that seemed to be taking place. This led to the launch of the Russian Labour Flexibility Survey in October 1991, which collected detailed labour and economic data from 501 industrial enterprises (establishments) in three oblasts (Moscow City, Moscow Region and Leningrad), covering over half a million workers.[6] Since then, five further rounds of the RLFS have been carried out, and the recent work has been conducted in collaboration with the Centre for Labour Market Studies in Moscow, which deserves most of any credit for the fieldwork.

The RLFS has evolved to cover eight oblasts in RLFS6, and the data from this will be used in the following consideration of the character of labour surplus in industrial enterprises of the type that still

---

[6]   As the fieldwork for RLFS1 ended in January 1992, the survey had the odd character of beginning in one country and ending in another, and beginning in one city and ending in another.

dominate the Russian labour market. The characteristics of the RLFS are summarised in Table 3.5.

Table 3.5:   *Characteristics of the Russian Labour Flexibility Survey, 1991–96*

Round	Date	Reference period	Number of establishments*	Panel**	Workforce covered	Regions
RLFS1	1991–92	1990–91	501 (501)	—	529,250	Moscow City, Moscow Reg., St Petersburg
RLFS2	June, 1992	1990–92	200 (191)	109	166,895	Moscow City, Moscow Reg., St Petersburg
RLFS3	July, 1993	1991–93	350 (340)	240	308,969	Moscow City, Moscow Reg., St Petersburg, Nizhnii Novg.
RLFS4	July, 1994	1992–94	400 (384)	340	303,333	Moscow City, Moscow Reg., St Petersburg, Nizhnii Novg., Ivanovo
RLFS5	July, 1995	1993–95	500 (482)	380	322,240	Moscow City, Moscow Reg., St Petersburg, Nizhnii Novg., Ivanovo, Tatarstan, Vladimir
RLFS6	July, 1996	1994–96	500 (497)	338	289,287	Moscow City, Moscow Reg., St Petersburg, Nizhnii Novg., Ivanovo, Tatarstan, Vladimir, Chelyabinsk

Note: *   Figures in parentheses indicate number of establishments completed; the first figure is the initial sample for the round. The unit of observation is the establishment, not the enterprise, which may consist of more than one establishment.

       **   Number of establishments covered in the round that were in at least one other round.

Although the samples have been drawn randomly from the registers kept by Goskomstat, we cannot claim that they are fully representative, either within the selected oblasts or the Russian Federation overall. However, the samples were drawn as objectively as possible, and include all the main industrial sectors, size of manufacturing establishment and property form. The RLFS is more detailed and larger than any other comparable survey, and it is one of the few sources of detailed information on the evolution of the industrial labour market in this extraordinary period of economic, social and labour market restructuring.[7]

In the RLFS, information has been collected, *inter alia*, on the restructuring of firms and on the changing level and structure of employment. No attempt is made here to describe the range of data. An attempt is made merely to measure the extent of labour surplus and to examine how managements have responded to the slump in production and output.

Let us begin with a few stylised facts about the 'stress indicators' and 'restructuring indicators' of manufacturing firms in what are the main areas of industrial production in Russia. For brevity, this will be done in telegraphic form, recognising that to do the individual elements justice would require separate sections.

THE ENTERPRISE STRESS INDICATORS

The continuing economic slump in Russia has been reflected in all rounds of the RLFS. Once again, in 1996 the main economic problem identified by managers was inability to sell their output. Throughout the RLFS, a majority of firms have experienced declining sales in real terms. In RLFS6, although it reflected a modest improvement over 1995, nearly a third of factories (30.4%) reported that the volume of production had fallen over the past year, and nearly a third (31.2%) reported that they had expanded.

Perhaps also indicative of stress is that the percentage of output that was *bartered* rose from an average of about 13% of output in mid-

---

[7]   In the mid-1990s, several excellent sociological surveys have been launched, and in many respects these should be an advance on the RLFS, particularly in providing case studies. In the course of successive rounds of the RLFS, individual case studies based on repeat visits to selected factories have helped in refining the questionnaires.

1995 to nearly 16% in mid-1996 (Figure 3.2), with the share in Moscow rising from 9% to nearly 10%.

Figure 3.2: Output Bartered, by Industry, 1995–96, All Regions (%)

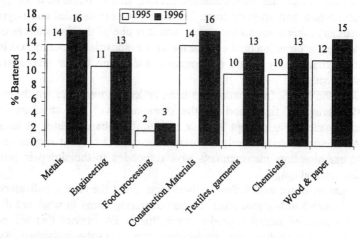

Source: RLFS6, n = 497

Figure 3.3:   Establishments Believing Bankruptcy Likely within a Year, by Region, 1996 (%)

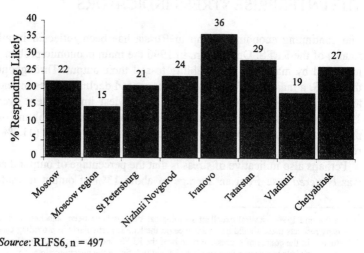

Source: RLFS6, n = 497

A feature of the economic upheavals in eastern Europe has been the emergence of substantial inter-enterprise indebtedness. In the RLFS6, the vast majority of firms had *debts*, with only 12.3% having no debts. Just over a third said that they owed more than was owed to them, 26.4% reported that their debts balanced the money owed to them, and 28% said they were owed more than their debts.

As perhaps the most significant indicator of stress, 23.5% of all firms thought it likely that they would go *bankrupt* over the next 12 months (Figure 3.3), 32.6% thought it was possible, 0.2% did not know, and 43.7% thought it unlikely. This was substantially more than in 1995. Of those fearing bankruptcy, 34.9% thought the main reason was difficulty in paying debts, 21.7% thought the main reason was the rising price of raw materials and 19.9% thought it was high taxes.

Throughout the 1990s underutilisation of productive apparatus has been a reflection of the economic slump, although many have suggested that much of the equipment is obsolescent. *Capacity utilisation* levels fell from a mean average of 60.9% in mid-1994, to 54.8% in mid-1995 and to 52.6% in mid-1996. These are extraordinarily low levels by international standards. The decline continued a decline that had been observed in 1991 and throughout the six rounds of the RLFS.

Figure 3.4: *Capacity Utilisation Rates, 1994–96, by Industry, All Regions (%)*

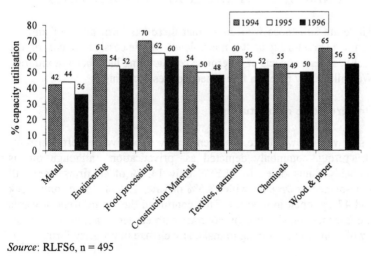

Source: RLFS6, n = 495

In sum, in terms of production, capacity, commercialisation, indebtedness and fears of bankruptcy, Russian industry in 1996 seemed to be as deep in economic crisis as in previous years. Whatever caveat one chooses, this is scarcely good news.

Figure 3.5:   Capacity Utilisation Rates, 1994–96, by Region (%)

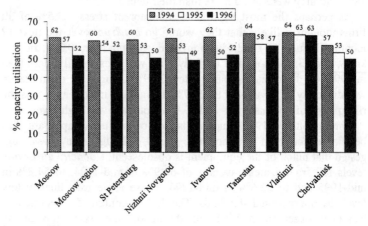

Source: RLFS6, n = 495

ENTERPRISE RESTRUCTURING INDICATORS

There are still those who doubt that there has been much of an economic restructuring at the micro-level. In successive rounds of the RLFS, several aspects of enterprise restructuring have been monitored. We will merely mention five aspects of restructuring.

Property form restructuring

As is well known, there has been a very pervasive property-form restructuring, commonly depicted as 'privatisation', although this is probably a misnomer. In RLFS6, only 14.7% of all firms were still state-owned or *arenda*, with 18.5% private, 19.6% closed joint stock and 47.1% open joint stock. This continued the strong trend towards the last-mentioned form. By contrast with earlier years, only a minority of firms were planning to make any change in property form.

Governance restructuring

Perhaps more significant than property form is the issue of management restructuring, or 'corporate governance restructuring'. This goes well beyond the issue of ownership.[8] Essentially, this is about accountability, entailing aspects of the range of responsibilities and controls exercised by management and workers, and the pressures influencing decision making within the firm. Long a neglected aspect of restructuring, it may prove more significant than the notion of 'privatisation'.

Rather than discussing the elements taken into account, as done elsewhere, we may merely note the classification of governance types. For assessing whether enterprise governance makes a difference to the firm's employment and labour market practices, account is taken of property form, character of share-owning and form of management appointment. As such, besides *foreign* firms, governance is classified into four main types:

– *State governance* is where the establishment is state-owned and where the senior manager was appointed by a line Ministry or local authority, or state-owned and where nominally the work collective and the Ministry or local authority are responsible for managerial appointment.

– *Private governance* is where there is private ownership or a joint-stock arrangement in which employees do not own more than 50% of the shares and where the manager is appointed by an enterprise board or at a shareholders' meeting, as long as employees do not possess more than 50% of the shares.

– *Employee governance* is where the property form is joint-stock, where the workers and management together own more than 50% of the shares, without the workers owning 50% or more, and where the top manager is appointed by an enterprise board, a shareholder meeting or some other non-state mechanism.[9]

– *Worker governance* is where the property form is joint-stock, where the workers own 50% or more of the shares and where

---

[8] For an extended discussion, see Standing, 1995b.

[9] Also included were a few cases where the management was appointed by a line Ministry or a local authority but where the establishment was a joint stock company with majority employee ownership. Such cases arose from the timing of appointment and timing of property form change, and it is assumed that behaviourally managers would adapt to the *current* governance form.

management is appointed by the workers or a shareholders' meeting.

As of mid-1996, the distribution of governance types in the Russian industrial establishments covered by RLFS6 showed that 20.5% were state governance structures, 23.9% were private governance, 30.6% were employee governance, 23.3% were worker governance structures, and 1.6% were foreign. This represented a shift from worker-governance to private from the pattern observed in 1995. There was not a neat mapping of property forms and corporate governance forms. Thus, for instance, 29.1% of open joint stock firms were effectively private in terms of governance, while 24.1% of worker-governance firms were private in terms of property form. The sample of 338 firms that were in both RLFS5 and RLFS6 suggested that there was considerable turbulence in governance forms, with some erosion in the share of worker controlled firms. We believe that ultimately corporate governance will prove to be a more appropriate way of classifying enterprises than ownership and that labour market behaviour will evolve differentially as the corporate governance forms evolve.

Intriguingly, capacity utilisation levels were lowest on average in the purely private firms and in the state-controlled factories, and were highest in the foreign-owned firms.

Sales restructuring

One aspect of restructuring is the redirection of output, notably towards *exports*. With the opening up of the Russian economy, it has been anticipated that the share of total output that would be exported would rise. There has been some rise observed over the six rounds of the RLFS. However, in 1996 the firms in RLFS6 exported merely 3.6% of total output to the CIS area and 4.6% outside that area, compared with 3.8% and 5.0% respectively in 1995.

Technological restructuring

A substantial number of firms had made some form of *technological change* in the past year – 48% had partly renewed their products, 10% had completely changed their products, 39.5% had introduced new technology in production and 32.1% had reorganised their work organisation in some way.

Institutional voice restructuring

The changing role of institutions in a labour market is indicative of its character. There have been changes in the role of employers and workers in this respect. Whereas employers and managers were traditionally linked to the Party and the central bureaucracy, their relations have become more selective and personalistic. They certainly have not organised into strong cohesive organisations. In the RLFS6, fewer than 10% of all managements belonged to any employer association, with about two-thirds of those being in the Association of Industrialists and Entrepreneurs. Only 4.4% of private firms were in any employer organisation.

More significantly is what has happened to the extent of *unionisation*. The data show that there has continued to be a strong decline in unionisation, so that whereas in 1992 about 95% of industrial workers covered in RLFS2 were in unions, by 1996 the figure for RLFS6 was about 62%. Although direct comparison would be misleading, since new areas had been added, this represents a rapid rate of decline of worker voice, which may or may not have been balanced by the growth of worker shareholding and what we describe as corporate governance.

In sum, there has been substantial restructuring in terms of ownership and corporate governance, and some technological dynamism and sales re-orientation. It would be surprising if there had been little change in employment and labour utilisation.

ESTIMATING LABOUR SURPLUS IN RUSSIAN FACTORIES

Russian industry in the Soviet era suffered from chronic excess employment, often described by analytical critics as 'labour hoarding', for reasons that have been extensively documented. With the slump in production in the 1990s, one could have anticipated that the extent of surplus labour would have increased, since in any economy employment cuts tend to follow falling output. Before considering how firms responded to the continuing crisis, an attempt is made to measure the extent of surplus labour in mid-1996, which may be compared with comparable estimates made in the RLFS for the previous few years.[10]

The concept of surplus labour is notoriously complex, and labour economists are unlikely to agree on any ideal measure. One should make a basic distinction between short-term (or 'static' or 'visible') and long-term (or 'dynamic') surplus labour, where the latter implies that time is allowed to adjust to higher levels of efficiency and better work organisation. There has been considerable scope for improving methods of production so as to raise labour productivity. But there is also evidence of surplus labour with existing arrangements. In some sense, this could be described as 'suppressed unemployment'. A difficulty arises in trying to combine forms of surplus into a composite index. In successive rounds of the RLFS, attempts have been made to do this. Recognising that no index is ideal, the elements have been presented separately. The first and last forms cannot be integrated into any index, while combining others raises questions about possible double-counting. Nevertheless, measurement of the various indicators should provide a sense of the extent of the problem and help identify trends and the changing incidence of labour surplus.

Figure 3.6:   *Percentage of Establishments that Could Produce Same Output with Fewer Workers, by Industry, 1996, All Regions*

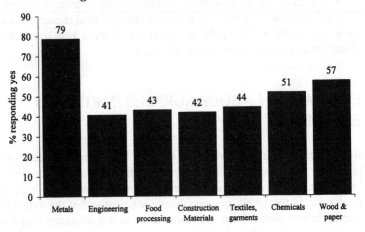

Source: RLFS6, n = 494

---

[10]   Since the RLFS started, several good surveys have attempted to assess labour surplus. Apologies are made to those who have conducted them for not reviewing them here.

Managerially-perceived labour surplus

In all rounds of the RLFS, managements have been asked if they could produce the same level of output with fewer workers. This is clearly a subjective measure, and one can have legitimate reservations about the exact interpretation one should place on the results.[11] In 1996, no less than 45.3% of managements said they could produce the same level with fewer workers (Figure 3.6), with 55.5% of firms with more than 500 workers stating that they could do so. The overall figure was ten percentage points more than in 1995.

Figure 3.7: *Percentage Fewer Workers to Produce Same Output, by Industry, 1996, All Regions*

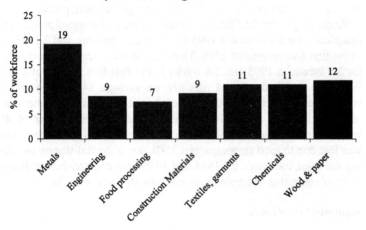

Source: RLFS6, n = 490

Overall, including firms that believed they needed all their workers, the average cut they believed they could make was 9.6%. This too was a higher figure than in 1995.[12] For those stating that they could produce the same level of output with fewer workers, the mean estimated

---

[11] The workers in question are production workers, and we believe that was understood as such. Of course, Russian factories have also had groups of workers on social functions, etc., and cutting those would presumably have little effect on output.

[12] Incidentally, in both years scarcely any firms reported any problem of labour shortage, in contrast with the situation in the first round of the RLFS.

cut they could make was 21.5%, ranging from 24.7% among textiles and garments manufacturers to 17.5% among food processing plants (Figure 3.7). Measured in this way, labour surplus was high in all property forms, was highest in large-scale factories, and was highest in Ivanovo (27.8%), lowest in Nizhniii Novgorod (16.9%).

Production stoppages

A more direct form of surplus labour arises from production stoppages. Because visits to factories and anecdotal reports suggested that this was becoming pervasive, since 1994 the RLFS has included questions about spells of complete stoppage and partial stoppage of production due to economic reasons, with the estimated percentage of the workforce directly involved if the stoppage had been partial.

According to the RLFS6, on average, firms had *stopped production completely* for 2.9 weeks in 1995 for economic reasons, and 2.3 weeks in the first five months of 1996. They had *partially stopped production* for 3.6 weeks in 1995 and 2.6 weeks in the first five months of 1996. For those that had stopped partially, on average 34.1% of workers were directly affected. All these figures were substantially higher than recorded in 1993 and 1994. If one assumed a working year of 48 weeks, then the figures imply that in 1996 about 7.7% of working time was lost due to total stoppages and 1.9% due to partial stoppages. Using the same measures for 1994 and 1995, one can conclude that this form of concealed unemployment was substantially worse in 1996.

Administrative leave

However, the main form of surplus labour identified in the mid-1990s has been long-term *administrative leave*, or lay-off. This arises from the common practice of management (or the union on their behalf) telling workers that they do not need to go to work, often for months. In the Russian context, the suggestion is that it is in practice a euphemism for 'unemployment', in that for many workers there is very little prospect of any return to employment with the enterprise. There have been financial incentives to induce firms to retain workers on such 'leave' for months, initially because it enabled them to deflate the average wage to reduce or avoid the excess wage tax and consistently because they do not have to pay 'severance pay' in such circumstances. Under the law, enterprises have had to pay any worker they redundant two or three months of his or her previous average wage. Thus, putting workers on unpaid leave (or with a minimal amount of conscience money) has been a way of avoiding costs, so that they do not have to face potential retribution while they wait for workers to 'quit voluntarily'. This is one reason for treating figures on reasons for departure from employment as dubious.

Figure 3.8: Working Time Lost due to Production Partially or Wholly Stopped, by Region, 1995–96 (whole year for 1995, first 5 months for 1996) (% of total employment)

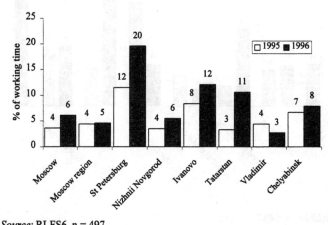

Source: RLFS6, n = 497

Unpaid leave was a major form of labour surplus in 1995. According to managements, in May 1995 it varied from 8.7% in textiles and garments to a low of 1.5% in food processing. In December 1995, it varied from 19.3% in engineering and 8.9% in textiles and garments to a low of 4.5% in food processing. But in May 1996, there was very little unpaid leave, with a maximum of 5.4% in wood products and none in food processing, and textiles and garments. What happened was that there was a shift from totally unpaid to *partially paid* leave, with the typical payment being the minimum wage, which was about 10% of the so-called 'physiological subsistence minimum' income. As a consequence, if one were to measure only totally unpaid leave, one would have a very poor estimate of the extent of administrative leave. There were a few workers put on fully-paid administrative leave, but this was very rare.

The total number of workers on administrative leave as a percentage of the labour force in May 1996 was high, as indicated in Figures 3. 9 and 3.10. And the total was considerably higher than in December 1995 or May 1995.

Figure 3.9:   *Workers on 'Administrative Leave', by Industry, 1995–96, All Regions (% of total on unpaid, partially paid and fully paid leave)*

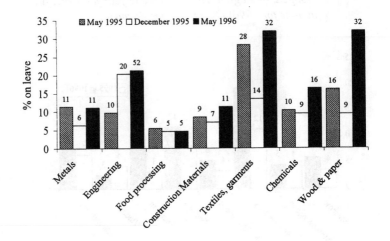

Source: RLFS6, n = 497

Short-time working

Another form of surplus consists of short-time working, which may overlap with non-working as a result of production stoppages. In the RLFS, an attempt to measure this form of surplus has been through asking managements what share of the workforce has been working shorter working weeks than the norm (contractual) for economic reasons. Clearly, this is an empirically tricky notion, although conceptually it makes sense.

Over successive rounds of the RLFS, it seems that working fewer days per week has been more common than working fewer hours per working day. Figure 3.11 suggests that in most sectors short-time working was greater in 1996 than in 1995.

Figure 3.10: Workers on 'Administrative Leave', by Property Form, 1995–96, All Regions (%)

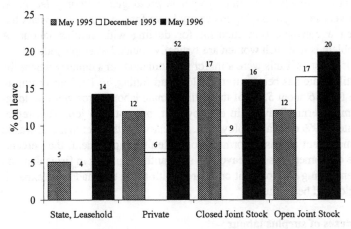

Source: **RLFS6**, n = 496

Figure 3.11: Workers on Short Time for Economic Reasons, by Industry, 1995–96, All Regions (%)

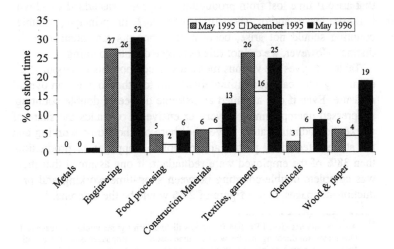

Source: **RLFS6**, n = 497

Maternity leave

Another feature of Russian industry that can be interpreted in part as a form of suppressed unemployment is *prolonged maternity leave*. At the very least, prolonging maternity leave for more than two years has been a convenient mechanism for dealing with surplus labour. A problem is that such women are typically counted as employed.

It is not as if this were a minor phenomenon. In a country where the fertility rate has been extremely low and falling, in 1996 according to the RLFS6 about 5.7% of the entire female labour force were on long-term maternity leave – in employment, but not in a job. This represented 2.9% of total employment. Indicative of the fact that this was to some extent at least a form of concealed unemployment, the percentage of women on such leave was substantially greater in firms that had been cutting employment compared with those that had been expanding or had been static.

Indexes of surplus labour

Identifying the various components of labour surplus leads to consideration of an overall measure of surplus. If we added administrative leave to short-time working would there be double-counting? Would that arise if time lost from production stoppages was added to administrative leave and/or short-time working? In principle, double-counting should not arise, because the concepts are intended to be distinct. However, we cannot rule out some double-counting.

Table 3.6 gives the various measures or components of labour slack separately. One cannot legitimately add all together to make an overall measure. Even if one assumed an extreme degree of double-counting, suppressed unemployment is very extensive. If one adds the share of workers on administrative leave, the share on short-time working and the share affected by partial and complete stoppages of production, then 38% of the employed were redundant. If one assumed that there was complete double-counting between short-time working and production stoppages, then a figure of 28% would be the outcome.[13]

---

[13]   Anyone who has visited Russian factories will find such figures intuitively reasonable. One reason for doubting that the working time lost due to stoppages is double-counting for short-time working *per se* is that firms that had one phenomenon tended to have little or none of the other. The averages in Table 3.4 are for all firms, including those which professed not to have any labour surplus.

Table 3.6a: Indicators of Surplus Labour, or 'Concealed Unemployment', in Russian Industry, 1996

Indicator	%*
1. Could produce same with fewer workers	
– % employment cut possible, if yes	21.5
– % employment cut possible, all firms	9.6
2. Labour unused due to full production stoppages	7.7
3. Labour unused due to partial production stoppages	1.9
4. Unpaid administrative leave	4.1
5. Partially paid administrative leave	14.1
6. Fully paid administrative leave	0.5
7. Short-time, working fewer days or hours per day	9.7
8. Maternity Leave	
– % of women	5.7
– % of all workforce	2.9
9. Unpaid employment	?

Note: * In full-time equivalent numbers for all firms, including those with zero. All figures are weighted estimates for size of firm, as of May 1996.

Table 3.6b: Indicators of Surplus Labour in Russian Industry, 1995–96

Indicator	1995*	1996*
1. Could produce same output with fewer workers		
– % employment cut possible, if yes	21.4	20.9
– % employment cut possible, all firms	8.2	9.7
2. Labour unused due to full production stoppages	4.7	8.3
3. Labour unused due to partial production stoppages	2.2	2.0
4. Unpaid administrative leave	4.1	4.3
5. Partially paid administrative leave	6.0	14.0
6. Fully paid administrative leave	0.0	0.5
7. Short-time, working fewer days or hours per day	8.7	11.1
8. Maternity Leave		
– % of women	5.3	5.5
– % of all workforce	3.2	3.0
9. Unpaid employment	?	?

Note: * In full-time equivalent numbers for all firms, including those with zero. All figures are weighted estimates for size of firm.

Source: Merged RLFS5–6, n = 338

Even if there were some double-counting, one still has to make allowance for the 2.9% on prolonged maternity leave and a phenomenon highlighted on the last row of Table 3.6. In terms of labour statistics, one has no easy way of taking account of workers expected and required to turn up for work who have not been paid or who have little or no prospect of being paid.

Bearing in mind these caveats, it might be of interest to estimate a composite index of labour surplus, which could be defined as follows:

> *Labour surplus =*
>   *% of time lost from total stoppages +*
>   *% of time lost in partial stoppages in full-time equivalent*
>   *terms +*
>   *% of workforce on administrative leave +*
>   *% of workforce on short-time in full-time equivalent terms.*

To estimate this requires a few assumptions. The data on production stoppages due to economic factors (not strikes) are based on a reference period of the past five months, whereas the other measures have the past month as the reference period. In effect, we assume that the percentage of time lost over the longer period can be regarded as applying to any particular month. Another assumption, just discussed, is that time lost from partial stoppages is separate from that lost to administrative leave or short-time working. It could be that such stoppages are the immediate cause of some administrative leave. Accordingly, we can estimate labour surplus as a composite index that excludes partial stoppages, as well as the index that includes them. Another assumption is that those on short-time are deemed to have worked half-time. Finally, to estimate the percentage of time lost from production stoppages, we again assume a working year of 48 weeks, which in itself tends to result in an understatement of lost time because the average work year is probably shorter than that.

If we include labour input lost due to partial and complete stoppages of production, the percentage of workers on administrative leave, and the full-time equivalent measure of labour input lost due to enforced short-time working, *in 1996 suppressed unemployment in Russian industry was over a third of the workforce.* In effect, over one in every three workers could be released from employment, and in many cases have been released short of being made openly unemployed. This excludes any unreal maternity leave and unpaid employment.

One should be wary about concluding that this experimental measure is appropriate. The double-counting mentioned earlier is likely to some extent, and the subjective estimate derived from the perceptions of possible employment cuts by managements, summarised in the first two rows of Table 3.6, gives a lower level of labour surplus. However, with respect to those, of course, many firms may have already regarded workers put on long-term administrative leave as effectively removed from employment.

Among the simple correlations that deserve further analysis are the following teasers:

- Labour surplus was highest in firms in which managers had been appointed for two years or less. Is pressing accountability to stakeholders conducive to retention of surplus workers?
- Labour surplus was relatively high in purely private Russian-owned firms, and lowest in foreign-owned firms.
- The share of the workforce on lay-off was highest in the purely private form of governance.

Whatever the level of labour surplus, one should recognise that a very large proportion of those counted as employed are not really in employment or earning wages that give them an adequate income. A puzzle is why the suppressed unemployment has persisted? Has it been because firms have held on to their workforces because there are cost incentives and because there are no pressures on them to pay such workers wages?

EMPLOYMENT CHANGES IN 1994–96

It would be a mistake to think firms have not been cutting employment. On average, in 1996 factories had cut employment by 6.3% over the past year, with firms in textiles and garments having cut their workforces by 12.6% on average (Figure 3.12).[14] It fell in all regions covered by the survey, by most in the well-known area of economic

---

[14] Note that the percentage employment changes for each group are from aggregated figures for all establishments in that category. Note that 5.7% of firms had detached a unit from the establishment in the past year, and the number doing so was higher among those that had cut employment. The average number of workers in detached units was 175.

decline, Ivanovo, but also by a considerable amount in the area of Nizhnii Novgorod, long regarded as the leading area of liberal economic reform and the recipient of a vast amount of foreign financial and technical assistance. Employment fell for all four property forms of establishment, and for all forms of corporate governance (Figure 3.13). Only foreign-owned firms showed a small net expansion.

Figure 3.12: Employment Change, by Industry, 1995–96 (%)

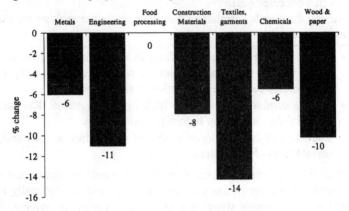

Source: RLFS6, n = 497

Figure 3.13: Employment Change, by Region, 1995–96 (%)

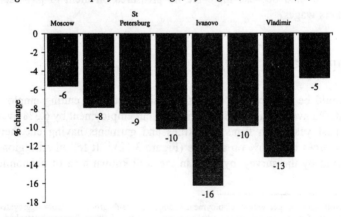

Source: RLFS6, n = 497

Figure 3.14: Employment Change, by Corporate Governance,
1995–96 (%)

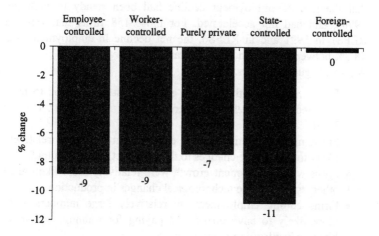

Source: RLFS6, n = 497

Figure 3.15: Women on Maternity Leave, by Employment Change,
1996, All Regions (%)

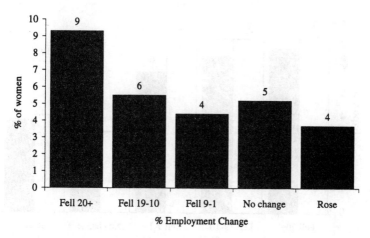

Source: RLFS6, n = 474

For firms included in both RLFS5 and RLFS6, total employment declined on average by 19.4% over 1994–96. It is important to note that the rate of employment decline had been steady through the 1990s, and had not accelerated. For those 158 firms that were in RLFS1 in 1991 and in RLFS6, the net decline in employment was 48.3% between 1990 and 1996, a total of 46,862 workers.

A few intriguing pointers:

- Firms making relatively large employment cuts tended to have exported a relatively high percentage of their output (Figure 3.16).
- Firms making relatively large employment cuts were relatively likely to have made changes to their product range of output.
- Firms with employment growth were relatively more likely than others to have made technological changes in production.
- Firms cutting employment by relatively large numbers were more likely to have abandoned paying for training, and more likely to be planning to cut training.

Figure 3.16: Sales Exported, by Employment Change, 1995–96, All Regions (%)

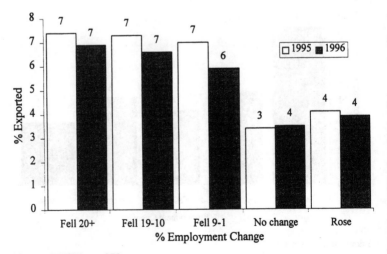

Source: RLFS6, n = 378

THE PUZZLE OF LABOUR TURNOVER: AN ASIDE

Implicit in the view that unemployment has remained low is that workers have held on to their jobs, 'preferring' wage cuts. A difficulty with this view is that *labour turnover* has been high. If so, then firms could cut employment primarily by not replacing workers who have left, whether 'voluntarily' (*sic*) or otherwise. If one continued to believe that unemployment was low and that there was little decline in employment, then what would need to be explained is why firms have recruited in the context of a prolonged and sharp decline in industrial production.[15] In any case, the *vacancy* rate in 1996 was less than 2%.

Issues of labour turnover are considered in terms of the *internal labour market* in the book to which this paper is linked, and will be considered in more detail in a forthcoming conference being organised by the Centre for Labour Market Studies in Moscow. However, according to the RLFS6, labour turnover has remained high (Figure 3.17), although it has declined in the 1990s.

Figure 3.17: Labour Turnover, by Region, 1995–96

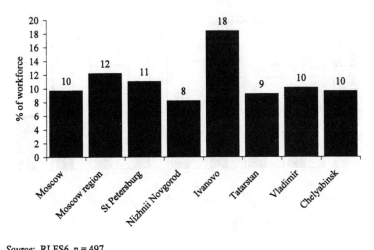

Source: RLFS6, n = 497

---

[15] Simon Clarke and his colleagues, in valuable on-going research, have focused on the recruitment process.

WAGE FLEXIBILITY

In another paper and in the book, it is argued that wages in Russian industry have been extremely downwardly flexible, and that this has limited the pressure on firms to raise labour productivity and to cut employment more drastically. The evidence will not be re-examined here. The most important points are that a sizeable minority of workers have been effectively at work without pay and that the non-payment of workers has grown and has been a means by which real unemployment has been 'suppressed'.

As shown in Figure 3.18, in all regions covered by the RLFS6 over a third of firms had been delaying the payment of wages regularly over the past year and many others had wage arrears a few times. On average, those firms that had not paid wages on time had not paid 66.7% of the total wage bill. The percentage was higher in those that had been cutting employment.

Figure 3.18: Establishments Having Wage Arrears, by Region, 1996 (%)

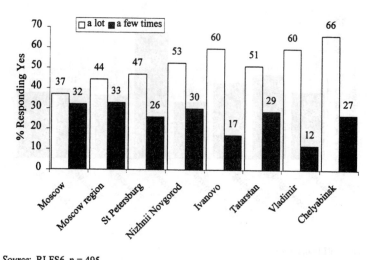

Source: RLFS6, n = 495

Besides the non-payment of wages through wage arrears and simple non-payment, a phenomenon observed in RLFS4 and RLFS5 is that firms have tended to put a significant number of workers on a minimal salary, typically well below the contractual wage rate and in some cases below the minimal subsistence level of income. That firms have been able to do this with impunity is indicative of 'wage flexibility', but the cost in terms of impoverishment at work is severe.

Figure 3.19: Establishments Having Wage Arrears, by Employment Change, 1996, All Regions (%)

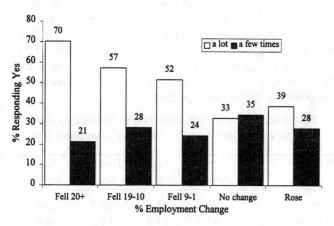

Source: RLFS6, n = 490

THE WITHERING OF ENTERPRISE WELFARE ?

An aspect of the wage system in Russia has been that wages have been a relatively small proportion of total remuneration. As in earlier rounds of the RLFS, in 1996 most firms formally provided entitlements to a wide range of benefits, showing that many industrial establishments were 'social enterprises' (Table 3.7). Access to such benefits was surely a factor in workers remaining with a firm even though put on unpaid leave or in precarious, low-wage positions.

Two trends observed through the RLFS since 1990 are that, first, after rising in the early 1990s, probably in response to misguided tax and regulatory policy, the provision of enterprise welfare has been declining. This is illustrated by Table 3.7, showing that for many forms of benefit, the number of firms providing workers with them declined in 1995–96. If we take the firms that were in both RLFS5 and RLFS6, the decline was quite widespread.

The second trend is the polarisation of the provision of benefits, or the contribution of the changing incidence towards the substantial increase in socio-economic inequality. Not only have certain groups of workers within firms been facing a much greater erosion of benefits than others, but there has been a growing divergence between those firms that pay relatively high wages and provide a wide range of benefits and those that pay low wages and provide relatively few benefits. Thus, as Table 3.8 shows, dividing firms into those paying less than 80% of the average wage, those paying between 80% and 120% of the average, and those paying more than 120% of the average wage, the probability of workers receiving a specific benefit entitlement has tended to be greater in the higher-wage firms.

Table 3.7a: Entitlement to Enterprise Benefits and Services, by Worker Category, All Regions, mid-1996 (% of firms providing)

1996	Admin. workers	Regular workers	Part-time workers	Temp. workers
Paid vacation	98.5	98.8	38.2	20.4
Additional vacation	47.3	61.2	16.0	4.4
Rest houses	37.0	36.4	15.4	5.9
Sickness benefit	92.3	92.0	36.1	31.1
Paid health services	41.7	41.7	16.9	7.4
Subsidised rent	8.3	9.2	4.4	0.0
Subsidies for kindergartens	29.0	29.3	10.4	5.0
Bonuses	62.1	63.9	25.7	17.2
Profit sharing	50.0	49.1	19.5	6.2
Loans	71.3	71.3	29.6	11.2
Retiring assistance	65.1	65.4	24.3	4.4
Supplementary pension	8.6	8.6	3.3	0.6
Possibility for training	60.4	65.1	24.0	9.2
Subsidy for canteen or benefit for meal	34.6	35.5	16.3	15.1
Subsidised consumer goods	5.6	4.7	3.8	3.6
Transport subsidies	24.0	22.2	8.3	3.0
Unpaid shares	13.6	13.6	7.1	0.6

*Table 3.7b: Entitlement to Enterprise Benefits and Services, by Worker
Category, All Regions, Change 1995–96 (change in % of
firms providing)*

Change 1995–96	Admin. workers	Regular workers	Part-time workers	Temp. workers
Paid vacation	-0.9	-0.6	2.4	2.1
Additional vacation	5.9	-1.2	3.6	1.7
Rest houses	-1.8	-2.7	1.2	2.6
Sickness benefit	0.0	-0.3	3.3	3.6
Paid health services	-5.6	-5.6	1.5	-1.2
Subsidised rent	-7.1	-7.4	1.4	-1.2
Subsidies for kindergartens	-4.7	-5.6	-2.0	2.3
Bonuses	1.7	3.2	2.9	1.5
Profit sharing	-3.8	-4.5	2.6	-3.0
Loans	-8.9	-8.9	1.1	0.8
Retiring assistance	-3.2	-3.2	-0.8	0.3
Supplementary pension	-0.3	-0.9	0.3	0.0
Possibility for training	6.0	5.9	6.0	2.1
Subsidy for canteen or benefit for meal	-9.8	-10.4	-1.5	-1.8
Subsidised consumer goods	0.0	-0.9	2.0	1.8
Transport subsidies	-2.9	-4.1	0.6	-1.7
Unpaid shares	-7.1	-7.1	1.8	-1.2

CONCLUDING POINTS

The rise of unemployment and the fall in employment in Russia have
been much greater than has been asserted by many commentators.
Beyond that, enterprises have retained substantial labour surplus, primarily because there are few inducements for them to shed redundant
workers and some incentives to keep their names on the books, just as
Gogol's landlords kept inflated lists of peasants. Workers, for their
part, have a disincentive to quit, in that they would be likely to lose
severance pay and the slim chance of recall to employment, and in that
they might have continued access to the social amenities, subsidised
stores and so on. However, it would be a misnomer to present all this
in terms of 'preferences' and 'flexibility'. It is a mess.

Several adverse economic and social consequences flow from the forms of dis-employment and their lack of transparency in conventional unemployment terms. Excessive wage flexibility means that there is an absence of one source of pressure on managements to raise labour productivity. If employers were genuinely obliged to honour employment and wage contracts, they would have been unable to retain on the books those they have not been paying and those they have been paying a minimal fraction of their contractual wage.

A second adverse consequence of the suppression and concealed character of 'unemployment' is that commentators, politicians, foreign technical advisers and the international community have been inclined to give very low priority to remedying unemployment. If there is very little unemployment, why worry about the low level of unemployment benefits or the inadequacy of the employment service?

Table 3.8: *Benefits Entitlements for Worker Categories, by Average Wages, mid-1996, All Regions*

Benefit	Administration			Regular workers			Part-time workers			Temporary workers		
Average wage	<80%	80<120	120%<	<80%	80<120	120%<	<80%	80<120	120%<	<80%	80<120	120%<
Paid vacation	97.1	98.7	100.0	97.6	98.7	100.0	36.6	35.9	39.0	15.6	18.3	23.5
Additional vacation	46.3	43.8	51.5	58.5	62.1	66.2	14.1	14.4	21.3	3.9	5.9	5.1
Rest houses	25.4	37.3	50.7	24.4	37.3	50.0	10.7	13.1	19.9	3.9	6.5	7.4
Sickness benefit	87.8	90.2	91.2	87.3	88.9	91.9	32.7	32.7	39.0	25.9	32.0	34.6
Paid health services	33.2	50.3	45.6	33.7	49.0	46.3	14.6	17.0	18.4	5.4	9.2	8.1
Subsidised rent	6.8	13.1	14.0	7.3	11.8	15.4	4.9	3.9	4.4	0.0	0.7	1.5
Subsidies for kindergartens	29.8	26.1	29.4	29.8	25.5	29.4	9.8	9.8	9.6	2.4	7.8	4.4
Bonuses	58.0	58.8	66.9	59.0	60.8	66.9	23.4	20.9	28.7	12.7	20.9	16.9
Profit sharing	42.4	45.8	55.9	42.4	43.8	52.9	16.1	15.0	21.3	5.4	7.8	6.6
Loans	67.3	69.3	74.3	67.8	70.6	72.8	25.9	23.5	32.4	7.8	13.7	14.0
Retiring assistance	59.5	66.0	70.6	59.5	66.0	70.6	20.0	21.6	27.2	2.4	8.5	5.9
Supplementary pension	7.3	4.6	11.8	7.3	4.6	11.8	2.9	1.3	5.9	0.0	0.7	2.2
Possibility for training	56.6	61.4	68.4	56.6	61.4	68.4	22.4	17.6	25.0	6.3	10.5	12.5
Subsidy for canteen/meal	28.8	33.3	39.0	28.8	33.3	39.0	12.7	14.4	18.4	11.7	12.4	17.6
Subsidised consumer goods	6.8	5.2	5.9	6.8	5.2	5.9	4.4	3.9	5.1	3.4	3.3	2.9
Transport subsidies	19.0	22.2	25.0	19.0	22.2	25.0	7.3	8.5	8.8	3.9	3.9	4.4
Unpaid shares	11.2	12.4	16.2	11.2	12.4	16.2	5.4	5.2	10.3	0.0	2.0	1.5

Source: RLFS6, n = 497

4 The Economic Development of Industrial Enterprises and the Dynamics and Structure of Employment

Pavel Smirnov
Senior Researcher, Centre for Labour Market Studies, Institute of Economics, Russian Academy of Sciences

ESTABLISHING AN INDICATOR OF THE ECONOMIC WELL-BEING OF INDUSTRIAL ENTERPRISES

During 1994–96 the Centre for Labour Market Studies carried out three surveys of industrial enterprises in Russian manufacturing industry. Over the course of the three surveys the number of surveyed enterprises varied between 384 and 500 and the regions surveyed were extended, but at the same time a 'nucleus' of 262 enterprises was retained which participated in the survey for three years in succession. Thus, data were at our disposal allowing us to estimate the size and dynamics of changes occurring at the same set of enterprises over a period of three years. We were most interested in investigating how employment at these enterprises changed and what structural shifts accompanied this process.

The surveyed enterprises are in five different regions of Russia, they cover all branches of manufacturing industry and the principal and most widespread forms of organisation (or patterns of ownership). At the same time, it seemed to us important to estimate the changes in employment at the enterprises not from the point of view of their branch or regional affiliation but from the point of view of the economic condition of the enterprises, the successes or problems of their economic development against the background of the catastrophic recession in Russia which has already lasted five years.

There is no doubt that the economic situation of the enterprises varies. Some have steadily reduced production and employment, others have overcome the consequences of recession, a third group has hardly been affected by it. The obvious question arises of whether it is possible to estimate the economic situation of the enterprise on the basis of a single indicator, for example, the change in the volume of sales, or the level of wages. It seems most unlikely that this will be possible since the characterisation of the 'economic well-being' of an enterprise is based on a combination of a definite set of parameters, which should satisfy the following requirements:

- They should include data on the position of the enterprise in relation to production ('capital') and the position of its employees ('labour').
- They should provide some kind of static characterisation of the economic situation of the enterprise at a particular point in time and be supplemented by dynamic characteristics so that one can evaluate its development over time.

A combination of such parameters would constitute the criterion for the comparison of enterprises according to the degree of their 'economic well-being' and the division of enterprises into different groups, depending on the significance of this criterion, could form the basis for the further analysis of their situation, in the first instance in relation to structural changes in employment.

At the first stage of the analysis we chose four parameters satisfying the criteria indicated above.

1. Current level of production of the enterprise as a percentage of its nominal capacity. This parameter defined the situation of the enterprise at the moment of survey.

2. Change of volume of production over the year previous to the survey (reduction, stabilisation, increase). This parameter defines the short-term dynamics of the enterprise.

3. Presence of production stoppages at the enterprise over the previous year and a half. This parameter characterises the rhythm of production and is also connected to the position of the enterprise's employees who, in the event of production stoppages, are sent on compulsory vacation or put on

short-time working, with a corresponding loss of income.

4. Average wages at the enterprise for May of the appropriate
    year (at the moment of survey) – the parameter which best
    characterises the current situation of the employees.

The method of factor analysis was then used to generate a single
criterion, which we have provisionally named the 'indicator of economic well-being' of the enterprises. This allows us to determine at
which enterprises things have turned out better than at others.

We found it most appropriate to divide the enterprises into three
groups according to the size of the indicator. Thus, relatively unsuccessful enterprises are found in the first group and relatively secure
enterprises in the third. From now on we shall call them 'bad',
'average' and 'good' enterprises for the sake of simplicity.

Table 4.1:   Changes of Category of Enterprises 1994–96 (%)

| | | 1996 | | | Number of |
		Bad	Average	Good	enterprises
	Bad	57.5	35.0	7.5	80
1994	Average	22.5	52.9	24.5	102
	Good	13.8	25.0	61.3	80

The parameters were calculated separately for each year. It is clear
that the unity of method did not exclude the possibility of redistribution of the enterprises between groups, while keeping the number of
enterprises in each group constant. The first results of such a distribution of the enterprises are presented in Tables 4.1 and 4.2 and in
Figures 4.1– 4.3.

From the data presented in Table 4.1 it can be seen that about 60%
of the enterprises have remained within the same group over the last
three years. However, this equally implies that about 100 industrial
enterprises have either worsened or improved their economic situation
in relation to others over the same period of time.

There is nothing unexpected in the distribution which emerges: the
degradation of light industry is reflected in its greater share of 'bad'
enterprises; in such a depressed region as Ivanovo over half the surveyed enterprises appeared among the outsiders.

At the same time it is necessary to pay attention to two interesting
features. First, the enterprises in the three groups are not significantly
different in the number employed. It seems probable that the industrial

flexibility characteristic of small enterprises is compensated to some extent by the 'economy of scale' enjoyed by the larger but less adaptable enterprises. Secondly, when we group enterprises according to their form of ownership, state and municipal enterprises on the whole look better than the mass of privatised enterprises, which are basically the open and closed joint-stock companies.

Figure 4.1: *Proportion of Enterprises of Various Types, by Region, 1994–96*

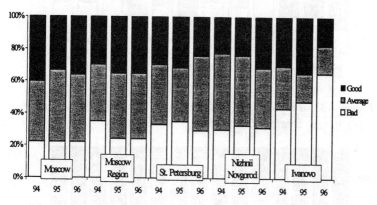

Table 4.2: *Proportion of Enterprises of Various Types, by Industrial Branch (1994–96, %)*

	Number of enterprises	1994			1995			1996		
		Bad	Average	Good	Bad	Average	Good	Bad	Average	Good
Metallurgy	10	60	30	10	30	50	20	20	50	30
Mechanical engineering	86	28	42	30	30	31	38	23	40	37
Chemicals	19	47	32	21	37	47	16	53	32	16
Wood manufacture	27	30	37	33	26	41	33	33	41	26
Building materials	21	48	43	9	43	43	14	48	33	19
Light	56	34	37	29	39	41	20	45	41	14
Food	43	9	40	51	14	42	44	9	37	54

Figure 4.2:   *Proportion of Enterprises of Various Types, by Form of*
                   Ownership, 1994–96

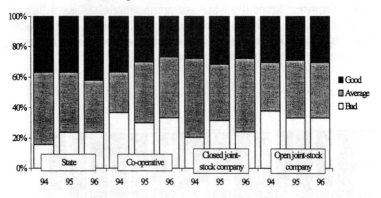

Figure 4.3:   *Proportion of Enterprises of Various Types, by Number*
                   Employed, 1994–96

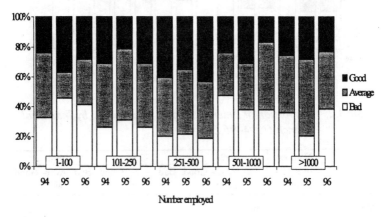

CHANGES IN THE STRUCTURE OF EMPLOYMENT
AT ENTERPRISES OF VARIOUS TYPES, 1994–1996

In Table 4.3 data on the structure of employment are presented covering three years. One can see, on the one hand, that this structure is slightly different for each of the groups of enterprises and, on the other, that it shows a particular dynamic within each of the groups. It is clear that during all three years the proportion of senior managers in the total number of employees was appreciably less at the 'good' enterprises, and this proportion remained stable at a level of 4.6–4.7%. In the other groups of enterprises the proportion of managers was significantly greater and this indicator fluctuated over the years.

Table 4.3: Structure of Employment at Enterprises of Various Types, (%)

	1994			1995			1996		
	Bad	Aver-age	Good	Bad	Aver-age	Good	Bad	Aver-age	Good
Central administration									
Chiefs	5.5	5.0	4.6	6.7	4.8	4.7	6.0	5.5	4.7
Specialists	7.7	7.9	7.8	8.3	7.5	7.6	7.5	8.1	8.0
Clerical employees	2.1	1.4	2.3	2.1	1.5	1.9	2.6	1.3	1.8
Shops Chiefs	4.1	3.9	3.5	4.4	4.1	4.0	4.9	4.2	3.8
Specialists	2.9	3.7	3.7	3.4	3.2	4.2	3.0	3.0	4.5
Skilled workers	65.1	65.7	67.6	60.6	67.6	64.1	63.6	65.7	61.7
Unskilled workers	12.7	12.4	10.6	14.5	11.3	13.4	12.3	12.1	15.1

In general, the aspiration to reduce the number of senior managers while increasing the proportion of specialists and technicians who directly manage or monitor the production process is expressed in the fact that the 'good' enterprises, while not increasing the number of shop chiefs (their share in employment each year was 3.5% – 4.0% – 3.8%), at the same time steadily increased the employment of shop specialists and technicians (3.7% – 4.2% – 4.5%) while conversely, at the 'bad' and 'average' enterprises the number of chiefs of shops and divisions grew while the proportion of shop specialists and technicians either remained stable or fell (to 3% in 1996, only two-thirds of the proportion at the 'good' enterprises). One could suggest that at the 'bad' and 'average' enterprises the prevailing tendency is the centralisation of production and personnel management, while at the 'good' enterprises, on the contrary, a decentralised type of management dominates with a higher degree of delegation of rights and responsibilities to lower levels of management. Simultaneously these same enterprises reduce, though not significantly, the proportion of employees engaged in low-skill non-manual work (typists, secretaries, couriers and so on). It would appear that some of their functions are included in the duties of the chiefs of divisions, and also of the shop specialists and technicians.

The data in Table 4.3 show that changes in the structure of employment over the last three years have also affected the most numerous categories of industrial employees – skilled and unskilled workers. One cannot fail to notice that the proportion of skilled workers at the 'good' enterprises has fallen significantly each year (by six percent over the years 1994–96) while the proportion of unskilled workers employed has correspondingly increased (from 10.6% in 1994 to 15.1% in 1996). The same tendency, although to a less dramatic degree, is characteristic of the surveyed enterprises as a whole. However, there is no doubt that it is precisely the changes in employment at the 'good' enterprises that dominates the dynamics of this process. This can be related to a process which is occurring nowadays in manufacturing industry of 'washing away' complex labour-intensive production for which there is no demand. In these conditions, naturally, the demand for skilled labour falls and the demand for low-skilled and unskilled labour increases relatively (and sometimes even absolutely). If the process continues at the present rate then soon the most 'effective' enterprises may be those making horseshoes and carts.

STRUCTURE OF SEPARATIONS

For the analysis of the structure of and reasons for separation of employees from the enterprises we have used our data for 1994–96 (Table 4.4).[1] It should be noted that the most stable category at all enterprises is the senior and middle managers. The non-production employees form an intermediate group and, finally, the skilled and unskilled workers leave the enterprise the most frequently. (We shall

---

[1]   We have collected data for separations for January to May of the given year. We have extrapolated these to annual totals which we relate to the total number employed on June 1 of the corresponding year. Of course such a method somewhat exaggerates the real figures but this will not affect the tendencies that we observe.

not consider changes in separations and recruitment of clerical employees because of the insignificant proportion of this category in the total number employed).

Table 4.4: *Separations of Particular Categories of Employee from Enterprises of Various Types (% of Total Employed in Each Category)*

	1994			1995			1996		
	Bad	Aver-age	Good	Bad	Aver-age	Good	Bad	Aver-age	Good
Central administration									
Chiefs	16.6	15.1	12.2	23.2	13.4	11.2	22.1	13.0	13.1
Specialists	28.2	22.5	23.1	34.9	22.0	16.6	92.2	24.2	17.8
Clerical employees	74.5	49.7	56.1	65.7	71.4	11.6	76.9	50.6	20.8
Shops									
Chiefs	27.4	19.7	16.1	36.4	12.6	8.3	27.7	16.2	11.6
Specialists	34.7	51.9	42.6	35.9	25.9	10.6	43.4	25.3	11.4
Clerical	44.1	100.7	39.1	8.5	82.1	16.3	13.6	84.8	38.6
Skilled workers	43.1	36.3	29.0	67.9	31.7	25.8	57.3	28.9	24.3
Unskilled workers	72.0	47.9	67.5	72.4	46.7	50.3	112.5	46.9	48.3
Total	42.3	33.4	30.1	52.4	28.9	23.6	56.0	26.4	22.8

At the same time, these data vary quite considerably from year to year. While 12.2–16.6% of managers left from all groups of enterprises in 1994, in 1995 and 1996 this figure rose to 22–23% in 1995 and 1996 in the 'bad' enterprises. Similar changes are characteristic of other categories of non-manual employees – approximately identical data for 1994 and sharp differences in 1995 and 1996. Thus, for example, shop specialists and technicians left the 'bad' enterprises in the final year almost four times as often as 'good' (43.4% and 11.4% correspondingly), and among the specialists working in the central administration the difference was more than five-fold (17.8% against 92.2%). This implies that virtually all engineers, economists and accountants left the 'bad' enterprises in the course of 1996.

As against the categories of employees mentioned above, rates of separation of skilled workers from the different groups of enterprises have always been substantially different. Moreover, it is striking that the traditionally high turnover among workers has even fallen somewhat at the 'good' enterprises (from 29% in 1994 to 24.3% in 1996). This means that in the present very difficult economic situation workers begin to value their jobs, above all if they receive relatively high wages and especially if wages are paid regularly. Our data show that the rate of separations of skilled workers, and also of engineering-technical employees who are not part of enterprise or shop management, serves as a reliable indicator of the state of affairs at the enterprise.

One also cannot disregard the lowest paid group of employees, the unskilled workers. As a whole they are distinguished by a considerably higher level of separations, which on the average was at the rate of more than 50% per annum during the last three years, and sometimes exceeded 100%. However, the general tendency of an increase in the separation rate with a deterioration of the economic situation of the enterprise also applies in this case. The only exception to this general tendency is a very high rate of separations for 1994 for the group of 'good' enterprises, which appears much closer to the figures of the 'bad' enterprises than to the 'average'. We shall try to provide some explanation for this phenomenon below.

THE MAIN REASONS FOR SEPARATIONS

Employees leave enterprises for various reasons. Some are not satisfied with the level of wages (or their absence), some have found themselves a new job, some have retired. At the same time, the economic forces determining the current situation at each particular enterprise or group of enterprises should certainly be reflected in the reasons for separation. The data on separations of employees of the surveyed group of enterprises are presented in Table 4.5.

The first and most striking point is the absolute prevalence of so-called 'voluntary separations', which amount to almost two-thirds of the total number of separations. Of course, a wide range of economic and personal reasons are hidden behind this formulation. The number really leaving voluntarily is substantially less. Thus, according to the data of a survey of the unemployed which was carried out by the Centre for Labour Market Studies in 1996 in Nizhnii Novgorod and Vladimir regions, no more than 20% of the total number of unemployed had in reality left work voluntarily, although even this figure is several times higher than comparable figures for economically developed countries.[2] But nevertheless it is appreciably less than the data given in the table. Unfortunately, the absence of detailed information forces us to use the official data of the enterprises corresponding to the formulations of the Labour Code. Nevertheless, even taking account of the points above, the data on voluntary separations is certainly of interest.

Table 4.5:   The Main Reasons for Separations from Enterprises (%)

	1994			1995			1996		
	Bad	Average	Good	Bad	Average	Good	Bad	Average	Good
Voluntary separation	59.9	63.0	65.3	65.4	62.8	69.7	59.7	65.4	64.9
Retirement	11.7	13.0	11.5	9.6	14.8	13.0	10.5	12.5	15.8
Disciplinary violations	4.7	3.7	6.7	4.1	4.7	4.6	6.3	2.9	3.5
Redundancy	12.4	9.0	2.2	10.5	5.3	2.2	15.1	6.5	6.8
Other	11.3	11.3	14.3	10.4	12.4	10.5	8.4	12.7	9.0

We can also see that through all three years of research the proportion leaving 'voluntarily' at the 'bad' enterprises was 4–5% lower than at the 'good'. There must certainly be some underlying reason for this stability, but for now we can say only that this problem requires more detailed study.

The second most significant reason for separation is retirement. This certainly does not mean that the employee immediately leaves the enterprise on reaching pension age. Indeed the proportion of pensioners in the labour force is quite large (see Table 4.6), although it is tending to fall. The tendency for 'good' enterprises to get rid of pensioners more actively than the other two groups also stands out clearly in the significant reduction in the proportion of pensioners among those employed at these enterprises, and in the gradual increase in retirement among the reasons for separation. It is likely that the directors of the more prosperous enterprises see an additional means of increasing productivity in such a re-structuring of employment.

Compulsory redundancy of employees is the third largest reason for separation. There is nothing surprising in the fact that the proportion of employees made redundant is much higher at the 'bad' enterprises than at the others, even exceeding the proportion leaving for

---

[2]   For example, in Ottawa, Canada, in the summer of 1996 we were told that the figure there does not exceed 5%.

retirement. A sharp reduction of production (on our data, the 'bad' enterprises are working on average at only 30% of capacity) forces their directors to get rid of surplus labour and to resort to such extreme methods. It should be noted that it is much more expensive for the enterprises to make employees redundant than to lose them by other means, since they have to pay at least three months' wages, quite apart from the moral costs of the process of redundancy itself. This means that if the enterprise resorts to such measures it implies that the situation is really critical and there is no possibility of finding work for these people either now or in the foreseeable future.

Table 4.6:   Proportion of Pensioners, among the Employed, at Various Types of Enterprises (1994–96)

	1994	1995	1996
Bad	15.4	14.3	13.8
Average	16.9	14.7	14.3
Good	16.4	13.4	13.1
Total	16.3	14.2	13.8

Finally, the fourth most frequent reason for separation is dismissal for infringement of labour discipline, as a rule, drunkenness, absenteeism and so on. It is interesting that for the 'good' enterprises the peak of dismissals for infringements of discipline came in 1994. That is the time at which the proportion of separations of unskilled workers at these enterprises was very large, as we have already mentioned above. There is undoubtedly a connection between these two facts. Thus, the unskilled workers who comprise 13–15% of the total employed at these enterprises, provided 18–20% of the total number of separations, and among the reasons for separation of this category, infringement of labour discipline accounts for more than 25%.

It is also quite interesting to note the sharp increase of this figure for the group of 'bad' enterprises in 1996. This increase is most probably connected as much with the fact that such a method of reducing numbers is cheaper and simpler than redundancy as with the aspiration of enterprise directors to maintain discipline at least at a minimally acceptable level.

HIRING OF NEW EMPLOYEES AND THE POSSIBILITY OF MANAGING THIS PROCESS

The renewal of the labour force of industrial enterprises is carried out through the regulation of both separations and hires, if such regulation is possible. In conditions of a constant outflow of staff from the enterprise the system of hiring acquires a special significance (see Table 4.7). Here, differences from the dynamics of separations are immediately obvious. First, in 'good' enterprises the hiring rate is significantly higher than in the other groups of enterprises. This makes sense – steadily working enterprises with quite high and regularly paid wages attract employees. On the other hand, the management of such enterprises has an opportunity to pursue a selective employment policy, choosing those who best satisfy its requirements from among the candidates for vacancies. Thus the level of hiring and separation, both for the enterprise as a whole and for the separate groups, remains balanced. The small excess, for example, of the hiring of shop technical specialists over their separations can be explained, in our view, by two reasons. First, the chiefs want to employ people in low-level engineering-technical positions so as to have a permanent reserve with which to fill higher level vacancies. This provides an incentive to encourage initiative and efficiency in the work of employees, that can promote the improvement of the economic condition of the enterprise as a whole. Secondly, the increase of hiring in comparison with separations may be a consequence of deliberate structural changes in employment undertaken at such enterprises, as has already been discussed above.

By contrast, at 'bad' enterprises a fairly high level of recruitment continues for only two categories of personnel. These are, first, senior managers at the factory level (although even here the ratio of hires to separations is still only 1:3). On all the evidence it is only the most senior posts in this group of enterprises that can attract candidates. Second is the category of unskilled workers, whose turnover in 'bad' enterprises is extraordinarily high. The total turnover of this category of employees each year is fifty per cent higher than the total employed. There is no possibility of conducting any kind of deliberate recruitment policy with this category of employees. The enterprise simply has to employ anyone they can get their hands on, with no possibility of reducing the turnover rate. In reality, for this group of enterprises, one can say that there is no deliberate recruitment policy, and this is the main determinant of the on-going degradation of their productive and labour potential.

Table 4.7:   Hiring Rate of Employees of Various Categories at Enterprises of Various Types (%)

	1995			1996		
	Bad	Average	Good	Bad	Average	Good
Central administration						
Chiefs	10.4	5.4	4.9	12.4	5.9	3.1
Specialists	8.8	11.2	17.4	6.5	9.8	10.1
Clerical	18.9	17.2	22.1	15.7	17.6	21.1
Shops						
Chiefs	7.2	9.5	6.1	5.1	13.4	9.1
Specialists	6.7	10.3	11.9	5.5	5.1	16.5
Clerical	8.4	52.9	17.0	65.2	36.2	60.3
Skilled workers	21.6	19.9	26.6	11.1	17.3	22.4
Unskilled	90.3	44.0	66.1	57.4	29.5	36.7
Total	21.2	19.5	22.2	16.1	16.3	19.9

CONCLUSION

The analysis offered above allows us to draw the following conclusions.

1. The economic situation of the enterprise has a fundamental impact on the structure and dynamics of employment in the enterprise.
2. The stable economic situation of an industrial enterprise allows its management to pursue a deliberate employment policy which harmonises levels of recruitment and separation in order to renew the staff so as to increase productive efficiency.
3. By contrast, the management of unsuccessful enterprises appears not to be capable of conducting a deliberate employment policy and cannot avoid losing a significant number of specialists and skilled workers each year without being able to find adequate

replacements for them. This aggravates the already very difficult situation of these enterprises.

In this paper I have made very little mention of the economic situation in relation to employment at the so-called 'average' enterprises. In the tables this group of enterprises almost always occupies an intermediate position in comparison with the other groups. Such a situation serves as an indirect confirmation of the appropriateness of the criteria of 'economic well-being' which we have selected, on the one hand, and allows us to conclude that there is a direct connection between the economic condition of the enterprise, the earnings of its employees and structural changes in employment, on the other.

5 How Vulnerable is Women's Employment in Russia?

Galina Monousova
Institute of World Economy and International Relations, Moscow

INTRODUCTION

Any economic reform divides the society into winners and losers. While some social groups gain status, power and wealth, others bear the painful burden of adjustment. Among those who are likely to be losers are women, pensioners, low-skilled workers and employees of obsolete industries.[1]

This paper looks at changes in female employment in Russia in the course of economic reforms in 1992–96. Most of the ECE countries undergoing transition have seen a significant growth in female unemployment and decline in employment (Flanagan, 1995). In these countries women are among the first who bear the transition costs. Is this the case for Russia as well? How are female employment and unemployment affected by the peculiarities of the Russian transition?

Labour market developments in Russia in general and concerning gender, in particular, differ from those in other countries (Commander and Coricelli, 1995; Layard and Richter, 1995). The data suggest that female employment has fallen relatively less, male unemployment exceeds female and lay-offs are quite rare. However, relatively favourable quantitative indicators of female employment may conceal very contradictory and painful trends in occupational segregation, an increasing wage gap between the sexes, growing psychological stress

---

[1] This paper was prepared on the basis of research conducted within the framework of a project on the restructuring of gender relations in Russia funded by the Nuffield Foundation and directed by Elain Bowers and Simon Clarke at the University of Warwick. The original version of the paper was presented to the conference of the British Association for Slavonic and East European Studies at the University of Cambridge in April 1997.

and expectations of forthcoming labour market failures.

This paper aims to look at how female employment in Russia has been adjusting to economic change under transition. In writing the paper I was departing from the following three hypotheses:

- the female unemployment rate does not exceed the corresponding male rate;
- the female labour force is being reallocated into the most low-wage and depressed sectors of the Russian economy;
- other factors being equal, employment conditions for women are deteriorating more rapidly than for men.

This set of initial hypotheses determines the design of the paper, which consists of three major parts. The first part deals with the scale and composition of female unemployment. The second part examines occupational and sectoral shifts in female employment and finally, in the third part, I discuss relative changes in wages and wage arrears.

The paper is based on several data sources. While the part looking at unemployment derives mostly from official sources such as the Labour Force Survey (LFS) and the statistics of the Federal Employment Service (FES), discussion of occupational shifts and working conditions relies largely on qualitative data. Here I refer to my interviews with key actors at selected enterprises in the Moscow, Kaluga, Krasnoyarsk and Kursk regions. To look at wages and wage arrears I use the Russian Longitudinal Monitoring Survey (RLMS) data set.

ARE WOMEN PUSHED INTO UNEMPLOYMENT?

The sharp rise in joblessness has rapidly replaced full employment in most of the transition countries. Almost everywhere, increasing unemployment concerns women more than men (Eastern and Central Europe, *Employment Observatory*, 6, Brussels).

The scenario of predominantly female unemployment was also expected in Russia. As soon as the Federal Employment Service, created in 1991, began to register the unemployed, the first data signalled a significant prevalence of women among the officially registered jobless. This was the only source of information available at that time and it provided grounds for many observers to speculate about the 'female face of unemployment'.

Table 5.1: Employment and Unemployment by Gender, 1992–96

	1992	1993	1994	1995	1996 (August)
Employment					
Total, million	71.3	69.9	67.4	66.2	65.9
men	37.1	36.6	36.1	35.1	35.0
women	35.0	34.3	32.4	31.1	30.9
Percentage of women	49	48	47	47	47
Unemployment rate (%)					
Registered, total	0.8	1.1	2.2	3.2	3.4
men	0.4	0.7	1.6	2.3	2.8
women	1.2	1.6	3.2	4.3	4.7
Percentage of women	72.2	67.9	64.2	62.5	60.3
ILO definition	4.7	5.5	7.4	8.8	9.2
men	4.7	5.6	7.5	9.1	9.3
women	4.8	5.5	7.3	8.5	8.6
Percentage of women	49.5	48.2	46.2	45.8	45.1

Sources: Goskomstat: *Trud i zanyatost v Rossii*, 1995; *Informatsionnyi statisticheskii byulleten'*, No.13, 1996

In October 1992 the Russian Federation held the first round of the Labour Force Survey conducted in accordance with the ILO guidelines and its results cast doubts on the idea that unemployment was mostly female. The data from the survey suggested a significantly higher rate of unemployment for both sexes, compared to the rates based on registration, and indicated that there were more men than women among the unemployed. Successive rounds of the LFS confirmed the tendency: survey unemployment was more a male phenomenon while registered unemployment remained strongly dominated by women. Moreover, the labour force surveys between 1992 and 1996 indicated a consistent decline in the proportion of women among the unemployed. This share amounted to 49.5% in 1992, 46.2% in 1994 and 45.1% in 1996. The proportion of men among the unemployed rose correspondingly (Table 5.1). Thus, in 1996 the rate of female unemployment amounted to 8.6% of the economically active population while that of men was 9.3%.

The registration data still show a different gender composition of unemployment. They continue to indicate a higher share of female unemployment and higher unemployment rate among women. However, even these data show a relative decline in the proportion of women in the total of registered unemployed. In 1996 women composed 60.3% of the registered unemployed while in 1993 they had accounted for 67.9%. The share of men increased correspondingly. Generally, we can say that the higher the level of registered unemployment, the greater the relative proportion of men. This is statistically proved by the significant positive correlation between the total rate of registered unemployment and the proportion of men, taken by region.[2]

Thus, we can see that the registration data based on personal applications of job-seekers to Employment Centres hide or underestimate male unemployment. The difference between registration data and LFS data is typical for many countries, but in Russia it is especially significant. This gap reflects a range of reasons due to which men who have lost their jobs are reluctant to apply to the FES. Among the reasons are such things as the red tape involved in the registration procedure, ignorance by the unemployed of their statutory rights, lack of hope in getting help and the image of unemployment as a stigma of shame. One of the most important factors restraining application to the FES is the extremely low level of unemployment benefit. Some unemployed people see little sense in spending time visiting the local employment office for the sake of these miserly subsidies. In some remote areas transport costs may exceed the level of benefits.

In 1992 under one-fifth of all the unemployed were registered in Employment Centres; by 1996 this indicator had risen to 37%. For women it increased from 25% to 55% in 1996, while for men it rose from 8.5% to 30%. Thus, the propensity of men to register if unemployed has been persistently lower than that of women. However, the lower propensity to apply to the employment centre does not mean lower actual unemployment.

Thus, unemployment in Russia does not look like a specifically female privilege; it seems to concern men to an even greater extent. How does this gender distribution of the unemployed fit with the data on employment decline? By 1996, compared to 1992, female employment had fallen by 12% while male employment had fallen by only

---

[2]   The correlation between the rate of registered unemployment and the share of women among the unemployed taken by regions is negative and statistically significant (r=-.33, p < .005).

6%. This may be explained by the different rate at which men and women left the labour force.

Let us look more specifically at the changes in proportions between the employed, unemployed and economically inactive population for the period 1992–95 (Table 5.2). Unfortunately, I have been unable to find corresponding data for a longer period. The female employment rate in 1992 was 61.5% of the population aged 15–72 (this age group is the base for defining economic activity in Russia) and the male employment rate was 72.7%; the corresponding unemployment rates were 3.0% for women and 3.6% for men so that the economically inactive made up 35.5% and 23.7% respectively. By 1996 these proportions had changed significantly.

Male employment declined by 4.5 points and two-thirds of this was accounted for by an increase in unemployment, with less than one-third being accounted for by an increase in economic inactivity. In the case of women the picture looks quite different. The total drop amounted to 7.8 points but only one-quarter of these people moved into unemployment. Over three-quarters of the employment decline was accounted for by an increase in the economically inactive population. Thus, although female employment declined more substantially than male, the major outflow went not into unemployment but out of the labour market. On the contrary, the outflow of men from employment was relatively limited but it went largely into unemployment.

The same picture can be shown in absolute figures (Table 5.3). For the selected period female employment fell by 4.0 million, only 1.2 million of whom became unemployed. The bulk of them, 3.6 million, simply left the labour market. Male employment declined by 1.7 million, but almost all of them (1.7 million) entered unemployment. Therefore, the outflow from employment has different directions for men and women. If men move from employment into unemployment, women are likely to leave the labour force.[3]

---

[3] Editor's note: Estimates of numbers of men and women employed based on the data in *Trud i Zanyatost*, 1996, p. 8 on participation rates derived from the Labour Force Survey are completely different from the distribution of the employed by sex derived from administrative statistics. The former show that slightly more men than women left the labour market between 1992 and 1995, with the fall in economic activity being heavily concentrated among pensioners and the under 19s. This data, which I would consider more reliable, and which is reinforced by the RLMS data, only strengthens the general argument of Galya's paper (see the discussion in the first chapter in this volume and Tables 2.2 and 2.3; see also Ashwin and Bowers, 1997). The same caveat applies to the data in Table 5.5, although this probably does not affect the inter-industry differences with which Galya is concerned.

Table 5.2:   *Changes in Labour Market Participation, Men and Women, 1992–95 (% of total population aged 15–72)*

	1992	1995	Change (1992–95)
Total	100%	100%	
Employed	66.9	60.6	-6.3
Unemployed	3.3	5.8	+2.5
Economically inactive	29.8	33.5	+3.8
Men	100%	100%	
Employed	72.7	68.2	-4.5
Unemployed	3.6	6.8	+3.2
Economically inactive	23.7	25.0	+1.3
Women	100%	100%	
Employed	61.5	53.7	-7.8
Unemployed	3.0	5.0	+2.0
Economically inactive	35.5	41.3	+5.8

Table 5.3:   *Changes in Labour Market Participation, 1992–95 (millions of individuals, 15–72 years)*

	1992	1995	Changes (1993–95)
Total population	107.9	109.6	+1.7
Economically active	75.7	72.8	-2.9
of which employed	72.1	66.4	-5.7
unemployed	3.6	6.4	+2.8
Economically inactive	32.2	36.8	+4.6
Men	51.0	51.9	+0.9
Economically active	38.9	38.8	-0.1
of which employed	37.0	35.3	-1.7
unemployed	1.8	3.5	+1.7
Economically inactive	12.1	13.1	+1.0
Women	56.9	57.7	+0.8
Economically active	36.7	33.9	-2.8
of which employed	35.0	31.0	-4.0
unemployed	1.7	2.9	+1.2
Economically inactive	20.2	23.8	+3.6

Source: author's calculations based on Goskomstat: *Trud i zanyatost v Rossii*, 1996.

The relatively lower incidence of female unemployment does not mean that women have better employment opportunities. If unemployed, women find it much more difficult to get back into employment. Table 5.4 shows that the period of job search for women is longer than that for men. This gap is quite persistent and more or less constant. However, it is narrowing, reflecting the relative worsening of reemployment opportunities for men.

Table 5.4: Average Duration of Job Search by Unemployed (months)

	1992	1993	1994	1995 October	1996 March
Total	4.4	5.8	6.7	7.5	8.2
Men	3.9	5.2	6.3	7.1	7.9
Women	4.9	6.4	7.1	8.0	8.6

Source: LFS data, various Goskomstat publications

Now I would like to shift the focus on to those who are still in employment. As I indicated at the beginning of the paper, the general deterioration of employment conditions is a price paid for saving jobs. This process may have two dimensions: the relative reallocation of female employment into more depressed sectors and worsening their employment conditions within enterprises.

THE REALLOCATION OF FEMALE EMPLOYMENT ACROSS SECTORS AND OCCUPATIONS

In this section I argue that the female labour force is being concentrated in the lowest-waged and most depressed sectors of the economy.

The 'traditional' breakdown of sectors into mostly male and female was quite stable over a long period. The proportion of women employed within particular sectors did not change while it varied significantly across sectors. In 1990 it varied from 20% in forestry to 90% in finance and insurance (Goskomstat, 1996e). Since the start of transition the female share has begun to rise in some sectors and to decline in others.[4] These changes have been happening against the apparent drop in employment in most sectors (Table 5.5).

---

[4]   Here I refer only to large and medium sized firms. Where small businesses account for a significant share of employment, as in trade, the tendency may differ.

Table 5.5: Total and Female Employment by Sectors, 1990–94
(million and %)

	1990			1994			changes 1994\1990		
	total mln	% women	women mln	total mln	% women	women mln	total mln	% women	women mln
Employed	75.3	52	39.1	68.5	51	34.9	-6.8	-1	-4.2
of which:									
Industry	22.8	48	10.9	18.6	45	8.4	-4.2	-3	-2.5
Agriculture	9.9	40	4.0	10.5	38	4.0	+0.6	-2	0
Construction	9.0	27	2.4	6.8	25	1.7	-2.2	-2	-0.7
Transport	4.9	25	1.2	4.5	27	1.2	-0.4	+2	0
Trade and catering	5.9	80	4.7	6.5	75	4.5	-0.2	-5	-0.2
Public utilities	3.2	52	1.7	3.0	44	1.3	-0.2	-8	-0.4
Public health	4.2	83	3.5	4.4	84	3.7	+0.2	+1	+0.2
Education	7.2	79	5.7	7.4	81	5.9	+0.2	+2	+0.2
R and D	3.1	53	1.6	1.8	52	0.9	-1.3	-1	-0.7
Finance	0.4	90	0.4	0.7	77	0.5	0.3	-13	+0.1
Administration	1.8	67	1.2	1.7	69	1.2	-0.7	+2	0

Source: author's calculations based on Goskomstat: *Trud i zanyatost v Rossii*, 1995b; *Informatsionnyi statisticheskii byulleten'*, No.13, 1996.

There are two ways in which the proportion of women employed in a given sector can rise. Either men exit the sector more rapidly than women do, or the inflow of women exceeds that of men. Correspondingly, it declines when either women leave more rapidly (while men stay) or men intensively enter the sector. In practice, of course, we have various combinations of all these options.

A rapid inflow of men in 1990–94 caused a significant decrease of female employment in finance and insurance (by 13 percentage points), where women had dominated. In its turn, the ouflow of men caused an increase in the proportion of women in transport. The female concentration increased in education and health care, affected mostly by an inflow of women.

To cut a long story short, the proportion of women employed rises in the most depressed sectors, and above all in budget-financed sectors. Correspondingly, where adjustment to the market goes more smoothly, the proportion of women employed goes down. This process is correlated with changes in the wage level.

The relationship between the share of female employment and relative wages can be illustrated in the following way. We can compare wage levels in heavily female (women comprise over 70% of the total employment) and male sectors (women make up less than 40%). The wage level relative to the average in the economy is higher in the male sectors and lower in the female (Table 5.6). This results in the growing gender gap in earnings and gives ground for conclusions about the 'feminisation of the poverty' (Rostchin, 1996). The tendency to the concentration of women in low-paid jobs is proved by enterprise survey data (Tsentr issledovannii rynka truda, 1995a; Standing, 1996b, Chapter 9).

Table 5.6: *Relative Wages in Predominantly Male and Female Sectors (as % of average wage in economy)*

	1991	1992	1993	1994	1996
Mostly male sectors (women comprise less than 40% of all employees)					
Gas	209	465	297	361	391
Coal mining	187	243	198	206	192
Oil extraction	241	331	275	255	278
Electricity	201	221	188	190	200
Mostly female sectors (women comprise over 70% of all employees)					
Textiles	122	81	71	49	52
Food processing	127	135	129	127	119
Electronics	77	58	83	55	...
Trade	78	73	81	83	...
Health care	69	60	78	80	79
Education	64	70	71	62	74
Culture	60	48	57	56	67

Source: Ekonomicheskie novosti Rossii i Sodruzchestva, No.1, 1995; *Informatsionnyi statisticheskii bulleten'*, No.13, 1996.

The effect of the concentration of female labour in particular sectors on wage differentials can also be illustrated by case studies. My research shows that women in industry get stuck in relatively low-paid occupations and corresponding jobs. If relative wages go up, jobs traditionally held by women are likely to be filled by men. Conversely, wage decline or wage arrears may lead to the feminisation of the jobs particularly affected.

During the period 1993 to 1995 I studied nine privatised industrial enterprises in various regions of Russia. The sample can be split into two groups: (A) enterprises employing mostly male labour and (B) those employing mostly female labour. The first group mostly comprised firms in engineering with relatively complex technology in which women accounted for fewer than 40% of all employees. The second group included a watchmaking factory and enterprises in the food, textile and clothing and footwear industries. They tended to employ mostly women (over 70% of all the personnel) who worked at low-paid and low-skilled jobs.

Let us look at differentiation between the major groups of workers from the point of view of their 'feminisation' and relative wages.

(A) Mostly male enterprises (metallurgy, shipyard, turbine manufacturer, engineering)

i. *Highly-skilled male main production shop-floor workers.* They (about 5–10% of all blue-collar workers) have firm-specific skills and possess occupations and experience which are in demand in the external labour market. Moreover, they are highly adaptable and are eager to change their job for a better paid one. Despite the fact that they are the best paid they tend to blackmail managers, trying to get even higher wages. This decreases the wage fund allocated among the other workers.

ii. *Semi- and low-skilled main production shop-floor workers.* Among these are both men and women but most of the women employed by the enterprises are concentrated in these jobs. They have no specific skills, and their labour turnover costs are very low. This makes them dependent and easily replaceable. Moreover, it is precisely these jobs that are the most sensitive to the decline in output and are easy to cut. Unpaid leave, short-term work and wage arrears are heavily concentrated in this sector of jobs. All this affects employment conditions and wages.

iii. *Highly-skilled auxiliary shop-floor workers (repair workers).* In all the firms studied this group is made up almost exclusively of men. Many repair workers have skills and occupations which are in demand outside the particular enterprise. At the same time these jobs have low elasticity in relation to changes in volumes of production and imply high labour turnover costs. This increases the bargaining power of these male workers and their wages, correspondingly.

iv. *Low-skilled auxiliary shop-floor workers.* They represent a mix of various low-paid occupations without any gender specification. They have very high labour turnover and they are easy to replace. Many of them work temporarily.

(B) Mostly female enterprises (food, women's wear, a watch-making enterprise).

Female labour prevails in the firms from this sub-sample. The production process here lacks flexibility and the equipment used needs medium level skills.

i.   *Highly-skilled main production shop-floor workers.* These were mostly women with long job tenures and they compose a minority of 2–3% of those employed in the sampled firms. Their work is largely manual, requiring firm-specific skills that cannot be obtained outside the firm. They play a key role in production and are rather well-paid. Wages in these jobs tend to rise and where this has occurred in the studied firms a gradual process of replacement of women by men starts. For example, in the footwear factory the proportion of men among employees in this occupational group increased from 20% to 50%. In the watch-making firm two-thirds of the highly paid watch assemblers are men while it had been mostly a female occupation before the relative wage went up.

ii. *Semi- and low-skilled main production shop-floor workers.* They are low-skilled, they undergo relatively simple and cheap training and are easy to replace. These workers are almost exclusively women of various ages. These jobs pay the lowest wages, at between a third and half the wage of highly paid workers.

iii. *Highly-skilled auxiliary shop-floor workers.* These are mostly men – repair workers (adjusters, welders, electricians, some metal workers, among others) maintaining and adjusting equipment. They have the highest skill level (within their enterprises) as well as the highest wages.

     This group of workers plays a very important role in enterprises of this second group. The equipment is quite old and needs a lot of maintenance and readjustment. This makes the main production workers dependent on adjusters and repair specialists, on their skills and motivation. Many of these occupations are in demand outside the firms studied, which gives these workers a strong bargaining position.

     While in 1992 the wage level of this group was lower than that of main production workers, by 1994 they had become the best paid. This was also caused by the shortage of some occupations in the face of demand from the better adjusting industries and the new private sector.

iv. *Low-skilled auxiliary shop-floor workers.* These are first of all male workers involved in loading/unloading operations. They do not need any skills but only physical strength, which makes them non-replaceable by women. Taking into account the low level of mechanisation of these operations, we can understand why they improve their bargaining position.

These intergroup differences can be illustrated with a diagram showing relative wages (Figure 5.1).

Figure 5.1: *Relative Wages of Major Occupational Groups, by Type of Enterprise (wage of low-skilled auxiliary workers in each type of enterprise equals 1)*

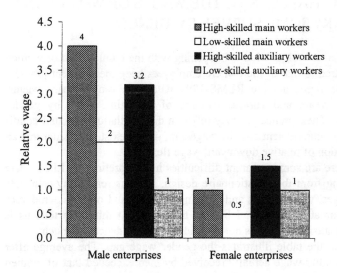

The tendencies discussed above are supported by the Goskomstat data. In 1992 in the women's wear industry the wage ratio between main and auxiliary workers was 1.2 but by 1995 it had fallen to 0.89 (author's estimates based on Goskomstat data). The same happened with repair workers from the first group of industries, although the wage difference of auxiliary workers from both groups is narrowing.

As we can see, in all the firms studied the wage differential between major groups of workers tends to grow. High labour turnover costs which make an employee hard to replace play a crucial role. These costs depend on the occupational structure of demand and supply, the existence of an occupational labour market and the composition of unemployment. As we can see, women mostly occupy jobs which do not provide their incumbents with significant bargaining power and as a result female employment becomes more vulnerable compared to that of men. This may lead to a growing gender gap in employment. The survey data which I am going to discuss below suggest that this is not always the case: the evidence is mixed and contradictory.

WHAT HAPPENS TO THE WAGES OF WOMEN IN WORK? SOME SURVEY EVIDENCE

Now let us look at what is happening with the employment of women compared to that of men where employees keep their current job. Using the representative RLMS-1995 data[5] one can compare wages, wage arrears and various patterns of short-time work by gender groups. These indicators may reflect a differentiation in actual conditions of employment and the wage gap, if they exist. I consider this an indication of relative downward wage flexibility.

There are some apparent difficulties in interpreting the RLMS data deriving from the questionnaire design. For this reason my estimates of wages, wage arrears and working hours should be considered very approximate. However, I believe the story that this table tells us is quite plausible and does not contradict other evidence too much.

First, the table illustrates the gender wage gap. The average after tax monthly wage actually received by men exceeded that of women by 60%. (Of course, the difference is affected by the sectoral distribution of male and female employment but the RLMS data set does not allow us to control for this). This gap is also reflected in hourly wage differentials adjusted to the number of actually worked hours. The female rate amounts to 76% of the male rate. This ratio suggests that the gap may be narrowing, having been 0.71 in 1992 and 0.70 in 1980 (Newell and Reilly, 1996, p. 341).

---

[5]   The Russian Longitudinal Monitoring Survey has been conducted since 1992. The 1995 data set includes over 4 thousand employed individuals.

Table 5.7: Indicators of Wages and Employment, by Gender, 1995

Variables	Total	Male	Female
Monthly post-tax wage, thousand rubles	539.8	671.7	422.8
Hourly wage, thousand rubles	3.2	3.7	2.8
Duration of usual working day, hours	8.3	8.7	7.9
Duration of actual working day, hours	7.6	8.2	7.0
Difference	0.7	0.5	0.9
% having wage arrears	41.5	44.6	38.6
Average wage arrears (for those with arrears), thousand rubles	801	1055	540
% receiving payment in kind	8.1	9.3	7.0
% having experienced unpaid leave	6.4	5.5	7.2
Duration of most recent unpaid leave, days (for those having had leave)	46	41	49

Source: RLMS-95, the author's calculations.

The real value of wages depends on whether wages are paid in time. This has become a very important dimension of employment conditions in the Russian economy, suffering from both wage arrears and inflation. The table suggests that over 40% of all respondents faced delays in wage payment. But both the share of those paid with delay and the average amount of arrears are significantly higher for men compared to women. Additionally, a higher proportion of men are paid in kind. The average amount delayed amounts to about 1.6 of the wage paid in the case of men and 1.3 in the case of women. The differences are likely to reflect the fact of the much higher initial male wage. This means that wage arrears may to some extent reduce the gender wage gap compared to the case when all wages are paid on time.

Another indication of employment vulnerability can be found in involuntary unpaid leave. Here we can see that women are more involved in forced vacations compared to men and their duration is longer. As to men, 5.5% of those interviewed had been on unpaid leave versus 7.2% of women. In this case women are more exposed to this version of lay-off, although the difference is not great.

Thus, we see that the RLMS data give a contradictory mix of evidence. On the one hand, men are likely to earn higher wages but the potential earnings are partially 'compensated' by the higher incidence and larger amount of wage arrears. This concerns only actual employment conditions. But how are they perceived by gender groups?

Both actual and perceptive dimensions are interconnected and mutually reinforcing. Thus, if an employee considers his or her labour market prospects as miserable he or she may prefer to stay at his or her current job regardless of the wage. This means that downward flexibility is likely to be accepted. Therefore, one can enter a vicious circle when a negative perception affects (directly or indirectly) the actual conditions which, in their turn, enforce an already negative perception of the future.

Much more pessimistic estimates of reemployment opportunities for women are illustrated by both the RLMS and VTsIOM data. Table 5.8 shows how women see their prospects and, therefore, why they are ready to keep their jobs at any price.

Table 5.8:   Perception of Employment Opportunities by Gender (%)

	Total	Male	Female
I am worried about losing my job*	59	56	62
If your enterprise is closed, how sure are you that you will find a new job? (absolutely sure + fairly sure)*	25	34	20
Do you think you might lose your job? (likely + very likely)**	36	34	40
If you lose your job will you be able to find a new one within the same occupation? (yes)**	52	65	40

Sources: * RLMS-95
             ** VTsIOM Bulletin, 4, 1996

CONCLUSION

How vulnerable is female employment in Russia? In conclusion let us give a short answer according to our hypothesis:

- Unemployment in Russia concerns both men and women, men leave employment for unemployment to an even greater extent.
- The share of female employment grows in the most depressed and,

primarily, the budget-financed sectors. In industry women are likely to get stuck in relatively low-paid occupations and corresponding jobs. If relative wages go up, jobs traditionally held by women may be filled by men. On the contrary, wage decline or wage arrears may lead to the feminisation of jobs particularly affected by it.

- Various data sources give different estimates of employment conditions for women and for men. Some of our evidence confirms the deterioration of labour conditions for women, other evidence does not. However, women estimate their current and future employment opportunities more pessimistically and tend to hold on to their jobs at any price.

6 Russian Unemployment in the mid-1990s: Features and Problems

Tatyana Chetvernina

Director, Centre for Labour Market Studies,
Institute of Economics, Russian Academy of Sciences

FEATURES OF THE RUSSIAN LABOUR MARKET IN THE 1990s

The main tendencies of the Russian labour market in the 1990s can be briefly characterised as follows.

First, economic decline was not accompanied by a commensurate reduction of employment. While GDP fell by 40% between 1990 and the middle of 1995 and the volume of industrial production fell by 51%, the reduction in employment in industry, according to the official statistics, was 23.2% and in the economy as a whole was 9% (Goskomstat, 1996d, pp. 54–6).

Second, alongside a low level of registered unemployment, the large gap between the level of registered and level of open unemployment has persisted, amounting in the middle of 1996 to a factor of 2.6.

Contrary to the common opinion, unemployment during the 1990s has grown quite rapidly (Table 6.1): registered job seekers (the number of people who have applied to labour exchanges in search of work) and registered unemployment have grown very rapidly over the past five years. While the number of registered unemployed has increased by 400% over the period from 1992 to the middle of 1996 (from 0.6 million in 1992 to 2.6 million people at the beginning of June 1996), the number of job seekers has increased by 290% and unemployment as defined by the ILO methodology has increased by 181%.

Table 6.1:   Number of Unemployed Registered with the Employment
Service and on ILO definition

End year	Registered job seekers (million)	Registered unemployed (million)	Registered unemployment (%)	ILO unemployed (million)	ILO unemployment (%)	Registered as % of ILO unemployed
1992	1.0	0.6	0.8	3.6	4.7	16.7
1993	1.1	0.8	1.1	4.2	5.5	19.0
1994	2.0	1.6	2.2	5.5	7.4	28.6
1995	2.5	2.3	3.2	6.0	8.3	38.3
1996	2.9	2.5	3.4	6.8	9.4	40.0

Third, a significant amount of hidden unemployment remains, several times greater than the level of registered unemployment.

According to the official data, the number of employees sent on compulsory leave by their employers increased from 2.1 million people in the second quarter of 1995 to 6.1 million in the same period in 1996. Over the same period the number of employees working short time on the initiative of the administration (a reduced working day or working week) increased by 1.5 times, from 2.0 to 3.3 million. Moreover, a significant proportion (40%) of these people did not receive any money at all, the remainder most often receiving payment only at the level of the minimum wage (Goskomstat, 1995c, p. 127).

Fourth, the specifically Russian mutant form of work without wages has grown steadily over the past few years. According to our calculations, 8.3% of all the employees in manufacturing industry alone were not receiving any monetary payment.

Table 6.2:   Distribution of Russian Regions by Level of Registered
Unemployment, 1992–96 (89 regions)

On 1.01	Number of regions with rate of unemployment of:					
	> 1%	1–2%	2–3%	3–5%	5–7%	> 7%
1992	89	-	-	-	-	-
1993	62	21	6	-	-	-
1994	47	23	8	9	2	-
1995	13	27	18	17	11	3
1996	4	18	21	19	13	14

Fifth, there is significant regional differentiation in the level of unemployment (from 0.9% in Moscow up to 26% in the Ingush republic) alongside an increase in the number of regions exceeding the 5% level of registered unemployment. The number of such regions has increased 6.5 times in comparison with 1994 (Table 6.2).

Sixth, interregional differentiation is also made more complicated by significant intra-regional differences in rates of unemployment. The system which developed in the Soviet period of a division of labour oriented to mono-industrial specialisation of districts has led to a substantial variation in rates of unemployment within one region. Thus, at the beginning of 1996, Vladimir oblast had a general level of registered unemployment of 8.7%, but this varied between 3.5% in Suzdal, an area specialising in tourism, and 17.5% in Kovrov, which is dominated by the textile industry (*Statisticheskii byulleten' Vladimirskoi oblastnoi Sluzhby zanyatosti*, Vladimir, 1996). A similar situation is characteristic of Nizhnii Novgorod oblast, which is generally considered to be one of the prosperous regions. Here the rate of unemployment ranged from 0.8% (in districts dominated by the food-processing industry) up to 12.9% in districts dominated by the military-industrial complex.

Seventh, the number of long-term unemployed has increased. On the figures of those registered with the employment service alone, the proportion of those who have been unemployed for more than one year has increased from 9% in 1994 to 15.7% in 1996. According to our research data, the average period between the moment of loss of work and the date of registration with the employment service is 3.7 months. Thus, the duration of unemployment may be considerably longer than is indicated by official sources.

Eighth, during the 1990s the material situation of the unemployed caused by deficiencies in the system of unemployment benefits worsened. In December 1993 the average unemployment benefit was equivalent to 1.1 minimum wages and amounted to 38% of the subsistence minimum.[1] In December 1994 the average payments to each unemployed person (including unemployment benefit, lump sum payments and allowances for dependants) had increased to 2.3 minimum wages, but the relative decline in the minimum wage meant that this

---

[1]   Here and elsewhere in this chapter the figures quoted for benefits are derived from the annual accounts of the Federal Employment Service for January to December 1995, *Statisticheskii byulleten'*, 12.

now amounted to only 36% of the subsistence minimum. In 1995 the average payment to the unemployed amounted to 96 thousand roubles (against 48.1 thousand in December 1994), equivalent to 2.2 minimum wages or 30% of the subsistence minimum.

If up to the middle of the nineties one can speak of the miserable size of unemployment benefits as a result of the high rate of inflation, a feature of the second half of the nineties has become the non-payment of unemployment benefits.

The tendencies in the Russian labour market outlined above allow us to assert, contrary to established opinion in state structures and the statements of a number of western experts, that the problem of unemployment is one of the most acute social problems in contemporary Russia, caused not only by the change of socio-economic system and the deep economic crisis in the economy, but also by the state's distancing itself from the resolution of these problems. The hushing up of the actual state of affairs ever since the existence of unemployment was first officially recognised in 1991 has resulted in the inability of the state not only to conduct any kind of effective active labour market policy, but even to provide a normal passive policy in relation to those who have lost their jobs or cannot find work in conditions of economic crisis for which the state cannot disclaim all responsibility.

PRIORITIES OF STATE LABOUR MARKET POLICY IN CONDITIONS OF SUSTAINED ECONOMIC CRISIS

Following the official recognition of unemployment it has become conventional to speak about the priorities of labour market policy. In statements of government officials from the Federal Employment Service and the Ministry of Labour and in the works of economists concerned with problems of unemployment, preference, as a rule, is given to active measures.[2] This would not give rise to any particular

---

[2]   It should be noted that in the majority of publications conclusions are drawn not on the basis of analysis of the expenditure and financial accounts of the employment fund or other sources of financing on the implementation of particular measures within the framework of the employment programmes, but only on the basis of the analysis of the textual exposition of the programmes, without any connection with their real

problems if it were not the case that the priority accorded to active policy is at the expense of the resources required for a passive policy.

Since existing perceptions of the forms of policy (especially active) which are actually implemented are rather dim, we shall consider in more detail not only their contents and effectiveness, but also the allocation of expenditure.

Expenditure from the employment fund can be divided into four principal components.

1. Expenditure for unemployment benefits, material help for the unemployed and payment of pensions for early retirees. These can all be categorised as passive policy.
2. Expenditure on retraining and public works. These forms of active policy follow from the existing Law on Employment (articles 23, 24.5 and 29), which means that they are obligatory for the Federal Employment Service.
3. Expenditure on financial support, purchase of financial securities and other costs. These particular forms of expenditure are united by the fact that they are not guaranteed by the Law but are incurred on the independent initiative of state and regional structures. In this context, expenditure under the heading 'financial support' can be considered as an active form of policy.
4. Expenditure on the development of the Employment Service – maintenance of the employment service, fixed investments, advertising, and so on.

Total expenditure for the first nine months of 1995 was distributed as follows:

> *Passive policy*: total 34.1%, including 29.2% on unemployment benefits.
> *Active policy, obligatory under the Law on Employment*: 8.5%
> *Active policy which is not prescribed by the Law on Employment*: 24.4%.
> *Support of the Employment Service*: 21%.

The remaining 12% of expenditure is funds accumulated in the federal part of the employment fund and redistributed to regions with a high level of unemployment.

---

implementation. In this context the most interesting publications are the articles of A. Dadashev in *Voprosy ekonomiki* (12, 1993 and 1, 1996), although the present author disagrees with the theses presented by A. Dadashev.

Thus, a little over half the expenditure (55%) comprises obligatory costs expended on those who are the *raison d'être* of the Employment Service, the unemployed and the employees of the services which are responsible for rendering assistance to the unemployed.

As far as active policy is concerned, the priority, as indicated by share of expenditure, is clearly those activities which are not legally obligatory, i.e. financial support, purchase of financial securities and other costs.

Expenditure for financial support for 9 months of 1995 amounted to 16.5% of the total expenditure from the fund. Of this 54.3% was spent on the preservation of jobs, 38.4% on the creation of additional jobs, 4.9% on compensatory payments to workers sent on administrative leave and 2.3% on supporting people establishing their own business.

Expenditure from the employment fund under this heading would seem to be inappropriate since it is not the responsibility of the Employment Service to struggle for economic growth and to solve the economic crisis but to work with that part of the population which requires the help of these state services in conditions of economic crisis.[3] That is, their job is not to struggle with the causes but to work with the consequences of economic recession. It would be more logical for this form of financial support (above all, the creation of jobs) to be financed from the budget of other departments, in particular, the Ministries of Economics and Finance.

Other doubts arise in relation to this category of expenditure. The creation of jobs is pretty expensive (according to the estimates of enterprise directors, the cost per job created is approximately equal to the annual expenditure on wages for each employee). If the state takes responsibility for the creation of jobs in conditions of economic recession, it should also accept responsibility for their maintenance and preservation for a certain period. Nobody calculates the effectiveness of job creation, which is why it turns out to be simply either a form of financial support for ailing enterprises or financial assistance for those who are closer to the regional authorities. One has to bear in mind that decisions about the allocation of expenditure for financial support in

---

[3]   A. Dadashev takes a different point of view, considering that policy becomes active when the distribution of expenditure from the employment fund is dominated by expenditure on the preservation of jobs (1), creation of additional jobs (2), provision of grants for the organisation of people's own business (3), cover of the costs of occupational training, retraining and vocational guidance (4). For more detail see: A. Dadashev, 1996, p. 79.

the majority of (debtor) regions is taken not by the regional employment service but by the regional administration and sometimes by the regional tripartite commission.

Although in various regions a whole procedure for granting financial help for the creation or preservation of jobs has been developed, experience shows that it is ineffective. Thus, in Vladimir oblast the allocation of resources from the employment fund for the creation of jobs for the unemployed is carried out on the basis of the examination of business-plans which are presented to the administration, together with full accounts. The final decision is taken by a commission of the administration with the participation of the regional trade unions. Thus the Employment Service does not bear any responsibility for the decision taken. On the basis of the commission's decision a contract is drawn up and financial support is allocated from the employment fund. It is important to emphasise that the financial support is provided on the basis of its repayment with interest, although the rate of interest is lower than the average rate payable to the banks. If the enterprise defaults on the terms and conditions of the contract it is obliged to return the money provided. According to the representatives of the regional employment service, the terms and conditions of contract are usually not observed. Thus, for example, the recipient might undertake to create several dozen jobs, but in reality create only a small fraction of these. The recipient is then obliged to return the money for defaulting on the contract. As a rule, such questions are decided through the courts. This means that only a portion of the money laid out by the employment fund at a low rate of interest is returned, by which time inflation has further eroded its real value. This sort of practice is mostly typical of small and medium enterprises.

As a rule large enterprises do not receive such support, although there are some exceptions to this. Thus, for example, the Vladimir tractor factory received financial support for three months in 1993 for the preservation of jobs at an annual rate of interest of 48%. During these three months the enterprise did not reduce the number of jobs, although it subsequently reduced the number of employees by more than 2,000 by the end of 1995. However, the money was not returned to the employment fund until the end of 1995, instead of after three months, and then only when the matter was about to be put before the court. The factory management, when asked why they had not repaid the money in time, replied that they regarded it as necessary first of all to pay off their debts to the bank, which charged an interest rate several times higher. That is perfectly logical from the point of view of the enterprise but it is not justified from the point of view of expenditure from the employment fund.

Table 6.3: Structure of Expenditure of the Employment Fund in Regions with Various Levels of Unemployment

Level of regional unemployment, %	Percentage of the employment fund spent on:			
	Passive policy	Active policy, legally prescribed	Active policy, not legally prescribed	Support of the employment service
Less than 1%	12.6	8.6	51.6	19.1
From 1 up to 1.9	23.0	13.3	18.9	25.4
1.9 - 2.8	34.2	8.8	19.3	23.0
2.9 - 3.8	44.0	9.5	9.2	24.3
3.9 - 4.8	51.0	7.4	13.4	20.0
4.9 - 5.8	58.8	7.8	4.7	25.5
5.9 - 6.8	61.7	4.2	12.9	17.0
6.9 - 7.8	64.5	2.7	7.6	19.1
More than 7.9	68.3	5.0	16.5	10.3
Russia average:				
9 months 1995	34.1	8.5	24.4	21.0
1st quarter 1996*	49.3	9.4	10.7	22.3

* The increase in the share of expenditure on passive policy is not a result of an increase in payments to the unemployed, but of the delayed payment of benefits due since November 1995.

The financing by the employment fund of payments to workers sent on administrative leave should equally be subject to criticism. Such an artificial maintenance of hidden unemployment (in essence these people are unemployed, receiving only the minimum unemployment benefit) over a period of several years simply makes the problem increasingly difficult since it slows down structural transformations in the enterprises and in branches, undermines their economic and financial position and consequently aggravates the subsequent resolution of the problem of unemployment even more.

The next item of expenditure from the fund – 'financial securities' – is no less dubious. There was probably some justification for investing money in the first years of unemployment, when the money in the fund was not all spent and the regional management regarded it as necessary to accumulate the resources of the fund in anticipation of the future growth of unemployment. However, in 1992–3, with a very high rate of inflation, it is difficult to regard such a use of the resources of the fund as properly thought out. It would have been more reasonable in this period to create a material base for future unemployment (to create and computerise the service, to recruit staff and so on). This is to say nothing of the fact that nobody monitored the return of the money or the rate of interest received.

The information on the expenditure of the employment fund for Russia as a whole is interesting in itself, however it does not reflect the regional priorities of policy. To show the specific features of regional policy in broad terms, we have divided all the regions of the Russian Federation into nine groups according to the rate of unemployment, in steps of one per cent, and have calculated the allocation of the employment fund to different types of expenditure in these groups (Table 6.3).

The accounts show that only one item of expenditure – money payments to the unemployed – is connected with the rate of unemployment in the region. Other costs have no direct connection with the rate of unemployment, but rather have a specifically regional orientation and express regional policy priorities. Thus, for example, among regions with a level of registered unemployment lower than 1%, in Belgorod oblast preference is given to financial support, while in Orenburg oblast to investments in financial securities. In the Ingush republic, where the level of registered unemployment is the highest in the country at 22.1%, a significant part of the employment fund is used for financial support – 24.9%. At the same time, only 2.1% is spent on retraining and public works. In Ivanovo and Vladimir oblasts, which are also included in the group of regions with a high level of unemployment, 8% of the resources of the fund are spent on financial support, while 7.9% and 7.2% respectively are spent on retraining and public works.

The highest levels of expenditure on the purchase of financial securities are shown by Moscow (25%), with a rate of unemployment of 0.5%, Vologda oblast (30.3%) with a rate of unemployment of 2.4%, Chita oblast (27.8%) with a rate of unemployment of 2.2%, and the Republic of Marii El (19.4%) with a rate of unemployment of 3.9%.

Thus, despite the existence of numerous programs, practice shows that the regional authorities consider the employment fund as an additional source of financing regional policies which are not always connected with the unemployed and their social protection. And the lower the rate of unemployment in the region, the more likely it is that the funds will not be spent for the use for which they were designated.

In regions with a high level of unemployment the priority in the activity of the employment service is the payment of benefits (passive policy). Though, in the opinion of their chiefs, this does not mean that it is necessary to reduce or terminate programs of training and retraining. As a rule, people who follow such training courses find a job, or at least increase their competitiveness in the future. At the same time, the data of the Federal Employment Service show that a large part of those who have undergone retraining, to all appearances, do no more than 'increase their competitiveness', since on average for Russia as a whole only 7% of the unemployed who have completed occupational training are found work. The highest rates of recruitment after completion of occupational training and retraining are in the Evenkiiskii Autonomous Region (49.2%), the Republic of Dagestan (22.7%) and the Tuva Republic (24.8%). The expenditure on retraining in these regions amounted to 11.2%, 1.6% and 7.6% accordingly. This can be regarded as a relatively efficient use of resources (in comparison with other), indicating the soundness of training programmes developed by the employment service which take into account the current situation in the local labour market.

In regions with a low rate of unemployment priority is given to the forms of active policy which are not required by the Law on Employment or by the state's obligations to those citizens who have lost their jobs.

Thus, it is possible to draw the following conclusions.

1. A significant part of the resources of the employment fund (by our calculation not less than 30% of the total fund) is spent inefficiently and for purposes which are not essentially the responsibility of the Employment Service.

2. There is no clearly expressed state policy for the allocation of the available resources and regional particularities can more accurately be characterised as regional arbitrariness in support of local authorities. How else can one regard the fact that, under its former chief, the Moscow employment service transferred

absolutely nothing to the federal (centralised) part of the fund during the whole period of its activity? Or why, until a sensational scandal in the summer of 1993, the item 'other costs' accounted for 62% of expenditure from the employment fund in St Petersburg, falling to zero by the end of the year. Or why the donor-regions (those with a low rate of unemployment) violate the law and transfer to the federal part of the fund, instead of the 20% laid down by law, only 2% (Sakha Republic), 4.2% (Belgorod oblast), 6.1% (Smolensk oblast). Or why in Novgorod oblast, where the rate of unemployment is above the average for the country, 88% of the unemployed receive the minimum unemployment benefit, while the resources of the fund are spent on so-called financial support (43.8%). The list of similar absurdities could be continued.

Therefore it is essential to define not only what policy is needed,[4] but also the sources of its financing and the allocation of the money available.

ADAPTATION TO UNEMPLOYMENT AFTER FIVE YEARS

Perception of unemployment by the population

As a reality of the transition period, unemployment could not but be reflected in the life of the majority of the Russian people and in their perceptions of the phenomenon. Whereas on the threshold of economic reform, according to the data of VTsIOM, 27% of respondents considered that a small amount of unemployment is useful and even necessary, by 1994 their number had already fallen to 21%, and the proportion of people considering unemployment inadmissible in our country had increased over the same period from 39% to 47%. The same data show that the unacceptability of unemployment has considerably increased since 1993. It is precisely in this period that the deterioration of the economic situation has resulted in the open dismissal of employees from enterprises, an increase in the proportion of

---

[4]   The long-term and intermediate term problems of state employment policy are described in a report of the Institute of Problems of Employment, 1995.

enterprises standing idle, a growth in the number of employees sent on administrative leave and the reduction of employment has been accompanied by a sharp increase in the rate of registered unemployment. It was in 1993 that people's perception changed radically and they really began to relate to unemployment as a real phenomenon of our life. The stereotypical perception of unemployment as an evil ('the birth-mark of capitalism'), which had grown up under the Soviet system of 'universal employment', persisted through inertia in the first years of reform, but was seen as external to our reality and specific to each of us. There were few at that time who could have imagined that by the middle of 1996 almost one in ten of the economically active members of our society would face the threat of losing their job or not being able to find work. In 1995 eight out of ten respondents said that their fear of losing their job had increased and the rise in unemployment had reached second place in the list of the most burning problems (*VTsIOM Bulletin*, 1994, 3, p. 21; 1995, 2, p. 36).

Therefore it is no wonder that in 1995 85% of Russians interviewed expressed the opinion that the state has a duty to provide a job for all those wanting to work, whereas in 1991 90% of the respondents had expressed the same view. This can hardly be treated as a lack of mental preparedness of Russians to live with this phenomenon because behind this opinion lies a real fear not only of losing but, more important, of not finding work.

Moreover, one can regard the fact that the share of the registered unemployed in the total number of unemployed (Table 6.1) has risen year by year as evidence that unemployment is gradually beginning to be seen by the population as a normal phenomenon and registration with the employment service as the first natural step in search of work. Confirmation of this is also provided by the results of our research. If in 1992 a significant proportion of job seekers did not turn to the labour exchanges for the reason that it was 'shameful to be unemployed', in 1996 nobody noted such a reason.[5]

The unemployed and the Employment Service

Alongside the gradual adaptation of the population to unemployment,

---

[5] For more detail see Institute of Economics, 1993, pp. 1, 11–13; data from research on the unemployed conducted at regional employment centres of Vladimir and Nizhnii Novgorod oblasts.

the perception of this phenomenon and of the unemployed themselves by employees of the employment service has also changed. In 1992 the widespread opinion among managers of the employment service was that it was mostly drunkards and layabouts who turned to them (Institute of Economics, 1993, p. 13), but by 1996 their position had changed. And though the directors of the service still consider that about one-fifth of their 'clientele' belong to that category, nevertheless for a greater part of the population registration at the exchange is considered as 'the last hope in the search for work', as 'an essential requirement for work as the source of existence or survival'. Indirect confirmation of this is provided by the data on the growth in the proportion of those applying to the employment service who register as unemployed: While in 1992 only 40% of those applying were officially registered as unemployed (the explanation of this phenomenon at the time was that the remaining 60% came to the service for advice, to find out about the Law on Employment or to find alternative work), in the middle of 1996 almost 90% were registered (Table 6.1).

One also cannot fail to note qualitative changes in the work of the Employment Service, the growth of their activity not only 'in breadth' (expansion of the network of the service, opening of additional branches in regions with a high level of unemployment or in locations remote from regional centres), but also 'in depth' through the establishment of closer relations with employers. The evidence of this is the growth in the number of enterprises hiring employees through the Employment Service, according to the panel data of the Russian Labour Market Flexibility Survey between 1993 and 1996 (Table 6.4).

Table 6.4: Proportion of Employees Hired by Enterprises Through the Employment Service

Hired through the Employment Service (%)	Proportion of industrial enterprises		
	1994	1995	1996
0%	61.2	61.2	57.5
Up to 10%	32.0	25.3	29.0
11–25%	2.9	6.2	4.8
26–50%	1.3	2.5	3.6
More than 50%	2.1	4.8	5.0

It is enterprises in the least successful branches of industry which more often resort to the help of the Employment Service. The constant 'client' of labour exchanges in hiring staff during the last three years has been light industry. Enterprises from the relatively prosperous food-processing industry use their services less often than others. Until 1995, engineering enterprises hardly ever resorted to the help of the employment service, but since 1995 26.6% of these enterprises have begun to employ up to 10% of their staff through state services. This can be explained partly by the fact that enterprises in this branch, with a traditionally highly-skilled labour force, have seen a significant simplification of production over the past few years, reducing their demand for skilled employees. At the same time, the growth of registration at labour exchanges, especially in regions with a high level of unemployment, has increased the supply of skilled labour on offer through employment centres, thereby increasing the likelihood of finding employees with the required qualifications. And, finally, enterprise management sometimes prefers to reduce labour turnover by hiring workers with low qualifications and limited ambition, willing to put up with the non-payment of wages and administrative leave for the sake of a regular job.

According to the panel data of the Russian Labour Market Flexibility Survey, the number of enterprises reporting vacancies to the employment service has increased (Table 6.5). The engineering industry reports vacancies more often than others, although they employ people through the employment services less often (traditional regularity), light industry reports vacancies the least often (because they hardly ever have vacancies) as does the food-processing industry, which employs staff through employment centres less often than others.

Table 6.5: *Vacancies Reported by Enterprises to the Employment Service*

Percentage of vacancies reported to the Employment Service	Proportion of enterprises		
	1994	1995	1996
Up to 10%	19.3	13.3	11.1
11–25%	6.6	5.0	5.9
26–50%	13.7	11.4	9.4
More than 50%	60.4	70.3	73.6

Thus, the need for an enterprise to hire through labour exchanges depends on the difficulty of the economic situation in their particular industry and on the demand for labour as a whole.

All that has been said above helps to explain the VTsIOM data showing an eight-fold increase in the 'popularity' of the employment service between 1991 and 1995. According to Goskomstat data, until 1994 the most important method of job search was 'personal connections' (approximately 37% of the unemployed during the last five years searched for work mainly using personal connections). Since 1994 application to the employment service has become the principal method of job search: in 1993 32% of the job-seeking population sought work only through the Employment Service, in 1994 – 39.8%, in March 1996 – 47% (*Obsledovanie zanyatosti Goskomstata v oktyabre 1993*; Goskomstat: *Informatsionnyi statisticheskii byulleten'*, 13, November 1996, p. 57).

WHAT INCENTIVE IS THERE TO REGISTER AT EMPLOYMENT CENTRES?

The official statistics show that there is still a big difference between the rate of unemployment calculated on the basis of the ILO methodology and the rate of registered unemployment (Table 6.1). This implies that a substantial proportion of those who lose their jobs for whatever reason have no incentive to register and acquire the official status of being unemployed. This situation is common to every region. So, for example, in Moscow, where the level of registered unemployment is the lowest among the 89 Russian regions, the rate of unemployment on the ILO definition is nine times the rate of registered unemployment. In regions with a high level of registered unemployment the difference between these two parameters still exists, although it is not so great (4–5%) as in Moscow.

Therefore, in analysing the data of our research on the unemployed conducted within the framework of the TACIS programme 'Structural reorganisation and unemployment in Russia', we have tried to answer the following questions:

- Do those looking for work have any incentive to register at a labour exchange?
- What are the current capacities of the Employment Service and are they able to cope with growing pressure in regional labour markets?
- How are the financial capacities of the Employment Service

correlated with the growing expenditure on labour market policies with rising unemployment?

Our main hypothesis was based on the results of research on industrial enterprises in eight regions of Russia during 1991–6 which had shown a substantial reduction in employment (35% on average for the given period). Our hypothesis was that one of the main reasons for the discrepancy between the large fall in employment and the small increase in unemployment is the underestimation of the level of unemployment which is the result of the operation of the Law on Employment and other normative documents related to the implementation of labour market policy. Moreover, since 1996 the understating of the rate of unemployment has become a deliberate policy of Russian state structures (above all, the Ministry of Labour of the Russian Federation), caused, apart from political ends, by serious financial problems – the growing deficiency of employment funds. Instead of developing an effective passive labour market policy (i.e. an effective system of unemployment insurance) the purpose of the policy adopted has become the resolution of the problem of unemployment at the expense of the unemployed, by minimising their number and minimising the amount of benefit paid. Such a policy is justified by declarative and unsubstantiated assertions that a passive policy strengthens the mood of dependence in society so that it should be reoriented towards an active labour market policy.

The research included two blocks of questions. The first was addressed to everyone who visited regional employment centres of both areas, the second to the chiefs of the regional services. The survey was conducted during two days of the last week of April 1996. As a result 75 chiefs of employment centres and 29,647 people who had visited labour exchanges over those two days were interviewed. The interviews were anonymous.

The choice of two Russian regions – Vladimir and Nizhnii Novgorod oblasts – was determined by a number of reasons. First, they are two of the largest industrial centres of the European part of Russia, both in terms of population and in the number employed in industry. Secondly, the economic situation of the two oblasts differs.

Vladimir oblast is one of the depressed regions of Russia, where the depth of economic recession and the decline in production are much greater than the Russian average while Nizhnii Novgorod oblast is around the Russian average in these respects. Moreover, Nizhnii

Novgorod was one of the first regions to conduct experiments in economic reform, so that it now has the reputation of being one of the leading regions in the progress to a market economy. Third, the structure of employment in the two regions differs (Table 6.6). Agriculture is the principal branch by volume of employment in 52% of the raions (districts) which make up Nizhnii oblast, while one-third of the raions in Vladimir oblast are concentrated around large textile enterprises, in which a large part of the population has been employed in the past. But both areas are also marked by the prevalence of industries of the military-industrial complex which is a legacy from the Soviet period. The formerly privileged military-industrial enterprises have been confronted by unfamiliar problems – a sharp reduction of state financing and a fall in production, accompanied in most cases by its simplification. The consequences have been a reduction of employment, loss of skilled employees and growth of unemployment.

Table 6.6: Distribution of 75 Raions of the two Oblasts by Predominant Branch (by Number Employed in this Branch) and by Rate of Unemployment in Each of These Groups

	Agriculture and forestry	Engineering	Light industry	Other industries
Proportion of surveyed raions, %	48.0	28.0	12.0	12.0
Registered unemployment in each group, %	6.5	6.5	11.1	8.0
Rate of unemployment in the opinion of directors of Employment Service,%	8.7	10.0	11.5	9.6
Percentage of women among the registered unemployed	46.1	51.8	54.0	47.3
Percentage of young people under 25 among the registered unemployed	27.2	27.3	29.5	26.1

Third, there are contrasts in the development of the labour markets of the two oblasts (Table 6.7), most notably in the rate of registered unemployment, although the differences in the rate of loss of jobs and in the rate of unemployment on the basis of the ILO definition are not nearly so striking. The registered unemployment rate in Nizhnii

Novgorod oblast is not much greater than the Russian average, while Vladimir oblast is one of those regions with the highest rates of registered unemployment. They also differ in the rates of increase of these parameters: the number of registered unemployed has increased by 266% between 1993 and 1996 in Nizhnii Novgorod and by 392% in Vladimir. However, the rate of increase in the level of ILO unemployment was hardly any different in these apparently polar areas – they appear to differ only in the rates at which those without work register. The explanation of this phenomenon might consist in the higher pressure on the labour market in Vladimir oblast, where recourse to the employment centre is considered as the first (or only) variant in search of a job, and in the more effective work of the employment service in Vladimir oblast.

Table 6.7:   Some Labour Market Indicators of the Surveyed Regions

	Nizhnii Novgorod		Vladimir	
	1996	% Change on 1993	1996	% Change on 1993
Total population, thousand	2,833	+2.7	1,251	+3.8
Economically active population, thousand	1,800	- 3.7	776	- 5.6
Employed, thousand	1,664	- 7.5	686	- 8.2
Activity rate, %	63.5	-3.6 points	62.0	-6.2 points
Number of registered unemployed, 1.04.96	64,785	+ 266	79,161	+ 392
Registered unemployment 1.04.96, %	3.5		10.2	
ILO unemployment, March 1996, %	8.7	+80	11.6	+100
Lowest rate of registered unemployment in oblast, %	0.8		4.7	
Highest rate of registered unemployment in oblast, %	12.9		23.6	

Source: Data provided by the analytical departments of the regional employment centres of Nizhnii Novgorod and Vladimir oblasts.

Interviews with the directors of the regional employment services have also shown that their valuations do not coincide with the

statistics recorded by their own services, and the divergence from
official statistics increases in accordance with the increase in the level
of registered unemployment. This is especially marked in the case of
the relatively 'prosperous' Nizhnii Novgorod oblast. According to the
official data only two raions of this oblast have rates of unemployment
of over 11%, but in the opinion of the directors there are five times as
many. In Vladimir oblast the divergences are not so great, but nevertheless they exist. On average almost one-third of the surveyed raions
in the two oblasts had a rate of unemployment of more than 11%, that
is 1.7 times the number according to registration statistics (Table 6.8).

Table 6.8:   *Distribution of Raions of the Surveyed Oblasts by Level of*
               Registered Unemployment, and Estimates of Director of
               Regional Employment Service (%)

Grouping of raions with a level of un-employment	Average rate of unemployment of both oblasts		Average rate of unemployment, Nizhnii Novgorod oblast		Average rate of unemployment, Vladimir oblast	
	Registered	Employ-ment Service estimate	Registered	Employ-ment Service estimate	Registered	Employ-ment Service estimate
Up to 1%	1.2	-	1.7	-	-	-
1–3%	14.9	4.3	19.3	5.8	-	-
3–5%	20.3	17.1	24.6	21.2	5.9	-
5–7%	25.7	14.3	29.8	17.3	11.8	5.9
7–9%	10.8	15.7	12.3	19.2	5.9	5.9
9–11%	9.5	18.6	8.8	17.3	11.8	23.5
More than 11%	17.6	30.0	3.5	19.2	64.7	64.7

**Social and demographic characteristics of those applying to
employment centres**

Fifty-two per cent of those applying to the Employment Service were
women. In spite of the fact that the proportion of women among the
registered unemployed is still higher than that of men, nevertheless the
thesis that unemployment in Russia has a 'female face' has gradually
been negated even in the labour exchanges. During similar research
conducted by us in collaboration with the ILO in 1993, women

accounted for 66% of those applying to the labour exchanges. The clients of the labour exchanges have also become younger in comparison with 1993. In 1993 the average age of men applying to the employment service was 40 and that of women 35, in 1996 the average age of men and women had fallen to 37 and 33 correspondingly. The educational characteristics of the job-seeking population had also changed a little: the number of people with elementary education had fallen and the number with middle special education had increased. But still the educational level of women remains higher than that of men.

Table 6.9: Distribution of Applicants by Educational Level (%)

	Men	Women
Elementary	16.1	7.3
Middle	50.0	44.0
Middle Special	27.1	38.6
Higher	6.8	10.0

Table 6.10: Distribution of Applicants by Marital Status (%)

Single	22.1
Married	60.0
Divorced	12.4
Separated	2.5
Widowed	3.0

The Law on Employment: the rights of the unemployed and main functions of the employment service

According to the existing federal Law on Employment all Russian citizens have the right to receive free consultation and information from the Employment Service with the purpose of choosing a line of business, recruitment and opportunities for occupational training (article 9 point 1 of the Law on Employment). To unemployed people the Law guarantees free career advice, occupational training, retraining and improvement of professional skills on the direction of the Employment Service; payment of unemployment benefits, grants during retraining; indemnification for expenditure incurred in connection with work or training in another district undertaken at the direction of the employment service; free health services and medical check-up on recruitment for work or assignment for training; payment of temporary invalidity; the opportunity of participation in paid public works (articles 12.2, 28 of the Law on Employment).

The law also defines the principal functions of the Employment Service (articles 15, 23, 24), of which the following are the main ones:

- Assistance in search of work.
- Organisation of career advice, occupational training, retraining and improvement of professional skills of unemployed citizens.
- Payments in the form of unemployment benefit, grants during training at the direction of the employment service, rendering of material help to the unemployed and dependent members of their families.
- Participation in the organisation of public works together with executive authorities.

Thus, the following might be reasons for turning to the employment service:

- To receive advice (under the current legislation, about job opportunities, training or retraining).
- To be registered as unemployed in order to have the right to receive unemployment benefit (it should be emphasised that all those seeking work and recognised as unemployed by the employment service have the right to receive benefit, irrespective of whether they have had work in the past, i.e. including those who are looking for work for the first time or who have taken a long break from work).
- To find work from among the vacancies available in the employment service.
- To undergo retraining.

Reasons for non-registration

A feature of the Russian situation, stable for many years among all categories of employees, is the prevalence of reductions in employment by voluntary severance rather than through compulsory redundancy. If one adopts the terminology accepted in international statistics, according to the formal criteria (applying to leave 'by their own will') 63.5% of those employees who left their jobs in industrial enterprises in the first half of 1996 did so voluntarily.[6] According to the data of our research in regional employment centres in the spring of that year, 56% of the unemployed, subsequently registered with the employment service and receiving unemployment benefit, fell into this category. However, more detailed analysis of the reasons for leaving their jobs showed that only 20.5% of the registered unemployed had really left for reasons which can be qualified as their 'own will': moving home, condition of health and family circumstances, conflict with management, dissatisfaction with working conditions and so on. The other 79.5% had left work for so-called economic reasons: because of low wages (their level was almost half that of those who had lost their jobs through redundancy or the closure of the enterprise), regular non-payment of wages, periodic stoppages of the enterprise and unpaid leave, remoteness from home and high transport costs.

The structure of the unemployed by reason for separation, according to the data of our research, is as follows:

- Dismissed (compulsory redundancies, closure of the enterprise): 38.3%
- Left for economic reasons: 44.6%
- Left voluntarily: 11.4%
- Termination of fixed-term contract: 5.2%.

Reason for visiting the Employment Service

The registered statistics show a difference between the number of people turning to the employment service and the number receiving unemployed status. Although the difference has fallen significantly, from 40% to 10%, nevertheless it requires explanation. As a rule the explanations offered by the employees of the Employment Service are that this ten per cent comprises those who have come for advice or those who have not yet completed the prescribed ten-day period between the moment of primary registration and receipt of unemployed status. Our data cast some doubt on this explanation – 94.2% of applicants had no work, 3.2% were counted as being employed but were on extended administrative leave without payment (i.e. were actually unemployed), 2.4% of the respondents were students and pensioners who were seeking additional employment (Table 6.11). From those who

---

[6] Data from research on industrial enterprises in 1996.

were on unpaid administrative leave, 39.7% had applied in search of
other work and 4.4% in the hope of receiving retraining to change
their occupation through the Employment Service.

*Table 6.11: Employment Status of Respondents at the Moment of
Application to the Employment Service, %.*

Employment status	Men	Women
No work	94.6	93.7
On unpaid leave	3.1	3.7
Students	1.3	1.7
Pensioners	1.0	0.9

*Table 6.12: Reason for Visiting the Employment Service for Those
Who had No Work at the Moment of The Visit*

Reasons for visit	% of respondents
Initial application	13.8
Receipt of status of unemployed	3.9
Re-registration and receipt of unemployment benefit	56.7
Search for vacancies	23.9
Registration for retraining through the service	0.9
Registration for premature pension	0.1
Other reasons	0.7

As to the reasons for visiting the employment service, it is interesting that a fairly high proportion (23.9%) of those who did not have
work had come in search of vacancies (Table 6.12). This contradicts
the view held by most government officials that the unemployed come
to labour exchanges not to search for work, but only to secure a comfortable existence at the expense of the state.

As noted above, the directors of regional services estimate the rate
of unemployment as being higher than reported in the official data. We
asked the directors about the reasons why the unemployed do not apply to the Employment Service. The answers were as follows:

- Prefer to search for work themselves: 52.7%.
- Have found themselves temporary alternative work: 29.7%.
- Do not have confidence in the chance of getting a job through
  the service: 14.9%.

- Remoteness of home from employment centre: 2.7%.

It is interesting that not one respondent gave such reasons as 'have not applied on principle – it is shameful to be unemployed' or 'do not know about existence of the Employment Service' which were quite common in 1993.

Period of unemployment, receipt of unemployed status and first unemployment benefit

According to the Law on Employment, receipt of unemployed status is possible on the tenth day from the moment of registration with the Employment Service, and the period of unemployment (and receipt of benefit) is counted from the first day of presentation of the documents indicated in the Law: passport, labour-record book or equivalent document, documents on professional qualifications, information on average earnings for the last three months at the last place of work and, for those seeking work for the first time or without any trade, their passport and educational record (article 3 point 2). Thus, if the Employment Service does not find a suitable job for a person without work within 10 days of the moment of their application, the date of their registration as unemployed should coincide with the date they received unemployed status and the date they received the right to unemployment benefit.

According to the date revealed by our research, the picture looks rather different:

Table 6.13: Delays in Employment Service Procedure (weeks)

Average period between:	Weeks
Loss of work and initial application to the employment service	17.4
Initial application to the Employment Service and receipt of unemployed status	1.2
Receipt of unemployed status and receipt of unemployment benefit	5.4

Thus, 6.8 weeks passes from the date of initial registration before the unemployed person receives their first unemployment benefit (in similar research in 1993 this period was 4 weeks;   Institute of

Economics, 1993, p. 13). Moreover, 19.5% of the registered unemployed had not begun to receive benefits two months after initial registration and half of these were still not getting benefit after three months. It would be logical to assume that the lengthening of these periods is connected with the growth of unemployment and the shortage of money in the employment fund, and thus with the attempt of the employment centres to postpone payment of benefits for as long a period of time as possible. However, it is interesting that there was no correlation between the length of these periods and the rate of unemployment in the raion. So, for example, in the raion with the lowest rate of unemployment (0.8%) the period between application to the service and receipt of unemployed status was 3.4 weeks (against the average for all raions of 1.2 weeks), while the same period was observed in a number of raions with a rate of unemployment of more than 7%.

Size of the benefit

Statements from officials of the Ministry of Labour to the effect that the existing system of payment of benefit encourages not the search for new jobs but a mood of dependence among the unemployed have become increasingly frequent (*Segodnya*, 48, 12 March 1997). An even more categorical point of view was expressed not so long ago by the President of the Moscow Confederation of Industrialists and Entrepreneurs, E. Panin: 'In Soviet times there was an article in the Code dealing with parasitism, now it [parasitism] is actually encouraged by the existing system of handing out unemployment benefits. They pay them to people who have deliberately chosen not to work'.[7] According to this leader of Moscow's businessmen (on whom, incidentally, the employment fund depends for the bulk of its receipts), this layabout can become rich by collecting almost one million roubles (approximately 200 US dollars) per year, when this 'enormous' amount of money could be directed to the creation of additional jobs in small and medium business.

Quite often experts can be found who share (maybe in not so categorical a form) this point of view. There is an established image of the prosperous Moscow unemployed coming to collect his benefit, which

---

[7]   Transcript of a meeting of the government of Moscow to discuss the programme of employment assistance, *Moskovskie novosti*, 6, February 1997, p. 11.

exceeds the national average wage, in his Mercedes or the shuttle trader who has an 'enormous' income and pretends to be unemployed.

As there is no official data on the size of unemployment benefits that are paid, nor data on the number of unemployed receiving the maximum unemployment benefit, we had some doubts about the validity of these claims. Therefore during our research we tried to find out in more detail what is the level of unemployment benefit and what is its relative importance as a source of income, for the sake of which people are supposedly ready not only to consider a period of unemployment as a privilege, but also to overcome the procedures laid down by our legislation in order to receive the desired status of unemployed. In other words, we tried to find out whether it is really so advantageous, in the material sense, to be unemployed.

The average size of unemployment benefit received in March 1996 was 142 thousand roubles in Nizhnii Novgorod oblast and 136 thousand roubles in Vladimir. One should take into account the fact that some of the unemployed were paid the delayed benefit for the previous month, so the average size of the monthly benefit is slightly overestimated. This explains the divergence in the answers of the directors of regional employment centres of Vladimir oblast and the unemployed on the question of the average size of the benefit – 103 thousand and 136 thousand respectively. In Nizhnii Novgorod oblast, where the problem of delay of payments of benefits had still not become serious in the spring 1996, there was hardly any divergence: 142 thousand according to the answers of the unemployed, and 144 thousand according to the chiefs of services. The more accurate sum, in our view, is that given by the directors, though this may be an overestimate as it probably reflects benefits due rather than benefits paid.

Thus, the average unemployment benefit in March 1996 amounted to 23% of the average wage in Nizhnii Novgorod and 19.5% in Vladimir oblast (under the Law on Employment the average benefit for one year should be 60% of the average wage), or approximately 40% of the subsistence minimum of both areas. Moreover, 40.5% of the recipients of benefit in March 1996 received it at a rate not exceeding the minimum wage, 38.1% – from one up to three minimum wages, 8.9% – between three minimum wages and the subsistence minimum of the region and only 12.5% at a rate between the subsistence minimum and the average wage.

If we take into account the fact that these data relate not to all those

Table 6.14: Distribution of Unemployed by Size of Benefit Received in March 1996 by Region (% of Total Unemployed in Oblast)

	Nizhnii Novgorod	Vladimir
Has received nothing	50.7	58.7
No more than the minimum wage	18.8	17.7
Between one and two minimum wages	11.9	9.7
Between two and three minimum wages	7.7	5.3
Between three minimum wages and the subsistence minimum	4.7	3.4
Between the subsistence minimum and the average wage	6.0	5.1

Notes: 1. *The minimum wage is equal to the minimum unemployment benefit, which in March 1996 was 64 thousand roubles.*
   2. *The subsistence minimum in March 1996, according to Goskomstat data, in Nizhnii Novgorod oblast was 289 thousand roubles and in Vladimir oblast was 308 thousand roubles.*
   3. *The average wage in March 1996, according to Goskomstat data, in Nizhnii Novgorod oblast was 621 thousand roubles and in Vladimir oblast was 527 thousand roubles.*

who were unemployed with a right to benefit in the period under consideration, but only to those who actually received it, the situation looks even more depressing: 50.7% of the unemployed in Nizhnii Novgorod and 58.7% in Vladimir oblast had not received any benefit (Table 6.14). The statistical average portrait of the unemployed person who had not received benefit is as follows: a married man, 34.8 years old, with two other adult family members and 1.5 children under 18 years old, with a monthly income per head of 129.1 thousand roubles on which to live.

The reasons for non-payment can be divided into two fundamentally different categories. The first are those which accord with the Law on Employment, which cover only 28.1% of cases of non-payment:

- Receipt of benefit from the enterprise (5.3%).[8]
- Suspension of payment because of dismissal under articles of

---

[8] Since May 1996, as a result of amendments to the Law on Employment, the receipt of redundancy payments from the enterprise cannot form the basis for non-payment (suspension of payment) of unemployment benefit.

the Labour Code, failure to re-register in time, refusal of two suitable job offers (7.6%).

- Has not reached or is beyond the term during which payment is due (15.2%).

The second category, amounting to 71.9% of the non-payment, is connected with the absence of money in the regional employment funds.

This reason for non-payment of benefit is most common among the rural unemployed and in raions in which light industry is the dominant branch – 60% and 60.3% of the unemployed respectively. The difficult financial situation of the employment funds has resulted in a tightening of the criteria for the payment of benefit. So, payment of benefit to the unemployed for failure to re-register in time was found more often in village areas (5.7% of cases), which in itself is not surprising because of the significant geographical dispersion of rural settlements, difficulties with transport and high transport costs. In the same areas a more strict approach was taken to the unemployed dismissed under articles of the Labour Code – 6.1% were not paid benefit for this reason.[9]

Quite often, theoretical discussions of the principles of determination of the size of unemployment benefits underline the disincentive effect of high social payments of long duration and, above all, of unemployment benefits. However, the data on the actual size of benefits testifies that the Russian unemployed provide no grounds for disquiet on this score: for half of them there is simply nothing to provide an incentive or a disincentive since benefit is not paid to them. For approximately one-third of the unemployed the benefit is a major, and sometimes the only, source of existence of the family, and to the extent that the role of the earnings of other members of the family is reduced, unemployment benefit takes on the leading role as the source of subsistence. For the greater part of the population without work and looking for a job without the help of state services, the size of the benefit paid is apparently not even a sufficient incentive for them to go to the employment centre.

---

[9]   According to the Law on Employment, payment of benefit can be suspended for a period of up to three months in the case of persons dismissed from their last place of work under the articles of the Labour Code and who have received the status of unemployed. The decision about the fact and the period of suspension is taken by a commission of the employment service in each particular case.

Unemployment benefit and the situation of families of the unemployed

As the average income per head of families of the surveyed unemployed amounted to 124 thousand roubles, which is only one-third of the subsistence minimum, the question naturally arises of how these families survive. Part of the answer to this question is given by the data on the main sources of the family budget, which those interviewed filled in themselves (see Table 6.15). The wages of employed family members were the main source of the family budget for just over half of the unemployed people (53%); for 4.4% of families of the unemployed this source was second in importance and for 2.8% of families it came third.

Table 6.15: Main Sources of Subsistence of Families of the Unemployed (as a % of the Total Number Interviewed), in Which No Family Members Received Wages

	First	Second	Third
Pensions, grants	29.7	15.2	4.9
Unemployment benefit	27.2	29.4	19.3
Individual subsistence production	19.2	12.1	17.8
Casual earnings of family members	6.5	4.5	3.1
Child benefit	5.9	25.0	24.2
Help from relatives	4.9	7.3	15.9
Income from individual subsidiary activity	3.2	1.3	2.6
Alimony	1.3	2.5	6.1
Monetary savings	1.1	1.2	2.1
Sale of accumulated property	0.7	1.3	3.7
Other	0.3	0.2	0.4

But an especially difficult situation arises in:

1. Families, where the wages of family members were not a significant source of the family budget (13%).
2. Families, where unemployment benefit is the most important source of the family budget (14.8% of families).

In the first group of families the average income per head of a family of three persons amounted to 106.2 thousand roubles, or 2.8 times less than the subsistence minimum. The average income per head of a family of the average size, 2.6 people, was even less – 98.3 thousand roubles, or three times less than the subsistence minimum. Among those to whom benefit was not paid, men were in a small majority (51%), but among those unemployed in whose families nobody received a wage, women were in the majority (56%), and were twice as likely to be divorced or separated.

It should be noted that among those families of the unemployed who did not indicate a wage as a source of the family budget, 69% had no employed family members. Of the remaining 31% of families, 66% had one person employed, 28.5% had two employed and 5.5% had more than two. However, these employed family members did not receive any income from their employment, i.e. on our classification (see the section on hidden unemployment), they were unemployed.

Thus, the main source of subsistence of families in which nobody is employed is various sorts of social payments – pensions, allowances, grants. Alongside this, unemployment benefit which, in the month previous to the research, amounted on average to 73.1 thousand roubles (or approximately 15 US dollars a month), plays an essential role for such families (Table 6.15).

The offer of vacancies

The offer of vacancies is one of the main responsibilities of the Employment Service, and one of the main determinants of the effectiveness with which the employment centres find jobs for those who apply to them. Moreover, the level of vacancies available in the Employment Service is the basis on which one of the most important indicators, that of labour market pressure (the number of unemployed per vacancy) is calculated. But, as we have already noted earlier (Institute of Economics, 1993, pp. 22–3), the data on vacancies in the Employment Service are incomplete since many enterprises either do not report vacancies at all or provide incomplete information, as a rule only for the low prestige and low-paid jobs. This is also supported by the data of Table 6.16, which shows that more than a quarter of enterprises provide only truncated information on vacancies. It is also necessary to remember that such information is given to the Employment Service mainly by medium and large concerns and, as a rule, by those in a difficult economic situation facing major financial problems. Directors of the raion employment services themselves have a low evaluation of the vacancies submitted to them. The Nizhnii Novgorod directors consider that only 43.8% of available vacancies reach them, those in Vladimir, 60.1%.

It is no wonder, therefore, that the possibilities of the Employment Service offering vacancies are limited. According to the data of our research more than 40% of the unemployed were never offered any vacancies (Table 6.16). Moreover, vacancies were offered more often in Vladimir oblast – a region with a high level of unemployment. In Nizhnii Novgorod oblast, in 15 of 57 raions more than 60% of the unemployed were not offered vacancies. One might assume that the activity and overall performance of the Employment Service of Vladimir oblast was higher both in seeking out vacancies available in the region and in the placement of people through these services. However, further analysis shows that agriculture is the main branch by volume of employment in the majority (90%) of these 15 raions of Nizhnii Novgorod oblast and agriculture, as a rule, does not inform the Employment Service of available vacancies for the reason that there aren't any. This, probably, also explains the fact that the lowest level of offers of vacancies is found in agricultural areas.

Table 6.16: Offer of Vacancies by Employment Service (% of Total)

Number of vacancies offered	Average for two areas	Nizhnii Novgorod oblast	Vladimir oblast	Women	Men
Were never offered any	43.1	47.8	31.4	43.3	42.8
1 vacancy	31.7	30.8	34.0	30.9	32.5
2 vacancies	12.1	11.1	14.8	12.4	11.9
3 vacancies	5.2	4.5	6.9	5.4	5.0
More than 3 vacancies	7.9	5.8	8.1	8.0	7.8
Average no.	1.2	1.0	1.6	1.2	1.1

Vacancies are offered most frequently in raions dominated by the engineering industry. According to our data, 78.8% of the unemployed in these districts were offered at least one vacancy. However, it was precisely in these districts that the unemployed more often (43.5%)

refused the vacancy offered because of low wages. It was in the same districts that the unemployed more often (18.9%) came back with nothing, as the vacancies turned out to have been filled.

Employers refused to take on 4.1% of the unemployed because they did not have the necessary qualifications, while 1.5% of the unemployed rejected the offer of a job because the workplace proposed did not pay wages regularly. It is not clear whether the latter should be considered a 'refusal of suitable work' which could provide a legal basis for withdrawal of official registration as unemployed.

The main reasons for the rejection of job offers by the unemployed were distributed as follows:

- Low wages: 41% of the unemployed.
- Distance from home and high transport costs: 15.7%.
- Not satisfied with character of the work: 12.4%.
- Heavy conditions of labour: 8.8%.
- Condition of health: 2.3%.
- Other reasons: 0.7%.

Thus, the most numerous reasons for the rejection of job offers from the Employment Service corresponded to the main reasons for employees' leaving their jobs 'at their own will' – low wages and high transport costs (quite often the monthly costs for city transport can amount to the average wage of some categories of employees in the budget sphere, light industries and so on).

Training and retraining

It is well known that employment programmes ascribe considerable importance to spending on professional training or retraining. Although expenditure from the employment fund under this heading is insignificant, nevertheless it has increased. The capacities of the Employment Service have increased correspondingly, as is shown by our research data. While in 1993 only 1% of unemployed women and 2% of unemployed men received retraining through the Employment Service, three years later already 32.8% of women and 28.2% of men were offered retraining. Slightly more unemployed people were offered training in the depressed Vladimir oblast – 31.4% – than in Nizhnii Novgorod – 30.2%. This can partly be explained by the fact that Vladimir oblast receives grants from the federal part of the employment fund and is developing a network of retraining for the growing number of unemployed not so much in the hope that they will more rapidly find work, as to provide a break in the period of unemployment and remove for a time the psychological stress on the unemployed themselves.

When questioned, 28.6% of the unemployed said that they would like to undergo retraining and 19.1% were not sure. Thus, about half the registered unemployed could apply to undergo a course of training or retraining through the employment service. In fact, 30.6% of the unemployed were offered the chance of retraining. It is obvious that the limited availability of training is connected with the shortage of money in the employment fund not only for the payment of grants to the unemployed, but also for the expansion of the training network.

Table 6.17: Attitude of the Unemployed to Retraining Through the Employment Service (% of Unemployed Questioned)

Would you like to undergo a course of retraining?	Nizhnii Novgorod oblast	Vladimir oblast	Men	Women
Yes	26.8	32.3	25.2	31.7
No	54.0	48.7	57.8	47.2
Have not decided	19.2	18.9	17.0	21.1

At the same time, significant differences of opinion concerning retraining were observed among the unemployed. So, in regions dominated by light industry many more of the unemployed refuse retraining (47.6%) than want it (33.0%). In rural districts, on average 31.1%, and often as many as 90%, wanted to follow a retraining course and 35.3% did not. The most positively oriented to retraining are those unemployed in areas dominated by the engineering and chemical industries. One can assume that rural inhabitants have no incentive to change or to acquire any other speciality or trade. Since they are unlikely to find work in a new trade in their district and migration to another district is difficult because of the high cost of housing and transport, they are more likely to look to self-employment in their own agricultural district. Registration with the Employment Service may be seen by them as the only possible way of receiving 'live' money. This is partly confirmed by the fact that the main reason for refusal of retraining is the absence of any guarantee of finding a job (see Table 6.18).

While women more often refused retraining because of the absence of any guarantee of a job (33.1%), the majority of men (36.2%) did not want to change their trade or profession.

Thus, as the data show, the chance of obtaining retraining through the Employment Service does not provide a strong incentive for registration as unemployed. And it is doubtful that it can provide such an incentive, especially in Russia, where there is almost no interregional labour mobility. Thus, the acquisition of a trade in Vladimir oblast is hardly likely to change the status of the unemployed. Positive examples are fairly rare and concern a limited circle of the registered unemployed. For example, the efficiency of retraining in one of the oblasts was maximal when the employment centre trained 20 unemployed people as trolley bus drivers, on the orders of the municipal authorities, with a guaranteed job at the end. In the overwhelming majority of cases the period of retraining can be considered only as a period of psychological relief for the unemployed.

Table 6.18: Reasons for the Unemployed's Refusal of Retraining Offered by the Employment Service.

Reasons for refusal	% refusing retraining
There are no guarantees of a job after retraining	28.0
No desire to change speciality	27.7
The proposed speciality was not suitable	23.2
The place of training is located far from home, high transport costs	17.5
Family circumstances	1.9
Other	1.7

It is obvious that the capacities of the Employment Service are fairly limited, and not only financially. In developing a network of retraining, they make little attempt to study the demand for labour in the region, to say nothing of their limited knowledge of the state of affairs even in the next oblast, let alone in the country as a whole. The retraining courses differ little from one another and usually train the same type of specialists, complicating an already tense situation in the labour market.

Retraining would probably be more effective if the unemployed themselves could choose in what trade to be trained and where, instead of having to select from the list of trades offered by the Employment Service. The unemployed themselves might even pay for such courses, or take out loans from the Employment Service, if they knew that the new specialism, trade or skills obtained would help them to find desirable work. The Employment Service could help the unemployed to orient themselves to the current situation in both their own regional labour market and those of other regions, and could also help with payment of removal costs to a new job and home. High transport costs will inevitably impose a burden on the employment funds, but expenditure on unemployment benefits would be saved. But more important, pressure on their own regional labour market will decrease and intra-regional and interregional labour mobility will be increased, which will help to overcome concentrations of unemployment which are characteristic of the majority of Russian regions.

Public works

There have been fundamental changes in the situation regarding public works over the last three years. During our research in 1993 we discovered that not one person registered as unemployed with the Employment Service had been offered participation in public works and this was mainly because of the indeterminate status of public works and sources of their financing. Three years later, according to the data of comparable research, 28% of the unemployed had already been offered participation in public works (28.4% of men and 27.6% of women). Public works were offered more often in Nizhnii Novgorod (33.5%) than in Vladimir oblast (16.4%). And though a lot still remains unclear in the definition of public works, sources of financing have been identified, depending on the economic situation in the particular oblast and in the particular raion. In 1993 enterprises were expected to pay 60% of the cost of public works, with the remaining 40% divided between the Employment Service and the local administration. In the past three years of economic recession the situation has changed fundamentally. First, enterprises have ceased to finance public works – they do not have enough money to pay their taxes or even to pay wages to their employees. Secondly, the non-payment of taxes has had an impact on the resources of the employment fund. Problems with the financing of the employment fund first arose in the autumn of 1995 and universal delay in the payment of the miserly unemployment benefits became a feature of 1996. Therefore the main role in the financing of public works has now been assigned to the local budget. In those areas where taxes can be more effectively collected, the municipal authorities can allow themselves to allocate a small amount of money to the organisation of public works. Nizhnii Novgorod oblast is an example of this, being able to conduct public works in areas with a high level of unemployment and in mono-industrial areas. The situation in Vladimir oblast, a depressed subsidised region of Russia, is quite different. Here a very small amount of money is spent on public works, mainly in the summer months to employ young people with no training and no trade who are virtually unable to find work in this oblast. The summer period is preferable, first, because from June there is a sharp increase in the number of young people applying to the Employment Service (after leaving school or ending the academic year), and, second, the costs of public works are lower than in the autumn and winter. In addition, people who have finished their period of entitlement to unemployment benefit or young people under 18 (students during the vacation or those who have refused training), rather than registered unemployed, are quite often sent on public works.

The tables show that the capacity to organise public works grows in accordance with the growth of the unemployment rate, but only up to a definite limit – 5%. Beyond that the capacity to provide public works falls, especially when the unemployment rate exceeds 9%.

Table 6.19: Distribution of 75 Raions by Rate of Unemployment and Involvement of the Unemployed in Public Works

Groups of raions with the given level of registered unemployment:	Proportion of the unemployed who had been offered participation in public works (%)
Up to 1%	27.7
From 1–3%	30.7
From 3–5%	37.8
From 5–7%	31.5
From 7–9%	34.1
From 9–11%	18.9
More than 11%	20.9

The grouping of raions by their principal industry shows that the highest level of unemployment is found in raions which had until recently been dominated by light industry. The reduction of employment, compulsory leave, growing non-payment of wages and production stoppages in these enterprises have all had an impact on unemployment in these districts, while sharply reducing the amount of money received by the local budgets and by the employment fund. This has correspondingly reduced the capacity of both the local authorities and the regional Employment Service to undertake such measures as public works with the unemployed. Therefore, participation in public works was lower in those districts dominated by light industry – 17.6% of the unemployed. Public works were offered twice as often in agricultural districts (35.7% of the unemployed – the highest rate of all areas), which is most probably connected with the indeterminate status of 'public works'.

According to the newly amended version of the Law on Employment, the unemployed who are directed to public works lose their unemployed status for the duration of their participation in such works. This innovation is one more mechanism for reducing the level of registered unemployment and leads to the further deterioration of the economic situation of the unemployed by reducing the size of their unemployment benefit.

The demands of the unemployed

It is clear, contrary to the opinion common in bureaucratic circles, that the Russian unemployed cannot in any way be accused of unwillingness to work or passivity in search of work: 45.1% of women and 38.3% of men are ready to work at any speciality, if only they are provided with regular and adequate earnings. It should be noted that one of the reasons for the refusal of a job offer is low pay. The refusal can be 'accepted' by the Employment Service if the wages offered are lower than those recorded as having been paid at the last place of work. Otherwise, under the Law on Employment, it can be qualified as a refusal of offered work. Two such refusals are the basis for suspension of the payment of benefit and consequently for the deprivation of unemployed status. Now, when a large proportion of the unemployed are leaving closed or potentially bankrupt enterprises it is obvious that their final earnings are very low. If to this is added long delays in the payment of wages, and their partial payment, one can assume that the recorded payment in their last job for the majority of unemployed will be below the level at which anyone could be expected to agree to work full-time. Nevertheless, formally, all those unemployed who refuse to work for a low wage, but one which is greater than that in their record, can lose both unemployed status and unemployment benefit. In Moscow oblast, for example, the unemployed are refused registration if they reject work with a salary at the average level for the oblast even if their earnings at their last place of work were above that average.

Table 6.20: Preference for Specialism (% of Those Questioned)

	Total	Men	Women
Would like to work only at my own speciality	45.0	50.2	40.2
Would like to change speciality	5.7	4.6	6.6
The speciality is not important, I would work for normal payment	41.9	38.3	45.1
The speciality is not important, I need any work	7.5	6.9	8.0

Table 6.21: Preference for Work Regime (% of Those Questioned)

	Total	Men	Women
Would like to work only full-time	37.4	46.5	29.0
Would prefer full-time work, but would agree to a part-time job.	22.0	15.8	27.8
Would like to work only part-time	5.1	3.0	7.0
It doesn't matter	35.5	34.7	36.2

More than half the unemployed were willing to work at any speciality and under any work regime (Tables 6.20 and 6.21). Women were more flexible in this respect, being willing more often than men to change their existing specialism (Table 6.20).

The demands of the unemployed concerning the minimum wage they will accept can be treated from two points of view. For the bureaucrat who wants to get the unemployed off the register their demands may be considered excessive, especially in depressed Vladimir, where the unemployed demand the average wage for the oblast

(Table 6.22). From the point of view of a normal person, particularly if they have a family and children, the minimum pay demanded is only one and a half times the regional subsistence minimum, which cannot possibly be regarded as an excessive aspiration.

Table 6.22: Minimum Wage for a Suitable Job, Thousand Roubles

	Minimum wage for a suitable job	Average wage for the oblast	Subsistence minimum for the oblast
Average	500.3	-	-
Nizhnii Novgorod	484.1	621.0	289.0
Vladimir	533.9	527.0	308.0
Men	589.0	-	-
Women	417.8	-	-

CONCLUSION

The growth of unemployment in Russia is occurring against the background of the state removing itself from the resolution of this most acute social problem. Unable or, rather, unwilling to undertake realistic and effective measures for the social protection of unemployed citizens, government officials prefer to resolve problems of the unemployment at the expense of the unemployed.

During the spring of 1997 two main theses were actively propagandised by the Ministry of Labour and Social Development: that rates of unemployment in Russia are much lower than in European countries and that the existing system of benefit payments encourages a mood of dependence in society.[10]

As to a low rate of unemployment, the data discussed above have shown the groundlessness of such an assertion, above all because the unemployed do not have any incentive to turn to the Employment

---

[10]   See, for example: 'Protection of capitalist labour'. Transcript of a meeting of the Government of Moscow to discuss the Program of Employment Assistance, *Moskovskie novosti*, 6, February 9–16 1997; A. Tkachenko, 'The forgotten labour market', *Nezavisimaya gazeta*, 12 March 1997; speech of Deputy Minister of Labour M. Moskvina at a meeting of the duma 'Social benefits breed dependency', *Segodnya*, 48, 12 March 1997; statement of M. Moskvina and Minister of Labour G. Melik'yan to the government commission, *Kommersant-Daily*, March 1997.

Services since the latter only 'guarantee':

- A miserly unemployment benefit, which for the last year has only been paid from time to time.
- Little chance of finding a job, since the database of the Employment Service is quite poor and access to it is extremely limited (only through the employees of the Employment Service or advertisements which are sometimes posted in the premises of the Employment Service).
- Ineffective retraining organised, as a rule, without regard for the current and long-term development of the regional labour market, which is why it cannot offer significant prospects for the unemployed either from the point of view of increasing their chances of finding a job or from the point of view of investment in their 'human capital'.

It is very sad that the state is not interested in changing the situation that has emerged, especially in the light of chronic non-payment and the absence of money in the employment fund. It has been simpler to use all the means put at their disposal by the Law on Employment to understate the rate of unemployment. Officials have appeared at their most inventive in looking for new methods of further reducing the rate of unemployment. Amendments to the Law on Employment are now proposed which would tighten the conditions of benefit by depriving those who leave work voluntarily of the right to benefit, which would remove any incentive for around a third of the currently registered unemployed to apply to the Employment Service. A further six per cent would lose their incentive to register under a proposed amendment which would restrict the maximum level of unemployment benefit to the subsistence minimum for the region (while now it is limited to the average wage paid in the region).

The adoption of these amendments would once again enable the state to confirm the myth common in the West that Russia has not only a low but even a falling rate of unemployment.

The claim that the existing system of benefit payments leads to the proliferation of social dependency is not only denied by the reality in which the unemployed are on the boundary between survival and extinction, but above all testifies to the cynicism of the Russian authorities, who could otherwise be accused of incompetence and of distancing themselves from reality.

7 Economic Restructuring and Employment Promotion in a Russian Crisis Region: The Case of Ivanovo

Maarten Keune
ILO Central and Eastern European Team, Budapest

INTRODUCTION

The profound economic and social changes the Russian Federation has been experiencing since the start of the transition process have had an uneven impact in the different geographical regions of the country.[1] As in other transition countries, clear regional disparities concerning economic and enterprise development, employment and income have emerged (or in some cases intensified). Although the country in general is in a state of economic depression, certain crisis regions can be identified which suffer disproportionally from employment losses, poverty and economic recession.[2]

Multiple causes determine these regional disparities. The main cause should be sought in the way industrialisation took place in the USSR, creating a high number of mono-structural regions in which the economy, employment, income, education, infrastructure and other socio-economic factors were often dependent on only one or two industries. The various industries have been affected in different degrees by the declines in domestic demand, the break up of the USSR and the

---

[1] Since October 1994, the Central and Eastern European Team of the ILO, based in Budapest, has been assisting Ivanovo Oblast in the framework of a technical co-operation project. This project has resulted among other things in a series of papers and an advisory report (ILO-CEET, 1996a). The present paper is to a large extent based on these materials.

[2] See, for example, Russian Ministry of Labour, 1996.

256

CMEA and the resulting loss of export markets and increasing foreign competition. This has been reflected in greater losses of production, employment, income and investment in the regions mainly dependent on the most affected industries, notably textiles and engineering. However, other factors also play a role, for example the availability of raw materials, location, climatic conditions or population density.

This is consistent with the developments in other transition countries, where in general the metropolitan cities, benefiting from international ties, increasing joint ventures, highly-skilled labour forces and better services are comparatively more dynamic and have lower unemployment, whereas old industrial regions or agricultural regions have often become problem regions with high unemployment levels.[3]

Here we will analyse the economic and employment developments of one of the crisis regions in Russia, Ivanovo oblast, which has been one of the most affected regions during the transition to a more market oriented system. We will discuss the restructuring of industry and employment, and the emergence of high unemployment, and show that this problem is due to become even more serious in the near future. Then we will discuss a number of policy fields that will have to be attended to in order to start to work on the recovery of Ivanovo.

ECONOMIC AND SOCIAL CRISIS IN IVANOVO

Ivanovo: a textile-dominated industrial region

The Ivanovo oblast is one of the 89 Russian administrative regions and has a population of around 1,274,000. The capital of the region, the city of Ivanovo, has a population of around 550,000 and there are 16 smaller towns. Ivanovo is the historical centre of the Russian textile industry, the first textile activities dating back some 300 years. During the centrally planned period the role of this industry was further bolstered and the region became the country's main supplier of cotton cloth, responsible for one out of every three meters produced in Russia in 1990. Moreover, it produced 9.3% of Russia's woollen cloth and considerable amounts of linen and silk cloth. An important part of the

---

[3]   See, for example, Sengenberger and Keune, 1996 or Russian Ministry of Labour, 1996.

cotton companies in the region integrate spinning and weaving, and only a few are dedicated exclusively to one of these activities.

Table 7.1:   *Employment by Industry in the Ivanovo Region, 1990 (thousands and %)*

	Thousand	%		Thousand	%
Total employed	667.5	100	**Employed in industry**		
Industry	269.1	40.3	Total industry	269.1	100
Farming	65.2	9.8	Textiles	121.1	45.4
Transport and communications	39.3	5.9	Engineering	63.0	23.4
Construction	45.6	6.8	Others	84.0	31.2
Trade, public catering and public utilities	54.8	8.2			
Non-productive sphere	155.6	23.3			
Private farming	0.1	–			
Individual business	1.3	0.2			
Other	36.5	5.5			

Sources: Ignatov, 1994, Rasumov, 1995.

As far as employment was concerned, Ivanovo became strongly dependent on industry, providing 40% of total employment in 1990, and in particular on the textile industry, accounting for 45.4% of industrial employment (Table 7.1). On the other hand, garment production hardly developed. Apart from textiles, engineering played an important part, with 23.4% of industrial employment, and to a minor extent also the chemical, woodworking and food industries. The dominance of the textile industry is further underlined by the fact that a number of other industries, especially the chemical industry, construction, engineering and transport were partly linked to textile activities.[4]

The textile enterprises were normally large to very large enterprises, resulting in a strong urbanisation of the region with 81% of the

---

[4]   The Ivanovo engineering industry produced, among other things, tools, parts and machines for the textile enterprises. However, the links between engineering and textiles were not at all as strong as could be expected. For example, Ivanovo produced only 2.9% of Russian looms.

population living in urban areas, often depending on one or two enterprises which apart from employment and income also constituted the basic structure for housing, social protection, health care and cultural activities and were main investors in the local infrastructure, education and other important areas.

Problems in the textile industry

Through the years Ivanovo became a typical example of the Soviet-type of industrial development and, as it has turned out, extremely vulnerable to economic change. Using the terminology of Rehfeld, Ivanovo developed into a highly specialised region, but with a very low degree of functional differentiation.[5] It came to depend mainly on the textile industry which was focused almost exclusively on the mass production (manufacturing) of low quality cloth and covered only a limited part of the production chain.[6] As indicated before, the production of machinery and tools for the textile industry was performed only to a moderate extent in Ivanovo itself. Apart from the fact that garment production was hardly present in the region, the relations with suppliers of inputs or with receivers of the products were underdeveloped (they were mainly managed by the central government) and the innovative capacity of the region was very low. The enterprises themselves had hardly any R&D capacity and the links between the enterprises and the Textile Academy, the main relevant Ivanovo based academic institution, were very weak.[7] The mentality in the region was (and to a large extent still is) a typical 'producer mentality', focused on manufacturing without substantial involvement in product innovation or design, raw material purchasing, distribution of products in and outside the country, marketing, or further processing of the textiles produced.

---

[5] Rehfeld (1995) groups regional economies along two axes: specialisation (indicating to what extent different branches or sectors are represented in the regional economy) and functional differentiation (indicating to what extent different production phases and other elements of the production chain are performed in the region).

[6] Besides the production itself, elements of this production chain are those functions preceding and following production, and those necessary to carry out the manufacturing process and the integrative function of standardisation, e.g. R&D, machine and tool production, marketing, etc. (Rehfeld, 1995).

[7] They were weak in the field of R&D. On the other hand, practically all enterprise managers and textile specialists had their education in the Textile Academy and its students had compulsory practical placements in the enterprises.

In the first years of transition, industrial production in Russia declined rapidly and by 1994 it had fallen to 47% of its 1990 level (Table 7.2). When looking at the different branches we see that light industry (including textiles) was the biggest loser with production reaching only 26% of its 1990 level. Engineering also suffered severely.

Table 7.2: Index of Industrial Production, 1994 compared to 1990 (%)

Light industry	26
Engineering	32
Wood and paper industry	38
Construction materials	42
Chemical industry	45
Food industry	55
Iron and steel	55
Non-ferrous metals	65
Oil, gas and coal	73
Industry total	47

Source: Götz, 1995.

Table 7.3:   Production in Industry as a Percentage of 1990, Ivanovo region 1990–95

	1990	1991	1992	1993	1994	1995
Industry	100	98.1	65.3	56.1	39.0	34.2
Textiles	100	97.8	58.2	46.2	33.3	32.9
Mechanical engineering	100	102.4	89.3	84.6	56.7	52.6
Construction	100	115.8	91.1	64.8	48.5	n.a.

Source: Rasumov, 1995 and 1996.

Within this context Ivanovo soon suffered the consequences of its narrow economic base and industrial decline was much steeper than the national average. Total 1994 industrial production in the region reached only 39% of its 1990 level, 8 percentage points lower than the national figure, and fell further to 34.2% of 1990 in 1995 (Table 7.3). This was caused mainly by the strong decline of textile production, falling to only 32.9% of its 1990 level in 1995. Although this was more favourable than the national average decline in light industry in this period, the dominance of the textile industry in Ivanovo made it a disastrous development. Ivanovo's engineering industry performed significantly better than the national average, maintaining 56.7% of its 1990 level in 1994 and 52.6% in 1995.

Labour market developments

Naturally, the developments described above have strongly influenced the labour market situation in Ivanovo. One of the most noticeable expressions of labour market changes has been the explosive growth of registered unemployment, non-existent before 1991 but amounting to 11.8% at the end of 1995 and to 13.7% (or 87,510 persons) on 1 April 1996. This made Ivanovo the second-highest unemployment region in the country. National registered unemployment was only 3.2% and 3.7% respectively on these dates.[8] Also within the region there are substantial differences in unemployment levels, with registered unemployment being relatively low in, for example, Ivanovo City (7.6% in 1995) while in some other, smaller towns, especially those dependent on only one or two large enterprises now in decline, reaching very great heights.

The decline in industrial production has resulted in massive dismissals of redundant workers with only very little prospect of finding alternative employment. The number of registered unemployed per vacancy rose to 169.5 in April 1996, compared to 10.3 for Russia. Of the registered unemployed, in April 1996, 42.5% were women, 32.8% were young people, and 15.5% of unemployed were registered for more than a year. The high percentage of young unemployed and the high unemployment in certain localities are maybe the most alarming aspects of the labour market developments in Ivanovo.

Still, the increase of registered unemployment, dramatic as it is, does not sufficiently indicate the aggravating labour market situation in the region. Total employment has declined much more than registered unemployment has increased, from 667,500 in 1990 to 429,600 in 1995, a loss of 237,900 jobs, almost one-third of total

---

[8] It should be noted here that registered unemployment strongly underestimates the real extent of unemployment in Russia. For example, at the end of 1995, national unemployment measured through the Labour Force Survey was more than twice as high, 8.2%. As we will see later, the same is likely to be true for Ivanovo. Registered unemployment data are used here for reasons of availability. For an extensive discussion of the reasons why registered unemployment in Russia is so low see Standing, 1996b.

employment. Considering that registered unemployment was around 75,000 at the end of 1995, this leaves a gap of some 150,000 persons (twice the number of registered unemployed!) not formally employed but not registered as unemployed either. A few of them may simply be unaccounted for by the statistical methods even if they are formally employed or self-employed, some may have become inactive and others may have taken up informal activities. Still, it is very likely that most of them are out of a job but see no reason for registering at the employment office or face obstacles in doing so. They would inflate the unemployment figure enormously.

Figure 7.1: Production and Employment in the Textile Industry, Ivanovo Region, 1991-95 (1990=100)

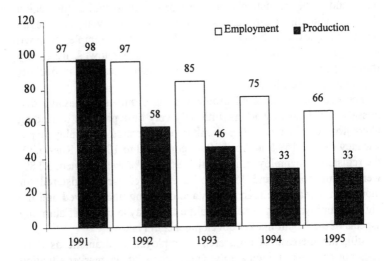

Sources: see table 7.3.

Moreover, there are strong indications that the level of labour hoarding is very high in Ivanovo. This can be illustrated by production and employment development data on the dominant industry in the region, the textile industry (Figure 7.1). After 1990, both production and employment started to decline rapidly. However, the decline in production has been much stronger than the decline in employment. Where production was at 32.9% of its 1990 level in 1995, employment was still at 66.4% of its 1990 level, suggesting very extensive labour hoarding.

In other sectors and branches there have been similar developments, although the extent of labour hoarding seems to be less. For example, in engineering the decline in employment followed the decline in production more closely: production dropped to 56.7% of its 1990 level in 1994, while employment fell to 67.6% of 1990.

The preservation of employment, including the high level of labour hoarding, is the result of a joint effort by the Ivanovo enterprises, trade unions, authorities and the Regional Employment Office to avoid mass lay-offs, although sometimes with different motives.[9] This is an important observation, especially considering that the enterprises are practically all privatised. It seems that on the side of management the wish to save on severance payments and paternalistic attitudes prevailing from the past (the management of the enterprises has often not changed) in many cases predominate over attempts aimed at profound restructuring of enterprises.

Several strategies have been used to preserve employment. First of all this is being done through paying very low wages as compared to the rest of the country, or through the non-payment of wages, allowing enterprises to maintain more workers in employment. The average monthly wage in Ivanovo in 1995 was 304,751 roubles compared to 472,392 roubles for Russia, and the average industrial wage in Ivanovo in 1995 was 304,255 roubles, compared to 521,994 roubles for Russia (Rasumov, 1996). Many textile enterprises, however, pay much lower wages, even below the minimum wage level. Moreover, the payment of wages is often delayed and a number of enterprises have huge wage debts to their workers. In May 1995, 11 Ivanovo textile enterprises had not paid wages for three to six months.

A second instrument used to avoid dismissals are employment subsidies. In 1995, 98 enterprises in the Ivanovo region (including 32 textile enterprises) received subsidies from the Regional Employment Fund, involving 31,420 employees. This form of employment protection had a significant effect on the labour market situation considering that the number of jobs preserved equalled some 40% of registered unemployment.

---

[9]   For example, workers may not want to lose their jobs because of the income or the social benefits they provide, while enterprises in some cases do not want to lay off workers because of the severance payments this would imply.

The third strategy observed is the reduction of working time. A very large part of the workforce is forced to work shorter hours (estimated at 87% of employed in the textile industry), to take partially paid or unpaid administrative leave, or to take extended maternity leave. In the first half of 1995, the number of persons on administrative leave varied from 80,000 to 120,000 every month. Moreover, overtime and irregular weekend work were abolished, and the number of shifts was brought down.

The last strategy observed is the diversification of activities of the enterprises. Some of the engineering companies started to make washing machines and bicycles instead of their traditional products. Moreover, a number of textile enterprises started the production of consumer goods (often garments, but also woodwork), engaged in agricultural activities, or started to provide repair services. Still, diversification has been very limited, both in terms of the number of enterprises engaged and the jobs involved.

All in all, it is clear that labour hoarding has reached great heights. If the jobs preserved through employment subsidies and administrative leave in 1995 alone were to become open unemployment and the workers involved were to be registered as unemployed, the unemployment rate would jump to 30% or more.

The possibility of hidden unemployment becoming open unemployment is very real. Because of the low and declining production levels, low productivity and increasing competition enterprises will in the long run not be able to support the present number of jobs. On the other hand, because of the low wages or non-payment of wages it becomes increasingly unattractive for workers to be formally employed. Some of the efforts to preserve jobs are more likely to cost employment in the long run than to save it, as they obstruct enterprise restructuring and diminish the chances for the enterprises to survive in the new, competitive environment they have to face. As a result, some 30% of industrial enterprises in Ivanovo fear bankruptcy within a year (Standing, 1996b).

It can be concluded that the employment situation in Ivanovo is very alarming and may become worse in the near future. The seriousness of the problems is only partially revealed by the registered unemployment figures as total employment declined much more than unemployment data would suggest and the level of hidden unemployment is high. Huge efforts are needed to prevent Ivanovo from falling into total crisis. In the following section we will discuss some of the employment related policy fields which should be addressed to start the recovery of the region.

TOWARDS EMPLOYMENT PROMOTION

The need for active policies

As shown in the previous section, the economic and employment situation in Ivanovo has become more and more difficult during the last five years, and it has become one of the main crisis regions of the country. Also, it was argued there are reasons to believe that the worst of the crisis is yet to come and that unemployment may rise considerably. Most enterprises suffer from high labour hoarding and low productivity, external competition and indebtedness, and do not have the strength to overcome their problems by themselves. Moreover, the general environment for future development is not very favourable. There is a high degree of industrial mono-structuring, the skills and competences on the regional labour market have a limited and one-sided composition, the technical and social infrastructure are in a bad state, the service sector is hardly developed, incomes are low, there is little capital available in the region and so on.

To avoid such a crisis and curb the downward spiral, Ivanovo would undoubtedly benefit from improvements in the general economic and social conditions in Russia. Political stability, economic growth, clear and enforced laws and regulations and the strengthening of the economic relations with former and new international partners are only some of the factors that could contribute to reversing the present developments in the country and in Ivanovo as well.

However, without wanting to minimise the importance of this national and international dimension, here we want to emphasise the decisive role of a specific regional dimension in addressing the problems of Ivanovo. There are two main reasons to do so.

First, the experience in Western and transition countries shows that even if the national economy manages to get on a path of growth, this does not automatically trickle down to the country's problem regions. Once a regional economy has started to seriously lag behind the national developments it faces enormous difficulties in catching up, among other things because the depressed environment does not stimulate economic dynamism and resources are scarce.

Second, there is a growing recognition of the fact that besides the national government, regional and local authorities and local economic institutions have a decisive part to play in economic and employment policy (Sengenberger and Keune, 1996).

Therefore, efforts should be made to develop a comprehensive package of policies aimed at initiating a process of restructuring and revitalisation of the regional economy, to adapt it to the new circumstances it faces. There is little hope that a passive or re-active attitude will bring positive results for Ivanovo as shown by the recent developments. Such a package would include a profound restructuring of the dominant textile industry but also various other fields of intervention. Attempts should be made to strengthen the economic base of the region to make it less vulnerable, increasing the functional differentiation of the economy and reducing the degree of specialisation. The general economic environment and business climate are in need of improvement and attempts should be made to create new competitive advantages for the region.[10] Likewise, the role of the economic and social actors and institutions in the region and the relations between them would have to be redefined and new objectives formulated. Here we want to provide some considerations on some of the elements of what could be called a restructuring strategy.[11]

The textile industry

A first and most important part of the restructuring of the Ivanovo economy would be the restructuring of the textile industry. Further or renewed industrial development would to a large extent have to be based on this industry (complemented by the engineering industry) if it were only because it has constituted the economic backbone of the region for so long, the skill structure of the workforce is based on it and there is no alternative readily available. At present the textile industry is largely based on standard mass production building on low factor costs, especially low labour costs.[12] This is, however, not a

---

10   Scott, 1995, argues that 'regional development is – and to an ever increasing degree – based on competitive advantages that are socially and politically created, and not simply given by nature'.

11   For a more detailed discussion on this subject, see ILO-CEET, 1996a.

12   As far as the cost of other inputs is concerned, the Ivanovo enterprises, contrary to earlier

unique advantage, Russia shares it with many other textile and garments producing countries, notably in Asia, and Ivanovo shares it with
other regions in the country. Moreover, the real advantage of low
labour costs in Ivanovo is reduced by the low levels of productivity.

As Cooke observes in a study of successfully restructured old industrial regions in Western Europe, it makes little sense to try to
develop a totally new (modern) industry out of nowhere. Efforts
should rather be made to upgrade existing industries. Moreover, he
underlines the importance of diversification:

> Fundamentally, if older industrial regions, dependent on too-narrow a base in
> declining industries such as coal mining, steel making, shipbuilding or textiles,
> are to survive and prosper, they must diversify, either vertically or laterally, and
> preferably both. Vertical diversification means two things:
> Firms can diversify into new products in the same branch. The classic instance
> is where a steel firm that traditionally specialised in bulk steel production diver-
> sifies into special steels, such as stainless steel or one or more of the variants of
> anodised steel, or even into steel alloys. This is a relatively narrow form of ver-
> tical diversification.
> Another, broader form of vertical diversification is where such a firm ... diversi-
> fies into the production of a processed product that embodies steel but was not
> hitherto produced by the company. This will almost certainly occur through ac-
> quisition.
> Lateral diversification is the even broader extension of a firm's activities away
> from its basic origins. (Cooke, 1995, Introduction)

The implications for Ivanovo could be threefold. First, the existing
textile industry should make attempts to upgrade its production and
improve its competitiveness. It is forced to do so because of the
opening up of the Russian economy and increasing domestic and foreign competition. The producer mentality would have to be abandoned
and more attention given to what to produce and for whom. Moreover,
productivity, quality and flexibility should be improved, e.g. through
investment in up-to-date technology, the reduction of labour hoarding,
outsourcing of non-core activities, improvement of work organisation
and skill levels, and the transfer of social infrastructure to for example
municipalities. This would improve the competitiveness of the enterprises based on more factors than only low labour costs. It would also
provide opportunities to improve the income of workers.

---

practices, now have to buy raw material (mainly cotton) at world market prices. Certain
subsidies, e.g. on energy or through preferential credits, do exist but their continuity is not
guaranteed.

Second, the textile industry should aim to achieve a higher degree of diversification by diversifying its textile production and, possibly more importantly, by developing textile-based production. The expansion of the garment and knitwear industry seems to be an obvious step in this direction. Its products are less cyclical than luxury goods, it has relatively low entry barriers in terms of knowledge and investment, it can consume part of the output of the textile enterprises, and it may absorb high volumes of labour. It can become an important supplier for the domestic market and has the potential of becoming an important export product, possibly replacing some Asian producers on the European market. Co-operation with West European producers could be envisaged, considering the low labour costs in Ivanovo and its relative proximity. Also, modernising and diversifying the textile industry would promote other activities, like services, to develop.

Third, to further decrease the vulnerability of the industry and lessen the focus on production, forward and backward linkages to production are to be developed to provide the full repertoire of business functions to local firms. This would include several additional elements of the textile and garment production chain like innovation and design, raw material purchase, market research and marketing.[13]

Both upgrading of the textile industry and diversification require investments which can hardly be expected from the existing enterprises or other local actors. Support from the federal and regional budget, possibly in the form of preferential investment credits and other promotional schemes will be indispensable. It could be considered only to provide financial support to those enterprises and investors which submit a viable restructuring or investment plan. Also, attempts should be made to attract capital from outside the region. Other ways of supporting the textile and garment industry can also be considered, for example through (temporary) trade regulations, training for workers and management, or improvement of the general economic environment.

The competitiveness of the region

Restructuring of the textile industry, even if fully successful, will

---

[13]   Although the enterprises in the present economic system are in competition with each other, they could to a certain extent benefit from co-operation in some clearly defined areas, especially raw material purchase and market research.

resolve only part of the region's problems of employment, unemployment and underemployment. The technological upgrading and rationalization of the industry can be expected to have a major labour-saving effect and even if part of this labour will be employed in the garment and knitwear sector, and possibly in services, this will certainly not be enough to productively employ similar numbers of workers as in the past.[14]

In view of this situation, restructuring of the textile industry will have to be complemented by other efforts aimed at generating new employment both related to and independent from the textile industry. As the negative employment effects of any kind of restructuring will materialize faster than the positive ones and unemployment is already high, short-term measures of employment creation will be required. Also additional longer-term initiatives aimed at the other economic activities, notably engineering, should be designed, promoting restructuring at the enterprise level, new businesses, productivity improvements and strengthening of competitiveness in the whole region.[15] Sectoral policies, focused on the textile and engineering industry, should be complemented by broader scoped regional policies, directed to all aspects and opportunities relevant for the region's future development. This emphasises the importance of endogenous, bottom up regional policies, based on Ivanovo's specific needs, resources and knowledge, looking to stimulate local initiatives, and taking into account the advantages the region can take from external conditions.[16] It does not mean, however, that the region can be left alone to solve its

---

[14] For a comparison of what the impact of rationalisation through information technology and organisational improvements on employment may be, take the case of West Germany: whereas total output slightly increased in the textile and garment industry between 1970 and 1992, employment shrunk from 845,000 to 337,000. It can be expected that the labour saving effect in Ivanovo will be smaller due to the lower wage level, but still it is likely to be important.

[15] See for example: Pyke, 1995, who argues that now, more than ever before, the competitive capability of individual firms depends on having ready access to equally competitive producers of supplies and services. The clear implication for Ivanovo is that policies should be aimed at raising the standards of whole networks of firms. This means broad scale policies aimed at raising quality, productivity, capacity to innovate, design, commercialisation and other areas.

[16] As indicated earlier, Ivanovo's social and economic well-being is obviously conditioned by numerous external factors that to a certain extent determine the possibilities for economic growth, employment generation and improvement of income in the region. They put important constraints on the scope and direction of action of the regional actors. On the other hand, external developments may also provide opportunities. Ivanovo may benefit for example from new markets outside the region or attract knowledge or capital from abroad.

problems. As indicated before, extensive support from especially the federal government is needed. Some of the areas to be attended in what could be a restructuring programme for a region like Ivanovo would be the following.

Active employment policy
The restructuring of enterprises and the creation of new employment opportunities can be supported by a package of active employment policies. The Regional and Local Employment Centres could intensify their co-operation with enterprises, trade unions, local and regional authorities, vocational training institutes, and others to adapt existing programmes to the new economic conditions. For example, the earlier described employment protection subsidies should be reassessed in the light of their real effect on enterprise restructuring and long-term job preservation. Financial support should be given on the basis of sound restructuring proposals including personnel plans. Redundant workers or workers who will become redundant in the near future could be given support in finding new jobs or starting their own activities, through retraining, use of non- or under-utilised enterprise premises and machinery, start-up credits or other assistance. Labour market training for the unemployed could be fine-tuned with the needs of the enterprises and general courses in modern skills scarcely available in the region could be offered (e.g. bookkeeping, languages, computer skills, marketing). Short-term employment creation can be stimulated by job creation programmes including subsidies to employers for new jobs or seed capital for small enterprises. Public works schemes could further soften the immediate unemployment problem and stimulate productive activities in areas where private activities are unlikely to develop, for example infrastructure, social care, housing, or environmental improvements. Apart from the employment objective such activities would improve the general living and economic environment in the region. Employment policies should give special attention to certain more vulnerable groups, especially young unemployed people who are threatened by exclusion from future employment opportunities, and to mono-structural localities with very high unemployment.

Small and medium-sized enterprise (SME) promotion
The experience in other transition countries shows that the SME sector can have a high capacity to create new employment. Although, on the

one hand, their development is hindered by the low production level of the large enterprises and the low income of the population, on the other hand they have had good opportunities in several sectors, in particular consumer and production-oriented services, the productive artisan trades, the professions, transport and construction – in short those firms supplying principally local and regional markets and whose development was particularly restricted by the Soviet-type economic system (OECD, 1996a). They normally have the advantage of low start-up costs, among other things because of low capital investment. Moreover, they can fill small market niches and adapt flexibly to changes in demand and other conditions. In Ivanovo, some 2,340 SMEs were registered in 1995, employing 19,000 persons on a steady basis and 9,000 through freelance or other arrangements. Their further development aimed at employment expansion could be an important policy objective. Apart from these existing enterprises, new enterprise formation can be promoted, especially for the underdeveloped service sector or in small scale industrial activities like wood working or food processing. SMEs can be related to the restructuring of the big enterprises in the region through subcontracting mechanisms concerning garment production or services formerly performed by the big firms. Further SME promotion can include improving access to (preferential) credits and capital, a key policy area, including loans, grants, or temporary share holding, which could be channelled for example through a Regional Development Bank or Entrepreneurial Fund.[17] It can also include the public creation of business centres, service centres or other support units which can provide SMEs with information on legal and financial regulations, information on developments in specific markets and industries, consultancy services aimed at productivity improvements and making contacts with suppliers, clients and possible business partners or investors. An additional function could be the provision of business and management training, aimed at successfully starting and running a small enterprise.

Education

Ivanovo has the second highest number of students per capita of all regions in Russia, a clear advantage which should be exploited to the

---

[17] An interesting example could be the Fund to Support Socio-economic Development, Entrepreneurship and the Development of Competition in Novgorod, financed by the local budget and providing funds mostly to small-scale projects on a matching basis. For a complete description see Halligan, Teplukhin and Willer, 1995.

maximum extent. Still, the output of the educational system does not always correspond to the current and future demand on the changing labour market. In this respect it would be important to review the educational institutions and the programmes they offer in the light of the existing restructuring plans and other expected developments. New professions like marketing or accountancy should get a place in the educational plans and the curricula of existing programmes should be adjusted, incorporating the new skills required.

Infrastructural improvements

A good technical infrastructure, including transport facilities, communication facilities and utilities (water, energy, heating, etc.), is a basic condition for a well functioning economy and one of the most important prerequisites for new enterprise creation.[18] It is evident that the present state of the technical infrastructure in Ivanovo needs attention. There is substantial scope for the improvement of road and rail transport of persons, products and materials, and a major investment in reconstruction, combined with regular maintenance, seems necessary. Similar comments could be made on the communication facilities and utilities. Apart from the technical infrastructure, attention should be given to the social infrastructure of the region, including housing, health services, sports and cultural facilities, and educational and training institutions. A good quality social infrastructure is beneficial as such and also has a direct impact on the quality of the labour force, on the intellectual and physical capabilities and on the creativity, motivation and initiatives.

Involvement of regional actors

An important subject is the changing roles and increasing responsibilities of the regional actors in Russia in general and in Ivanovo in particular. Because of the increasingly limited role of national actors and a tendency to greater decentralisation, regional and local authorities, employment offices, trade unions, employers and other interest groups now have to develop a large part of the economic and social programmes and strategies to promote economic restructuring and

---

[18]   See for example: Huber, 1995. This study concludes that infrastructure is one of the main variables in new business formation and that policy makers in transition countries should give preference to infrastructure development when attempting to increase new business formation

employment creation in their own regions. In previous paragraphs it was argued that the Ivanovo industry should restructure and the competitiveness of the region be improved. This will require a strong involvement and interventions from the side of the regional and local actors, not only the enterprises themselves but also others. Such policies need the support of the local leaders and interest groups and their success depends on the strength of these regional and local actors and on their input in the policy making process utilised to develop and implement a restructuring programme.

Moreover, especially in high-unemployment regions like Ivanovo, restructuring of the economy is a very complex and painful process, which may cause considerable discontent and desperation among the population. It deeply affects the lives of individuals and social groups. Passive, unproductive attitudes or even obstruction from their side may be expected if they are not actively involved and convinced of the need for change.

Therefore, similarly as in many Western countries, restructuring policies should be designed and implemented through the co-operation of a variety of actors, belonging to different groups or institutions of the Ivanovo society. They would include the enterprises but also the regional and local governments, education institutions, labour offices, unions, financial institutions, etc. This could further imply a new role for the regional authorities: the regional government could act as an orchestrator, bringing the regional actors together for discussion and consensus building. It could be considered to institutionalise such co-operation in something like a regional social and economic council or another type of 'regional forum of strategic choice and action' (Scott, 1995). According to Scott, such a forum can be essential for regional economic success in the modern world. It can be of limited scope but can also be more ambitious, as in the case of the regional economic councils (in Germany, for example) that regularly bring together major local constituencies (e.g. employers, banks, workers' organisations and municipal government) to debate questions of long-term industrial order and that seek to forge viable strategies of regional management. Apart from examples in Western Europe and the USA, more and more examples of this kind of regional bodies dedicated to dialogue on economic and social questions can be found in transition countries.[19]

---

[19]   See, for example, Keune and Nesporova, 1996; Nesporova and Kyloh, 1994; Sengenberger and Keune, 1996.

SUMMARY AND CONCLUSION

This paper gives an overview of recent employment developments in the Ivanovo region, a Russian region traditionally dominated by the textile industry that has been suffering from severe economic and social problems since the start of the transition process. The narrow base of the regional economy has made it exceptionally vulnerable to the economic changes of the transition period and the region has entered a situation of crisis. Production in the textile and other, often related, industries in Ivanovo has plummeted in the last five years, resulting in strongly growing unemployment, 13.7% in April 1996, including very high youth unemployment and localised pockets with much higher than average levels. However, unemployment figures do not sufficiently indicate the seriousness of the employment situation in the region, considering the fact that total employment has fallen much more than unemployment has increased and the high levels of hidden unemployment. There is a real possibility that open unemployment will further sharply increase when enterprises cannot further sustain this high level of hidden unemployment.

It has further been argued that in order to avoid such developments there is an urgent need for a comprehensive package of active restructuring and employment promotion policies, backed up by financial means from, among others, the federal and regional budgets. They should aim to strengthen the economic base of the region to make it less vulnerable, increasing the functional differentiation of the economy and reducing the degree of specialisation. The general economic environment and business climate are also in need of improvement and attempts should be made to create new regional competitive advantages.

The backbone of this restructuring process would have to be the textile industry itself. It would have to upgrade its production and improve its competitiveness to become less dependent on low labour costs and create genuine competitive advantages. Also the industry could diversify its production and develop forward and backward linkages to production. Moreover, broader scoped regional policies would be required to promote further employment creation and increase the competitiveness of the region. This would include, among other things, active employment policies, SME promotion, upgrading of the educational system and infrastructural improvements.

Such a process demands a strong, active involvement and interventions from the side of the national, regional and local actors and it is vital that the restructuring policies count on the support of the local leaders and interest groups. Its success depends to a large extent on the strength of regional and local actors, their input into the policy making process and their ability to build a strong coalition devoted to the region's development.

At present a number of the above mentioned policy areas are increasingly being addressed by the regional and local authorities and other regional and local actors while others receive less attention. Also, the federal government recently announced a package of support measures for Ivanovo, including investment projects in the textile industry. At the moment one cannot evaluate the likely results of these efforts, but the seriousness of the situation in Ivanovo suggests that recovery of the region will be a very long-term process. It would be important, though, to give a clear direction to this process as early as possible, to avoid the situation becoming even more difficult. Clear policy choices, combined in a comprehensive, mutually reinforcing policy package will have to be made on the direction and type of the future development of the region and all available resources mobilised to restructure and upgrade the region's economy. A passive, re-active approach has to be rejected as it has proven to be unsuccessful.

The case of Ivanovo is not unique, several similar cases can be found both in Russia and in other transition countries. They urgently need attention. The further they fall behind the main stream developments, the harder it will be to get them back on track, with all the risks of growing unemployment, poverty and social tension.

8 Aspects of Official Unemployment in Moscow and St Petersburg: The Views of the Registered Unemployed

Kathleen Young
University of Glasgow

The employment policies adopted by the Russian government in the transition largely reflect the position of the Organisation for Economic Co-operation and Development (OECD): that structural barriers to employment mobility are a primary cause of persistent unemployment, and that unemployment can be overcome on a background of sound macroeconomic policy, by combining labour market deregulation and carefully targeted active labour market policies (OECD, 1996b, p. 6).[1] The Russian legal definition of unemployment differs from OECD and International Labour Organisation (ILO) standards in that, for an unemployed person to be officially considered as unemployed, they must register with the State Employment Service. The Russian government has been able, in effect, to target its active policy programmes in this manner. The numerous and formidable disincentives to registration on the part of the unemployed were illustrated by Guy Standing and the ILO Job-seeker Survey of 1993, which concluded that official unemployment levels understated real levels of unemployment because of psychological, practical, and administrative barriers to registration and

[1] This research was made possible through the support of BASEES and the Institute of Russian and East European Studies, University of Glasgow. The author would like to express her gratitude to the staff of the Employment Services of St Petersburg and Moscow, particularly Tamara Chekulaeva, Nina Rusinova and Ludmilla Panova of the St Petersburg branch of the Institute of Sociology, Russian Academy of Sciences; and Nikolai Feodorov and Veronika of the Institute of Employment Problems, Russian Academy of Sciences, Moscow, without whose assistance these surveys would not have been possible.

the receipt of unemployed status; that the system of unemployment benefit was inadequate; that only a small proportion of individuals turning to the Employment Service was referred to vacancies or active employment measures; and that the unemployed were realistic in their aspirations and active in their approach to seeking employment.[2]

Official registered unemployment rates in Russia continue significantly to under-report real levels of unemployment, as determined by the Goskomstat Labour Force Survey. In the first quarter of 1996, the Labour Force Survey indicated that 8.4% of the workforce was unemployed, whereas official registered unemployment stood at only 3.9% (*Russian Economic Trends*, Vol. 5, No.1, 1996, p. 95). This was compounded by the additional 4.6% of the labour force determined to be under-employed on the basis of an involuntary administrative leave or a reduced work schedule. Consequently, in directing active labour market policies to reduce unemployment primarily towards the registered, or official unemployed, the Russian government restricts access to programmes to less than half of those deemed by international definitions to be unemployed. However, although official unemployment represents only a part of total unemployment, the study of this group of unemployed remains important. Firstly, this category of unemployed represents the intended recipients and main beneficiaries of Russian unemployment policy. Secondly, employment restructuring can not be achieved without taking into consideration the human aspect.

Employment restructuring comes at a human cost, the scope of which is exhibited in rising unemployment figures. While statistical analysis of the dynamics of employment restructuring and enterprise and manager behaviour is crucial to the greater understanding of processes at work in the Russian Federation, such procedures largely conceal the impact of restructuring on its casualties, the unemployed. The views and behaviours of the unemployed must also be considered in considering the problem of employment restructuring. Are the unemployed becoming demoralised, inflexible, and unemployable, behaving in a manner that creates barriers to their own employment? Is the current network of unemployment policy succeeding in returning the unemployed to work? This chapter examines the behaviours, experiences and views of a sample of registered unemployed in

---

[2] For details of these barriers, see Standing, 1995a, pp. 7–9, Standing and Chetvernina, 1993, Standing, 1994d.

Moscow and St Petersburg, as revealed in survey evidence, to assess the impact of the behaviour and the views of this category of unemployed.

The purpose of the survey forming the foundation of this paper was to provide a broader picture of the registered unemployed than was expressed in official statistics. The surveys form part of a larger study of the formulation and implementation of unemployment policy, with particular focus on St Petersburg. The motivations, attitudes, and behaviours of the unemployed must be acknowledged and understood if unemployment policy is to prove effective.[3] Fears that mass open unemployment may finally emerge in Russia in the near future make this understanding crucial. Further strains on the carrying capacity of Employment Centres are likely to force an even narrower targeting of resources, and for this to be achieved successfully, there must be an awareness of the experiences, attitudes, and behaviours of the registered unemployed. Another aspect of unemployment addressed by the survey is the question of the relationship between unemployment and the potential for social unrest. To this aim, the survey assesses the profile of the registered unemployed, their previous employment conditions, their job search experience and experience of the Employment Service, the household economic situation of respondents, and their attitudes on employment, political, and economic matters.

Moscow and St Petersburg were not chosen as survey sites for being representative of the situation in the country as a whole. The extreme variation in labour market conditions between regions in Russia renders the selection of 'representative regions' impracticable. On the contrary, the unrepresentative labour market conditions in the

---

[3]   One example of the effect on policy of a poor understanding of the motivations and desires of the unemployed was exhibited in 1994 by the St Petersburg Committee for the Labour and Employment of the Population (SPKTZN). In its 1994 Employment Programme, the SPKTZN sought to provide financial assistance to 1,500 unemployed persons to support entrepreneurial activity and self-employment, to be given in the form of block grants based on the annual unemployment benefit to which the applicant was entitled. At the end of the year, the programme to support entrepreneurial activity only managed to support the employment of 39 previously unemployed persons, at a cost of over 30 million roubles. The SPKTZN acknowledged the failure to fulfil the Employment Programme, attributing it to the lack of an appropriate normative-legal base for support of such activities, the psychological unpreparedness of the unemployed for entrepreneurial activity, insufficient matching funds on the part of unemployed clients, and poor development of business centres in the city (SPKTZN – FES, 1995, p. 28). Greater research on the part of the SPKTZN into the motivations and desires of the registered unemployed could have revealed the low level of demand for support for entrepreneurial activity.

capital cities, in comparison to other regions, was one of the motivations for surveying the registered unemployed of these cities. The
Employment Services in Moscow and St Petersburg are considered in
both Russia and the West to be two of the more pro-active and innovative services, relative to other regions in Russia, in their approaches
to the problem of unemployment and the application of active labour
market policies to alleviate unemployment. In addition, the inhabitants
of Moscow and St Petersburg face fewer structural rigidities in their
labour markets than are faced by inhabitants of other regions of Russia. Employment in these cities is distributed amongst a range of
economic sectors. The share of employment in private enterprises is
growing. Opportunities for entrepreneurial activity exist and, within
these cities, there is a small, albeit poorly developed, housing market.
The confluence of these factors results in increased opportunities for
employment, relative to other regions, making it easier to discriminate
between barriers to employment caused by labour market conditions,
and barriers whose source lay in the inflexibility of the registered unemployed themselves.

The information presented in this paper is based on personal interview surveys of officially registered unemployed persons conducted in
the branches of the State Employment Service in June to August 1995,
using a standardised questionnaire. Due to the sample size (St Petersburg n=172, Moscow n=189), geographical limitations, and the nature
of the sample, the results of the survey should be interpreted as a case
study of official unemployment in the capital cities, and should not be
extrapolated to the regional or national level, nor should they be con-
strued to represent other types of unemployment. In St Petersburg, the
sample selection was based on interviews conducted at the Kalininskii
raion employment centre, chosen for being broadly representative of
the city according to the sex and age profile of the registered unemployed in the area at the time of the survey. In Moscow, the survey was
conducted with the assistance of the Institute of Employment Problems, Russian Academy of Sciences, and selection was distributed
proportionally to the population in the geographical regions of the city.
The information provided herein is largely limited to a summary of the
aggregate survey results and conclusions. However, due to the distinct
natures of the two cities, where significant differences in results occur
they will be noted and tables of results include both aggregate figures
and figures for each city.

EMPLOYMENT CONDITIONS PRIOR TO THE SURVEY

National indicators

Official unemployment rates have remained low throughout the transition, rising from 0.8% at the beginning of 1993, to 1.1% at the beginning of 1994, to 2.2% at the beginning of 1995. This contrasts with survey-based measures of unemployment using ILO definitions that showed an increase in estimates of real unemployment from 4.7% at the beginning of 1993, to 5.5% at the start of 1994, and 7.4% for the beginning of 1995. On top of this, estimates of hidden unemployment of the working population rose from 1.8% to 5.3% from 1993 to 1994, but then fell to 4.5% at the beginning of 1995, and have remained fairly level since (*Russian Economic Trends*, Vol. 5, No. 1, 1996, p. 95). Levels of unemployment vary significantly from region to region. The capital cities enjoy relatively low rates of registered unemployment compared to other areas of the country. On 1 June 1995, the rate of official unemployment for St Petersburg was 2.1% of the economically active population, and was lower still in Moscow at 0.4% (Federal Employment Service, 1995a, p. 19).

Declines in industrial output have far outpaced declines in industrial employment. In 1993, industrial production dropped by 16%, but industrial employment declined by 5% (Marnie and Motivans, 1995). From 1991 to 1993, employment declined by 1% for every 5.3% decrease in industrial production (*Finansovye izvestiya*, 27 December 1994). The levels and structure of employment were slowly shifting. Although the share of working age population has not decreased significantly, labour resources and the total number in employment declined from 1992 to 1995 by 6.9%, or 5 million workers.[4] A corresponding rise has not occurred in either the rates of official unemployment, or in levels of unemployment determined through survey-based measurements, possibly indicating either that people are dropping out of the labour force, or that the informal sector is absorbing more employment than labour resource statistics can capture. The structure of employment is also shifting slowly away from

---

[4]   *Russian Economic Trends*, Vol. 5, No. 1, 1996, p. 99. Labour resources are calculated by adding the total working age population to the numbers of those in employment who are above or below the working age, less the total of working aged disabled.

concentration in industrial production. The dynamics of employment are illustrated in the table below. Employment in industry, construction and science has contracted over this period, while employment in the non-productive sector has expanded.

Table 8.1: Dynamics of Employment in Russia 1992–95

	1992	1993	1994	1995
Labour resources (million)	86.1	86.2	83.8	84.1
Total employed (million)	72.1	70.9	68.5	67.1
% of total employed in:				
industry	29.6	29.4	27.1	25.7
agriculture	14.3	14.6	15.4	15.7
transport/communications	7.8	7.6	7.8	7.9
construction	11.0	10.1	9.9	9.7
trade/catering	7.9	9.0	9.5	9.7
commercial services	4.1	4.2	4.4	4.9
health/social services	5.9	6.0	6.4	6.7
education/culture	10.4	10.2	10.8	11.3
science	3.2	3.2	2.7	2.5
credit/finance/insurance	0.7	0.8	1.1	1.3
public administration	2.1	2.3	2.4	2.5
other	3.0	2.6	2.5	2.1

Source: Goskomstat: *Rossiya v Tsifrakh*, 1996a.

The Federal Employment Service

The Russian Federation's Law on the Employment of the Population, passed in 1992 and based on the 1991 USSR Law on the Employment of the Population, recognised unemployment for the first time and provided for the establishment of the Federal Employment Service, built on the base of job placement and training centres which existed in the Soviet system. The Federal Employment Service is the primary government agency charged with dealing with the issue of unemployment. Only unemployed persons registering with the Centres of the Federal Employment Service are recognised as unemployed and official unemployment statistics are based on the information gathered by the Federal Employment Service.

The legally mandated responsibilities of the Federal Employment Service and its objectives are quite extensive, but can be reduced to four main spheres of activity. The first sphere of activity is that of facilitating the job-matching process. Active measures are emphasised in job matching, with the Federal Employment Service organs providing information for both job seekers and employers in an attempt to balance and service the needs of employers for suitably qualified workers and the needs of job seekers for employment appropriate to their skills, experience, and preferences. Where necessary, job training, counselling, aptitude tests and special assistance are utilised to achieve this goal and to make the period of job search or unemployment as brief as possible.

The second function of the Federal Employment Service is to provide social protection for the unemployed, which is achieved through a combination of passive and active measures. Unemployment benefits and supplementary material assistance to the unemployed, illustrative of passive measures of social protection, are supplemented by the use of active measures, such as: the development of temporary public works programmes and forms of temporary employment for school leavers and new graduates and specialised assistance for socially vulnerable groups, in the form of vocational training or re-training specifically for those falling into this category (youth, single parents, two parent households with a high number of dependants, women with pre-school children, parents of disabled children, disabled people, long-term unemployed, refugees, and those persons nearing pension age).

The third function of the Federal Employment Service is to develop human resources through professional training. Vocational training or retraining is directed toward those individuals who, because of the nature of their profession or skills, are unable to find employment locally, or those that lack or have lost their professional qualifications or skills. The final role of the Federal Employment Service is to gather and analyse labour market information for use in the development and execution of labour market policies, as well as in the development of general economic policy and regional development policies (OECD–CCET, 1994, p. 9–11).

Unemployment in Moscow

The demographic portrait of the unemployed remained fairly static in Moscow in 1995. According to official statistics, a registered unemployed individual was more likely to be a woman aged 45 to 55 with higher or specialised secondary education, had more than 20 years work experience, and was bringing up one or two children ('Sostoyanie stolichnogo rynka truda', *Chelovek i trud*, No. 2, 1996, p. 32). The survey data confirmed this portrait of the registered unemployed in the city. On 1 June 1995, 46,802 individuals were registered with the Moscow arm of the Employment Service as seeking employment, 23,947 or 50% of whom were officially registered as unemployed (Federal Employment Service, 1995a, pp. 5–7). Four-fifths of those registered as unemployed from 1 January to 1 June 1995, or 18,913 individuals, had benefits formulated for them in this period (ibid., p. 7). Of those receiving benefits, 31% were receiving the minimum level of benefit, equivalent to the minimum wage (ibid., p. 9). An average of 249 individuals per month were in receipt of supplementary material assistance, available only to those unemployed no longer entitled to receive benefits.

Although the Moscow Employment Service had listings of over 63,000 vacancies on 1 June 1995, the majority of these vacancies were for blue-collar employment, showing a clear discrepancy between the character of vacancies and the qualifications of the registered unemployed (ibid., p. 11). Although there were three vacancies for every registered job-seeker, there were two job-seekers for every white-collar vacancy. From 1 January to 1 June 1995, a total of 4,864 registered jobseekers were placed in employment, only 2,523, or 51.9% of whom were officially registered as unemployed (ibid., p. 13).

Of the 15,334 individuals removed from the unemployment register from January to June 1995, 2,702 were directed to vocational training or retraining at the expense of the Employment Service (ibid., pp. 7, 15). Of the 2,411 completing training or retraining in this period, only 822 were subsequently found employment (ibid., p. 15). Over half of the individuals offered training or retraining were women aged 30 to 50 with dependant children ('Uchit'sya nikogda ne pozdno', *Chelovek i trud*, No. 2, 1996, p. 39).

Public works programmes were considered to be largely inappropriate to the needs of the registered unemployed in Moscow, given their educational profile (Eremeeva, 1996, p. 34). Moscow was one of four constituent elements of the Russian Federation where the share of registered unemployed participating in temporary public works programmes declined from 1 January to 1 June 1995 in comparison with participation in the corresponding period of 1994. On 1 June 1995, 408 persons were participating in public works programmes in Moscow (Federal Employment Service, 1995a, p. 17).

Unemployment in St Petersburg

The demographic portrait of the registered unemployed in St Petersburg reflected that of Moscow in that a registered unemployed individual was more likely to be a woman with higher or specialised secondary education, and bringing up one or two dependent children (SPKTZN - FES, 1995, p. 72). The registered unemployed of St Petersburg, however, were more likely to fall in the 36 to 45 age bracket, and have 16 to 20 years work experience. The survey data also reflected this profile. A greater share of registered jobseekers in St Petersburg was officially registered as unemployed. On 1 June 1995, 61,866 jobseekers were registered with the St Petersburg Committee for the Employment of the Population, approximately 81% of whom, or 53,943, were officially registered as unemployed. Just over 88% of those registered as unemployed from 1 January to 1 June 1995 had been formulated unemployment benefits. Of those formulated benefits, 35.1% were receiving the minimum level of benefit. Supplementary material assistance to the unemployed was applied less frequently than in Moscow, with only an average of 30 individuals per month receiving such assistance during the aforementioned period (Federal Employment Service, 1995, pp. 5–7).

Unlike the situation in Moscow, the number of registered unemployed outstripped the number of vacancies by a ratio of 3.1 to 1. Like Moscow, however, the majority of these vacancies were for blue-collar employment. The registered unemployed in St Petersburg formed a larger share of the total number of individuals finding employment with the assistance of the Employment Service. Of the 20,385 registered jobseekers placed in employment from 1 January to 1 June 1995, 16,675, or 81.8%, were officially registered as unemployed (ibid., pp. 11, 13).

The proportion of individuals removed from the unemployment register as a result of being directed to vocational training or retraining was similar to that of Moscow. Of the 40,144 removed from the register during the January to May period, 9,249 had been directed to retraining, and of the 7,828 completing their training in this period,

2,583 were subsequently placed in employment. Temporary public works programmes were also of limited application in St Petersburg although, unlike Moscow, participation in such programmes had increased from the corresponding period of 1994. On 1 June 1995, 912 unemployed individuals were participating in public works programmes (ibid., pp. 7, 15, 17).

SURVEY RESULTS

Previous employment profile of the registered unemployed

The overwhelming majority of respondents (93%) were in employment up to the time of their unemployment registration. Of the 7% who had not been in employment prior to their registration, more than half were school leavers (81% in St Petersburg, 50% in Moscow). Of those formerly in employment, most had been employed by state-owned enterprises. For one-quarter of the sample, the last employer was a joint-stock company. Private companies employed only one in ten respondents. The growing share of the unemployed previously employed by other forms of enterprises than state or municipally owned indicates that privatisation has progressed, at least formally, in Russia.

Table 8.2:   Ownership of Previous Employer

	Total n=336	Moscow n=180	St Petersburg n=156
State-owned	60	64	56
Privately owned	11	10	12
Joint-stock	25	22	29
Combined	1	1	1
Other	3	3	3

The respondents were workers of some considerable experience. The average work experience, or *stazh*, was 20 years. A breakdown of the data shows that workers of over 10 years experience predominated amongst the sample, and that the largest share of respondents had 21 to 30 years work experience. This would seem to imply that older, more experienced workers are registering with the Employment Service on becoming separated from employment. Thus, the picture of the registered unemployed emerging from the survey results are that they are mature workers of extensive work experience.

Table 8.3:   Work Experience (stazh)

	Total n=350	Moscow n=178	St Petersburg n=172
< than 1 year	7	5	10
1–5 years	6	3	9
6–10 years	10	6	13
11–15 years	10	10	11
16–20 years	16	14	18
21–25 years	18	21	15
26–30 years	15	19	12
31–35 years	11	14	8
36–40 years	5	6	4
41–45 years	1	2	1

The predominance of respondents who were of an age and level of experience considered to be the prime of working life contrasts with the experience of the West, where these groups are less represented among the registered unemployed. In the assessment of the 1993 ILO Jobseekers survey, two possible explanations were put forward. Firstly, that there existed the possibility of a generational effect, where individuals entering the work force in the 1960s and 1970s were characterised by a poor attitude to work and were consequently more vulnerable to redundancies in the 1990s. Alternatively, it was suggested that the younger unemployed were seeking unemployment in the informal sector, while older workers are being directed to early retirement on a state pension (Standing, 1994d, p. 39).

Both these propositions may also suggest a generational effect of a different sort, determined less by poor work practices than by experience of official policies of full employment and its effects on the attitudes of the unemployed. Individuals whose lifetime experience has been based in a society of state dependency, full employment, and relative economic stability, i.e. those entering employment in the 1960s and 1970s, have been dependent on the state for their livelihood for the greater share of their lives and upon becoming unemployed turn to the state, their 'benefactor', for assistance. In contrast, the younger unemployed, entering the work force in the 1980s and 1990s, have less experience of the 'nanny state' and fewer expectations of state assistance and paternalism and, consequently, seek employment independently or through the private or informal sector.

Table 8.4: Branch of Industry

	Total n=336	Moscow n=180	St Petersburg n=156
Heavy industry	6	8	3
Defence industry	21	18	24
Light industry	12	11	14
Building/construction	10	8	12
Transport/communications	9	9	8
Trade/catering	10	9	11
Utilities/communal services	6	7	5
Health/education/culture	13	12	14
State administration	2	4	1
Armed/security forces	2	3	1
Other	10	10	9

The profile of respondents based on the branch of industry in which they were previously employed shows that quite a large share (40%) were employed in what could be termed as 'core industries', or industries which were closely tied to the state structure (defence, transport/communications, utilities/communal services, state administration, and armed/security forces).[5] The largest group of respondents (21%) had been employed in the defence industry. Other well-represented sectors of previous employment in the capital cities were health, education, and culture at 13%; light industry at 12%; trade and catering at 10%; and building and construction at 10%. While conclusions drawn on the basis of form of ownership can be misleading during the course of privatisation, one can see that a large share of respondents was previously employed in branches of industry closely linked to the state structure. The high representation of persons previ-

---

[5] The proportion of those previously employed in state-linked enterprises was higher in Moscow, at 41%, than in St Petersburg, at 38%. This difference may be attributable to the concentration of such branches of industry in the capital. Heavy industry was not included in this figure, but would raise the share of total respondents to 46%.

ously employed in 'core industries' supports the proposition that the nature of the individual's previous relationship to the state may be a factor in their behaviour on becoming unemployed.

The predominance of white-collar workers amongst the registered unemployed was reflected in the results of the survey. The significant representation of white-collar workers amongst the registered unemployed is characteristic of the capital cities. The majority of respondents were formerly employed in white-collar jobs and over one in five (23%) were previously employed as an engineer or engineering technician. Clerical and accounting workers composed 18% of the sample. The positions previously held by respondents broadly reflected their educational background, with the largest share (46%) previously employed as a specialist with higher education. Considering that the majority of vacancies reported to the Employment Service are for blue-collar positions requiring a low skill level, the prospects for the registered unemployed of finding appropriate employment through the Employment Centre are limited. The large share of white-collar workers amongst the registered unemployed in this stock-based sample may be reflective of the limited opportunities for the job placement of such workers through the public employment service.

Table 8.5: Previous Position

	Total n=331	Moscow n=175	St Petersburg n=156
Manager/assistant manager	13	12	15
Specialist with higher education	46	55	35
Technical personnel	15	17	14
Skilled worker	13	7	20
Unskilled/auxiliary worker	5	1	9
Self-employed/entrepreneur	1	1	0
Other	7	7	7

The size of the previous employer was well distributed amongst the sample: 39% worked in companies having less than 200 employees, 23% worked in enterprises employing 200–1000 individuals, and 38% in enterprises employing over 1000 persons.

The experiences of the respondents would seem to indicate that their previous employers did not display attitudes of paternalism towards their employees. The majority of respondents (55%) had indicated that in their last six months of employment mass redundancies had occurred at their previous place of employment. A considerable proportion of the respondents also had personal experience of hidden unemployment prior to their registration with the Employment Service. One in five (21%) had been placed on unpaid administrative leave at some time during the last six months of employment. The share of respondents placed on unpaid leave in St Petersburg was higher than that of Moscow (24% versus 19%). Of those placed on unpaid leave, 45% were on leave for less than one month, 46% were on leave for one to six months, and 9% were put on leave for more than six months. One in four respondents (25%) were working a reduced work schedule in their last month of employment. In addition to being subjected to forms of hidden unemployment, respondents also faced irregular payment of wages. Only 69% of respondents were paid in full and on time in their last three months of employment. An additional 14% received their wages in full, but not on time, while another 17% received only partial wages, of which approximately three-quarters received less than 50% of their wages. Failure to receive wages in full or on time may have led many workers to leave voluntarily, or may indicate financial difficulties at the previous place of employment for workers made redundant.

Table 8.6: Duration of Involuntary Administrative Leave

up to 1 month	45
1–3 months	33
4–6 months	13
> 6 months	9

Although the predominant official reason for unemployment, as cited in the labour book, was personal desire (48%), a significant proportion became unemployed as a result of staff reductions (36%), or liquidation of the enterprise (6%). When asked to give the main reasons for their separation from employment, the majority cited worsening economic conditions (40%) or a reduced volume of production in the workplace (36%). A further 10% felt that conflicts with the employer were a cause of their unemployment, and 6% felt that their unemployment was caused by a mismatch between their qualifications and new skills demanded in the work place (27% stated that there were other reasons for their unemployment, usually personal).[6]

Table 8.7:   Official Reason for Loss of Employment

	Total n=335	Moscow n=180	St Petersburg* n=155
Personal desire	48	44	52
Staff reduction	36	40	32
Liquidation of enterprise	6	6	7
Completion of work contract	4	3	5
Violation of discipline	0	0	1
Other	6	7	4

*Columns do not add precisely to 100 per cent due to rounding.

There may be two conflicting explanations for these results. The large share of the registered unemployed voluntarily leaving their previous employment seemed to indicate that individuals whose working life was shaped by official policies of full employment expected to find new employment within a relatively short span of time. The discrepancy between official reasons for unemployment and perceived reasons, when viewed in respect of indicators of hidden unemployment, may also shed doubt on the real proportion of persons voluntarily becoming unemployed. It has been proposed that through use of administrative leave, late or partial payment of wages and reduced work schedules enterprise management is able to discharge workers without being liable to the payment of severance pay. Workers leaving voluntarily are not entitled to the two to three months severance pay allocated to workers made redundant. Through these administrative measures they can be sure that at least a proportion of workers will leave of their own accord, thus sparing them this additional expense. How voluntary does unemployment become when the employee is neither working nor receiving wages? Anecdotal evidence also suggests that some workers made unemployed prefer to have their official reason for separation recorded in their work books as 'voluntary', fearing that redundancy will affect their chances of finding new employment.

---

[6]   Respondents were to choose all reasons they considered appropriate.

Experiences of unemployment and the Federal Employment Service

Most of the respondents were in receipt of unemployment benefits and found them easy to obtain. The overwhelming majority intended to stay in the labour force and most were unemployed for six months or less. Over two-thirds began their search for employment within two weeks of becoming unemployed and were not passive in their search, utilising additional methods to find employment while registered with the Employment Service. Although the receipt of benefits was a powerful incentive for registering with the Employment Service, the largest share of respondents turned to the Employment Service in hopes of finding appropriate work. A large proportion of the respondents claimed that in their initial visits to the Employment Service they were offered vacancies inappropriate for a variety of reasons. However, as the majority of respondents had never refused an offer of appropriate employment, it does not seem that the registered unemployed have unrealistic expectations in their job search. Although few were willing to move to another location to work, two-thirds of the respondents were willing to undergo retraining, showing a certain degree of occupational flexibility, if not geographical flexibility. Three-fifths of the respondents expressed satisfaction with the work of the Employment Centre, but were less certain that they would be able to find appropriate employment through the Employment Service.

Of the registered unemployed, 73% said that they were currently in receipt of unemployment benefits. The share of the registered unemployed in Moscow receiving benefits was, at 81%, higher than the share of the St Petersburg sample, which stood at 66%. A further 2% of total respondents had received benefits in the past, but were no longer entitled to receive them. Those not receiving benefits at the time of the survey, but who would be receiving benefits in the future (new registrants with the Employment Service whose benefits were not yet calculated, and those still in receipt of severance pay), totalled 11% of the sample. Benefits were not received by 14% of respondents. This represents a narrowing in the gap between the officially registered unemployed and the unemployed receiving benefits. Despite the low levels of benefits in relation to the subsistence minimum and the average wage, 44% considered the benefit to be a significant contribution to household income. This indicates that the welfare of households with an unemployed member is dependent on the receipt of unemployment benefit to maintain at least some standard of living, albeit minimal. The majority of respondents who were in receipt of benefits found obtaining benefits somewhat easy (37%) or very easy (41%), whereas only 12% found it difficult to obtain benefits. The growing share of the registered unemployed receiving unemployment benefits and the ease with which they are obtaining benefits may indicate that the Employment Service itself is treating unemployment less as an aberrant behaviour, as was concluded by the 1993 ILO study, and more as a product of economic transition. While the gap between persons not in employment registering with the Employment Service and those receiving official unemployed status revealed by official statistics is narrowing, this gap, nevertheless, remains.

The overwhelming majority of the registered unemployed intended to remain in the labour force. Most respondents had been registered as unemployed for six months or less, and had begun their job search soon after becoming unemployed. Only a small proportion of respondents stated that they would not persist in looking for employment (3%) and 94% stated that they would continue to look for appropriate work for as long as it took. Another 4% found it difficult to say whether or not they intended to remain in the labour force.

The average length of time the respondents had been registered with the Employment Service was 4.9 months for Moscow and 4.2 months for St Petersburg. The largest share of respondents (35%) had been registered with the Employment Service for one to three months and the majority, at the time of the survey, had been registered for six months or less. Approximately one in five (19%) had been on the register for less than one month and another one in five (20%) was registered for four to six months. Those registered with the Employment Service for more than six months but less than a year was 21%, and the share of respondents among the long-term unemployed, registered for one year or more, was 5%.

Certain reservations of the ability of official unemployment statistics accurately to portray the scale of long-term unemployment must be expressed. A high proportion of those removed from the unemployment register are removed 'for other reasons' (approximately 25% in St Petersburg). This category does not include those found employment through the Employment Service, those referred to vocational training, or those given early retirement. The Employment Service claims that most of those removed from the register find employment independently, but provides no supporting evidence of this. The share of the number removed from the register who remain unemployed is unknown, as dropping off the register does not necessarily indicate a move out of unemployment. Low levels of benefits and the mismatch of vacancies to registrants would seem to provide a disincentive for remaining registered with the Employment Service upon the expiry of benefit entitlement. It is hoped that further research on hidden unemployment will reveal the share of hidden unemployed previously counted amongst the registered unemployed.

Most respondents who had previously been in employment did not wait an extended period of time before beginning their search for work. Within two weeks of becoming unemployed, 67% were searching for work and another 16% began their search for employment within the first month of becoming unemployed. Another 17% waited longer than two months after becoming unemployed to begin their job search. Thus, we can see from the survey evidence that the majority of those registering with the Employment Service begin an active job-search soon after becoming unemployed. This would refute claims of a tendency toward passivity amongst the registered unemployed.

Table 8.8:   Duration of Registration with Employment Service

	Total n=361	Moscow n=189	St Petersburg n=172
< 1 month	19	15	23
1–3 months	35	35	35
4–6 months	20	15	24
7–9 months	14	22	6
10–12 months	7	8	6
13–18 months	4	3	4
> 19 months	2	2	2

First time entrants to the labour force and those returning to the labour force after an extended absence tended to turn to the Employment Service after not being able to find employment independently: 78% of first time entrants and re-entrants to the labour force had been registered with the Employment Service for one to three months, but only 52% had been searching for employment for the same amount of time, while 30% had been looking for employment for four to six months and a further 17% had been looking for employment for more than six months.

A considerable proportion of the respondents did not rely on the Employment Service alone to find employment. In addition to turning to the State Employment Service, 65% actively checked newspapers, notice boards and the mass media for information on employment opportunities, 69% actively used personal contacts to try to find employment, 37% approached potential employers directly and 5% used other additional methods to find employment. In this regard, the registered unemployed were not passive in their job search, particularly as the use of personal contacts has become a significant means to find employment. According to the data, the registered unemployed in St Petersburg were more active in their use of additional methods to find employment.

Table 8.9:   Additional Methods Used to Find Employment.

	Total n=358	Moscow n=186	St Petersburg n=172
Media advertisements	65	59	72
Personal contacts	69	65	73
Direct approach to employers	37	33	42
Other	5	3	6

Respondents were to choose all applicable methods. Results are given in percentages of all respondents indicating that they utilised the given method in their job search.

Motivations for registering with the Employment Service varied significantly between the two cities. The survey did not support the proposition that the main motivation for turning to the Employment Service was to receive benefits, although close to half did state that the receipt of benefits was one of the motivations for turning to the Employment Service. The share of respondents indicating that they were motivated to register with the Employment Service by the possibility of receiving benefits was higher in St Petersburg than in Moscow. The predominant reason for registering, cited by over two-thirds of the respondents, was the hope that they would find appropriate employment through the Employment Service. Here, the percentage of respondents in Moscow citing this as a motivation for registration was higher than in St Petersburg. An additional 36% stated that they turned to the Employment Service to receive vocational training or retraining. In St Petersburg, the share of respondents citing the possibility of receiving retraining as a motivation for turning to the service was more than double that of Moscow. It is unclear which factors cause motivation for registration to diverge so greatly between the two cities.

Table 8.10: Motivations for Turning to the Employment Service

	Total n=360	Moscow n=188	St Petersburg n=172
Unemployment benefit	48	40	56
Receive retraining	36	20	54
Find appropriate work	70	79	59
Receive initial training	0	0	1
Other	3	3	4

Respondents were permitted to choose all applicable motivations. Results are given in percentages of respondents agreeing that they were motivated by the given option.

Motivations to register with the Employment Service did not correspond to the assistance offered in preliminary visits to the Employment Centre. Respondents stated that, on their initial visits to the Employment Centre, they were offered work inappropriate for a variety of reasons, the most prevalent being work inappropriate to their qualifications, or work with an inappropriate wage. The Russian Federation Employment Law guarantees and defines what constitutes appropriate employment according to qualifications and wages. Approximately one in five was offered vocational retraining. As shown in motivations for turning to the Employment Service, the share of respondents offered retraining was significantly less than that desiring retraining in St Petersburg and somewhat less than those hoping for retraining in Moscow. The share of respondents indicating that they were offered nothing by the Employment Service in their initial visits was low within the total sample, but higher in St Petersburg than in Moscow. Responses to this question may, however, present a misleading picture of the assistance offered to the registered unemployed, giving the impression that the registered unemployed are offered few appropriate vacancies. As the study represents a survey of a stock of unemployed persons, rather than a tracer survey chronicling the job search of an unemployed person over a period of time, those who have successfully found employment through the Employment Service are not represented here.

Table 8.11: Assistance Offered in Initial Visits to the Employment Service.

	Total n=346	Moscow n=176	St Petersburg n=170
Retraining	21	18	23
Heavy physical or dangerous labour	3	2	5
Work requiring a move	1	1	2
Work not appropriate to qualifications	28	32	25
Work with inappropriate wage	36	39	34
Offered an interview with employer – not hired	3	4	2
Offered an interview with employer – job already filled	4	3	5
Early pension	1	2	1
Nothing	12	7	17
Work inappropriate for other reasons	13	18	8

Respondents were permitted to choose up to two of the listed options

The registered unemployed can refuse up to two offers of appropriate work before their entitlement to benefits and unemployed status is affected. In the main, the registered unemployed do not seem to be excessively selective in their refusal of employment offered by the Employment Service. An interview for a vacancy was never refused by 49% of respondents, while 14% stated that they had yet to be offered a placement. One-quarter of respondents had refused one possible placement, with the share of those refusing one offer of employment higher in St Petersburg (31%), than in Moscow (19%). Only 12% refused more than two offers of possible employment.

Poor geographical mobility remains a significant obstacle to employment mobility in Russia. However, only 24% of respondents said that they were prepared to work in worse conditions in their own city rather than move. Respondents in Moscow showed greater inflexibility than those in St Petersburg, with 27% willing to compromise their working conditions, as opposed to 20%. A very small proportion, 4%, were willing to move to another city or region to work. The largest share, or 73%, found it hard to say whether they would be willing to move or not. Anecdotally, some of those who found it hard to answer the question stated that moving was not a realistic option, given limitations to geographical mobility in Russia at the time of the survey (e.g. low availability of suitable housing, poor information on job opportunities in other regions), but that were the circumstances to change they would be willing to consider the possibility. Survey evidence from general population surveys shows that the share of registered unemployed unwilling to move is similar to that of the general population, indicating that lack of geographical mobility is not a problem solely amongst the registered unemployed.[7] The registered unemployed showed more flexibility when it came to occupational mobility. When asked if they would be willing to undergo retraining if they could not find employment appropriate to their qualifications, 66% would agree to undergo retraining, while 16% were not willing to change their specialisation, and a further 18% of respondents were unsure if they would be willing to retrain. Respondents from St Petersburg were more amenable to retraining, with 80% expressing willingness, as opposed to 54% in Moscow. In comparison with surveys of the general population, the registered unemployed would appear to be more willing to adapt their skills to the changing economy.[8]

Satisfaction with the work of the Employment Centres was high. Three-fifths of total respondents expressed satisfaction, of whom 30% were very satisfied and 31% were mostly satisfied. Moscow respondents were generally more satisfied with the work of the Employment Service, with 72% expressing that they were mostly or very satisfied, as opposed to 48% in St Petersburg. Only 15% stated that they were mostly or very dissatisfied, while another 24% found it difficult to say. Anecdotally, many of those who expressed satisfaction with the Employment Centres felt that the centres and their staff provided what assistance they could, but were constrained by official policy.

Despite high levels of satisfaction with the work of the Employment Centres, respondents were less sure of the ability of the centres

---

[7] Boeva and Shironin, 1992, p. 20; Rose, 1995, p. 15. In 1992 a representative survey of the population found that 9% were willing to take up employment in another town, whereas in 1995 only 2% in a similar survey were willing and likely to take up employment in another town.

[8] Rose, 1995. In the 1992 survey, 28% of the sample expressed the desire to learn a new skill and in 1995 17% either had learned or were likely to learn a new skill.

to assist them in finding appropriate work. Only 22% felt that they would be able to find work through the Employment Centre within the next three months, 9% felt that it would take three to six months, 5% felt that it would take more than six months, and 13% felt that they would never find appropriate work through the Employment Centre. A further 51% found it hard to say when they would find work through the Employment Service.

It would appear that, amongst the registered unemployed at least, the stigma attached to unemployment has faded. When asked to evaluate their attitude or emotional response to being unemployed, the largest share of respondents (35%) expressed anger about being unemployed. Another 27% had an attitude of indifference, feeling that unemployment was something that could happen to anyone, while 24% felt depressed about being unemployed. Only 7% were ashamed to be unemployed, and 1% felt that being unemployed suited them fine. Having spent most of their working lives under official policies of full employment, the anger and depression expressed as a result of becoming unemployed would seem to be a reasonable response to a lack of stability.

Household economic situation

The transition process has intensified the problem of poverty in Russia, and the unemployed are particularly vulnerable. The levels of unemployment benefits in Russia appear generous on paper, but inflation, the benefits structure and entitlement conditions have eroded their value. The level of benefit received by most respondents stood at a fraction of the subsistence minimum. Two-thirds of respondents stated that their benefits did not meet the cost of food. For the nearly one-third of respondents who stated that no member of the household was working, and the 5% of respondents whose sole household income was unemployment benefit, the economic position of the household was precarious indeed. Households having other sources of income are also vulnerable to poverty. Just over three-quarters of respondents had a per capita monthly income below the subsistence minimum. Although a larger share of the registered unemployed was receiving benefits, the level of benefits relative to the subsistence minimum and the average wage show that the unemployment benefit system continues to provide insufficient support for the unemployed and does not adequately fulfil its role as a social safety net.

The average amount of benefit received monthly by the respondents was 146,037 roubles, well below the subsistence minima at the time of the survey. The average benefit level of Moscow respondents (161,853 roubles) was higher than the average benefit of 127,940 roubles in St Petersburg. Of those receiving benefits, 20% were receiving the minimum benefit, equivalent to the minimum wage, which was 43,700 roubles in June and July 1995, and 55,400 roubles from August 1995. The share of respondents receiving benefits at a level between the minimum wage and the subsistence minimum at the time of the survey was 62%. When viewed in relation to the average subsistence minimum, the level of benefits was inadequate to support the majority of the registered unemployed. The average subsistence minimum for June 1995 was 277,400 roubles, increasing to 293,400 in July and reduced to 286,100 in August. In all, 82% of the respondents were receiving unemployment benefits at a level below the subsistence minimum. In comparison, the average wage for June was 495,000 roubles, 499,500 in July and 520,600 in August. Thus, the minimum wage, or floor on the level of unemployment benefit, comprised only 16% of the subsistence minimum in June 1995 and 11% of the average wage. Those receiving benefits falling between the subsistence minimum and the average wage constituted 18% of the respondents.

Table 8.12: Benefits Received from Previous Employer

	Total n=331	Moscow n=176	St Petersburg n=155
Medical services	32	36	28
Pre-school care	4	5	3
Sanatorium/rest home visit	20	22	19
Goods	1	0	1
Free transport	4	2	5
Food	3	0	7
No benefits received	56	56	56
Other benefit	3	2	3

Respondents were asked to choose all benefits offered amongst the given options. Results indicate the number of respondents stating that they were offered the benefit by their previous employer.

As discussed in regard to the experience of the unemployed of the

Federal Employment Service, 44% considered unemployment benefits to be a significant contribution to household income. When asked to evaluate the level of benefit they received, 10% stated that the benefit level they received was sufficient for food and communal services. The number of respondents stating that the level of benefit was sufficient for the purchase of food alone was 23%, while the majority, 67%, stated that the level of benefit they received was not enough even for food.

Although unemployed persons have the right to receive certain non-wage work-based benefits from the former employer for a period after becoming unemployed (such as child care and medical services), the survey revealed that relatively few of the respondents were offered any benefits through the employer even while still employed. The majority of respondents (56%) claimed that they received no employer benefits in the previous place of employment. Medical services and sanatorium and rest home visits were the most common benefits provided while employed. This would seem to imply that enterprises in a financially difficult position are cutting back on employee benefits first, before making workers redundant. It may also indicate, when coupled with the high proportion of registered unemployed who left their employment voluntarily, that workers not satisfied with their conditions of

Table 8.13: Sources of Household Income in Addition to Unemployment Benefit

	Total n=335	Moscow n=169	St Petersburg n=166
Wages of other household members	64	62	66
Private farming	22	17	27
Pension	21	18	24
Stipend	6	5	7
Odd job income	15	15	15
Help from relatives	16	16	17
Personal savings	16	12	19
Other benefits	12	6	19
Other income	5	3	6

Respondents were asked to indicate all forms of additional household income. Results indicate the percentage of respondents' households having additional income from each source.

employment are behaving in a manner reminiscent of their experience of full employment, leaving with the expectation of finding better employment elsewhere within a short span of time.

The low level of state benefits in relation to the subsistence minimum, not just of unemployment benefit but of other state benefits such as work and disability pensions, stipends, and child benefit, increases the importance of income from employment of other household members to maintaining the standard of living of the household. Most of the respondents had one wage earner in the household, with 47% stating that this was the case. However, 30% stated that there was no wage earner in the household.[9] Households in St Petersburg were more likely to have no member working (34%), than those in Moscow (27%). Two or more persons were working in 19% of respondents' households, and three or more persons were working in 4% of respondents' households.

Respondents were asked what other sources of income the household had, given the loss of regular income through the unemployment of one household member. Nineteen respondents, or 5% of the sample, had no household income other than unemployment benefit. The majority of households (64%) had the wages of other family members. Private farming, most of which was for household consumption rather than to be sold, provided additional income for 22% of respondents. Another 21% of households received income in the form of a family member's pension. Other main sources of income were financial assistance from relatives not a part of the immediate household, personal savings and income earned from odd jobs.

Such sources of additional income did not ensure the financial security of the household. The average household per capita monthly income was 233,907 roubles. Again, the per capita monthly income was higher in Moscow (267,885 roubles) than in St Petersburg (195,739 roubles). Per capita monthly income was below the subsistence minimum for 76% of respondents, and only 24% had a per capita monthly income above the subsistence minimum. A larger proportion of respondents from St Petersburg, 83%, had per capita monthly incomes below the subsistence minimum, whereas in Moscow, 65% were below the subsistence minimum.[10]

---

9 For the purpose of the survey, the household was defined to be persons living together in the same domicile under the same household economy (including, children, parents, and other close persons).

10 These figures are calculated on the basis of the average subsistence minimum. The

Attitudes of the unemployed

Much has been made of the social tension that could potentially erupt as a result of mass open unemployment. The potential for the economic hardships of the transition to affect political stability has also been recognised, a sign of which could be seen in the success of the Communist Party in the December 1995 Duma elections. Despite fears of a social explosion in Russia, there are few signs that open unemployment, as yet, will prove to be a catalyst. The experience of Western Europe shows that the open unemployed do not tend to engage in radical political activity, or that open unemployment on its own rarely leads to social unrest.

The attitudes of the registered unemployed appear to have been formed by their experience of official policies of full employment. Most respondents favour equality of opportunity in hiring for both sexes and across age groups and support interventionist methods to reduce levels of unemployment. They believed that unemployment in the country would become worse in the coming years and were broadly split between those unsure that economic reforms should continue and those who support the continuation of reforms. Many felt that the government was performing poorly in regard to unemployment and should step down from power. The largest shares of respondents felt that unemployment, poor or worsening standards of living, the economic situation in the country, inflation and low wages were the problems in Russian society most likely to lead to conflict. Although a large share of respondents felt that protest actions were likely in their city, fewer respondents were personally willing to take part in such protests. More respondents approved of legal forms of political expression and protest, and those expressing willingness to participate in actions of protest were more likely to use legal means. Although the largest share of respondents was mostly interested in politics, few could identify with the programme of a political party at the time of the survey. Less than half of the respondents could state with certainty that they had voted in the 1993 Duma elections and less than two-fifths asserted that they would be taking part in the 1995 Duma elections.

Respondents showed a general trend toward equality of opportunity

---

subsistence minimum is calculated at different levels for able-bodied men, able-bodied women, pensioners, children under the age of 7 and children aged 7 to 15 years.

in terms of hiring, which would seem to be characteristic of their experience of full employment policies and the high participation rates of women in employment. When asked whether priority in hiring should be given to men, women, or extended equally across the sexes, 91% felt that men and women should be treated equally in hiring, while 7% felt that men should be extended priority in hiring, and 2% felt that women should be given priority treatment. When asked the same question in respect to age, 80% felt that both the elderly and the young should be given equal treatment in terms of hiring, while 18% felt that priority should be extended to young persons, and 2% felt that priority should be extended to elderly persons.

Table 8.14: Approved Measures for the Reduction of Unemployment

	Total n=338	Moscow n=175	St Petersburg n=163
Reduce pension age	18	27	9
Extend vacation	7	8	6
Reduce work week	12	14	9
Reduce number of shifts	4	5	3
Benefits to private enterprises for job creation	35	31	38
Subsidies to state enterprises for job creation	36	34	39
Improve geographical mobility	6	1	10
Establish system of public works	15	11	18
Perfect retraining system	28	19	37
Administrative measures to guarantee work	32	32	31
Other	10	8	11

Respondents were permitted to choose more than one response.

Respondents were asked to choose from a selection of measures to reduce unemployment that had their approval. Measures to reduce unemployment receiving the highest degree of approval were those which favoured state interventionism, reflecting the belief that it is the responsibility of the state to ensure the employment of the population. Subsidies to enterprises to preserve jobs were approved by 36% of respondents. Benefits to private enterprises for the creation of jobs were approved by 35%. Administrative measures to guarantee employment were approved by 32%. Improving the system of training and retraining was seen as a means to reduce unemployment by 28% of respondents. All of these methods, except for measures to guarantee employment, formed a part of the national platform of unemployment policies. Other measures supported by at least 10% of respondents included a reduction in the pension age, improvement of the programme of public works and reduction of the work week.

Pessimism reigned amongst the sample when the future path of unemployment in general was considered. The majority of respondents felt that unemployment was not likely to improve in the future. Optimists accounted for only 15% of the respondents, who felt that the unemployment situation would improve greatly or improve slightly in the next few years. The situation would remain much the same according to 29% of the respondents, whereas 27% felt the situation would get slightly worse, and 29% felt that things would get much worse in the coming years. The respondents were less sure of whether economic reform should continue. Two in five (40%) found it hard to say whether or not economic reforms should continue, while 48% said that reforms should continue and 11% felt that they should not.

Table 8.15: Should Economic Reform Continue?

	Total n=355	Moscow n=185	St Petersburg n=170
Yes	48	45	52
No	11	18	5
Hard to say	40	37	43

Attitudes to the government and political situation were less than charitable amongst the respondents. While 13% of respondents felt that the government's activity in relation to unemployment was good or very good and 27% felt that the government was performing satisfactorily in regard to unemployment, 25% evaluated the government's performance as bad and 15% felt its performance was very bad (20% of respondents found it difficult to evaluate the government's performance). When asked to give an appraisal of their general support for the government, only 2% of respondents fully supported the Russian government, whereas 28% disagreed with some of its activities, and 41% felt that the government should stand down from power (30% found it difficult to give their evaluation of support for the government). When asked to evaluate the political situation in the country at the time of the survey, only 2% felt that the political situation was satisfactory, whereas 54% characterised the situation as tense and 32% characterised it as critical or dangerous.

Respondents were asked in an open question which problems they felt caused most people to be dissatisfied and were the most likely to lead to situations of conflict in the nation. Economic issues dominated the responses. The five problems cited most by the respondents were: unemployment (19%), worsening or poor standards of living (16%), economic reform or the economic situation in the country (12%), low wages (12%) and inflation (11%). In Moscow, the most predominant responses were: high prices (15%), worsening or poor standards of living (14%), unemployment (12%) and low wages (11%). Other responses supported by at least 9% of the sample as additional sources of dissatisfaction that could lead to conflict in Russia included: instability, the national economic situation, crime and lawlessness and material and financial difficulties. In St Petersburg, the most commonly cited sources of public dissatisfaction were: unemployment (27%), inflation (19%), worsening or poor standards of living (18%), the national economic situation (15%) and low wages (12%).

Following their assessment of problems likely to be a source of conflict, the propensity of the unemployed to participate in actions of protest was assessed. When asked if they believed protests, demonstrations, meetings or other actions of protest were likely to occur in their city in response to declining standards of living, 42% of respondents felt it likely, 34% felt that such protests were unlikely, and 25% found it hard to say. A smaller proportion of respondents were likely to participate in actions of protest, should they occur: 16% said that it was more than likely that they would participate, 61% said they would probably not participate and 23% were not sure. In the view of the respondents the likelihood of actions of protest coming as a response to unemployment, rather than declines in living standards, was less: 27% felt such protests were likely, 48% felt they were not likely to occur and 25% found it difficult to answer. Anticipated participation in such protests was likely for 18% of respondents, unlikely for 57% of respondents and 25% found it difficult to answer.

Respondents were then requested to choose up to three forms of protest that they approved of and those forms of protest in which they would be willing to participate personally. Legal forms of protest received the most support from respondents and were the forms of protest they were most likely to participate in themselves, but there was some limited support for extra-legal and more radical actions of protest. The forms of protest most likely to be supported in general by respondents were the signing of petitions (27%), legal meetings and demonstrations (24%), boycotts of elections (15%) and legal strikes (11%). One in four (25%) did not approve of any of the forms of protest listed and 23% found it hard to say which forms of protest they approved of in general. When asked which forms of protest they would be willing to participate in themselves, 32% said they would not participate in any of the enumerated forms of protest, 22% found it had to say, 29% would be willing to sign a petition, 20% would participate in legal meetings or demonstrations, 14% would boycott elections and 7% would participate in legal strikes. The survey results suggest there was little likelihood that the registered unemployed would take part in illegal or radical forms of political expression.

Table 8.16: Actions of Protest Approved and In Which Respondents Would Participate

	Total		Moscow		St Petersburg	
	n=355	n=352	n=183	n=181	n=172	n=171
	approve	participate	approve	participate	approve	participate
Legal meetings/ demonstrations	24	20	21	16	27	25
Sign petition	27	29	25	23	30	36
Illegal strikes	6	2	8	2	4	1
Occupy govt. premises	1	1	1	2	1	0
Illegal meetings/ demonstrations	3	2	3	2	3	2
Picket buildings of organs of power	5	3	6	3	5	2
Legal strikes	11	7	8	4	13	9
Take to streets/march	1	1	2	0	1	1
Boycott elections	15	14	10	11	20	17
None of the above	25	32	26	34	24	30
Hard to say	23	22	27	28	19	15

Respondents seemed to be evenly split between those citing a general interest in politics and those expressing little or no interest in politics. When asked which party's programme they identified with the most, 60% found it hard to say, 23% said that they identified with none of the existing parties, 7% felt closest to Yabloko, 3% felt closest to the Communist Party of the Russian Federation and 1% each felt closest to the Liberal Democrats and Our Home is Russia. Approximately one-quarter of respondents (26%) stated that the issue of unemployment would change the way they voted in the next Duma election, while 33% answered that it would not effect the way they voted and 42% found it difficult to answer. Respondents were then asked to evaluate their general interest in politics. Those stating that they were interested in politics (23%), or usually interested in politics (22%) composed 45% of respondents, while those indicating that they were not interested (19%) or not usually interested in politics (28%) composed 47% of respondents and 8% found it difficult to evaluate their political interest.

The political participation of the registered unemployed was then assessed by looking at their behaviour in the 1993 Duma elections and their attitudes to the 1995 Duma elections. When asked if they had participated in the 1993 Duma elections, 48% of respondents indicated that they had, 42% indicated that they had not and 11% stated that they did not remember if they had participated. Of those that did participate, 57% could not remember for whom they had voted. Of those that did remember, support was strongest for Yabloko (14%), Russia's Choice (6%) and the Communist Party of the Russian Federation (5%).[11] Of those that did not participate in the 1993 Duma elections, 38% felt that none of the parties knew what it was doing or how to solve the most pressing problems, lack of interest in politics was cited by 34% of respondents, mistrust of politics was cited by 28% and 17% felt that none of the parties represented their interests.[12]

When asked if they intended to participate in the December 1995 Duma elections, 39% indicated that they would, 25% indicated that they would not and 36% had yet to decide. Of those that intended to participate, 67% were not sure which party they would be supporting. Of those intending to participate, the most frequently supported parties were Yabloko with 10%, the Communist Party of the Russian Federation with 8% and Our Home is Russia with 3%. Of those not likely to vote in the elections, 43% felt that none of the parties knew what it

[11]   Percentages are of the total stating that they did participate in the election (n=207).
[12]   Respondents were able to choose all responses they felt to be applicable.

was doing, 29% did not trust politics, 28% were not interested and 20% felt that no party represented their interests. From 1993 to 1995, disinterest in politics declined, but the belief that none of the political parties knew what it was doing increased. It would seem that support for the Communist Party of the Russian Federation grew amongst the registered unemployed, but it would be tenuous to conclude that this was a result of respondents' unemployment, in light of the small share of respondents indicating a vote or a proposed vote for a particular party. As a general conclusion, it seems clear from the survey evidence that there is a high degree of alienation from politics amongst the registered unemployed.

CONCLUSIONS

The age and employment profile of the sample showed that the registered unemployed come largely from generations governed by full employment policies of the Soviet period. Their employment experience has largely been one of the paternalist state, which not only employed them, but supported their welfare. A large share of the registered unemployed was leaving employment voluntarily, revealing expectations characteristic of full employment that they will find new employment within a relatively short span of time. Throughout most of their working lives, the respondents enjoyed the stability of employment granted by state full-employment policy and seemed to return to the state on becoming unemployed, hoping that they would be found appropriate employment through its agency, the Federal Employment Service. The registered unemployed advocated state intervention to relieve unemployment, appeared receptive to active unemployment policies, gave a generally negative assessment of the government's performance in regard to unemployment and considered economic problems to be the greatest source of dissatisfaction.

Although their experience of socialisation to full employment seems to have had an effect on their attitudes and beliefs, their behaviours in seeking employment were affected to a lesser degree. The registered unemployed did not appear to be characterised by inflexibility or passivity and seemed to be adapting to new conditions of employment. They were seeking employment through channels other than the Employment Service, were receptive to retraining, were not refusing an inordinate number of vacancies and were beginning their search for employment soon after becoming unemployed.

Another significant finding of the surveys is that, despite the existence of a social safety net for the unemployed, the structure of unemployment benefits is such that a large share of the registered unemployed was vulnerable to poverty. Not only were the four-fifths of the registered unemployed receiving unemployment benefit at a level below the physiological subsistence minimum exposed to poverty, but three-quarters of households having an unemployed member had a per capita income below the poverty line. The safety net for the unemployed remained insufficient.

The registered unemployed also seemed to be evenly split between those that felt alienated from politics and those that continued to show an interest and participate in elections. Although a small share of the registered unemployed was willing to engage in actions of political protest, the cohort that would take part in extra-legal or more radical forms of protest was quite small. Findings from the survey would seem to preclude the eruption of mass social unrest as a result of open unemployment where registered unemployment levels remain at a low proportion of the employed population.

Unemployment is not solely an economic issue, its impact extends to the political and social sphere. The survey shows that the economic position of the registered unemployed has declined further in the transition. Their experience of the Federal Employment Service appears to indicate that it was still finding it difficult to fulfil its job-matching and social protection functions, even when operating in an environment of low registered unemployment. Should levels of registered unemployment begin to rise, as is anticipated, or should even a share of hidden unemployment move to registered unemployment, the Federal Employment Service is likely to face considerable strains to its carrying capacity and resources. Although the survey suggests that mass social unrest attributable solely to open unemployment is currently unlikely, further declines in standards of living and a greater share of the population descending into poverty as a result of unemployment may alter the situation. Whether or not mass unrest results from rising unemployment, the social and political ramifications of an increase in registered unemployment have the potential to compound the difficulties of economic and employment restructuring in Russia.

9 Households' Experience of Unemployment in Moscow, St Petersburg, and Voronezh

Nick Manning
University of Nottingham

INTRODUCTION

This chapter presents some initial data from the first phase of a study of unemployment in Moscow, St Petersburg, and Voronezh.[1] Although the general study is concerned with such questions as the way in which social policy (including unemployment policy) has emerged in the 1990s, the general aims of policies, and the extent of support for policies, this chapter will focus specifically on households experiencing insecure employment of a variety of sorts.

The study has several distinctive features. It is designed as a longitudinal study of change to capture the rapid rate of change taking place in the labour market. In particular, it is a panel study – the sample, of 240, will be re-interviewed after 12 months to explore themes that arise out of the first round, and to identify the way in which households are responding to and dealing with social and employment change. The sample includes households experiencing four different types or stages of unemployment in three Russian cities. In addition a related panel of policy makers (industrialists, trade unionists, government officials, and politicians) are being interviewed and re-interviewed.

[1] I would like to thank the ODA and INTAS for funding this project, and the following colleagues in Russia and the UK for collaboration over the design of the project, and for undertaking the fieldwork and analysing the data: Ovsey Shkaratan, Nataliya Tikhonova, Nina Rusinova, Ludmilla Panova, Elena Pakhomova, Nadia Davydova, Tatiana Sidorina, Karen George.

BACKGROUND

An important question for recent studies of Russian social change is that of whether western social science explanations can be applied legitimately to post-socialist Russia. The big questions include, for example, whether the economy is functioning in response to neo-classical economic patterns, such as movement towards market equilibria, or rather has become enmeshed in institutional economic patterns locked into particular path-dependencies, including rent-seeking, corruption and crime (Hausner, Jessop, and Nielsen, 1995). A political example is provided by a previous study by this author and others, concerned with whether citizen actions such as social movements would develop to press particular interests in the political system, for example housing or environmental concerns, in a pattern common to societies in transition from dictatorship (Láng-Pickvance, Manning, and Pickvance, 1997). If this did happen, would this activism continue, and if so would it feed into any kind of party political process?

These questions resonate with perennial concerns in sociology over the relative dominance of structure or action in social life, and the extent to which the topic for study should be cultural continuities which shape behaviour, or the situational constraints and opportunities which a rational actor might consider, or the way individual characteristics might lead to certain patterns of individual action (Therborn, 1991).

There are related debates in social policy. What is or should be the relationship between welfare benefits and work (Deacon, 1994)? Does deregulation of the labour market promote flexibility and employment opportunities for all, or polarisation and restricted opportunities for many (McLaughlin, 1994)? If the latter is the case, what is and what should be the opportunity or even the right to employment for able bodied citizens (Marsh, 1991)?

The actions of Russian workers within the labour market and their strategies for economic survival raise these issues in a specific context. To what extent do individuals demonstrate a rational response to their social security or labour market situations? Are they influenced by cultural habits from the past? Do social policies operate in a predictable manner? Some answers to these questions will be illustrated with new data in this chapter.

A GENERAL PICTURE OF UNEMPLOYMENT

This study was conceived in the expectation, shared with many observers, that mass lay-offs would eventually appear in the Russian labour market. Indeed the non-appearance of mass unemployment, and the expected political, social and health consequences, particularly compared with other central European societies, has spawned a small 'where are they?' industry (Standing, 1994d). The reasons for this particular 'dog that didn't bite' are debated extensively elsewhere in this book.

The notion that workers in the past have stayed put (indeed a perennial policy aim since the labour laws of the 1930s (George and Manning, 1980)), and that their continued employment is a result of the absence of real labour movement, is false. The labour market is and has always been one of quite high turnover – now in the region of 20 per cent annually. This continues. In spite of the dramatic collapse in production of approximately 50 per cent, hiring continues at a high level.

The actual number of unemployed is particularly sensitive to definition. There are three different measures in general use. First is a measure of those actually registered as unemployed, either in order to receive benefit, or in order to gain employment. This is the measure used in the UK currently which has been subjected to so much criticism, since governments are tempted to massage this figure by removing potential applicants through, for example, special training schemes, through early retirement, and through an active discouragement to register, as with the new 'jobseekers' scheme in the UK. This is also the official measure of unemployment in Russia.

The second method is survey based. Instead of taking registration as the real test of people's situations, individuals are asked about their working situations and their aspirations about work. For example all countries in the EU undertake regular surveys of the labour force, which can provide this kind of information. In Russia, labour force surveys are also regularly conducted.

The third method can provide a more even-handed guide to the rate of unemployment. It takes a variety of measures and attempts to estimate various distorting effects before arriving at a potential range within which unemployment lies, but eschews the idea of a single definitive numerical measure. This approach is particularly important

with regard to Russia, since the very low rate of unemployment benefit, and the negative attitude that many employers have towards the
employment service, inevitably leads to a low rate of registration.

Standing (1996a) has constructed a particularly careful definition of
the factors that might be taken into account when considering the rate
of unemployment. To those registered with the Employment Services
should be added those on enforced leave, those on short-time, and
those not working due to production stoppages. Standing estimates
that 'suppressed unemployment' amounts in reality to 28 per cent of
the workforce (1996a, p. 23), rather than the 1995 survey based definition of 7.2 per cent unemployed.

Nevertheless, Standing observes that the covariance of the different
measures of unemployment suggests a probable systematic relationship between them. One consequence is that the slow rate of
unemployment growth has probably been real, and requires some explanation, since it stands in considerable contrast to other societies in
Eastern Europe, where mass lay-offs have developed since the early
1990s (ILO, 1995, p. 109).

Within the literature there are three contrasting views of this situation, represented in detail elsewhere in this book. First are those who
do not expect there to be a massive shakeout, since the labour market
is already making a successful adjustment to flexible restructuring.
The evidence for this is in terms of the rate of labour turnover, and the
adjustment of wages to market conditions (Lippoldt and Gimpel'son,
1996; Layard and Richter, 1994).

Second are those who believe that there is not yet a flexible labour
market, due to the continued hoarding of labour by worker controlled
managements (Commander, McHale et al., 1995). This situation will
eventually be forced to adjust, as inefficient firms are forced out of
business.

Third are those who argue that unemployment exists but is hidden
for a mixture of perfectly rational administrative reasons, which will
(and should) soon give way to mass unemployment. Roxburgh and
Schapiro (1996), for example, cite the effects of the wages tax as a
strong incentive to retain workers on low or no wages (e.g. through
compulsory 'leave') to keep down the average wage on which the tax
is calculated. Since this tax was recently overhauled, there is now an
opportunity to test the effects of this interpretation. A variant of this
view concerns the explanation as to what the rationality is for the

retention of labour – it is kept because the patterns of enterprise work (including the provision of social welfare services) would require too much investment of time and effort to change: 'enterprises retain labour because they need it and it costs them little to keep it' (Clarke, 1996d, p. 52). In this view there is no particular prescription to shed labour, unless the investment necessary to create alternative activities were forthcoming.

One consequence of this 'hidden unemployment' is that most actual movers report that they have taken their decision voluntarily. But in many cases this will be because the threat of redundancy, late pay, and extended leave have encouraged them to jump before they are pushed. We have aimed to capture these 'voluntary' unemployed in our sampling structure.

DETAILS OF THE TWO SURVEYS

Although most people do not get jobs through the Employment Services, in common with most countries, and especially since labour turnover is high at 20 per cent per year, there is still between 3 per cent and 8 per cent of the workforce unemployed, and this has been rising steadily, whether one takes a broader or narrower definition.

The unemployed are a sub-category of those who change jobs, defined by the time period between jobs. For many this time is effectively zero. For the unemployed, however, the time period is some significant period between jobs, extending for some to 'long-term' – usually taken to be more than 12 months. In fact the typical period of time for unemployed people in Russia currently, using the period of registration with the Employment Services as an indicator, is between 1 and 6 months.

However, not everyone registers with the Employment Services. How can we look at the unemployed? First we have taken into account the points made by Standing and others about the particular meaning of unemployment in the Russian context, and we have aimed to sample different kinds of 'unemployment'. The initial idea was to sample at three different points of the job-change cycle. This would start at the point of possible *redundancy*, move through the stage of *unemployment*, to *re-employment*. The widespread use of wages arrears, and particularly leave, as a way of managing budgetary constraints and labour surpluses lead us to include those *on leave* as a fourth group.

These groups might be conceived as being at different stages or samples of a single cycle for some purposes. But since workers can join or leave the groups in different ways, particularly in the context of a widespread turnover in the labour market, this may not always lead to clear differences between the groups in some respects, as is apparent from the data below. There are nevertheless important and systematic differences between the groups which will be presented.

However, the turbulence or 'churning' in the labour market can also be put to good use, since in the light of the relatively short periods of time for which the unemployed are registered, we can expect those in our sample to have changed their employment situation over the course of 12 months, and there is great merit in taking this sample as a small panel to be followed up. Moreover, all extant surveys that we have seen have been cross-sectional, whether conducted by Goskomstat, VTsIOM, ILO, or OECD. We are unable from these to trace the same individuals as they move through the labour market. We have therefore set up a small panel of interviewees that we will re-interview after one year, and ideally for several years after.

The four groups therefore include firstly those who have been given notice of possible *redundancy* but are still employed – the insecurely employed. Second, those who have been put on extended leave – *on leave*. Third, those who are currently registered as unemployed – *the unemployed*. Fourth, those who have been registered as unemployed but are now re-employed – *the re-employed*.

A further important feature that is increasingly appearing in the literature is the recognition that there are sharp regional variations in the Russian labour market. While some general surveys try to capture the picture across the whole Federation, others have focused on particular areas. The annual Russian Labour Flexibility Survey conducted by the ILO started with Moscow and St Petersburg in 1991, but has now moved wider to include also Nizhnii Novgorod, Ivanovo, Vladimir, and Tatarstan (Standing, 1996a, p. 2). Young's study (this volume) remained with Moscow and St Petersburg. Others have sought to target more provincial cities: Clarke (1996d) – Samara and Kemorovo; Gimpel'son and Lippoldt (1996) – Kaluga and Krasnoyarsk; Keune (this volume) – Ivanovo. Clearly Moscow and St Petersburg are important for understanding Russia, but so are the provinces. Our survey similarly therefore covers both Moscow and St Petersburg, but also Voronezh to represent the Russian provinces. More details on the differences between these three cities will be given towards the end of this chapter. We are concerned to identify differences in these labour markets as the context in which households and policy makers are acting.

The questionnaire covers a broad range of elements including work histories, job-seeking, Employment Services, household structure and survival strategies, attitudes, health status, and so on. The sample size consisted of a total of 240 heads of household, spread between Moscow (100), St Petersburg (80) and Voronezh (60), and equally across the four types of unemployment in each city (25 in each category in Moscow, 20 in each in St Petersburg and 15 in each category in Voronezh). Those on leave were identified through local enterprises in the three cities; the rest were contacted via Employment Services files.[2]

In order to identify the views of significant policy actors surrounding the unemployed, we have also set up a panel of interviewees drawn from industrialists, trade unionists, Employment Service officials, and government officials. Here we have aimed at recording knowledge of and attitudes to and, where relevant, use of social policy, including employment services, and views about what direction new policy should go in. This panel will also be followed up after one year; however there will not be sufficient space in this chapter to report on this section of the project.

---

[2]   For the registered unemployed, we took a random sample on Employment Service premises. The interview took place only after agreement to co-operate in the long-term had been obtained. For those who had received redundancy notices, and for people who were re-employed after a period of unemployment, addresses were supplied by Employment Service staff. From this, we selected our sample. In rare cases we went out to an enterprise which had implemented mass staff redundancies: the main instance of this was in Voronezh, but even there the number of respondents was no more than one-third of the redundant sample. Gaining the sample of those on leave was the most complex task – these respondents were by definition absent from the workplace. The Russian project team members had to make use of personal contacts and enterprises. The actual number of direct workplace interviews was no more than 15 in Moscow and Voronezh taken together.

GENERAL CHARACTERISTICS OF UNEMPLOYMENT

We can look initially at the general characteristics of our overall sample – combining the four types of 'unemployed' in the three cities. What would one expect the characteristics of this group to be? If unemployment were the consequence of mass lay-offs, then one would expect there to be broad similarity between the unemployed and the rest of the labour force. In fact the unemployed are falling out from a situation of rapid turnover, combined with significant levels of wage arrears and forced leave. In addition, the majority of those changing jobs are getting rehired without appearing in the unemployment statistics. In these circumstances one might expect the unemployed to reflect those vulnerable to being on leave, and those unable to get rehired having 'chosen' to quit. Moreover one might expect that those taking up employment after a period without work might either have fewer skills, or suffer from acute poverty, forcing them to take whatever work was available.

Other surveys of the Russian situation have suggested that those who register are not those we would expect in other countries, i.e. older and younger men with low education and skill (Greg and Wadsworth, 1995). Standing (1994d) reports from the 1993 ILO Job Seeker Survey that the unemployed are more likely to be skilled women, and to be middle-aged. Young's survey of St Petersburg and Moscow reports a similar pattern for 1995 (this volume). Our own data for the three cities in this survey for 1996 confirm this pattern.

Overall there is a concentration towards middle-aged workers – confirming this very distinct Russian pattern of unemployment. With mortality rising (Ellman, 1994), particularly for men, and the option of pensionable retirement for older workers, the predominant group in the unemployed are middle-aged workers, and to a certain extent women. At the other end of the age range, younger workers have been able to benefit from the rapid rate of labour turnover, and take a greater share of the hiring opportunities, particularly where previously valued skills and capacities are less in demand. This interpretation is supported by the pattern of education and career grade amongst the unemployed: a high level of education, with nearly half the sample having had higher education, even though they are an older group. In addition, nearly half the sample are managers or specialists.

Table 9.1:   Demographic Pattern for the Overall Sample (n=240)(%)

Age	under 21	3
	21–25	10
	26–30	8
	31–40	30
	41–50	32
	51–60	16
	over 60	1
Sex	Male	45
	Female	55
Education	Basic secondary	4
	Specialised secondary	30
	Higher	44
Current/previous employment	Manager	10
	Specialist	33
	Technical (white collar)	22
	Blue-collar	23
	Unskilled	4
	Self employed	0.4
	Other	7

This peculiar pattern of unemployment enables us to consider alternative explanations. For example, is there a clear change in the pattern of industrial employment, such as the collapse of the defence industry, which might account for this pattern, or is there something intrinsically different about this group, in terms of their adaptability to the labour market changes that have occurred in recent years? In other words, does this unusual pattern help us to consider whether individuals or structures account for unemployment? Can we explain those in our sample in terms of their individual characteristics, such as work and personal attitudes, or work skills and capacities, or alternatively in terms of their alternative opportunities or relative poverty? Or is the structure of changes in the local labour market the key?

Our sample across different types of unemployment, and different cities sheds some light on these questions.

DIFFERENT TYPES OF UNEMPLOYMENT

We might expect the four types of 'unemployment' to be quite different. For example, those threatened with redundancy may 'choose' to join the great mass of labour turnover, and never become registered as unemployed. On the other hand, those who are re-employed after having been registered may have been driven to take any kind of work through poverty. We can show that indeed their general characteristics vary sharply. In the following sections differences between the four sub-samples of the unemployed are highlighted.

Personal and work demography

The age distribution varies markedly between the four sub-groups. The currently unemployed are markedly less likely to be in their early twenties, and more likely to be in their forties than the re-employed. Young people have been the most successful in our sample in getting back into work.

Table 9.2: Age and Unemployment (%)

Age	Unemployed	Re-employed
21–25	2	15
41–50	41	27

However, this might be the result of other attributes of younger workers. For example they might be compelled to take work for reasons of poverty. Alternatively they may possess characteristics that favour them in the labour market in terms of skills, education, or work attitudes. Cross-tabulating age with these factors indicates there are systematic differences which are consistent with differences in labour market success:

Table 9.3: Age, Skills and Discipline (%)

Age	Skills	Discipline	Skills Deficit
21–25	80	35	50
41–50	55	18	24

Younger workers consider that skills and discipline are assets for securing a job, and that skills deficits have in fact been a handicap on their success in the past. This is not the same as formal education however, where older workers have a clear advantage – over 50 per cent of them have higher education compared with a quarter of younger workers.

However, it does appear that poverty may have also driven young workers into work. In 1990 older workers were much more likely to judge their families to be better off than others, compared to young workers. By 1996 young workers' judgements have increased slightly, but older workers' have collapsed.

Table 9.4:   Age and Family Circumstances

Age	Better than others (1990)	Better than others (1996)
21–25	21	25
41–50	47	9

In terms of current/previous employment, we see a clear difference between those being put on leave as a prelude to unemployment, and those who have managed to get back into work. Only 30 per cent of the re-employed are managers or specialists, compared with 55 per cent of those on leave. This fits closely with a model of employment losses as occurring in the defence industry, where specialists' skills are no longer in demand, but re-hiring is taking place into less skilled positions. For example, those re-employed are likely to be in the trade/catering or education/culture sectors of the economy, whereas those unemployed are mainly from the defence sector, and those on leave or notice of redundancy are also from heavy industry or defence.

This pattern also fits with the ownership and size of firms in which the re-employed have found work. Within the sample, a disproportionate number of the re-employed are in privately owned firms compared with the other three groups who work or worked predominantly in state or joint-stock companies. The majority of the re-employed and those facing redundancy are also more likely to be in small firms, with less than 50 employees compared to the other two groups where between 70 per cent and 80 per cent have worked in big firms with more than 200 employees.

Turning to differences between men and women, women are particularly over-represented amongst those faced with redundancy (68 per cent), and the unemployed (62 per cent). Since the former are actually still working, this may indicate that the industries in which women work are particularly vulnerable. For example, as might be expected men are more likely to be found in heavy industry and construction, whereas women are more likely to be found in trade and catering, education/science and culture, and state administration. However, when asked whether their enterprises or industrial sectors have had difficulties, women report a lower rate than men's: 40 to 48 per cent for enterprises; 37 to 43 per cent for industrial sectors.

Alternative explanations might include the possibility that they are differentially targeted to leave, or that having lost their jobs their skills are not in demand in the labour market. Certainly there is a sense for some women that family responsibilities can result in job loss (10 per cent), and contribute to difficulties over finding new work (15 per cent) – both factors that not a single male respondent noted. Looking particularly at the unemployed, women reported that they were more likely to have been the target of selective staffing cuts than men (44 to 36 per cent), and more likely to have been compelled to take leave (35 to 28 per cent).

This is not because women have experienced more conflicts at work – they have had less (10 to 16 per cent), nor that they feel that there are particular factors militating against them getting jobs in the future compared to men. Indeed on all such factors where men and women disagreed, women were less likely to feel barriers to getting work: lack of jobs, poor skills, poor discipline, and even personality factors.

Conclusion

There appears to be a general pattern here of younger, less well qualified people being more likely to move through this process of job loss and/or re-hiring, often into smaller privately owned firms, whereas older, better qualified people, especially women, are less likely to. In the case of women it is difficult not to come to the conclusion that they are being eased out of work for reasons of perceived family obligations, rather than any less gendered factors.

Is this due to personal or market causes?

Personal factors

A very common issue in looking at the unemployed in any study is the question of whether they have personal characteristics that are associated with job loss. *Health* is a good example. For the overall sample, current health is worse than it was at the beginning of their careers:

Table 9.5:   Self-reported Health Status (%)

	Now	(At career start)
Very poor	2	(0)
Poor	17	(1)
Satisfactory	62	(30)
Completely healthy	19	(69)

It would be difficult to disentangle this from the general bias towards middle age in the sample, however, since health tends to decline with age. Nevertheless, if health factors were related to unemployment we would expect reported health status to vary between the groups. In fact about 80 per cent in each group have reported satisfactory or good health – a high level in comparison with community surveys in other societies (for example Hannay, 1979). In addition, when asked about their own view of the causes of unemployment, almost none felt that this was due to poor health; indeed taking the unemployed group alone, the main likely cause for job loss was stated by 20 per cent to be 'conflicts at work'.

Another common factor that we might expect to find to vary between the groups is *age*. As we have seen already, the older unemployed do differ noticeably from the younger re-employed in this respect, and this is also reflected in the two thirds of the unemployed who also actually feel this to be a major problem – which is not found to be the case in the other groups.

Turning to other personal factors affecting employment, such as skills and connections, we find that those who are the least concerned currently with finding a job consider the lack of *job search skills* is the problem, namely those on leave and those who are re-employed and who thus in principle have jobs already. Presumably they consider it is the lack of such skills in others that holds them back. A critical variant of job search skills is the accessibility of contacts and *connections* in finding work. The common assumption is that these are (and were, as Shlapentokh, 1989, showed) important in getting access to scarce resources (now including work). This is certainly true across all the subsamples – more than two thirds in all groups considering that connections are the key to getting jobs. This is very clearly the most commonly cited factor.

Market factors
Considering the labour market itself, there was a common perception amongst all the groups that suitable jobs were in short supply. Thus only one third of all but the re-employed felt that lack of skills was the problem. By comparison a half to two-thirds across all the groups felt there is a lack of suitable jobs. This is not surprising in view of the age and sex distribution across the four sample groups – younger and less well qualified applicants are being re-hired. Since we know that labour turnover is relatively high, it is not necessarily the absence of jobs *per se* (although see the discussion of the different cities below), but the mismatch between previous employment and job availability that is striking.

Turning to the changes within enterprises that were felt to be the cause of unemployment, we find sharp variation in the reasons cited. We can distinguish here between specific changes within the patterns of work within and beyond the enterprise. For example, manufacturing activities may have been restructured to produce different goods for which there is a perceived growth in markets, or activities such as social welfare functions may have been hived off outside the enterprise. Almost none of our sample reported this kind of change as the cause of job losses. This is quite consistent with the debate cited earlier in this chapter and elsewhere in the book about the reasons enterprise managers might have for retaining workers.

A more common reason, cited by between a third and half of the sample, was the view that the whole sector was in difficulties, for example the defence industry; but the most common reason, cited by nearly two-thirds, was that the individual enterprise itself was in difficulties. This again is consistent with enterprise-based surveys already cited such as those carried out by Standing, but also the detailed case studies by the OECD and ILO (Lippoldt and Gimpel'son, 1996; Keune, this volume).

Conclusion

Inevitably, where there is a mismatch between jobs and workers, there will be some factors associated with the individuals who fail to find work. Given the high rate of labour turnover, most workers who leave their jobs, for whatever reason, are actually finding alternative work without becoming unemployed. Not all the personal factors that we might have expected amongst those unemployed groups we have studied here have been found in this sample – particularly those associated with poor health.

How does job-seeking activity vary?

Other than the re-employed, most of the other three groups are seeking work. Not surprisingly 80 per cent of the unemployed are looking for work, since the low rate of benefit makes this a requirement for many to be able to survive. On the other hand only 40 per cent of those on leave are job-seeking, with a very large proportion (33 per cent) of don't knows. This reflects the uncertainty of this group's future – leave doesn't necessarily mean impending job loss – indeed although less than 5 per cent of workers across Russia are on leave at any one time, it is a normal feature of current employment (Roxburgh and Shapiro, 1996, p 16). The normality of leave as an endemic feature of employment is also reflected in the fact that this group is far less likely to have information about alternative job opportunities, and more likely to hope that the enterprise will soon find them work, and also less likely to feel they have the necessary contacts to find work for themselves.

Just as there is no strong evidence that poor health is associated with unemployment in any of the groups, this is also the case in terms of job-seeking. Health is not reported to be a problem to job-seeking for 95 per cent of all four groups.

As to the pattern of job-seeking, most of our sample, except for those on leave, contacted the Employment Service. This of course is a consequence of the way the sample was derived. However, these are not the only actions taken. About two-thirds look for job advertisements and most, especially the re-employed, contact friends and acquaintances to identify employment opportunities that may not have been publicly advertised. This pattern might be considered typically Russian – or at least a continuation from the old system, where, as the old saying had it 'better a hundred friends than a hundred roubles'. Shlapentokh's (1989) review of evidence of daily life and survival under the old regime certainly confirms the crucial function of informal networks to getting resources, including work. Nevertheless, this pattern is not actually unique to Russia, but a well known pattern of employment in many industrial societies, identified for example in post-war studies of the East End of London (Young and Wilmott, 1957), and more generally discussed by Granovetter (1995).

Contacting enterprises directly however is a minority strategy, undertaken by less than a quarter of the sample. While this might be explained by lack of effort on the part of the individual, a better explanation would be that it relates to the hiring practices of enterprises. Even less (6 per cent) have tried to set up their own businesses – again arguably a reflection of opportunity rather than desire.

Conclusion

Job seeking appears to be quite widespread, perhaps not surprising in view of the rate of job turnover in the labour market generally.

How does family income and poverty vary between the groups?

The financial circumstances for many households in our sample are very difficult. We might expect this to be a major stimulus to job-seeking.

Table 9.6: Income Sufficiency (%)

	unemp.	leave	redundant	re-emp.
Insufficient for food	28	16	20	10
Food alone	32	15	20	26
Necessities(not clothes)	28	46	48	38
Clothes and more	12	23	12	26

Of those currently unemployed, over 60 per cent report that they only have enough money to buy food, but not enough for other necessities, let alone clothes. Twenty-eight per cent do not even have sufficient for food. This is almost exactly the same situation as Rowntree found in his classic survey of York at the turn of the last century, and which was unchanged in his follow up survey in the 1930s (Rowntree, 1901, 1941). The reason for this very deep poverty is probably a result of 15 per cent of this group who are trying to survive entirely on unemployment benefit, worth around 30 per cent of the average wage, and only two-thirds the official subsistence poverty level. They will have little recourse to the alternative incomes illustrated in Table 9.7.

This contrasts sharply with those who are now re-employed, where 90 per cent have enough money for food, and 64 per cent enough for basic necessities.

A similar variation appears from a number of detailed questions in the survey about food, clothing, and material well-being. It is difficult not to conclude that there is a very strong incentive for unemployed people to take whatever employment may be available. However, there are various ways in which household income is supplemented, which is likely to qualify the effect of unemployment on incentives to take employment.

Table 9.7:   Other Income from Self or Other Family Members (%)

	unemp.	leave	redundant	re-emp.
Dacha/plot				
– income	23	31	16	19
– kind	34	27	28	29
Pension	21	30	27	17
Wages	32	17	27	24
Casual earnings	26	48	9	24
Help from relations	31	35	16	26
Savings	7	10	9	26
Rent out car	1	10	4	11
Rent out flat	6	2	6	6

There are some interesting overall patterns and variations between the sub-samples in this table. The first point is that many households do have other means of support than the wages of the household head interviewed in the survey. This fits with other survey evidence, particularly the 'Barometer' surveys conducted by Richard Rose (Rose, 1993; Rose and Haerpfer, 1994). Rose has identified at least nine different income streams available to households in Russia, of which formal employment provides only one. Clearly the incentive to take work will be critically qualified by the availability of these other means of support.

Those on leave are the most likely to have additional income from their plot, casual earnings, a household pension, and help from relations. This must reduce their dependence on the head of household's employment, and will reflect their opportunity to survive in this condition. They will be able to put off 'volunteering' to quit, as so many are forced to do, and to put off signing on as unemployed and/or taking new employment.

By contrast, we can compare the unemployed and re-employed to show that in many respects the re-employed have less alternative support to employment, and will have been under greater pressure to take work. The re-employed are less likely to have income from a plot in either cash or kind, less likely to have wages from other household members, less likely to have casual earnings, less likely to have a pension coming into the household, and less likely to have help from relations.

It would seem therefore that those continuing to stay on leave, and those remaining unemployed or moving to re-employment, appear to be responding rationally to their household circumstances. Moreover those on notice of redundancy are of course still drawing a wage, which is why they have far lower need to seek casual earnings than those in the other three groups.

Conclusion

Clearly poverty is widespread and, for a substantial minority, deep. However, it is also clear that households have a variety of means of survival, and that this appears to be closely related to their labour market strategy. Adjusting benefits or wages on their own may not necessarily change incentives and behaviour as expected in this situation, and it cannot therefore be assumed that lack of response to incentives is a result of cultural inertia, where there are complex and overlapping household circumstances and opportunities.

Different types of labour market

The four groups of 'unemployed' are of course spread across three different labour markets. What are the characteristics of these different markets? This brief picture draws in part on the project's interviews with local policy makers, not otherwise presented in this chapter. First the rate and structure of unemployment varies markedly. Although the official rate of unemployment underestimates the likely real rate, as discussed earlier, nevertheless it varies considerably between a high of 3 per cent in Voronezh, 2.2 per cent in St Petersburg and low of 0.6 per cent in Moscow. This has been caused by the growth of services and construction in Moscow, sufficient to absorb employment losses from manufacturing industries.

With a very active city government, Moscow can be characterised as 'municipal capitalism', with an economic atmosphere and labour market reminiscent of a free-wheeling boom town. Policy makers do not in general perceive social and employment problems here, so much as complain about the expenditure of tax income on the Employment Services, which are regarded by employers as almost universally ineffective (not a view shared by most of the unemployed in our sample, incidentally).

The contrast with Voronezh could not be sharper. Here the crisis in industrial production is not matched in any way by the growth of alternative economic activity. The Voronezh region is the biggest in the 'Central Black Soil Area' of Russia, with a standard of living in seventieth place amongst the Russian regions. It has suffered a larger than average loss of production, with little immediate hope for change. This has led perhaps not surprisingly to a desire, absent amongst policy makers from the other two cities, to return to the old regime. The dominant theme is a conservative concern to rescue the past, or to reinstate the past, with a concern that the central and regional authorities are not doing or spending enough to solve problems – a much more dependent approach to the future than was found in the other two cities.

The general preference for future employment policy matched these characteristics – more active in St Petersburg and Moscow, especially in favour of SME development in the latter, but more conservative in Voronezh, favouring the prevention and relief of mass unemployment through large scale government intervention, including benefit provision.

Are there overall differences between the cities, irrespective of the types of 'unemployment'? The picture here is mixed. There are almost no differences in terms of the distribution of educational achievement in the different cities, nor are there great variations in proportion of men and women, although the proportion of women reaches two thirds in Voronezh. However, the Moscow sample reports rather less poor health than the other city samples, which would not be anticipated from our characterisation of the Moscow labour market as vacancy rich where all those who are able to work can find jobs.

On other dimensions the inter-city variation is clearer, and more consistent with the differences in the three labour markets. For example, differences in the relative proportions of white and blue collar unemployed workers in samples from Voronezh and St Petersburg are striking:

Table 9.8: Previous/Current Employment in St Petersburg and Voronezh

	St Petersburg	Voronezh
Technical (white collar)	18	33
Blue-collar	29	17

Another striking variation manifests itself in the age structure of the overall sample, where there is a clear gradation between the cities, with Moscow exhibiting a pattern more typical of the west, where we would expect older and younger people to feature strongly amongst insecure and unemployed people. Voronezh on the other hand shows a much more 'Russian' pattern of fewer younger or older people. St Petersburg is in between:

Table 9.9: Age Structure in the Three Cities (%)

	Moscow	St Petersburg	Voronezh
Under 25	19	9	10
Over 50	20	24	3
Total	39	33	13

In many respects Moscow and Voronezh now represent polar types of labour markets in Russia. Whereas Voronezh respondents were more likely to report that their employment problems stemmed from a contraction of the whole sector in which their enterprise was located, the Moscow pattern was reported as much more likely to have resulted from an individual enterprise suffering difficulties. Strategies for getting work are consequently different. In Moscow skills and connections are far more likely to be felt to be effective in getting work – mainly because much more work is available. And in actual fact the Moscow respondents were consistently more active in using the whole range of job-seeking: the Employment Service, adverts, friends and relatives, starting businesses, doing work 'on the side'. While it could be argued that these might reflect cultural differences between the cities, there are real economic differences to which the unemployed have to respond. It is unlikely that cultural differences can explain the apparently greater passivity of the Voronezh sample, as we expect to be able to show from the second round of interviews.

One consequence is that family income and poverty is far more spread out in Moscow than Voronezh; that is, inequality is greater. There are many more deeply poor families and relatively comfortable families in Moscow. While the affluent in Moscow will be benefiting from the successful local economy, reflected in greater access to casual work, and a higher level of savings, it appears from our survey that poorer households in Voronezh can better protect themselves through the wages of other family members, income from plots, and access to pensions than their Moscow counterparts.

Conclusion

Just as there are systematic variations between the four types of unemployed people in the sample, there are also systematic differences between the three cities. While it may be tempting in principle to characterise the unemployed in Moscow as necessarily failures in the context of a generally active labour market, this appears not to be the case in terms of their comparative job-seeking activities. Conversely, while the unemployed in Voronezh are less likely to be self-selected in the face of widespread economic difficulties, and in principle therefore more likely to be active, they are not. Perhaps this is merely a perfectly rational response to the limited opportunities they face. However, cultural differences in attitudes towards employment will be explored as an explanation after the second round.

GENERAL CONCLUSION

Much of the overall sample was collected through the Employment Services, which, while reviled by many outside it, are regarded very positively by those who use it. Given the relatively short time that Russians are unemployed, and the slow but steady rise in unemployment, a substantial minority of Russian workers will have had this experience by the end of the century.

In order to develop and sustain effective policies to deal with unemployment, it is important to know how and why unemployed workers feel, think and act in the labour market. It is the general conclusion of this chapter that, as is the case in other countries, they react rationally to the circumstances in which they find themselves. It is important in this respect to understand the complex situations through which Russian households are trying to survive their current economic circumstances, and particularly the varied constraints and opportunities of different households.

There is considerable evidence here that policy should be considered, in terms of its potential effectiveness, in the context of a detailed understanding of household circumstances. The follow-up of the households described here in the second phase of the survey will give a great deal more knowledge about this dynamic interplay.

If there is an equivalent of 'path dependency' at the level of households – in other words an institutionally and culturally constrained set of reactions to unemployment – this cannot be assumed. As evidence accumulates of the rationality of these actors in their various situations, we can feel encouraged in our efforts to understand enough of the daily life of those households suffering at the sharp end of economic and social change to design policies that might work.

References

Alashaev, S. (1995) Informal Relations in the Process of Production. *Management and Industry in Russia: Formal and Informal Relations in Transition.* S. Clarke, ed. Cheltenham. Edward Elgar.

Alashaev, S. (1995) On a Particular Kind of Love and the Specificity of Soviet Production. *Management and Industry in Russia: Formal and Informal Relations in Transition.* S. Clarke, ed. Cheltenham. Edward Elgar.

Ashwin, S. and E. Bowers (1997) 'Do Russian Women Want to Work?' in M. Buckley, ed. *Post-Soviet Women.* Cambridge. Cambridge University Press.

Aslund, A. (1993) *Systemic Change and Stabilization in Russia.* London. Royal Institute of International Affairs.

Aslund, A. (1996) Is Russia Threatened by Economic Crisis? Carnegie Endowment for World Peace. 12 September 1996, reported Johnson's Russia List. 13 September.

Aukutsionek, S. (1995) Wasteful Production in Russian Industry, *Russian Economic Barometer*, IV, 2.

Aukutsionek, S. and R. Kapelyushnikov (1996) Labour Hoarding in Russian Industry, *Russian Economic Barometer*, V, 2.

Barberis, N., M. Boycko, et al. (1995) How Does Privatization Work? Evidence from the Russian Shops. NBER Working Paper.

Baskakova, M.E. (1996) *Current Tendencies in the Position of Women in the Sphere of Employment and in the Labour Market.* Gender research in Russia: problems of interaction and prospects of development. Moscow. Moscow Centre for Gender Research.

Boeri, T. (1994) Labour Market Flows and the Persistence of Unemployment in Central and Eastern Europe. *Unemployment in transition countries: transient or persistent?* OECD. Paris. OECD.

Boeva, I. and V. Shironin. (1992) Russians Between State and Market: The Generations Compared. Centre for the Study of Public Policy. University of Strathclyde. *Studies in Public Policy* No. 205.

Brown, J.D. (1996) Excess Labour and Managerial Shortage: Findings from a Survey in St Petersburg. *Europe–Asia Studies*, 48, 5, pp. 811–35.

Burda, M.C. (1993) Unemployment, Labor Markets and Structural Change in Eastern Europe. *Economic Policy*, 16, pp. 101–37.

Chetvernina, T. (1994) Minimal'naya zarabotnaya plata v Rossii. Conference on tripartism and the politics of incomes. Moscow. ILO–CEET.

Clarke, S., ed. (1995) *Management and Industry in Russia: Formal and Informal Relations in Transition*. Cheltenham. Edward Elgar.

Clarke, S., ed. (1996a) *Conflict and Change in the Russian Industrial Enterprise*. Cheltenham. Edward Elgar.

Clarke, S., ed. (1996b) *Labour Relations in Transition: Wages, Employment and Labour Relations in Russian Industrial Enterprises*. Cheltenham. Edward Elgar.

Clarke, S., ed. (1996c) *The Russian Enterprise in Transition: Case Studies*. Cheltenham. Edward Elgar.

Clarke, S. (1996d) Structural Adjustment Without Mass Unemployment? Lessons from Russia in S. Clarke, ed. 1996e.

Clarke, S., ed. (1996e) *The Restructuring of Employment and the Formation of a Labour Market in Russia*. Centre for Comparative Labour Studies. University of Warwick.

Clarke, S., V. Borisov, and P. Fairbrother (1995) *The Workers Movement in Russia*. Cheltenham. Edward Elgar.

Clarke, S., P. Fairbrother, V. Borisov and P. Bizyukov (1994) The Privatisation of Industrial Enterprises in Russia: Four Case Studies. *Europe–Asia Studies,* 46, 2, pp. 179–214.

Commander, S. and F. Coricelli, eds. (1995) *Unemployment, Restructuring and the Labor Market in Eastern Europe and Russia*. Washington D.C.. EDI. World Bank.

Commander, S., S. Dhar and R. Yemtsov (1995) How Russian Firms Make Their Wage and Employment Decisions. Mimeo.

Commander, S., S. Dhar and R. Yemtsov (1996) How Russian Firms Make Their Wage and Employment Decisions, in Commander, Fan and Schaffer, 1996.

Commander, S., Q. Fan and M. E. Schaffer (1996) *Enterprise Restructuring and Economic Policy in Russia*. Washington D.C.. The World Bank.

Commander, S., L. Liberman and R. Yemtsov (1993) Wage and Employment Decisions in the Russian Economy: An Analysis of Developments in 1992. Washington, D.C. EDI.

Commander, S., J. McHale and R. Yemtsov (1995) Russia. in Commander and Coricelli, eds, 1995, pp.147–91.

Commander, S. and R. Yemtsov (1995) Russian Unemployment: its Magnitude, Characteristics and Regional Dimensions. Mimeo. EDI, World Bank.

Cooke, P. (ed.) (1995) *The Rise of the Rustbelt*. UCL Press. London.

Dadashev, A. (1996) Employment of the Population and Unemployment in Russia: Problems of Regulation. *Voprosy ekonomiki*, 1. Moscow.

Deacon, A. (1994) Justifying workfare: the historical context of the debate in M. White ed. *Unemployment, Public Policy and the Changing Labour Market*. Policy Studies Institute, pp. 53–63.

Doeringer, P.B. and M.J. Piore (1971) *Internal Labor Markets and Manpower Analysis*. Lexington. Heath.

Dolopyatova, T. and I. Evseeva (1994) *Strategii vyzhivaniya gosudarstvennykh i privatizirovannykh predpriyatiy promyshlennosti v perekhodny period*. Moscow.

Donova, I. and E. Varshavskaya (1996) Secondary Employment of Employees of Industrial Enterprises, in S. Clarke, ed., 1996e.

Ellman, M. (1994) The Increase in Death and Disease under Katastroika. *Cambridge Journal of Economics*, 18, pp. 329–55.

Eremeeva, V. (1996) Gorod i bezrabotitsa. *Chelovek i trud*, 2.

Federal Employment Service (1995a) *Osnovnye pokazateli deyatel'nosti organov gosudarstvennoi sluzhby zanyatosti*. January-August. Moscow.

Federal Employment Service (1995b) *Monitoring of employment at industrial organisations and in the construction complex organisations of Russia*. Third quarter of 1995. Moscow.

Flanagan, R. (1995) Labor Market Responses to a Change in Economic System. *Proceedings of the World Bank Annual Conference on Development Economics, 1994*. The World Bank. Washington D.C.

Garsiya-Iser, M., O. Golodets and S. Smirnov (1995) Chto skryvaet skrytaya bezrabotitsa. *Segodnya*. 22 December. Moscow.

Garsiya-Iser M., O. Golodets and S. Smirnov (1996) *Kriticheskie yavleniya na regional'nykh rynkakh truda*. Moscow.

George, V. and N. Manning (1980) *Socialism, Social Welfare and the Soviet Union*. Routledge and Kegan Paul. London.

Gimpel'son, V. (1993) Economic Consciousness and Reform of the Employment Sphere in B. Silverman, R. Vogt and M. Yanowitch, eds *Double Shift*. Armonk, NY. M.E. Sharpe.

Gimpel'son, V. (1994) Why is There no Mass Unemployment in Russia. *Business and the Contemporary World* VI, 3, pp. 98–112.

Gimpel'son, V. (1996a) Is Employment in Russia Restructured? Mimeo. Moscow.

Gimpel'son, V. (1996b) Chastnyi sektor v Rossii: zanyatost i oplata truda. Mimeo. Moscow.

Gimpel'son, V. and D. Lippoldt (1996) Dvizhenie rabochei sily v Rossii. Paper presented to OECD–Goskomstat seminar on 'Dynamics of the Russian Labour Market'. Moscow. 9 December.

Gimpel'son, V. and V. S. Magun (1994) Uvolennye na rynke truda: novaya rabota i sotsial'naya mobil'nost. *Sots zhurnal* 1.

Gorbacheva, T., B. Breev et al. (1995) Bezrabotitsa: metody analiza i prognoza. *Voprosy statistiki*, 8, pp. 3–12.

Goskomstat (1990) *SSSR v tsifrakh*, 1990. Moscow. Goskomstat SSSR.

Goskomstat (1995a) *Osnovye pokazateli po statistike truda*. Moscow. Goskomstat Rossiya.

Goskomstat (1995b) *Trud i zanyatost v Rossii, 1995*. Moscow. Goskomstat Rossiya.

Goskomstat (1995c) *Sotsial'no–ekonomicheskoe polozhenie RF v yanvare–yune 1995*, 6. Moscow. Goskomstat Rossiya.

Goskomstat (1996a) *Rossiya v Tsifrakh, 1996*. Moscow. Goskomstat Rossiya.

Goskomstat (1996b) *Metodolicheskie polozheniya po statistike*. Moscow. Goskomstat Rossiya.

Goskomstat (1996c) *Maloe predprinimatel'stvo v Rossii v 1995 godu*. Moscow. Goskomstat Rossiya.

Goskomstat (1996d) *Osnovnye sotsial'no–ekonomicheskie pokazateli razvitiya Rossiiskoi Federatsii v 1995*. Moscow. Goskomstat Rossiya.

Goskomstat (1996e) *Trud i zanyatost v Rossii, 1996*. Moscow. Goskomstat Rossiya.

Goskomstat (1997) *Rossiya v Tsifrakh, 1997*. Moscow. Goskomstat Rossiya.

Goskomstat *Sotsial'no-ekonomicheskoe polozhenie Rossii*, monthly. Moscow. Goskomstat Rossiya.

Goskomstat *Informatsionnyi statisticheskii byulletin'*, monthly. Moscow. Goskomstat Rossiya.

Gotz, R. (1995) *Strukturwandel, Deindustrialisierung und Strukturpolitik in Russland*. Bundesinstitut fur ostwissenschaftliche und internationale Studien. Koln.

Granick, D. (1987) *Job Rights in the Soviet Union*. Cambridge. England. Cambridge University Press.

Granovetter, M. (1995) *Getting a Job*. Chicago. University of Chicago Press.

Greg, P. and J. Wadsworth (1995) A Short History of Labour Turnover, Job Tenure and Job Security. 1975–93. *Oxford Review of Economic Policy*, 11, 1, pp. 73–90.

Gruzdeva E. (1996) *Zhenskaya bezrabotitsa v Rossii*. Moscow.

Halligan, L., P. Teplukhin and D. Willer (1995) Subsidisation of the Russian Economy. Paper presented at the conference on Social Infrastructure and the Russian Enterprise: the Human Resource Dimension. Moscow. December 1995.

Halligan, L., P. Teplukhin and D. Willer. (1996) Subsidization of the Russian Economy. *Russian Economic Trends* 5, 1, pp. 109–28.

Hannay, D.R. (1979) *The Symptom Iceberg, a Study of Community Health*. Routledge. London.

Hanson, P. (1986) The Serendipitous Soviet Achievement of Full Employment: Labour Shortage and Labour Hoarding in the Soviet Economy, in D. Lane, ed. *Labour and Employment in the USSR.*. Brighton. Wheatsheaf, pp. 83–111.

Hausner, J., B. Jessop and K. Nielsen (1995) *Strategic Choice and Path-Dependency in Post-Socialism*. Edward Elgar. Cheltenham.

Hedlund, S. and N. Sundstrom (1996) The Russian Economy after Systemic Change. *Europe–Asia Studies*, 48, 6, pp. 887–914.

Hendley, K. (1993) The Quest for Rational Labour Allocation within Soviet Enterprises in S.G. Solomon, ed. *Beyond Sovietology*. Armonk, NY. M.E. Sharpe.

Horton, S., R. Kanbur, and D. Mazumdar (1994) *Labour Markets in an Era of Adjustment*. Washington, D.C. EDI, World Bank.

Huber, P. (1995) Stylized Facts of New Enterprise Formation in Central and Eastern Europe. How Different are the Czech and Slovak Republics? Institute for Advanced Studies. Vienna. September.

Ickes, B. and R. Ryterman (1994) From Enterprise to Firm: Notes for a Theory of the Enterprise in Transition. in G. Grossman, ed. *The Post–Communist Economic Transformation*. Boulder. Westview Press.

Ignatov, V. (1994) *Description of the Labour Market in the Ivanovo Region*. Paper presented at a workshop on the restructuring of the textile industry in the Ivanovo region. Moscow, 4–5 October 1994.

ILO (1995) *World Employment, 1995*. ILO. Geneva.

ILO–CEET (1996a) *Economic Restructuring and Social Dialogue in the Ivanovo Oblast, Russia*. Budapest.

ILO–CEET (1996b) *For More and Better Jobs in the Russian Federation*. Budapest.

IMF/World Bank/OECD (1991) *A Study of the Soviet Economy*, 3 volumes.

Institute for Strategic Analysis and Development of Entrepreneurship (1995) Malyi biznes Rossii: adaptatsiya k perekhodnym usloviyam. *Voprosy statistiki*, 9, pp. 19–68.

Institute of Economics, Russian Academy of Sciences (1993) People in Search of Work [Chelovek v poiskakh raboty]. Results of research into regional employment centres of Leningrad oblast in February–March, 1993.

Institute of Economics, Russian Academy of Sciences (1996) *Polozhenie zhenshchin v reformiruemoi ekonomike: opyt Rossii*. Moscow.

Institute of Problems of Employment, Russian Academy of Sciences (1995) Problems of employment and unemployment in conditions of transition to the market. *Rossiiskii sotsial'no–politicheskii vestnik*, 2, pp. 5–11.

Jackman, R. (n.d.) Economic Policies, Employment and Labour Markets in Transition in Central and Eastern Europe. Centre for Economic Performance. LSE.

Jackman, R. (1994) Economic Policy and Employment. *International Labour Review* 133, 3.

Jackman, R. and C. Pauna (1996) Labour Market Policy and the

Reallocation of Labour across Sectors. Mimeo.

Kabalina, V. (1996) Privatisation and Restructuring of Enterprises: Under Insider or Outsider Control? in S. Clarke, ed. *Conflict and Change in the Russian Industrial Enterprise*. Cheltenham. Edward Elgar.

Kapelyushnikov, R.I. (1994) Problema bezrabotitsy v Rossiiskoi ekonomike. Moscow. Mimeo.

Kapelyushnikov, R.I. (1997) Job and Labour Turnover in Russian Industry. *Russian Economic Barometer*, VI, 1, pp. 31-51.

Kapelyushnikov, R.I. and S. Aukutsionek (1994a) The Russian Enterprises Behaviour in the Labor market: Some Empirical Evidence. Moscow. Mimeo

Kapelyushnikov, R.I. and S. Aukutsionek (1994b) The Russian Labor market in 1993. *RFE/RL Research Report* 3, p. 29.

Kapelyushnikov, R.I. and S. Aukutsionek (1994c) Labor Market in 1993. *Russian Economic Barometer*, III, 1.

Kapelyushnikov, R.I. and S. Aukutsionek (1995a) Labour market in 1994. *Russian Economic Barometer*, IV, 2.

Kapelyushnikov, R.I. and S. Aukutsionek (1995b) Rossiiskie promyshlennye predpriyatiya na rynke truda. *Voprosy ekonomiki* 6, pp. 48–56.

Keune, M. and A. Nesporova. (1996) *Promoting Economic and Social Restructuring in the Spis Region, Slovakia*. ILO–CEET. Budapest.

Kharkhordin, O. (1996) A System of Responsible Dependency: The Collective as an Object of Knowledge and Action. University of California. Berkeley.

Khibovskaya, E. (1994a) Vtorichnaya zanyatost. *VTsIOM Bulletin*, 5, pp. 35–40.

Khibovskaya, E. (1994b) Dobrovol'naya trudovaya mobil'nost. *VTsIOM Bulletin*, 4.

Khibovskaya, E. (1995a) Rossiyanie stali bol'she opasat'sya poteryat rabotu. *Segodnya*, 26.

Khibovskaya, E. (1995b) Secondary Employment as a Method of Adaptation to Economic Reforms. *Voprosy ekonomiki* 5, pp. 71–9.

Khibovskaya, E. (1996a) Trudovaya motivatsia i zanyatost. *VTsIOM Bulletin* 4, pp. 32–4.

Khibovskaya, E. (1996b) Secondary employment in various economic sectors. *VTsIOM Bulletin* 3, pp. 24–7.

Khotkina, Z.A. (1996) Otverzhdennye. *Nezavisimaya gazeta*, Moscow.

Klopov, E. (1996) Vtorichnaya zanyatost' kak forma sotsial'notrudovoi mobil'nosti, in Trudovye peremeshcheniya i adaptatsiya rabotnikov. Moscow. IMEMO, pp. 21–39.

Koen, V. (1996) Russian Macroeconomic Data: Existence, Access, Interpretation. *Communist Economies and Economic Transformation* 8, 3.

Kozina, I. (1996) Changes in the Social Organisation of Industrial Enterprises in S. Clarke, ed. *Labour in Transition: Wages, Employment and Labour Relations in Russian Industrial Enterprises*. Cheltenham. Edward Elgar.

Kozina, I. and V. Borisov (1996) The Changing Status of Workers in the Enterprise in S. Clarke, ed. *Conflict and Change in the Russian Industrial Enterprise*. Cheltenham. Edward Elgar.

Kupriyanova, Z.V. (1996) Rynok truda v 1995g. *VTsIOM Bulletin* 1.

Láng-Pickvance, K., N. Manning and C. Pickvance, eds (1997) *Environmental and Housing Movements, Grassroots Experience in Hungary, Russia and Estonia*. Aldershot. Avebury.

Layard, R. and A. Richter (1994) Labour Market Adjustment in Russia. *Russian Economic Trends*, 3, 2.

Layard, R. and A. Richter (1995) How Much Unemployment is Needed for Restructuring: the Russian Experience. *Economics of Transition* 3, 1, pp. 39–58.

Lehmann, S. (1995) Costs and Opportunities of Marketization: an Analysis of Russian Employment and Unemployment. *Research in the Sociology of Work*, 5.

Linz, S.J. (1995) Russian Labor Market in Transition. *Economic Development and Cultural Change*, 693–716.

Linz, S.J. (1996) Gender Differences in the Russian Labor Market. *Journal of Economic Issues*. XXX, 1 March.

Lippoldt, D. and V. Gimpel'son (1996) *Labour Restructuring in Four Russian Enterprises: A Case Study*. Paris. OECD.

Malle, S. (1986) Heterogeneity of the Soviet Labour Market as a Limit to a more Efficient Utilisation of Manpower in D. Lane, ed. *Labour and Employment in the USSR..* Brighton. Wheatsheaf, pp. 122–42.

Malle, S. (1990) *Employment Planning in the Soviet Union.* Basingstoke. Macmillan.

Marnie, S. and A. Motivans (1995) Women in the Labour Market and Female Unemployment in Russia, Latvia, and Uzbekistan. Paper presented to the World Bank Europe and Central Asia Region Seminar on Gender in Transition. Bucharest. Romania. February 1–2.

Marsh, C. (1991) The Right to Work: Justice in the Distribution of Employment in N. Manning, ed. *Social Policy Review 1990–91.* London. Longman, pp. 223–42.

McLaughlin, E. (1994) Flexibility or Polarisation? in M. White, ed. *Unemployment, Public Policy and the Changing Labour Market.* Policy Studies Institute, pp. 7–28.

Metalina, T. (1996) Employment Policy in an Industrial Enterprise in S. Clarke, ed. *Labour in Transition: Wages, Employment and Labour Relations in Russian Industrial Enterprises.* Cheltenham. Edward Elgar.

Monousova, G. and N. Guskova (1996) Internal Mobility and the Restructuring of Labour in S. Clarke, ed. *Labour in Transition: Wages, Employment and Labour Relations in Russian Industrial Enterprises.* Cheltenham. Edward Elgar.

Mosley, P., J. Harrigan and J. Toye (1995) *Aid and Power: The World Bank and Policy-based Lending.* London. Routledge.

Nesporova, A. and B. Kyloh. (1994) *Economic and Social Dialogue in the Ostrava–Karvina Region.* ILO–CEET. Budapest.

Newell, A. and B. Reilly (1996) The Gender Wage Gap in Russia: Some Empirical Evidence. *Labour Economics,* 3.

OECD (1995a) *Wage Formation During the Period of Economic Restructuring in the Russian Federation.* Organisation for Economic Co-operation and Development. Paris.

OECD (1995b) *Economic Surveys: The Russian Federation.* Organisation for Economic Co-operation and Development. Paris.

OECD (1996a) *Small Business in Transition Economies: The Development of Entrepreneurship in the Czech Republic, Hungary, Poland and the Slovak Republic.* Organisation for Economic Co-operation and Development. Paris.

OECD (1996b) *The OECD Jobs Strategy: Pushing Ahead with the Strategy.* Organisation for Economic Co-operation and

Development, Paris.

OECD (1996c) *Short-term Economic Indicators – Transition Economies*, 3, 1996. Organisation for Economic Co-operation and Development, Paris.

OECD–CCET (1994) *Enhanced Labour Market Monitoring: Unemployment in the Russian Federation*. Organisation for Economic Co-operation and Development. Centre for Co-operation with Economies in Transition. Paris.

Oxenstierna, S. (1990) *From Labour Shortage to Unemployment: Soviet Labour Market in the 1980's*. Swedish Institute for Social Research.

Popov, A. (1995) Predlozhenie i spros na rynke truda v Rossiiiskoi federatsii: kolichestvennaya otsenka. *Voprosy statistiki* 6, pp. 26–8.

Pyke, F. (1995) *Ivanovo, Some Considerations on Future Actions*. Paper prepared for a meeting on restructuring in Ivanovo held in Budapest, 28–9 September.

Rasumov, A. (1995) *An Analysis of the Labour Market of the Ivanovo Region and Production Trends in the Textile Industry of the Region: Some Conclusions and Observations*. Paper prepared for a meeting on restructuring in the Ivanovo region. Budapest, 28–9 September.

Rasumov, A. (1996) The Current Situation on the Labour Market and Economic Policy in the Textile Industry of the Ivanovo Region. All–Russia Centre of Living Standards. Moscow. Mimeo.

Rehfeld, D. (1995) Disintegration and Reintegration of Production Clusters in the Ruhr Area in P. Cooke, ed., 1995.

Romanov, P. (1995) Middle Management in Industrial Production in the Transition to the Market in S. Clarke, ed. *Management and Industry in Russia: Formal and Informal Relations in Transition*. Cheltenham. Edward Elgar.

Rose, R. (1993) Is Money the Measure of Welfare in Russia? *Studies in Public Policy*, 215. Centre for the Study of Public Policy. University of Strathclyde.

Rose, R. (1995) New Russia Barometer IV. *Studies in Public Policy*, 250. Centre for the Study of Public Policy. University of Strathclyde.

Rose, R. and C. Haerpfer (1994) New Democracies Barometer III: Learning from What is Happening. *Studies in Public Policy*.

230. Centre for the Study of Public Policy. University of Strathclyde.

Rostchin S. (1996) *Zanyatost zhenshchin v perehodnoi ekonomike Rossii.* Moscow.

Rowntree, B.S. (1901) *Poverty: A Study of Town Life.* London. Macmillan.

Rowntree, B.S. (1941) *Poverty and Progress: a Second Social Survey of York.* London. Longman.

Roxburgh, I. and J. Shapiro (1996) Russian Unemployment and the Excess Wages Tax. *Communist Economies and Economic Transformation,* 8, 1, pp. 5–29.

Russian Ministry of Labour (1996) Employment Policy in the Russian Federation, in ILO–CEET, 1996b.

Ryzhykova, Z. and M. Fidler (1995) O dinamike i struckture bezrabotitsy v Rossiiskoi federatsii. *Voprosy statistiki* 2, pp. 21–5.

Samara Research Group (1996) Two Military–Industrial Giants in S. Clarke, ed. *The Russian Enterprise in Transition.* Cheltenham. Edward Elgar.

Scott, A. (1995) The Geographic Foundations of Industrial Performance, *Competition and Change,* Vol.1, pp. 51–66. Chur, Switzerland. Harwood Academic Publishers.

Sengenberger, W. and M. Keune (1996) The Role of Proactive Policies for Employment Generation at the Industrial and Regional Level – International Experience, in ILO–CEET, 1996b.

Shlapentokh, V. (1989) *Public and Private life of the Soviet People.* Oxford. Oxford University Press.

Smith, A. (1910) [1776] *The Wealth of Nations.* London. Dent.

SPKTZN – FES (1995) *Sluzhba zanyatosti sankt peterburga v 1994 godu.* Department for Analysis of the Labour Market. St Petersburg.

Standing, G. (1991) *Structural Adjustment and Labour Market Policies: towards social adjustment?* Geneva. ILO.

Standing, G. (1992) *Employment Dynamics of Russian Industry.* Conference on Employment Restructuring in Russian Industry. ILO.

Standing, G. (1994a) Labour Market Implications of Privatization in Russian Industry in 1992. *World Development* 22, 2, pp. 261–70.

Standing, G. (1994b) Labour Market Dynamics in Russian Industry in 1993: results from the Third Round of the RLFS.

Standing, G. (1994c) Employment restructuring in Russian Industry. *World Development* 22, 2.

Standing, G. (1994d) Why is Measured Unemployment in Russia so Low? The Net with So Many Holes. *The Journal of European Social Policy*, 4, 1, February, pp. 25–49.

Standing, G. (1995a) *Enterprise Restructuring in Russian Industry and Mass Unemployment: The RLFS Fourth Round, 1994.* Employment Department. ILO. Geneva.

Standing, G. (1995b) *Promoting the 'Human Development Enterprise': Enterprise restructuring and corporate governance in Russian industry.* Geneva. ILO Labour Market Papers 8.

Standing, G. (1996a) *The Shake-out in Russian Factories: The RLFS Fifth Round, 1995.* Geneva. ILO Labour Market Papers 14.

Standing, G. (1996b) *Russian Unemployment and Enterprise Restructuring: Reviving Dead Souls.* Basingstoke. Macmillan.

Standing, G. and T. Chetvernina (1993) Zagadki rossiskoi bezrabotitsi (po materialam obsledovaniya Tsentrov zanyatosti Leningradskoi oblasti). *Voprosy ekonomiki*, 12, pp. 86–93.

Stavnitskii, A. and A. Solov'eva (1994) *Politika zarabotnoi platy i sotsial'noe partnerstvo.* Conference on tripartism and the politics of incomes. Moscow. ILO–CEET.

Tartakovskaya, I. (1996) Women's Career Patterns in Industry: a Generational Comparison. *Gender, Generation and Identity in Contemporary Russia.* H. Pilkington. London and New York, pp. 57–74.

Therborn, G. (1991) Cultural Belonging, Structural Location, and Human Action. *Acta Sociologica*, 34, pp 177–91.

Tkachenko, A. (1996) Vyborochnye obsledovaniya zanyatosti svidetel'stvuyut. *Chelovek i trud* 1.

Toye, J. (1995) *Structural Adjustment and Employment Policy: Issues and Experience.* Geneva. ILO.

Tsentr issledovannii rynka truda (1995a) *Mekhanizmy adaptatsii vnutrennego rynka truda predpriyatii k novym ekonomicheskim usloviyam.* Moscow. IE, RAN.

Tsentr issledovannii rynka truda (1995b) *Obsledovanie rynka truda v promyshlennosti Rossii v 1994 godu.* Moscow. IE, RAN.

UN–ECE (1996) *Economic Survey of Europe in 1994–1995*. Geneva.

UNDP (1997) *Human Development Report: The Russian Federation.* New York and Moscow. UNDP.

Vinogradova, E. (1996) Rossiiskie predpriyatiya: zanyatost', zarabotnaya plata, sotsial'naya infrastruktura. Rossiiskii sotsial'no-politicheskii vestnik, 1-2.20:22.

Vychislitel'nyi tsentr (1994) *Dvizhenie rabotnikov i nalichie svobodnykh rabochikh mest.* January–December. Moscow. Goskomstat.

World Bank (1995) *Workers in an Integrating World.* New York. Oxford University Press for the World Bank.

World Bank (1996) *From Plan to Market.* New York. Oxford University Press for the World Bank.

Yemtsov, R. (1994) Masshtaby i formy bezrabotitsy. *VTsIOM Bulletin* 5, pp. 40–43.

Young, M. and P. Wilmott (1957) *Family and Kinship in East London.* Harmondsworth. Penguin.

Zaionchkovskaya, Z. A. (1994) *Migratsiya naseleniya i rynok truda v Rossii.* Moscow. INP, RAN.

Zaslavskii, I. and M. Moskvina (1989) Kto ostanetsya za porogom prokhodnoi? *Sots issled* 1.

Zdravomyslova, E. A. (1995) Women Without Work. *All people are sisters.* St Petersburg.

Index

age, 54, 61, 63–4, 66, 69–2, 74, 75–7, 85, 99, 125, 132, 136–7, 139, 142, 150–54, 189, 191, 193, 195, 204, 235, 279–80, 282, 284, 286, 302–4, 308, 317, 319, 322–3, 329
agriculture, 23–4, 26, 40, 65, 67, 76, 97, 131, 246, 281
  subsistence, 3, 12, 55, 65, 76, 79–80, 94, 128, 139
arrears
  unemployment benefit, 78, 180, 201, 208–9, 212–15, 314, 317
  wages, 44, 68, 78–9, 93, 118, 140–41, 180, 201, 213, 241, 251
Ashwin, S., 75, 204
Aslund, A., 21, 49, 147
Aukutsionek, S., 31, 32, 34, 36, 37, 39, 40, 43, 47, 59, 67

banking system, 28, 32, 107, 120, 222, 273
bankruptcy, 16–17, 26, 56, 61, 90, 141–2, 161–2, 252, 264
barter, 19, 80, 128
Boeri, T., 21
Boeva, I., 297
Bolshevik, 1
Borisov, V., 23, 99
Bowers, E., 5, 75, 200, 204
Breev, B., 64
Brown, J. D., 36, 67

budget constraints
  hard, 9, 16, 21, 26–7, 51, 82, 90, 104–5, 212, 297–8, 304–7
  soft, 10, 17, 20–21, 25, 28, 91, 93, 148

capacity utilisation, 39, 93, 110, 164
capital markets, 14, 91, 106
capitalist, 1, 2, 28, 52, 105, 108, 254
case study, 4–5, 38–9, 42, 59, 95, 97, 99, 101, 103, 109, 113, 115, 125, 131, 159, 208, 279, 323
Central Europe, 3, 19, 21, 45, 201
Centre for Labour Market Studies, xiii, 29, 30, 35, 37, 38, 43, 98, 99, 119, 124, 157, 179, 186, 194, 208
Chetvernina, T., xiii, 6, 53, 216, 277
churning, 40, 154, 315
Clarke, S., xiii, 1, 2, 3, 9, 32, 36, 87, 93, 100, 101, 106, 117, 118, 179, 200, 314, 315
collective bargaining, 15, 145
Commander, S., 9, 10, 16, 17, 19–22, 30–35, 37–8, 40, 48, 56, 64–5, 90, 95, 200, 313
Communist Party, 16, 24, 29, 33, 34, 139, 165, 302, 307

conflict, 32, 34, 37, 126, 237, 302, 305
construction, 23–4, 29, 40–42, 67, 84, 97, 112, 119, 140, 146, 258, 271, 281, 287, 321, 328
Cooke, P., 267
Coricelli, F., 16, 95, 200
credit, 19–20, 26, 40, 46, 54, 62, 90, 107, 157, 281
crime, 13, 76, 156, 305, 311
Czech Republic, 19

Dadashev, A., 220, 221
Deacon, A., 311
dead souls, 73, 111, 115
debt, 11–12, 19, 87, 118, 141
dependence, 231, 240, 254, 327
dependency culture, 6
deskilling, 5, 52, 56–7, 130
Dhar, S., 17, 22, 31, 33, 34, 38
dismissal, 34, 48, 82
distribution, compulsory, 133
Donova, I., xiii, 4, 56, 87

economic crisis, 4, 75, 162, 219, 221
economic reform, 176, 200, 226, 232, 302, 304–5
economically active population, 3, 10, 41, 63, 66, 69, 97, 202, 280
economy, 1, 2, 9–13, 16, 18, 20, 24–5, 33, 37, 41, 50, 52, 54, 58, 61, 80, 82–4, 88, 89, 103–6, 108, 112, 119, 124, 137, 141, 143–7, 164–5, 189, 201, 206, 208, 213, 216, 219, 232, 256, 259,

265–7, 272–5, 297, 301, 311, 320, 330
EDI, 19, 31, 32, 90, 91, 95
education, 40, 45, 63, 64, 73, 76, 116, 129, 138, 207, 235, 256, 259, 273, 281, 283–4, 287–8, 317, 319–21
Ellman, M., 317
employment
    decline, 17, 19, 27, 39, 70, 93, 183, 231
    industrial, 19, 20, 40, 57, 90, 258, 280, 318
    secondary, 4, 47, 51, 54–5, 64–5, 70, 73, 77–8, 95, 97, 102–3, 110, 113, 127–30, 134, 137, 145, 149, 282–3
    short-time, 59, 217, 330
    structure of, 5, 40, 101, 159, 190, 192, 232, 280
    temporary, 24, 32, 42, 46–7, 58, 60, 62, 66, 77, 124, 141, 143, 236, 238, 268, 271, 282–3
employment centre, 203, 227, 229–34, 237, 239–45, 249, 279
employment fund, 62, 219–26, 231, 240, 243, 247–8, 250, 252, 255
employment opportunities, 206, 215, 270, 294, 311, 324
employment policy, 5, 35, 47, 59, 108, 110, 116–24, 141, 143, 145–6, 197–8, 226, 266, 270, 308, 328
employment restructuring, 2–5, 17, 38–47, 49, 95–9, 101,

102, 103, 123, 139, 141, 277
Employment Service, 6, 15, 18,
 37, 42, 45, 55, 61, 62, 96,
 98, 100–102, 113, 118, 122,
 132, 133, 136–7, 148, 154,
 156, 184, 201, 218–39, 243,
 245, 247–8, 280–88, 291,
 300, 308–9, 313, 316
 regional, 6, 222, 233
enterprise directors, 18, 20, 25–
 7, 29–34, 37, 116, 126, 195,
 196, 221, 228, 232–3, 238,
 241, 246
enterprise restructuring, 100,
 162–5, 264, 270
enterprises
 corporate governance, 84,
  109–10, 163–5, 175–6
 state, 10, 16–19, 21, 24, 27,
  39, 42, 46, 50, 54, 56, 66,
  73, 84, 90–93, 98, 105,
  115–17, 125, 137, 143–5,
  303
 successful, 5, 10, 12, 25, 37,
  40, 48, 80, 83, 98, 103–5,
  108–9, 116, 119–23, 130,
  133, 136, 139–40, 144,
  146, 228, 268, 313, 319,
  330
 unsuccessful, 5, 12, 48, 98,
  103–5, 107–8, 116, 119–
  23, 125, 130, 139, 188,
  198, 275
 workers' control, 20, 28–37,
  164, 313
entrepreneurs, 79
Eremeeva, V., 283
excess wage tax, 67, 112, 114,
 150, 168

export, 12, 17, 88, 118, 257,
 268
extractive industries, 16, 17,
 89, 143

Fairbrother, P., 106
Fan, Q., 9, 30
Flanagan, R., 200

Gaidar Institute, 29
GDP, 9, 19– 20, 41, 63, 89, 216
gender, 5, 54, 63, 69, 71–2, 75,
 85, 99, 129, 137–8, 154,
 200, 202–04, 208–09, 212–
 4, 279, 323
George, V., 310, 312
Gimpel'son, V., 22, 34, 40, 41,
 46, 65, 109, 313, 315, 323
globalisation, 12
Golodets, O., 37, 56
Gorbachev, M. 53
Gorbacheva, T., 64
Goskomstat, 9, 19–20, 24, 29,
 39–40, 43–6, 53–5, 58–9,
 63, 66–79, 93, 113, 115, 150,
 152–3, 159, 202, 205–7,
 211, 216–17, 230, 242, 277,
 281, 315–16
Gotz, R., 260
Granick, D., 24, 26, 27
Granovetter, M., 325
Greg, P., 317

Haerpfer, C., 326
Halligan, L., 26, 271
Hannay, D.R., 322
Hanson, P., 22, 27
Harrigan, J., 82
Hausner, J., 311

health, 23–4, 45, 90, 109, 140,
145, 182–5, 207, 236–7,
247, 259, 272, 281, 287,
312, 316, 322, 324, 329
Hedlund, S., 9
Hendley, K., 134
Horton, S., 144
households, 17, 33, 63, 79, 282,
292, 300–01, 309–10, 316,
325–7, 330–31
housing, 23, 24, 40, 45, 90,
110, 116, 117, 140, 145, 248,
259, 270, 272, 279, 297, 311
Huber, P., 272

Ignatov, V., 258
ILO, 3, 9, 18–20, 29–32, 37,
38–9, 48, 52, 56, 63, 65, 92,
202, 216–7, 230, 232–4,
256, 266, 276, 280, 286,
292, 313, 315, 317, 323–8
IMF, 18, 27, 42, 43, 147
incentives, 3, 52, 105, 144, 153,
168, 175, 183, 326, 327
income, 7, 41, 79, 291, 298,
300–01, 326
industry, 4, 9, 16, 24, 29, 35–6,
39, 41, 56, 59, 61, 67, 70,
80, 90, 97, 99–100, 102,
104, 148, 157, 186, 188,
197, 208, 228, 231–2, 237,
264
    light, 17, 23, 54, 89, 188,
    229, 243, 248, 252, 260,
    287
    textile, 6, 209, 218, 232,
    257–69, 274–5
inequality, 13, 53, 75, 79, 81,
90, 94, 148, 182, 330

inflation, 13, 18–20, 27, 33, 44,
49, 75, 89, 112, 120, 213,
219, 222, 224, 298, 302, 305
information sources, 26, 30, 66,
93, 111, 113, 132–3, 148,
159, 195, 201, 224, 235,
239, 245, 269, 271, 279,
281–2, 294, 297, 312, 324
Institute for Strategic Analysis
and Development of
Entrepreneurship, 73, 74
Institute of Economics, Russian
Academy of Sciences, xiii,
29, 35, 119, 186, 216, 227,
228, 240, 245
Institute of Problems of
Employment, Russian
Academy of Sciences, 226
ISITO, xiii, 100
Ivanovo, 6–7, 43, 45, 103, 158,
168, 176, 188, 224, 256–75,
315

Jackman, R., 17, 40, 144
Jessop, B., 311
job search, 63, 98, 110, 131,
206, 230, 278, 282, 291,
292–5, 322
job tenure, 40

Kabalina, V., xiii, 66, 87, 98,
100
Kanbur, R., 144
Kapelyushnikov, R. I., 19, 22,
31, 32, 34, 36, 37, 38, 39,
40, 41, 43, 45, 47, 49, 55,
59, 67, 98
Kemerovo, xiii, 4, 87, 99, 100,
102–04, 109

Keune, M., xiii, 6, 256–7, 266, 273, 315, 323
Kharkhordin, O., 34
Khibovskaya, E., 42, 56, 65
Klopov, E., 56
Koen, V., 9
Kornai, Janos, 25
Kozina, I., xiii, 4, 23, 87, 99, 100, 112
Kyloh, B., 273

labour
  ancillary, 23–5, 29, 36, 44, 107
  auxiliary, 23–5, 36, 45, 128, 209–11, 288
  casual, 3, 10, 12, 21, 40, 51, 54, 56, 60, 65–6, 71–2, 76–9, 92, 129, 139, 141, 143, 157, 327, 330
  clerical, 25, 44, 54, 193
  core workers, 23, 88, 99, 108, 120, 124–6, 135–6, 267, 287
  costs, 31, 37–8, 57, 59, 109, 266–8, 274
  disabled, 24, 36, 45, 128, 154, 280, 282
  discipline, 24, 34, 42–4, 62, 102, 113–15, 120, 128, 196, 290, 320, 321
  hoarding, 3, 10, 17, 20–37, 60, 67, 90–92, 95, 165, 262–5, 267, 313
  migration, 40–41, 50, 248
  reserve, 23, 57, 61
  shortage, 22, 25–6, 31, 116, 122, 167
  skilled, 15, 18, 23, 28, 31,
  35–8, 50–52, 60, 84, 106–9, 118, 121–9, 132–7, 142–4, 146, 148, 192–3, 198, 200, 209–11, 229, 232, 235–6, 250, 253, 257, 265, 270, 272, 282, 288–9, 297, 317–23, 329
  social, 24
  surplus, 6, 18, 22–31, 34–7, 56–7, 60, 67, 88, 93, 148, 157, 159, 165–9, 172, 174–5, 183, 196, 315
  turnover, 5, 21, 40, 42, 91, 93, 99, 101, 111, 118, 121, 133, 154, 179, 209, 211, 229, 313–4, 317, 319, 323–4
  unskilled, 24, 37, 45–6, 50–52, 107, 118, 128, 132, 136, 142, 192, 194, 196–7
labour book, 43, 72, 73, 102, 114, 115, 289
labour collective, 34, 51, 107, 116–21, 124–5, 135, 139, 140
  degradation, 5, 51, 109, 130, 188, 198
labour exchange, 102, 132, 216, 227–31, 234, 238
labour force
  composition, 5, 113, 119
  inactivity, 75–6, 204–5, 262
  stratification, 4, 98
labour market
  flexibility, 2–4, 6, 10, 14, 18, 21, 38–61, 76, 80–4, 87–95, 128, 135, 140–43, 181, 183–4, 212, 214, 279, 291, 297, 311, 313

internal, 126–7, 134–6
segmentation, 97, 127–8, 132
labour market policies, 8, 10, 15, 62, 88, 90, 94, 132, 231, 276, 277, 279, 282
  active, 15, 48, 62, 88, 90, 122, 219–21, 225, 231, 265, 274, 276–7, 279, 330
  passive, 219–20, 223, 225, 231
  public works, 50, 145, 220, 224, 236, 250–52, 282–3, 285, 303–4
  training, 7, 15, 47, 50, 116, 125, 132, 138, 178, 182–5, 210, 220–25, 235–8, 247–51, 255, 268–72, 281–4, 291–2, 295, 297, 303–4, 308, 312
  regional, 7, 224
labour mobility
  geographical, 40, 90, 296
  external, 4, 110, 135, 136
  internal, 4, 97, 110, 129, 134–6
  promotion, 25, 135, 265, 270–71, 274
  transfers, 21, 42, 97, 129, 134, 135
labour placement bureaux, 18, 24, 46, 62
labour recruitment, 5, 24, 30, 34–7, 39, 42, 44–7, 50, 62, 82, 93, 95, 101, 110–15, 121–6, 131–3, 136, 138, 140, 179, 193, 197–8, 225, 228, 229, 235, 302–3, 312, 317, 320–21, 325

family, 40, 63, 65–6, 69, 70, 74, 125, 237, 242–5, 254, 301, 321, 325–6, 330
friends, 65, 76, 124–5, 129, 131–3, 141, 324, 330
from the street, 98, 108, 132, 137
patronage, 11, 15, 51, 130, 132, 151, 225, 254, 259, 263, 270, 282, 309
personal connections, 51, 97, 124, 131, 133, 136, 230
law, 27, 60–61, 67, 94, 144, 149, 220, 225, 228, 231, 235, 239, 241, 242–3, 247, 252, 255, 271, 276, 278, 281, 295, 302, 306, 309
Layard, R., 3, 10, 48, 49, 50, 52, 53, 54, 56, 91, 94, 144, 147, 200, 313
lay-off, 18, 33, 49, 56, 58–9, 118, 120, 127, 153
leave
  administrative, 6, 7, 44, 48, 50, 54, 56–60, 67, 69–71, 77, 92, 113, 118, 127, 141, 168–70, 172–5, 187, 217, 221, 223, 227, 229, 237, 252, 264, 277, 289, 290
  maternity, 70–71, 172, 174, 264
  unpaid, 31, 43–4, 70, 140, 169, 181, 213, 237–8, 289
liberal economics, 1, 87
Liberman, L., 20–21, 31, 35, 40
life expectancy, 53, 154
Linz, S. J., 22
Lippoldt, D., 41, 109, 313, 315, 323

loans, 31, 61, 250, 271
local government, 6, 23–4, 26, 40, 90, 102, 117–18, 132, 145, 189, 249–50, 273, 328

Magun, V. S., 40, 46
Malle, S., 26, 27, 35
management, 27, 142, 163, 277, 288
  line, 31, 36, 121, 123, 126
  strategy, 4, 38, 120–21, 125
Manning, N., xiii, 7, 310, 311, 312
market economy, 13, 18, 24, 50, 54, 61, 80, 103, 105–6, 108, 112, 124, 137, 232
Marnie, S., 280
Marsh, C., 311
McHale, J., 17, 30, 32, 37, 313
McLaughlin, E., 311
men, 5, 40, 44–5, 53, 66, 69, 75, 79, 85, 86, 137–8, 152, 154, 156, 201–4, 206, 207, 208–15, 234, 245, 247, 249, 250, 252–3, 302–3, 317, 320–21, 328
methodology, 4, 29, 40, 63, 68, 95, 99, 101, 216, 230
Ministry of Labour, 219, 231, 240, 254, 256, 257
monopoly, 21, 39, 106, 109, 142
Monousova, G., xiii, 5, 113, 200
moral economy, 20
mortality, 53, 154, 156, 317
Moscow, xiii, 2, 7, 29, 35, 41, 43, 45, 53, 54, 65–6, 68, 74, 100, 148, 152, 157–8, 160, 179, 201, 218, 224–5, 230, 240, 253–4, 276, 278–306, 310, 315–17, 328–30
Moskvina, M., 27, 254
Mosley, P, 82
Motivans, A., 280

Nesporova, A., 273
new technology, 39, 164
Newell, A., 212
Nielsen, K., 311
Nizhnii Novgorod, 158, 176, 194, 218, 227, 231–4, 241, 242, 246–8, 250, 254, 315

OECD, 9, 14, 26, 34, 48, 63, 65, 69–70, 74, 271, 276, 282, 315, 323–31
overtime, 55, 264
ownership, 20, 119–20, 163–5, 186, 189, 287, 320
Oxenstierna, S., 22

parasitism, 49, 62, 140, 240
Pauna, C., 17, 40, 144
pensioners, 24, 44, 62, 64, 66, 76, 77, 79, 107, 111, 132, 142, 195, 200, 204, 237, 302
pensions, 3, 76, 77, 80, 153, 220, 245, 301, 330
perestroika, 27, 52, 84
Pickvance, C., 311
planning, 18, 22, 23, 25–29, 37, 63, 102, 103, 105, 110, 113, 118, 162, 178, 257, 268
politics, 1, 4, 6, 11, 13–16, 18, 30, 35, 41, 52, 82, 94, 104–6, 109, 112, 118, 132, 142, 145–7, 184, 231, 278, 302,

304–12
Popov, A., 46, 75
poverty, 12, 16, 23, 28, 40, 42, 52–3, 78–81, 105, 146, 148, 151, 169, 208, 255–6, 275, 278, 286, 297–8, 302, 305, 309, 317–25, 327–8, 330
price liberalisation, 11, 14
private sector, 16, 21, 39, 42, 49–51, 54, 56, 67, 73, 77, 88, 92, 94, 112, 117, 124, 143, 144, 210
privatisation, 11, 20, 31–2, 37, 54, 90, 98, 106, 117, 142, 162–3, 189, 208, 263, 285, 287
production decline, 9, 17, 19, 38–9, 232
productivity, 3, 23, 24, 26–31, 36, 38, 52, 81, 109, 166, 180, 184, 195, 264–71
profit, 34, 61, 105
property form, 29, 56, 109, 110, 159, 162–4, 168, 176
protectionism, 11, 132
protest, 302, 305–6, 309
   strikes, 32, 174, 306
Pyke, F., 269

Rasumov, A., 258, 260, 263
reform, 9, 14–21, 25, 27–8, 30, 36, 38–44, 49, 53, 63, 82, 88–90, 117, 119, 121, 133, 150, 176, 200, 226, 232, 302–5
Rehfeld, D., 259
Reilly, B., 212
Richter, A., 10, 49, 50, 52, 53, 54, 56, 144, 200, 313

Romanov, P., 119
Rose, R., 297, 326
Rostchin, S., 208
Rowntree, B.S., 325
Roxburgh, I., 67, 313, 324
Russian Economic Barometer, 29, 30, 31, 32, 34, 36, 37, 38, 39, 40, 43, 47, 67, 80, 110
Russian Labour Flexibility Survey, 4, 78, 148, 157, 158, 159, 161, 162, 164, 166–8, 170, 181, 315
Russian Longitudinal Monitoring Survey, 33, 40, 55, 65, 69, 70, 71, 72, 74, 76, 77, 78, 79, 86, 133, 201, 204, 212, 213, 214
Russian Ministry of Labour, 219, 231, 240, 254, 256, 257
Ryzhykova, Z. 66

Samara, xiii, 4, 87, 99–100, 102–3, 315
Scott, A., 266, 273
Sengenberger, W., 257, 266, 273
separations, 5, 21, 34–5, 42–4, 47, 67, 113, 121, 123, 136, 192–4, 196–7
   compulsory, 17, 21, 43, 44, 60, 114, 236, 237
   redundancy, 7, 17, 21, 31, 32, 34, 36–7, 40, 43–5, 48–9, 60, 97, 107, 113–14, 118, 195–6, 236–7, 242, 286, 289–90, 314–16, 319–21, 327
   voluntary, 34, 43, 114, 194

service sector, 16–17, 51, 54, 70, 88, 97, 138, 265, 271

Shapiro, J., 67, 324

Shironin, V., 297

Shlapentokh, V., 323, 325

small enterprises, 14, 27, 39, 47, 54, 67, 70, 73, 89, 102, 113, 116, 118, 189, 206, 270

Smirnov, S., xiii, 4, 29, 38, 48, 110, 119, 186

Smith, Adam, 11, 13, 81

snowdrops, 111

social and welfare apparatus, 24, 45, 90, 110, 117, 145

social network, 4, 40, 68, 96, 126–7, 228, 248–9, 277

social safety net, 15, 17–18, 90, 299, 309

Solov'eva, A., 40

St Petersburg, 7, 29, 43, 67, 74, 158, 226, 276, 278–80, 284–306, 310, 315–17, 328–9, 356

stabilisation, 1, 2, 9, 11, 13–14, 16, 20, 82, 87, 89, 187

standard of living, 11, 55, 83, 292, 301, 328

state expenditure, 11, 89

statistics, 3–5, 8, 19, 38, 42–3, 53, 58, 66–71, 75, 85, 90, 93–5, 99, 100–102, 109–15, 132, 136, 147, 149, 151, 153–4, 157, 174, 201, 204, 216, 230, 234, 236–7, 242, 262, 277–8, 280–82, 292, 317

status, 23, 25, 37, 63, 71, 114, 132, 134, 137, 200, 230, 237–43, 249–52, 277, 292, 296, 316, 322

Stavnitskii, A., 40

stoppages, 44, 56, 58, 92, 110, 168, 170, 172–4, 187, 237, 252, 313

structural adjustment, 1–3, 10–17, 48, 50, 80, 82–3, 87–92, 139, 144

students, 46, 62, 64, 156, 237, 251, 259, 271

subsidies, 6, 17, 26, 35, 37, 89–90, 93, 105–6, 118, 120, 146, 182–5, 203, 263–4, 267, 270

suicide, 156

Sundstrom, N., 9

survey data, 3–7, 9, 18–20, 22, 29, 30–47, 49, 52–6, 58–75, 77–8, 80, 93–5, 102–3, 109, 113, 119–21, 138, 148, 151, 156–7, 159, 166, 175, 186–8, 194, 202, 208, 212, 231, 276, 278–80, 283–4, 286, 288, 291–5, 297, 299–306, 308–9, 312–17, 322, 323, 325–6, 330–31
   labour force, 9, 19, 45, 55, 59, 61–6, 68–75, 93, 113, 121, 151, 202, 312

survival strategies, 8, 316

taxation, 31, 46, 51, 54, 56, 61, 67–8, 72–3, 110–11, 114–15, 118, 120, 143–4, 150, 168, 181, 212–13, 313, 328

Teplukhin, P., 26, 271

Therborn, G., 311

Tkachenko, A., 69, 254

Toye, J., 82, 144

trade unions, 15, 32–4, 37, 48, 81, 88, 148, 222, 263, 270, 272, 310, 316

UNDP, 148
unemployed
  registered, 3, 7, 41, 44, 46, 63–5, 121, 137, 156, 203, 216, 227, 232–4, 237, 240, 248–51, 255, 261–2, 277–9, 283–6, 288, 290–302, 306–9, 316
  registration, 43, 62–4, 76, 140, 151, 202–3, 218, 227–9, 234, 236–9, 247, 249, 253, 276, 285, 289, 294, 312–14
unemployment, 3–7, 9–21, 33–4, 38–9, 41, 43–52, 55–66, 69–71, 74–6, 78–83, 88, 90–92, 94, 98, 101, 103, 121, 126, 131, 136–7, 139–40, 142, 144–5, 148–57, 166, 168, 172, 174–5, 179–80, 183–4, 194, 200–206, 212, 214, 216–55, 257, 261, 263–5, 269–70, 273–86, 288–331
  benefit, 3, 7, 15, 24, 47–51, 62–5, 72, 76, 79–82, 88, 91, 117, 120, 132, 140, 143, 151, 184, 203, 218–20, 223, 225–6, 231, 235–45, 250–55, 268–9, 277–8, 283–4, 291–5, 298–301, 309, 312–13, 317, 324, 326, 328
  concealed, 56–7, 168, 172
  frictional, 61
  hidden, 3, 56, 60–61, 217, 223, 245, 264, 274, 280, 289–90, 293, 309, 314
  ILO, 9, 65, 217, 233
  mass, 10, 17–18, 20, 48–50, 92, 103, 140, 144, 312–13, 328
  open, 4, 18, 41, 56, 61, 92, 94, 139, 142, 216, 264, 274, 278, 302, 309
  rate, 7, 10, 14, 21, 41, 45, 61, 64–5, 69, 76, 91, 151–3, 201–4, 217–18, 224–6, 230, 231, 232, 234, 238, 240, 251, 254–5, 264, 277, 280, 312–13, 328
  structural, 61
  suppressed, 3–4, 57, 59, 166, 172, 174–5, 313
  transitional, 15
Union of Industrialists and Entrepreneurs, 30, 34
United States, 14, 81, 91

vacancies, 15, 22, 46, 113, 133, 136, 197, 229, 236, 238, 245–7, 277, 283–4, 288, 291, 293, 295, 309
Varshavskaya, E., 56
Vinogradova, E., 39
Vladimir, 7, 22, 103, 158, 194, 218, 222, 224, 227, 231, 233, 234, 241, 242, 246, 247, 248, 249, 250, 253, 254, 315
Voronezh, 7, 310, 316, 328, 329, 330
VTsIOM, 33, 40, 42, 46, 53, 55, 64, 65, 78, 214, 226, 230, 315

Wadsworth, J., 317
wage
  minimum, 49, 60, 78, 91, 144, 169, 217–18, 241–2, 253, 263, 283, 299
wage fund, 25–7, 150, 209
wage reform, 27
wages
  flexibility, 15, 21, 48–50, 57, 83, 91, 181, 184, 212
  low, 6, 10, 21, 36, 38, 40, 42–3, 47, 49–53, 55–6, 58, 60, 65, 78–9, 83, 92, 114, 137, 140–41, 144, 169, 182, 218, 237, 241–2, 244–5, 247, 252, 254–5, 263–4, 291, 298–9, 301–2, 305, 309
  real, 19–20, 53, 118, 149
  relative, 40, 207–9, 211, 215
welfare provision, 13, 17, 57, 80, 116–17, 140, 151, 180–83, 185, 244, 300–301
Willer, D., 271
Wilmott, P., 325
women, 4–5, 22, 40, 44–5, 53, 66, 69–71, 75, 79, 85–6, 110, 127–8, 137–8, 148, 154, 156, 172–3, 200–215, 232, 234, 245, 247, 249, 250, 252, 261, 282–3, 302–3, 317, 320–21, 328
work regime, 63, 253
working conditions, 5, 24, 42, 46, 52, 63, 80, 113, 136, 145, 201, 237, 296
working day, 44, 58, 170, 213, 217
World Bank, 3, 9, 12, 14, 16, 19, 20, 29, 30, 31, 33, 34, 37, 38, 46, 48, 49, 52, 56, 90, 91, 147
world market, 10, 11, 16, 89, 123, 143, 267

Yeltsin, 18, 30, 119, 120
Yemtsov, R., 35, 46, 48, 56, 64, 65
Young, K., xiii, 7, 276
Young, M. , 315, 317, 319, 325

Zaionchkovskaya, Z. A., 41
Zaslavskii, I., 27